Workbook & Grammar Book

Jenny Dooley

Published by Express Publishing

Liberty House, Greenham Business Park, Newbury,
Berkshire RG19 6HW, United Kingdom
Tel.: (0044) 1635 959 759
email: inquiries@expresspublishing.co.uk
www.expresspublishing.co.uk

First published 2018
Sixth impression 2023

Made in EU

ISBN 978-1-4715-7082-7

Acknowledgements

Author's Acknowledgements
We would like to thank all the staff at Express Publishing who have contributed their skills to producing this book. Thanks for their support and patience are due in particular to: Megan Lawton (Editor in Chief); Viki Davies (senior editor); Michael Sadler and Steve Miller (editorial assistants); Richard White (senior production controller); the Express design team; Warehouse (recording producers); and Kevin Harris, Kimberly Baker, Steven Gibbs and Christine Little. We would also like to thank those institutions and teachers who piloted the manuscript, and whose comments and feedback were invaluable in the production of the book.

The authors and publishers wish to thank the following who have kindly given permission for the use of copyright material.

Module 1: ***Reading 1a:*** 11 Ways in Which Travel Has Changed my Life © Lauren Juliff, neverendingfootsteps.com on p. 5; ***Skills Work 1:*** Love Paris like a local: tour the city with an insider guide © Guardian News & Media Ltd 2018 on p. 13; **Module 2:** ***Reading 2a:*** 10 Habits of the World's Greatest Learners © Saga Briggs, InformED, an Open Colleges blog on p. 17; **Module 3:** ***Skills Work 3:*** Forget Goths, punks and emos, these are the new teenage tribes © Joanna Mathers on p. 37; **Module 4:** ***Reading 4a:*** How has Technology Changed our Lives? © Tech Spirited, techspirited.com on p. 40-41; ***Skills Work 4:*** Languages: The secret extinction © Paul Simpson, Wanderlust Travel Magazine on p. 49; **Module 6:** ***Reading 6a:*** Motivational posters: do they actually work? © Guardian News & Media Ltd 2018 on p. 64-65; ***Skills Work 6:*** I Hired a Millennial Life Coach © Amanda Shapiro, Vice Magazine, vice.com on p. 73.

Photograph Acknowledgements
Vocabulary 4b: Nyan Cat © Rob Bulmahn/Flickr.com/photos/rbulmahn.

The authors would also like to thank Shutterstock for images used in this book.

Contents

1a Reading

How TRAVEL has Changed My Life

"Three years ago, I stepped on a plane in the hope that it would change my life. Here's how it has ..."

Multiple choice

Preparing for the task

Remember!

First determine what the question is testing (opinion, detail, comparison, etc) in order to know what kind of information to look for in the text. Then find the relevant information in the text and underline it. Choose the answer that best represents the information in the text.

1 **a) ★ Read the question stem below. Is the question testing for opinion? detail? exemplification or comparison?**

In the second paragraph the writer mentions an incident on a boat in Thailand to

A highlight the dangers that travellers can face.
B illustrate the importance of survival skills.
C show that she started to confront daunting situations.
D point out the variety of exciting experiences she had.

b) ★ Now read the second paragraph paying attention to the underlined sections. Which is the correct answer?

2 **★★ You are going to read a blog entry about travel. For questions 1-6, choose the answer (A, B, C or D) which you think fits best according to the text.**

1 What does the writer say in the second paragraph about her difficult experiences while travelling?
A Her anxiety was triggered after experiencing them.
B It required a lot of effort to overcome them.
C There were always worse experiences that could have happened.
D The more she experienced them the less anxiety she had.

2 The writer mentions calamari in the third paragraph in order to
A demonstrate how misinformed she had been about her diet.
B illustrate her illogical fear of unusual food.
C explain why she was afraid of exotic food.
D to show the strange types of food her friends had encountered.

3 The writer says compared to other world cuisine, Vietnamese food
A was less intimidating with fewer unusual items.
B was too spicy for her to eat.
C took more time for her to like than other dishes.
D was the ideal challenge offering safe options.

Before I started travelling, anxiety had control of my life. It sent me **spiraling out of control**, and left me unable to function at times. Travel helped me manage my anxiety by giving me control of things. In the beginning, I was running away from my fears, but later, I began to run towards them.

When travelling, I found myself having to face these fears **on a daily basis** – after all, I was terrified of everything. While I could have run away from them, it **got to the point** where I no longer wanted to. So I took a bus instead of spending 10 times as much on a plane ticket, and I was fine. I ate a cockroach and didn't get food poisoning and die. My boat started to sink in Thailand and I put on my life jacket and survived. After so many horrible experiences, I realised that my anxiety was nearly always caused by me worrying about the worst case scenario. As it happened, the worst case scenario often actually did come true! Yet, it was never as bad as I thought it would be. I'd take a deep breath, I'd deal with it and I'd move on. After doing that several hundred times, I began to stop worrying so much.

For most people, the best part of travel is getting to sample delicious food **along the way**. I used to listen to people gush about the joys of travelling for food and wonder what was wrong with me. I had spent my whole life eating bland food and been perfectly happy with it. I didn't know any different. During my first week on the road, I tried calamari for the first time and freaked out because I thought the tentacles might stick to my throat and suffocate me!

Vietnamese food, though, was perfect for me because everything that scared me came **on the side**. I could order a bowl of pho and know that it would be edible, but accompanied with a plate of chillies and limes and... other, leafy things. I could grow accustomed to the bland version of the food, and then add a single chili. I was able to increase my spice tolerance while remaining in control. When I realised that this was the case for most Vietnamese dishes – especially soups – I went crazy. I started picking out random items on menus that didn't have English translations. To my delight, I would adore every dish I ordered. Most of the time, I'd have no idea what it even was!

Besides having a lot of fears, I wasn't the most confident of people. I used to walk with a hunchback and stare at my feet. I avoided eye contact and mumbled. I stayed away from social situations that made me uncomfortable. Staying in hostels changed all that. For the first few months of my trip I chose to stay in 6 to 10 bed dorms. Every time I stepped inside, I'd have someone asking me where I was from, where I had been, where I was going. After a while, I became that person who was asking the questions.

I walk differently now. I **hold myself up**, and look straight ahead. I make eye contact with people. I tell jokes and ridiculous travel stories without fear of being judged. I no longer try and squash my personality down so that nobody really knows who the real me is.

And then there was the kindness of strangers. People who had never spoken to me, knew nothing about me and didn't owe me a thing would often **come to my rescue**. There was the girl who approached me when I was lost on the streets of Taichung to help me figure out where I was going. There was the man in Thailand who helped me push my luggage to safety while we were being evacuated after the tsunami – not knowing if he was endangering his life in doing so. **Time and time again**, I've been astounded by the friendliness and compassion that has been shown to me by people who had no idea who I was and had no reason to ever help me. Now, I try not to judge anyone I meet, instead thinking only about ways in which I can help other people.

It's a cliché but when I left to travel, I hoped that it would help me find out who I am. I wanted to heal myself and become the person I knew I could be. I hoped to **rid myself of** anxiety and stop being frightened of everything. I still have lots of work to do but I feel like I'm **getting there**. I know I'll never be perfect but I'm determined to be the best possible version of myself. As soon as I conquer one hurdle, I'm setting the next one down. Most of all, I'm the happiest I've ever been. Here's to the next three years!

4 What does the writer suggest about dorm rooms?
- **A** They were instrumental in helping her improve her social skills.
- **B** They were vital for getting information about travel.
- **C** They are the best place to swap travel stories.
- **D** They are the perfect environment to be yourself in.

5 What main point does the writer make in paragraph 7 about the locals she has met?
- **A** Some were overly judgmental of her without cause.
- **B** They rarely spoke to her but were always kind.
- **C** They would repeatedly go out of their way to help her.
- **D** Their behaviour was surprising and odd at times.

6 In the final paragraph, the writer refers to 'a cliché' to show that
- **A** her initial expectations are shared by many other people.
- **B** the result of her travel experience was not a surprise.
- **C** her travel choices overseas were not interesting or novel.
- **D** the things that she experienced while travelling were quite dull.

3 ★★ **Match the phrases in bold in the text to their meanings below.**

- repeatedly • reached the stage
- making progress • separately
- quickly becoming chaotic • help me
- stand confidently • be free of
- during the process • every day

4 ★★ **The following words are found in the passage. Look at their standard definitions, then explain their meaning in the context of the passage. How are these words being used? Why?**

1 **run away** (paragraph 1): to leave a place suddenly
2 **squash** (paragraph 6): to crush or squeeze sth
3 **show** (paragraph 7): to make sth be seen
4 **heal** (paragraph 8): to treat an injury/sickness
5 **conquer** (paragraph 8): to take control of a land or people by force

1b Vocabulary

1 ★ **Choose the correct answer.**

1 We were impressed by the **impeccable/appreciative/low-cost/priceless** service at the hotel and would definitely stay there again.

2 We got a **severe/poor/desolate/raw** deal when we booked our accommodation and ended up paying through the nose for it.

3 As a **scheduled/weary/unwary/seasoned** traveller, he knows how to get the best deals on flights and accommodations.

4 These are only **conventional/provisional/provincial/existential** plans for the trip and they may change.

2 ★★ **Replace the word(s) in bold with a word from the box.**

• quaint • renovated • converted
• impoverished • lush • secular

1 The jeep tour is set up to help **poor** villages in the countryside by bringing tourist money to these areas.

2 This tour visits a variety of both religious and **non-religious** attractions in the city.

3 I suggested this travel package as it provides accommodation at a recently **improved and restored** hotel in the city centre.

4 Our guide took us on a canoe trip through the **very green and thick** vegetation of the valley.

5 We stayed at this **charming and old-fashioned** bed and breakfast while in Vermont.

6 The restaurant is a **transformed** theatre from the early 19th century.

3 ★★ **Fill in:** *in (x2), at (x2), through, down, up, over.*

1 Travel, ... essence, is the discovery of new places and cultures.

2 Tourists, ... the very least, should be somewhat familiar with local customs.

3 .... the end, the exchange between tourists and locals should be a positive experience.

4 We asked the taxi driver to pull .... at the museum.

5 We were held .... in traffic on our way to the airport.

6 Be careful crossing the road; people in this country often race down the street .... full speed.

7 It's easy to flag .... a taxi outside the street market.

8 We sailed .... customs at the airport without a problem.

4 ★★ **Fill in:** *handle, life, kite, face, tide.*

1 Implementing a tourism tax flies in the .... of plans to increase tourism in the area.

2 Mike apologised to the personnel at the front desk for flying off the .... when there was a mix up with his booking.

3 Time and .... wait for no man, so don't miss this opportunity to see the Amazon.

4 The disgruntled passenger was so upset that he told the airport security to go fly a ....!

5 She had the time of her .... on the cruise ship.

5 ★★ **Fill in:** *ordinary, vibrant, unbeatable, beaten, luxurious, far-flung, tedious, receptive.*

Break FREE!

These days we seem to be spending more time planning our holidays than enjoying them. With the plethora of travel websites and blogs at our fingertips, offering the inside scoop on the most **1)** .... accommodation and how to get **2)** .... prices on practically all your travel needs, there is more choice than ever. Whatever happened, though, to throwing caution to the wind and just heading off to some **3)** .... location completely plan free?
These kinds of holidays can be extremely refreshing and full of adventure as you have no idea what will happen next. They offer you the chance to discover something out of the **4)** .... in places which can often lie off the **5)** .... track and are populated by **6)** .... communities full of fun-loving, colourful people. These **7)** .... locals are ready to welcome you in and show you an authentic cultural experience. Spur-of-the-moment travel sometimes results in long and extremely **8)** .... journeys but it's worth all the trouble when you return home with some amazing stories to tell.

Topic related vocabulary

Tourism

6 ★ **Choose the correct item.**

1 The work of the local artist **embeds/embarks/embodies/exemplifies** the spirit of the city and appeals to tourists.
2 A dramatic fall in tourism will have serious **outcomes/devastations/damages/repercussions** on the local economy.
3 This resort **brags/boasts/gloats/asserts** a number of top-rated restaurants.
4 The village is a **microscopy/microclimate/microscope/microcosm** of traditional Italy.
5 It's important to stay hydrated while trekking in the mountains as the exertion **dwindles/drains/diminishes/dissipates** your body of vital fluids.

Collocations

7 ★ **Choose the odd one out.**

1 The Ecolodge I stayed at is a **main/excellent/prime/fine** example of a sustainable hotel.
2 We had a **narrow/tight/close/lucky** escape when the coast guard rescued us from our sinking sailboat.
3 Tourism has had a **desired/desirable/dramatic/decisive** effect on the local economy.
4 There is a **strong/likely/fair/sheer** chance that we can catch the last plane if we leave for the airport now.

Phrasal verbs

8 ★★ **Fill in:** *off, out (x3), on.*

1 Inflation has driven .... the locals leaving only those working in the tourist industry in the town.
2 After walking for over an hour, it dawned .... the group of tourists that they had been going in the wrong direction.
3 The tour went .... as planned in spite of the weather.
4 The planned resort will wipe .... the wetlands.
5 The tour guide will set .... the exact plan of the tour when we meet.

9 ★★ **Fill in:** *mass, package, tourism, tourist, financial, wildlife, seasonal, working.*

The Price of Progress

The recent submission of plans by the Willowview council to increase the budget for further development of the **1)** .... sector in our area has raised some alarm bells. Even though an increase in this industry will undoubtedly result in a **2)** .... gain for the town with direct employment and an increase in business for the service and retail sectors, most of this new employment will consist of **3)** .... jobs with low pay and often poor **4)** .... conditions. If our town becomes a major **5)** .... destination, experiencing **6)** .... tourism, it will lead to increased pollution not to mention the impact on our mountain parks as **7)** .... tours make the area easily accessible. What will be done to ensure **8)** .... conservation in our mountains? Only time will tell what the true price of this progress will be.

Word formation

10 ★★ **Complete the sentences with words derived from the words in bold.**

1 The number of tourists visiting the area is expected to double in the .... future. **(SEE)**
2 Raising ticket prices when tourism numbers are already down seems .... in the long run. **(PRODUCE)**
3 The service at the resort was ....; we can't praise the staff enough. **(STAND)**
4 There has been a drop in visitors to the country due to recent political .... **(STABLE)**
5 The tourism industry was affected badly by the severe weather, with .... cancellations at hotels and resorts. **(NUMBER)**
6 The campsite was .... by car so we had to go on foot. **(ACCESS)**
7 It's a(n) .... tour that allows visitors to get involved in the different aspects of the production line. **(ACT)**
8 The council tried to .... the negative effects that tourism has had on the city. **(PLAY)**
9 A travel advisory has been released by .... at the embassy. **(OFFICE)**
10 The resort .... a complete makeover and reopened last month. **(GO)**

1c Grammar in use

Present tenses

1 ★★ **Put the verbs in brackets into the correct present tense.**

A: Hi, Jane. Have you booked your holiday yet?
B: No, unfortunately not. Peter **1)** .... **(always/change)** his mind about where he wants to go! To be honest, we really need to hurry up because it **2)** .... **(get)** more and more difficult to find good deals now.
A: Yes, you're right. I mean, If you **3)** .... **(wait)** too long, you'll need to reconsider your plans altogether. Jack made that mistake last year and really **4)** .... **(regret)** it now.
B: Really? That's terrible. Well, ... on the positive side, we **5)** .... **(agree)** on a country to visit already. But, since it's the first time the two of us **6)** .... **(ever/travel)** together, it's proving impossible to compromise on a city.
A: Ah, ... I see. The first holiday together is always a challenge. It took Kevin and I weeks to agree! **7)** .... **(you/use)** travel websites and travel agents on the high street lately?
B: Yes. We **8)** .... **(check)** holiday brochures for months. But I **9)** .... **(always/feel)** like it's one step forward and two steps back!
A: Maybe you just have to pick at random.
B: Perhaps you're right. After all, fortune **10)** .... **(favour)** the bold, as they say!

Stative verbs

2 ★★ **Write the meaning of the verbs in bold.**

1 **a** I **see** what you mean!
....
b I**'m seeing** my cousin when I go to Toronto.
....

2 **a** This dress **fits** me perfectly!
....
b Martin **is fitting** a trailer on his jeep.
....

3 **a** Prague **looks** like a beautiful city to visit.
....
b Jake's outside; he**'s looking** at the view.
....

4 **a** This Chinese silk scarf **feels** incredibly soft.
....
b Ellen **is feeling** the fruit at the bazaar.
....

Past tenses – *used to* – *be/get used to* – *would*

3 ★★ **Put the verbs in brackets into the correct past form.**

1 A: Do you remember when William .... **(fly)** to Switzerland with me and then .... **(stay)** in Lausanne for a few days by himself?
B: Yes, I do! Actually, I .... **(mean)** to stay in Lausanne with him but my plans fell through. We .... **(do/return)** together, though, at the end of the trip.

2 A: I can't believe we are standing outside the house where Tolkien .... **(write)** *The Lord of The Rings*!
B: Yes! Just imagine, decades ago he .... **(work)** in that drawing room creating Middle Earth while the seasons .... **(change)** around him! It's amazing to think that he .... **(procrastinate)** for years before he finally sent it to publishers.

3 A: Excuse me, ... **(you/consider)** a package holiday to Spain? We have some great summer offers in Madrid at the moment.
B: Well, if I .... **(not/visit)** Spain last Easter, and if I .... **(not/go)** there again next Christmas, I definitely would be! It's my favourite place!

4 ★★ **Fill each gap with the correct form of** ***be/get used to*** **or** ***used to*****. Where can you replace** ***used to*** **with** ***would*****?**

1 Ellen didn't like the hostel at first, but she .... it in time.
2 When Andre was a teenager he .... spend summers in Ireland.
3 Jackie found it difficult to .... travelling so much for work.
4 Bill and his wife didn't .... like cruise holidays, but now they love them.
5 Vicky is an experienced flight attendant, so she .... always being on the move.
6 Martin .... have a gold card with the airline when he travelled for business.
7 No matter how hard she tried, Ann couldn't .... foreign food.
8 Jack .... visit Europe more often when he had relatives there.

5 ★ Choose the correct item.

1 This is the bumpiest flight we **have ever encountered/are encountering/encountered/had ever encountered**.
2 Charles Darwin **was exploring/had been exploring/explored/had explored** the Galapagos Islands.
3 Oh no! There **is going/goes/has gone/went** the last train for the evening!
4 When Ian **had realised/realised/had been realising/was realising** that he would need to cook his own meals, he cancelled his reservation in the villa.
5 Having lived in Jamaica for several years, James now **has been knowing/is knowing/has known/knows** Patois, which is quite different from English.

6 ★ Underline the correct word/time expression.

1 I packed my bag, **then/when** I headed directly to the train station.
2 Haven't you posted pictures online from your holiday **yet/since**?
3 **After/Before** I met Julian, I had never considered cycling around Europe.
4 Jade **always/still** travels first class every time she goes overseas!
5 I have **yet/just** finished writing a review of the holiday resort; I loved it!

7 ★★ Put the verbs in the correct present or past form.

Hi bloggers!

I've got to be honest with you... this trip is the most difficult trek I **1)** .... **(ever/do)** in my entire life! And I **2)** .... **(hike)** ever since I was a small child! I didn't expect it to be easy of course, but I never **3)** .... **(imagine)** it would be so challenging when I **4)** .... **(organise)** it last October. Earlier today, I **5)** .... **(ask)** my climbing partner Bill if he felt the same while we **6)** .... **(catch)** our breath after a particularly hard afternoon. He admitted that he **7)** .... **(not/experience)** anything else like it either during his outdoor career. This is remarkable considering that he usually **8)** .... **(climb)** the highest mountains in the world. On the plus side, though, by pushing ourselves so hard, we **9)** .... **(get)** stronger and stronger mentally every day. Check back tomorrow for another update once we **10)** .... **(reach)** the next camp!

Key word transformations

8 ★★ For questions 1-5, complete the second sentence so that it has a similar meaning to the first sentence using the word given. Do not change the word given. You must use between three and eight words, including the word given.

1 The last time I spoke to James was months ago. **ANYTHING**
I .... months.
2 Janet thinks the only thing she can do is cancel her skiing holiday. **ALTERNATIVE**
Janet thinks she .... to cancel her skiing holiday.
3 Paul was delighted to engage in long conversations in Italian while he was in Rome. **DELIGHT**
Much .... in long conversations in Italian while he was in Rome.
4 When Henry was offered the chance to work on a cruise ship, he took it without hesitation. **HESITATE**
When Henry was offered the chance to work on a cruise ship, ... it.
5 I don't think Andrew will want to come back from Alaska – he's never enjoyed anything as much as this holiday. **TIME**
I don't think Andrew will want to come back from Alaska – he .... life!

Grammar in Focus

★★ Fill in the gaps with the correct word. Then put the verbs in brackets into the correct form.

Nowadays, holidays **1)** .... **(reach)** a threshold, where few destinations are considered as exotic as they **2)** .... to be in the past. In such a climate, where the demand for ever more adventurous experiences is relentless, tour companies **3)** .... **(now/offer)** increasingly unusual options and thus, opening the door to new travel possibilities their clients **4)** .... **(ignore)** up until now. Extreme tourism fills a gap in the market and takes bold travellers to exciting new destinations. These destinations are often places that traditional tour companies **5)** .... **(avoid)**, rather than advertising or promoting, **6)** .... many years. But **7)** .... days, abandoned cities, isolated regions, and desolate environments **8)** .... **(grow)** more and more popular and attractive to a community of dedicated thrill seekers.

1d Listening skills

Multiple choice

Remember!

The answer will often be paraphrased so read the options before you listen and think of what you will be listening to. While you listen, work out which answer is closest in meaning to what the speakers say. Also, be aware that the speakers will mention words or phrases related to the other options that are intended to distract you. Remember, you must listen very carefully as only one option is correct.

1 **a) ★ 🎧 You will hear two short segments from a radio programme. The programme is called 'Learning from the Experts.' You will hear what two different radio guests have to say about two different topics. From the three answer choices given, you should choose the one that best answers the question according to the information you heard.**

Segment 1

1 According to the speakers, what information did ABTA unearth?
- **A** Fewer young people are travelling abroad.
- **B** Many young people aren't covered when they travel.
- **C** Most young people nowadays travel to Europe on holiday.

2 According to the survey, what mistake did people make about health cover abroad?
- **A** They believe the EHIC gives the same level of protection as travel insurance.
- **B** They assume the country they are travelling to has the same health system as Britain.
- **C** They think that the EHIC affords them the same medical coverage abroad as at home.

3 What is an issue faced by people travelling to rural areas?
- **A** the difficulty of finding private care
- **B** hospitals do not accept the EHIC
- **C** the lack of government hospitals

4 What did the speaker mean by worst case scenario?
- **A** having a terrible experience on holiday
- **B** having the extra cost of returning home
- **C** having poor treatment while in hospital

5 According to the speaker, why are some claims invalid?
- **A** because the policy did not cover certain activities
- **B** because the policy did not contain any excess
- **C** because the policy holder was liable for the costs

b) ★ 🎧 From the three answer choices given, you should choose the one that best answers the question according to the information you heard.

Segment 2

1 In addition to being useful, what may come from learning a language?
- **A** It allows people to travel to more countries.
- **B** It can prevent the onset of age-related illnesses.
- **C** It can make one's work more interesting.

2 According to the speaker, why do adults find it difficult to learn a language?
- **A** because their minds don't work the same way as children's
- **B** because they have other obligations to fulfil
- **C** because language courses are not designed for them

3 Under what circumstances do students on an immersion course learn?
- **A** They only hear and communicate in the language they are learning.
- **B** They are only taught by native speakers of the language.
- **C** They learn the language alongside children.

4 What did the speaker mean by 'being thrown in the deep end'?
- **A** being left to study the language on your own
- **B** being given little support while learning
- **C** being unable to rely on your own language to help

5 What is the main advantage of the immersion method?
- **A** belief in all one's abilities increases
- **B** native proficiency of the language
- **C** greater understanding of one's mother tongue

Speaking skills 1e

Making and responding to suggestions

1 **a) ★ Read the dialogue about holiday ideas. Use phrases (a-e) to complete the dialogue.**

- **a** sounds perfect!
- **b** let's find some other sites.
- **c** I'm not sure about that.
- **d** no, I don't think so.
- **e** how about

A: Hey, what are you looking at?
B: A travel website. I'm searching for holiday ideas for me and my family but I haven't found anything interesting yet.
A: Well, **1)** .... How about a wildlife and safari holiday? Do you fancy that?
B: **2)** .... They're a bit too extreme for us.
A: I see. Would you be interested in a city touring holiday?
B: To be honest, **3)** .... We prefer beach holidays that combine swimming and water sports.
A: OK, **4)** .... this all-inclusive package holiday to Mexico? It includes flights, accommodation as well as water activities at a sensible price.
B: Now, that **5)** .... I'm going to bookmark this site so I can check it out later.
A: Good idea.

b) ★★ Which phrases in Ex. 1a are making suggestions and which are responding positively/negatively?

Suggestions	1 ....
Responding positively	2 ....
Responding negatively	3 ....

Asking for and giving personal information

2 **★ Match the questions (1-6) to the correct responses (A-F).**

1 ☐ What do you like most about where you're living?
2 ☐ What is your taste in music?
3 ☐ What can you learn from travelling abroad?
4 ☐ What has motivated you in your work or studies?
5 ☐ How easy or difficult is it for young people to find a job in your city/area?
6 ☐ Can you tell us what you and your friends do to relax?

A I'm inspired by coaching a sales team to meet and exceed targets. I work closely with my team to ensure that they develop the negotiation skills they need to succeed. This gives me a sense of pride to be part of this professional development.

B After a busy week I like to unwind by spending quality time with my besties. We usually enjoy hanging out together by going to the cinema or to our favourite restaurant or café to catch up.

C Honestly, I like every genre but my favourite will always be country because that is what I grew up listening to. Every time I hear a good old-time classic, it really reminds me of my childhood, the best years of my life.

D For me, there is no greater enjoyment than packing up and leaving my comfort zone to experience unfamiliar places and customs. It helps me to learn and respect how others live in various regions.

E It is getting hard to find work in my area nowadays due to the high unemployment levels and for the few jobs available, it is extremely competitive with so many other qualified applicants.

F Well, residing near the city centre is amazing because there are many shops and public transport options within walking distance of my flat. I also love living in a building where there are diverse people willing to strike up a friendly conversation.

3 **★ Choose the correct item.**

1 A: Would you be interested in going to Peru?
B: **a** That would be lovely.
b You're probably right.

2 A: What do you think about a walking tour?
B: **a** I don't think so.
b It's not my cup of tea.

3 A: Let's try to find a cheap package deal.
B: **a** It's a definite maybe.
b That's a great idea.

1f Writing An essay based on written input

1 ★ **Read the rubric and underline the key words. Then answer the questions.**

> Read the two texts below. Write an **essay** summarising and evaluating key points from both texts. Use your own words throughout as far as possible, and include your own ideas in your answers. Write your answer in 240-280 words.

1 What type of writing task is it?
2 What do you have to do to analyse the material?
3 How should the information in the text be presented?

2 ★★ **Read the two texts and answer the questions that follow.**

Text 1

In exotic lands

On the surface, travelling abroad is about seeing new places and discovering the wonders outside our country. But underneath, it offers so much more: opening our horizons to new experiences, cultures, cuisine and landscapes. This increases our cultural sensitivity, making us more open-minded, which helps us to adapt to different situations and it boosts our self-confidence at the same time. While photos provide a record of our various travel experiences, it is the transformation within that is often the strongest confirmation of why travelling abroad is so important.

Text 2

Staying local

Nowadays, more and more people are reaping the benefits of holistays, – a period in which an individual stays at home and participates in local leisure activities, rather than travelling internationally. With holistaying, people get all the fun of organising and enjoying a holiday, without the added travel and lodging expenses. Locals get a chance to explore their city as tourists and discover venues they never knew existed. With proper planning and the right attitude, a holistay can offer all the advantages of more far-flung holidays. Why, then, would anyone want to go abroad?

1 What are the key points of each text?
2 Are the key points in the set of texts opposing or complementary?
3 How many paragraphs will the essay contain?
4 What would you include in the introduction of the essay?
5 Do you need to evaluate the points raised?

3 ★★ **Read the sentences which are all paraphrases of the key points in texts 1 and 2. Which are the best paraphrases? Which are incorrect because of content and which are incorrect because of paraphrasing techniques?**

Text 1

Point 1

a Arguably, the end result of travelling internationally is the development of a global mindset which builds tolerance and character.

b Travelling abroad opens our eyes and gives us new experiences, which allows us to adjust to unfamiliar situations and raises our self-assurance.

Point 2

a The value of international travel is the reinforcement of personal growth.

b The most vital aspect of travelling abroad is the collection of memories obtained through travel experiences.

Text 2

Point 1

a Internal tourism can prove to be both recreational and easier on one's wallet.

b On holistays, people can enjoy planning and then having a holiday without extra costs for the trip and accommodation.

Point 2

a There is a shared consensus that people can convert their residences into holiday resorts for tourists who seek to explore the local culture.

b It is reasonable to suggest therefore, that creative holistay tourism offers as much or more than other holidays.

Your turn

4 ★ **Use the rubric in Ex. 1 and your answers in Exs 2 & 3 and one of the plans below to write your essay.**

Plan A

(Para 1) *Introduction (present the topic)*
(Para 2) *Summary of both texts*
(Para 3) *Evaluation of both texts*
(Para 4) *Conclusion (present your opinion)*

Plan B

(Para 1) *Introduction (present the topic)*
(Para 2) *Text 1 – summary & evaluation*
(Para 3) *Text 2 – summary & evaluation*
(Para 4) *Conclusion (present your opinion)*

Paris from the Inside!

Georges, a retired French general, is waiting outside the metro station in the Parisian district of Le Sentier, eager to show off the finer – and less refined – points of an area he knows 'like his pocket.'

Le Sentier is a curious mix of shabby and chic that stretches from the grand boulevards of Napoleon III's architect Baron Haussmann to the aristocratic Palais Royal, via the colourful and notorious Saint Denis district, with its nightlife and sweatshops. 'How long have we got?' Georges asks. I assume that there is not much I don't know about an area I've lived near for almost 15 years, and reply: 'Long enough.' Three hours later, and Georges is still showing me places on my doorstep I never knew existed.

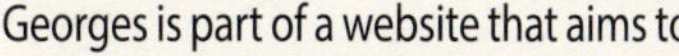

Georges is part of a website that aims to be the next big thing in tailored tours with private guides. The idea, developed by Bertrand Bazin, 23, a graduate of one of France's elite business schools, along with three friends, could hardly be simpler: take a city dweller who is passionate about their home and introduce them to visitors looking for insider knowledge. Since it started last July, the company has not stopped growing, and now has around 500 people worldwide in 100 destinations, from France and Spain, to India and Brazil.

Georges' tour is an eclectic mix of historical detail, little-known facts, quirky places (like the button and ribbon shop with stock from the 19th century, in rue Choiseul) and souvenir buying opportunities. His advice to visitors is simple: look up. He points out the characteristics of Haussmann's famous boulevards: the long avenues of ashlar-stone buildings between five and seven storeys high, each subtly different – the more spacious apartments with ornate wrought-iron balconies on the second floor, étage noble, with flats becoming more modest with each floor, up to the rooftop garrets.

He knows where to find the little-known passages, the many statues and carvings influenced by Greek mythology, or those that reflect the proprietor's trade or interests. Of the 150 or so covered passages that existed in Paris before Haussmann redesigned the city in the mid-19th century only 20 remain, among them the grand Galerie Vivienne (named a gallery not a passage, due to its proximity to the aristocratic Palais Royal) and the Prado and Brady passages in the less well-to-do 10th arrondissement, which is rough around the edges but increasingly trendy.

Georges points out the areas frequented by Toulouse-Lautrec, Guy de Maupassant and the Prince of Wales, later Edward VII. At the Palais Royal we gaze wistfully into the window of Le Grand Véfour – the celebrated cradle of French restaurant gastronomy, opened in the mid-18th century – at the €315 menu plaisir and dining salle where French literary giants Colette and Jean Cocteau entertained the Parisian beau monde, Georges reliably informs me.

These are the sort of details, Bazin says, that visitors love. 'Today, people are looking for far more than museums, culture and restaurants from a city visit, but they may be too timid or not have the opportunity to meet local people. So we are doing the introductions. Our guides are passionate about their city and are not just doing this for money.' So far, one-third of customers to the French site are foreign visitors, one-third are French nationals and the remaining third are locals wishing to rediscover their arrondissement. 'This is for people who really want to see the city through the eyes of a local person.'

Over lunch at a Mauritian restaurant that I didn't even know existed, Georges admits he speaks a little Russian and that during the cold war, as a young man in the French intelligence service, he spent time in Moscow. I say it makes him sound like a French James Bond. He smiles enigmatically.

Reading

1 **★★ You are going to read an article about a local tour guide. For questions 1-6, choose the answer (A, B, C or D) which you think fits best according to the text.**

1 What does the writer imply regarding his neighbourhood in the second paragraph?
- **A** He finds it to be run down and uninteresting.
- **B** He is surprised at how interesting it is.
- **C** He didn't expect to learn so much about it.
- **D** He is amazed at how long the tour of it took.

2 What does Georges point out to tourists about the local architecture?
- **A** the perfect uniformity of the building facades and design
- **B** the notoriety of the architect behind the buildings
- **C** the avenues lined with beautiful elaborate balconies
- **D** the simplification of flats as floors rise

3 Georges shows the writer around passages that
- **A** used to be full of tradesmen's stalls.
- **B** are secretly in use today.
- **C** existed before the city was redone.
- **D** are named after figures from ancient mythology.

4 The writer refers to various figures in French history in order to
- **A** show how historically important his neighbourhood is.
- **B** explain why Paris is a top tourist attraction.
- **C** describe places and how they were used in the past.
- **D** illustrate Georges' detailed knowledge of a place.

5 What point is made about tourists in paragraph 7?
- **A** Tourists often go out of their way to meet locals.
- **B** Mostly foreign tourists want to meet up with locals.
- **C** Tourists want more than the typical travel experience.
- **D** There are many ways for tourists to meet up with locals.

Language Knowledge 1

Word Formation

1 ★★ **For questions 1-8, read the text below. Use the word given in capitals at the end of some of the lines to form a word that fits in the space in the same line. There is an example at the beginning (0).**

TOURISM WITH A DIFFERENCE

Mass tourism has long been criticised as being **0)** *incredibly* destructive to the environment. Tourism, however, can prove to be **1)** .... to an area if developed in a way that isn't **2)** .... to the region. Known as CBT, Community Based Tourism is a community-led approach offering a genuine experience for the traveller while at the same time **3)** .... local people. Locals, who are often from **4)** .... communities, work together to invite tourists into their world. As well as sharing their culture, they also take care of the **5)** .... of accommodation and food. CBT can become a great source of **6)** .... income that locals can use to preserve their culture and environment. Schemes like CBT acknowledge the **7)** .... as well as the social value of areas, while creating a system that results in full **8)** .... and equality for everyone involved. Bringing tourism into the hands of the community in this way can safeguard a tourist destination for many years to come.

CREDIBLE
ADVANTAGE
DETRIMENT
POWER
MARGIN
PROVIDE
COMPLEMENT
COMMERCE
TRANSPARENT

Open cloze

2 ★★ **For questions 1-8, read the text below and think of the word which best fits each space. Use only one word for each space. There is an example at the beginning (0).**

Travelling Paws

Who said adventure and travel are only for people? One traveller, in particular, **0)** *would* highly disagree, if he could talk! This traveller, who likes to **1)** .... a walk on the wild side, is called Aspen and he is an adorable golden retriever who definitely proves travel can be for **2)** .... sorts of creatures. Along with his human partner, photographer Hunter Lawrence, Aspen has hiked **3)** .... some of the most spectacular scenery in the USA and Canada. Aspen **4)** .... advantage of his travels by swimming, snow-sledging and canoeing, and like most tourists, posing for a photo in front of his favourite spots! Hunter photographs Aspen basking **5)** .... nature in a way that doesn't take **6)** .... from the natural environment itself. The results are striking and heartwarming images that have made Aspen more popular on social media than many human travellers! **7)** .... he's at home in Colorado or on the road, Aspen doesn't plan to stop exploring **8)** .... soon!

Key word transformations

3 ★★ **For questions 1-6, complete the second sentence so that it has a similar meaning to the first sentence using the word given. Do not change the word given. You must use between three and eight words, including the word given.**

1 Non-passengers are strictly forbidden from entering the departure lounge of the airport. **NO**

On .... the departure lounge of the airport.

2 Nancy called her family regularly while she was travelling in Asia. **CONTACT**

Nancy .... her family while travelling in Asia.

3 I hope they will consider the environmental impacts when they start more tours in the Amazon. **ACCOUNT**

I hope the environmental impacts .... when they start more tours in the Amazon.

4 Steve was made responsible for the set-up of the camp on the trip. **CHARGE**

Steve .... the camp on the trip.

5 We were surprised at how in-depth the tour of the Tower of London was. **CAME**

It .... that the tour of the Tower of London was so in-depth.

6 Is it likely that we will get a seat on the next plane to Frankfurt? **CHANCES**

What .... a seat on the next plane to Frankfurt?

Grammar

4 ★ Choose the correct item.

1 Only after leaving for the airport .... she had left her passport at the hotel.
A she realised
B she had realised
C had she realised
D did she realise

2 The airport bus leaves at 10 am from the hotel unless you would rather .... by to get you.
A I passed
B my passing
C I had passed
D to pass

3 This website is the .... source that I trust for accurate travel information and hotel reviews.
A one only
B only and one
C one and only
D only one

4 Some tourists fail to understand the importance .... respectful to the environment when travelling.
A their being
B being
C to be
D of being

5 "Has Jerry made any inquiries about where to go on the trip?"
"No, all he does is .... about the cost of everything."
A complain
B complaining
C to be complaining
D complained

6 This time of year is the perfect time to take a trip to the coast as it .... in summer.
A ever hardly rains
B hardly ever rains
C rains hardly ever
D never hardly rains

7 I finally booked the safari! It's .... I've wanted to do since Carla told me about her safari experience.
A that
B which
C where
D what

8 The guide book advises .... near the port as it can be quite dangerous at night.
A not to stay
B not staying
C against to stay
D don't stay

9 At first I didn't like travelling by train but after having travelled by train all summer, I have finally .... it.
A been used to
B used to
C get used to
D gotten used to

10 This airline has .... service that I will highly recommend it to all my friends.
A such good
B such a good
C so good
D a good

11 "I forgot to book the airline tickets."
"Don't worry about the plane tickets now. I'll do the booking later, on ...."
A itself
B my own
C its own
D myself

12 .... the boat tour seemed very interesting, they chose to go on a walking tour of the city instead.
A Despite
B However
C Since
D Although

Vocabulary

5 ★ Choose the correct item.

1 We love travelling together; we have so much in ....
A relation
B common
C mutual
D parallel

2 There are several techniques you can use to .... your fear of flying.
A overcome
B surpass
C deal
D undo

3 The hotel .... to be a lot better than we expected.
A came across
B ended up
C turned out
D went on

4 Jim likes to become .... with the local culture by reading about it before travelling.
A aware
B familiar
C specialised
D accustomed

5 The hotel will not refund your booking if you cancel at short ....
A announcement
B response
C warning
D notice

6 The area is considered unsafe for tourists. That's .... why we chose to go somewhere else.
A directly
B particularly
C precisely
D namely

7 One of the .... of travelling abroad is meeting so many lovely people from different cultures and backgrounds.
A risks
B peaks
C perks
D extras

8 The resort's .... were top-notch and even included a golf course.
A features
B services
C resources
D facilities

9 The ancient fortress was designed to .... attacks from all sides.
A encounter
B withstand
C experience
D confront

10 It's important to keep a budget so as not to live beyond your ....
A means
B money
C funds
D allowance

11 Tom .... to be a travel blogger one day and travel around the world full time.
A inspires
B aspires
C pursues
D retires

12 We .... upon a quaint little café near our hotel.
A stumbled
B tumbled
C staggered
D tripped

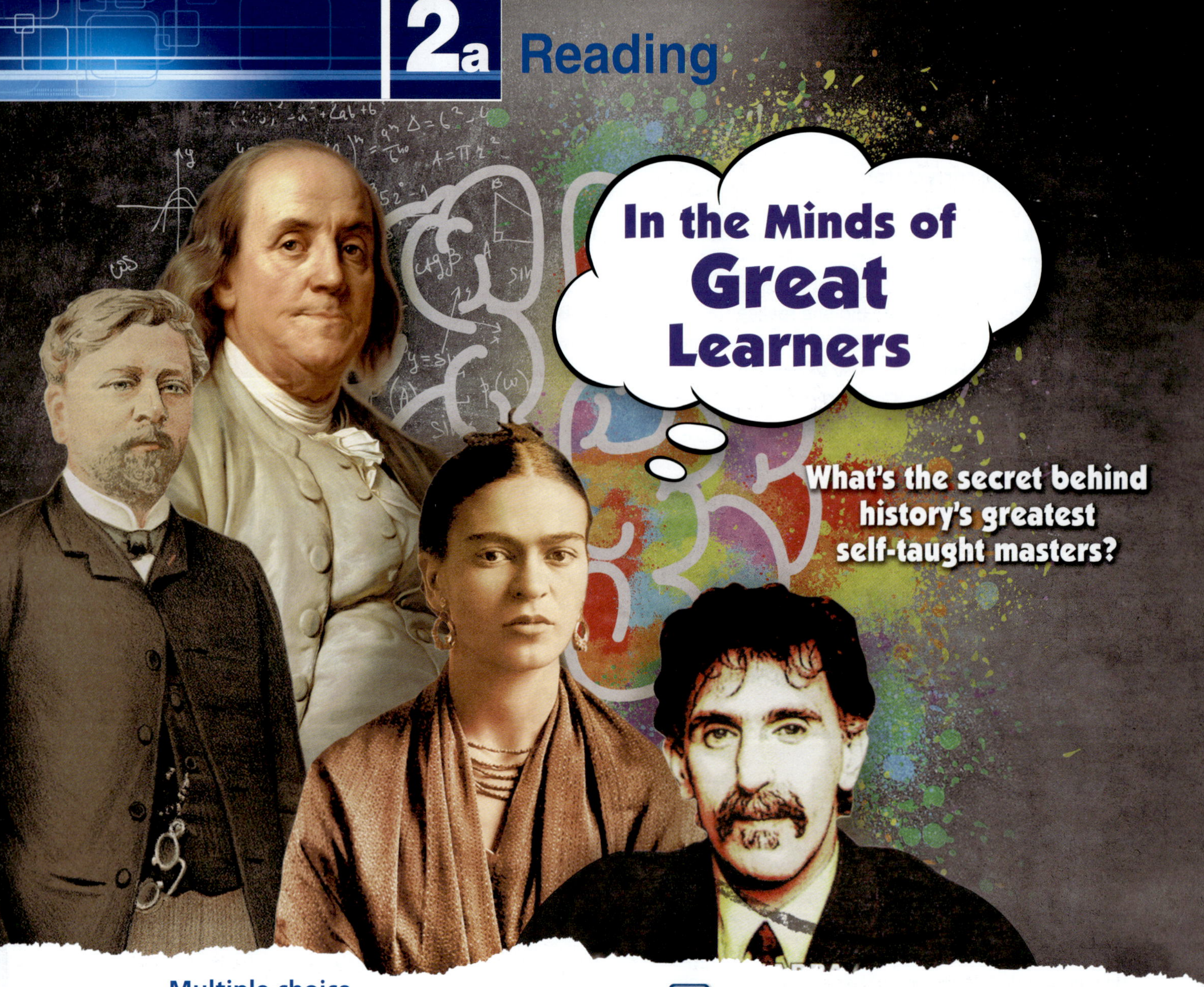

Multiple choice

Preparing for the task

Remember!

To underline the key words in the questions. Then look in the text for phrases and ideas with similar meanings to the key words. The exact same words will not appear in the question and text.

1 a) ★ **Read the two questions below and underline the key words.**

In which section does the writer mention

1 an expert's opinion on the number of autodidacts?
2 an expert's opinion on how people become autodidacts?

b) ★★ **Now read the highlighted section of section A of the text. Underline the key words that pertain to the two questions in Ex. 1a. Which question (1 or 2) does the highlighted section match? Why?**

2 ★★ **You are going to read an article about independent learners. For questions 1-10, choose from the sections A-E. The sections may be chosen more than once.**

In which section does the writer mention

an approach that likens learning to an equation?	1
the subtle difference between two similar principles?	2
the importance of a wide frame of reference?	3
an unusual technique that throws learners in the deep end?	4
the need to focus on individual tasks?	5
an overlooked truth that is often avoided?	6
the nature of self-taught learners?	7
a positive effect of a lack of conventional education?	8
a belief that something is not predestined but created?	9
the state that can cause learning to stop?	10

A History is filled with people called autodidacts, or individuals who teach themselves about a subject or subjects in which they have little to no formal education. Benjamin Franklin was an autodidact. So were Jorge Luis Borges, Eileen Gray, Gustave Eiffel, and Frida Kahlo. The original 'self-directed learners,' autodidacts possess intrinsic motivation, self-determination, and a true passion for learning.

'Look around,' says psychologist Annie Murphy Paul. 'We all know at least one successfully self-taught expert, and the tech world is teeming with them.' The question is, how'd they get that way? On this topic, Paul says, 'the psychological literature is largely silent.' Still, the psychology of motivation and interest suggests that 'self-directed learners are not only born, but can be made.' Bearing this in mind, what are the habits of the world's best learners and how do they do it?

B One important habit is to seek personal renewal. In a speech to a top consulting firm, the celebrated professor John W. Gardner explored this idea and the urgent need for leaders to commit themselves to continued learning and growing. 'We have to face the fact that most men and women out there in the world of work are more stale than they know, more bored than they would care to admit,' he said. So what is the opposite of boredom: the personal attribute that allows individuals to keep learning, growing, and changing, to escape their fixed attitudes and habits? 'Not anything as narrow as ambition,' Gardner explained to the crowd. He then offered a simple maxim to guide the accomplished leaders in the room. 'Be interested,' he urged them. 'Everyone wants to be interesting, but the vitalising thing is to be interested. As the proverb says, "It's what you learn after you know it all that counts."'

C Another useful habit is to calculate your motivation-to-inhibition ratio. This was a technique used by Kató Lomb, one of the first simultaneous interpreters in the world. She was able to interpret fluently in nine or ten languages. She learned these languages as an autodidact. Not believing in the so-called language talent, she tended to express language skill with a fraction, with motivation in the numerator and inhibition (the fear of starting to speak, of being laughed at) in the denominator. In her conviction, the stronger the motivation is within us, and the more we can put aside inhibition, the sooner we can take possession of the skill. Lomb also practised immersion, and one of her favourite study tricks was to try to read a novel in a language completely unknown to her as a way to decipher the language. 'We don't really need to look up each and every word in the dictionary: it only spoils our joy of reading. In any case, what we can remember is what we have figured out ourselves.'

D It's also vital to be open-minded. This trait is exemplified by American musician, songwriter, composer, recording engineer and film director Frank Zappa. In a career spanning more than 30 years, Zappa composed rock, jazz and orchestral works. As if all that weren't impressive enough, he also directed feature-length films. One of the secrets to his success was, ironically, the fact that he began his career with no formal training: 'Since I didn't have any kind of formal training, it didn't make any difference to me if I was listening to Lightnin' Slim, or a vocal group called the Jewels ... or Webern, or Varèse, or Stravinsky,' he said in 1989. 'To me, it was all good music.' It was his diverse musical influences that led him to create the music he became famous for–music that was often difficult to categorise.

E The last habit is to break up your goals, something pioneered nearly three hundred years ago by Benjamin Franklin, when he came up with an approach to changing habits called the list of thirteen virtues. These were character traits he took to be important, but in which he found himself lacking. He knew that nurturing these habits would bring about positive change in his life. Starting at the top of the list, Franklin spent one week working on each virtue. In the morning he thought about how he would reinforce the new habit throughout the day. During the day he looked at his notes to remind himself of the new habit. To accomplish his virtues, he broke them into small units of work, thinking only about one unit at a time. 'Spend most of your time working on the task in front of you,' he wrote, 'and avoid dreaming too much about the big goal.' Now that's sound advice, still valid even today!

3 ★★ **The words/phrases below appear in the sections indicated in brackets. What do they mean in the context of the text? Choose the correct meaning.**

1 silent (section A)
 A non-existent B unheard
2 face the fact (section B)
 A show the truth B confront the truth
3 take possession (section C)
 A acquire B own
4 spanning (section D)
 A enclosing around B extending across
5 reinforce (section E)
 A strengthen B support

4 ★★ **Fill in:** ***nurture, personal, accomplished, intrinsic, formal, possess, aid.***

Interestingly enough, most autodidacts have little to no **1)** .... education or training but **2)** .... self-determination, curiosity, true passion and a(n) **3)** .... motivation to learn. These **4)** .... attributes drive the self-taught to **5)** .... rather unique learning habits that **6)** .... them in achieving impressive learning outcomes. It's no surprise then, that most autodidacts are quite **7)** .... in their fields of study.

2b Vocabulary

1 ★ **Choose the correct answer.**

1 Teamwork requires that everyone is **plum/cushy/vital/amenable** to each other's ideas.
2 A skilled researcher can **attain/interpret/enfold/accomplish** data given to them and draw conclusions from it.
3 Candidates for the position of chief communications officer must be able to **cultivate/facilitate/articulate/allocate** ideas effectively.
4 Many young people feel a sense of **entitlement/aspiration/association/dedication** and don't believe they have to work hard.

2 ★★ **Fill in:** *down, in (x2), upon, on, into, away, off.*

1 He was asked to step .... from his position as president of the board of directors.
2 Most days Jim knocks .... work around 6 pm.
3 Examinations are held each term, ... accordance with the college's policy.
4 It took Kelly a while to settle .... her new role when she first joined the company but now she is a key member of staff.
5 The developer unexpectedly hit .... a great new idea for a software application.
6 The research team is .... the threshold of a major breakthrough in treating Alzheimer's.
7 College students should try to secure an internship .... their chosen field.
8 The sales team hammered .... at the new proposal in order for it to be ready for today's meeting.

3 ★★ **Complete the idioms with:** *pick, take, brought, slipped, racked, think.*

1 The meeting with the marketing department completely .... his mind.
2 Let's go for coffee so I can .... your brain about my new start-up.
3 As an app developer, it's essential to .... outside the box to come up with new innovative ideas.
4 He .... his brain for hours but couldn't remember where he left his thesis notes.
5 His lecture .... to my mind some research I did on cognitive conditioning years ago.
6 Let's go for a walk to .... your mind off your work for a while.

4 ★★ **Complete the sentences with a word from the box.**

• frank • blunt • unfettered

1 I hope you will be .... with me about my thesis; I really could use some honest feedback.
2 Kevin can be quite .... with his colleagues, often upsetting them.
3 The university allowed him .... access to the research material when he was writing his paper.

• composed • constituted • collated

4 The data will be .... in a report by the head engineer on the project.
5 Most of the report was .... of different surveys and the analysis of their results.
6 The oral exam .... fifty percent of the students' final mark last term.

• constantly • swiftly • literally

7 Education has .... become accessible to all; online opportunities have made this a reality.
8 He is .... promoting his company with various online activities.
9 The company will attempt to process all orders as .... as possible to ensure customer satisfaction.

5 ★★ **Fill in:** *cutting-edge, career, tired, key, blue-collar, tuition.*

Vocational Education – a practical path

In recent years, vocational training has seen an upsurge in its standing as a viable alternative to university. The **1)** .... cliché that it is only for those that aren't academically minded, and are only seeking **2)** .... jobs, is now outdated. A variety of qualifications from plumbing to journalism are available to those students looking to enhance their **3)** .... prospects by obtaining a practical skill set in their chosen field. Lower **4)** .... fees and the specialised nature of these courses, that are often delivered using **5)** .... technology, make vocational training a highly attractive option. In today's ultra-competitive job market, employers are looking for candidates with the skills to meet the challenges of the workplace. A vocational course may just be the **6)** .... component for job success!

Topic related vocabulary

2b

Success, Hopes and Dreams
Prepositions & Phrasal verbs

6 ★ **Choose the correct item.**

1 It's important not to be sucked **in/with/on** by conventional thinking when pursuing your dream.
2 Great people in history often leapt **on/at/over** opportunities when they presented themselves.
3 Success means thinking **beyond/ahead/over** and developing a logical plan.
4 Everyone was **at/on/in** awe of his strength and courage as an athlete.
5 She quit her job **on/in/over** impulse to pursue her dream of being a writer.
6 Through his foundation, he set **off/through/out** to help educate poor children throughout the world.

Words often confused

7 ★★ **Complete the sentences with a word from the box.**

• inspiration • stimulation • aspiration

1 Mary had a flash of .... and decided to write a book.
2 Her .... is to become a successful novelist.
3 Children need a lot of .... in class to prevent them from being distracted.

• achieved • encountered • overcame

4 Mark .... his physical limitations to become a star fencer.
5 Julia .... various obstacles that challenged her inner strength.
6 Ralph .... his life-long dream and competed in the Olympics.

• diligent • dedicated • driven

7 The researchers are .... to the cause of finding a cure for cancer.
8 They are .... to continue the work of their predecessors in the field.
9 He is .... about recording his experiments and never leaves out a detail.

Idioms

8 ★★ **Use the items in the list to complete the idioms in the sentences.**

• hopes • limit • back • pieces • sights • courage

1 The sky's the .... on what Janey can do; she's so talented.
2 When he sets his .... on something, there is no stopping him.
3 After dropping out of medical school, Nora had difficulty picking up the .... of her life.
4 I hope to pluck up the .... to apply for the position.
5 He got a pat on the .... for a job well done.
6 Harry pinned his .... on being accepted on the course.

9 ★★ **Fill in:** *passive, articulate, knowledgeable, humble, competent, focused.*

Get your Dream Job with an Impressive Interview

You've applied for the job and now it's time for that dreaded interview. This is the opportunity for employers to assess how **1)** .... you would be in the position.

Consider these tips:

• Always do your research. Employers want someone who is **2)** .... about the company and role so do your homework and prepare answers in advance.
• Being **3)** .... might seem like an attractive quality to have but employers want to know about your achievements, so you have to sell yourself.
• Don't be **4)** .... Engage with the interviewer and be **5)** .... when answering questions; you have to be able to express yourself with assurance.
• Finally, be **6)** .... on your goals. Someone who knows what they want is more likely to succeed!

Word formation

10 ★★ **Complete the sentences with words derived from the words in bold.**

1 The research team .... difficulties when they began analysing the data. **(COUNTER)**
2 The idea of realising our hopes and dreams is .... in Western culture. **(BED)**
3 Virtual technology has the potential to .... teaching methods. **(REVOLVE)**
4 To be successful at something it's important to recognise your .... **(WEAK)**
5 It takes a lot of .... to start a business. **(INITIATE)**
6 The launch of the new product was a(n) .... success and it sold out within hours. **(PRECEDE)**
7 He was .... to let go of his dream and continued to work hard. **(WILL)**
8 The idea of travelling the world was highly .... for her. **(PROVOKE)**

2c Grammar in use

Infinitive – Gerund (-*ing* form)

1 ★★ **Complete the short texts using the correct infinitive or -*ing* form of the verbs in brackets.**

A More and more colleges hope **1)** .... **(introduce)** virtual learning environments (VLEs) in the near future as they provide flexibility for staff and students alike. However, while evidence appears **2)** .... **(already/prove)** that they play an important part in modern education, some disagree. Critics of VLEs, many of whom admitted **3)** .... **(oppose)** to the idea from the outset, complain that the system makes students lazy. They claim that the material VLEs offer should **4)** .... **(prepare)** by students themselves anyway.

B In our modern age there's no point in **1)** .... **(fight)** change. This is a concept which many employers seem **2)** .... **(start)** to understand. Firms have changed their policies and employees appreciate **3)** .... **(offer)** more flexibility, in terms of hours and working arrangements. Companies are also pleased **4)** .... **(gradually/increase)** their productivity for so long since introducing these measures.

2 ★★ **Put the verbs in brackets into the correct infinitive or -*ing* form.**

1 Make sure you don't forget .... **(order)** more office supplies tomorrow.
2 I'll never forget .... **(graduate)** from university; my parents were so proud!
3 I'm sorry .... **(hear)** that the conference has been cancelled; I was looking forward to it.
4 The clients are sorry for .... **(alter)** the project brief, but their CEO demanded last minute changes.
5 The delegate pack omitted .... **(mention)** that some of the talks had been cancelled.
6 The university are omitting .... **(say)** that tuition fees could increase next year.

It – There

3 ★ **Choose the correct word(s).**

1 I would appreciate **it/there** if you could help me prepare my speech.
2 **It's/There's** no choice but to cancel the conference; the venue's double-booked.
3 **It's/There's** no good complaining.
4 **It appears/There appears** that Mr Lewis left his laptop in the meeting room.
5 **There/It** comes a time when you have to re-evaluate your career choices.

Future tenses/other future forms/ the future in the past

4 ★★ **Put the verbs in brackets into the correct future form.**

1 a It's four o'clock already; Jane .... **(hand)** in her essay by now.
b We all expect that Professor Jackson .... **(hand)** us our new assignments in Friday's morning class.
2 a I'm sorry to disturb you, but .... **(you/work)** during the weekend, Sir?
b By the end of the week, the team .... **(work)** on the proposal for several months.
3 a Mrs Erikson believes that Tony .... **(not/finish)** the sales report on time.
b Staff believe that the company .... **(not/finish)** the refurbishments by the time they are due to move into the new office venue.
4 a The visiting professor's flight .... **(arrive)** at 3 pm.
b The students .... **(arrive)** in Glasgow on Wednesday morning.

5 ★★ **Use the words in bold to rewrite the sentences. Make any necessary changes.**

1 She was just about to hand in her notice when her boss offered her a new contract. **(point)**
....
2 The CEO will be opening the new flagship store next month. **(is to)**
....
3 The company are going to break into the European market any day now! **(verge)**
....
4 Emily will definitely go to Oxford; she's a very gifted student. **(sure)**
....

Grammar Revision 2c (Modules 1-2)

1 **★★ Put the verbs in brackets into the correct tense.**

1 Jason .... **(regret)** his decision to study in his hometown now that his friends have gone away to university.
2 The project leader .... **(probably/arrange)** a review meeting tomorrow morning.
3 We .... **(spend)** hours going through all these applicants; just look at all those CVs!
4 I .... **(sit)** in my office when the firm's record profits were announced.
5 They .... **(not/finalise)** the research application until this afternoon.
6 Jane .... **(revise)** all day so she was exhausted.
7 The government .... **(agree)** to support the economy by investing in banks.
8 My college .... **(run)** the same courses for years!
9 Amy .... **(constantly/boast)** about how qualified she is!

2 **★★ Tick (✓) the correct sentences.**

1 a My MBA course is the most difficult thing I had ever done. ☐
b My MBA course is the most difficult thing I have ever done. ☐
2 a Louise used to have a very well-paid job. ☐
b Louise would have a very well-paid job. ☐
3 a It's no use to postpone the decision any longer. ☐
b It's no use postponing the decision any longer. ☐
4 a Mr Rivers would prefer to schedule the appointment for Monday. ☐
b Mr Rivers would prefer scheduling the appointment for Monday. ☐
5 a Eric got such good results because he has been studying hard for months. ☐
b Eric got such good results because he had been studying hard for months. ☐
6 a Karen was heard to talk about the new merger. ☐
b Karen was heard talking about the new merger. ☐

Key word transformations

3 **★★ For questions 1-5, complete the second sentence so that it has a similar meaning to the first sentence using the word given. Do not change the word given. You must use between three and eight words, including the word given.**

1 I'll wrap things up here and then I'll print you a copy of the sales figures to check. **SOON**
I'll print you a copy of the sales figures to check .... here.
2 Mr Vickers continued his presentation even though the committee seemed indifferent towards his proposal. **ON**
Mr Vickers .... the committee's indifference towards his proposal.
3 I'm ever so sorry but I totally forgot about our meeting. **CONFESS**
I must .... my mind.
4 I'm certain that the firm will reimburse you for the money that you lost. **BOUND**
The firm .... you for the money that you lost.
5 She's been doing her PhD for nearly three years. **STARTED**
It .... her PhD.

Grammar in Focus

★★ Fill in the gaps with the correct word. Then put the verbs in brackets into the correct form.

- It seems likely that the traditional letter grade system used in schools **1)** .... **(remain)** the benchmark for many more years to come. However, how useful is it in **2)** .... **(assess)** a student's progress? Some educators feel that the system we have been using **3)** .... decades needs urgent improvement. They argue that many types of learners **4)** .... **(overlook)** by the rigid one-dimensional view of letter grade systems. Instead, they hope schools **5)** .... **(look)** to standards-based grading systems as an alternative, a method that they believe **6)** .... bound to provide a more balanced view of a student's abilities.
- Many millennials who **7)** .... **(graduate)** from university recently, find themselves in a difficult situation. They are frequently being told that they are overqualified and inexperienced. But, how are these young people expected to be able **8)** .... get experience when they **9)** .... **(study)** for most of their lives? One solution is to pursue a vocational course that **10)** .... **(offer)** some practical experience **11)** .... the time a student graduates.

Listening skills

Multiple choice

Preparing for the task

STUDY SKILLS

Before you listen, read the rubric to get an idea of what you will hear. Then read the questions and the options to help you focus on what you will be listening for. In some tasks you may have to listen for what the speakers agree/disagree on. For these types of questions, pay attention to language indicating agreement/disagreement. Remember, while you listen, pay attention to the register and tone of the speaker as this can be useful in clarifying your answer.

1 **a) ★ Read the rubric and questions 1 and 2. Which question is asking about agreement and which about disagreement?**

You hear two people talking about holiday time.

1 Both speakers believe that holidays
   A can create stressful situations.
   B are necessary in order to be productive.
   C are difficult to arrange.

2 On which point do the speakers contradict each other?
   A the best way to de-stress
   B the appeal of foreign holidays
   C the effect holidays have on health

b) ★ Read the extract from an audioscript and answer the questions in Ex. 1a.

Woman: What are you doing, Bill?
Man: I'm just sorting out my days off. I've got a trip to Spain booked and I wanted to make sure that this project won't clash with it.
Woman: I love Spain.
Man: Me too, and I really need the break. My head's just not in the game right now.
Woman: I know what you mean. This job can be very stressful and you need some time to unwind if you want to be able to do the job properly. Although, I've noticed that often when I do unwind, I tend to feel under the weather.
Man: Really? I find the opposite is true. I often come back to work after a holiday feeling refreshed only to get ill after being in the office.

2 **★★ You will hear three different extracts. For questions 1-6, choose the answer (A, B or C) which fits best according to what you hear. There are two questions for each extract.**

Extract one
You hear two people talking about a work placement.

1 In the man's opinion, what was the most salient point to address?
   A the fine details
   B the choice of departments
   C the schedule of events

2 What do the two speakers agree about?
   A that they have confirmed the important aspects of the placements
   B that they need proper preparation in place before they begin
   C that they have finalised all the details for the placements

Extract two
You hear a careers councillor talking to students about job hunting.

3 What is the speaker doing when she mentions getting your foot in the door?
   A predicting a likely outcome of the process
   B demonstrating the need to be aggressive
   C highlighting the importance of getting a jump on things

4 Why does the speaker refer to her own job hunting experience?
   A to reassure the students that they are not alone
   B to warn the students that they are not prepared
   C to show the students the gravity of their situation

Extract three
You hear two people talking about evening classes.

5 The woman uses the term 'cost an arm and a leg' to illustrate
   A the expense of professional work.
   B the physical requirements of D.I.Y.
   C the importance of proper training.

6 The man thinks that courses that lack a practical application
   A allow people to improve themselves.
   B fail to prove their worth.
   C provide an artistic outlet.

Speaking skills

Offering/Responding to apologies & Reassuring

1 a) ★ Read the dialogue. Use phrases (a-e) to complete the dialogue.

a you needn't worry
b I completely overlooked it
c that is most regrettable
d my humblest apologies
e I appreciate your honesty

Mr Sanders: Jack, did you courier the files to our clients across town for their 2 pm meeting today?
Jack: Actually, no, **1)** .... I'm so sorry; it won't happen again.
Mr Sanders: Well, **2)** .... They just called me and were quite bothered about not having received them yet. They are key clients and we can't afford to lose their business.
Jack: Yes, I realise that. The fault is entirely mine but **3)** ....; there's still time. I'll take them over personally now.
Mr Sanders: Please do. **4)** ...., Jack.
Jack: Thank you, and once again, **5)** ....

b) ★ Replace the phrases (a-e) in Ex. 1 with the ones below.

• I'll rectify the situation • I can't apologise enough
• Thank you for your candour on the matter
• it totally slipped my mind • that is unfortunate

c) ★ Which phrases in Exs 1a & b are offering/ responding to apologies or reassuring?

Offering apologies	....
Responding to apologies	....
Reassuring	....

Comparing pictures

2 ★ Look at pictures A and C showing different styles of learning. Then expand the prompts to form sentences about the differences in the two teaching methods.

A

B

C

D

A traditional teaching method/effective/structured schedule/attend class/routine/face-to-face interactions/instructors/keep students/on task

C agree/but/online courses/students/study course materials independently/contribute/class discussions/assignments/offer/flexibility

3 ★ Now look at all the pictures. Use the list to put the advantages and disadvantages of each teaching method in the box below. Some may be used more than once.

• students work at their own pace
• conflicting schedules • active learning • spoon feeding of material • encourages cooperation
• no other student feedback • isolated learning environment • closes learning gaps

	Advantages	Disadvantages
Picture A		
Picture B		
Picture C		
Picture D		

4 ★ Choose the correct item.

1 A: Which picture portrays collaborative learning?
B: **a** The first picture is a good example.
b All the pictures are interesting.

2 A: Suggest another teaching method.
B: **a** Perhaps using tablets in the classroom.
b Technology would illustrate that aspect.

3 A: What may have happened after the picture was taken?
B: **a** I fail to see the point.
b I can't say for certain.

2f Writing Formal letters/emails

Rubric analysis

1 a) ★ Read the rubric and underline the key words. Then answer the questions.

An English language magazine is inviting readers to submit letters in response to the following excerpt from an article: '*The 21st century workplace requires more technological skills than ever before.*' You decide to submit a letter expressing your views. You should briefly describe your experiences using technology, explain the reasons why it has become important and assess the impact it has in the workplace. Write your **letter** in 280-320 words.

1 What greeting would you use?
2 What is the purpose for writing the letter?
3 What paragraph plan would you use?
4 How would you sign off the letter?

b) ★ Read the letter and choose the correct expressions.

Dear Sir/Madam,

Having thoroughly read your article on technology in the workplace in the last issue of your magazine, I would like to put forth my observations on the subject. New technological devices, considered to be innovative tools, have indeed revolutionised the way businesses operate. **1) It is my strong belief/In my view** that they will define the future of the workplace.

2) As far as myself/Personally, I have a lot of high tech experience and I am very confident in my ability to learn any new computing programs quickly. **3) While/In fact,** I cannot imagine living without my mobile phone as I frequently check status updates from various networking sites and keep in touch with my 100+ social media friends and followers.

There is no doubt that the adoption of sophisticated technology within the workplace has become essential in recent years. The apparent reason for this is that the latest tech tools allow employees and companies to be more efficient in the global marketplace. **4) This way/That being the case**, technological know-how is required for the majority of industries since it makes life easier for all working professionals.

It is my considered opinion that technology has impacted businesses significantly. **5) Like/As** markets shift with higher frequencies, businesses have become extremely reliant on technology. This is because computers and machinery perform many tasks and cut costs for businesses while increasing productivity. **6) Similarly/Yet** the Internet has improved communication since information can be transferred instantaneously, allowing businesses to offer their services across the globe.

7) Even though/On the whole, any businesses without some level of technical savvy are unlikely to succeed in the future. It is **8) although/therefore** critical that businesses embrace change and new technologies in the digital age to stay afloat. Thank you for considering my views.

Yours faithfully,
Martin Jones

2 ★ Read the model letter again and underline examples where the writer has used advanced grammatical/linking structures:

1 passive voice
2 fronting
3 reduced relative clauses
4 discourse markers

Your turn

3 ★ Read the rubric and underline the key words. Then answer the questions.

An English language magazine is inviting readers to submit letters in response to the following excerpt from an article: ***'Remote working will become more common in the future.'*** You decide to submit a letter expressing your views. You should briefly describe a remote working experience that you or someone you know has had. Explain the reasons why it will become more common in the future and assess the impact it will have on businesses. Write your **letter** in 280-320 words.

1 What greeting would you use?
2 What paragraph plan would you use?
3 What useful expressions could you use as opening and closing remarks?
4 How would you sign off the letter?

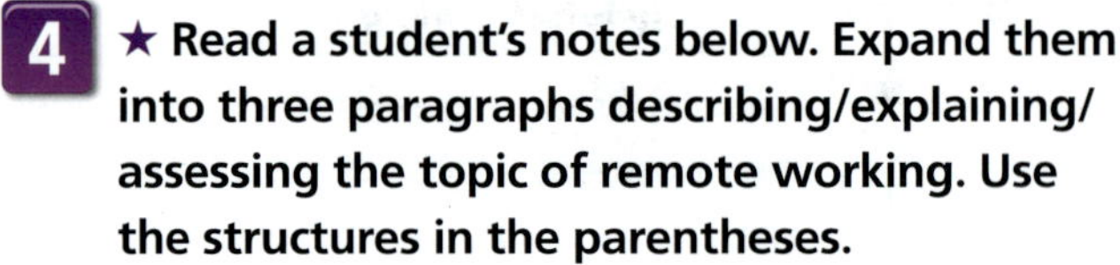

4 ★ Read a student's notes below. Expand them into three paragraphs describing/explaining/assessing the topic of remote working. Use the structures in the parentheses.

Para 1
1 have/set up work space/home – collaborate/colleagues online (fronting)
2 remain focused/non-work notifications/turn off (passive)

Para 2
3 remote work/flexibility/consider to be/the way of the future/no set schedule (reduced relative clauses)
4 travel time/reduce (passive)

Para 3
5 help companies grow/less expensive (discourse marker)
6 obtain/clear productivity gains (discourse marker)

5 ★ Use the model in Ex. 1, the ideas in Exs 3 & 4 and the plan below to write your letter.

Plan

Introduction

(Para 1)	*Greeting (opening remarks)*
(Paras 2-4)	*Development of the points raised in the rubric and analysis in different paragraphs*
(Para 5)	*Closing remarks (summary of opinion)*

Reading

1 ★★ **You are going to read an article about what makes a great boss. For questions 1-10, choose from the people A-D. The people may be chosen more than once.**

Which person gives each of these opinions about bosses?

The average boss fears losing their power.	1
Great bosses see employees as their peers.	2
Truly successful bosses take risks.	3
Good bosses know that constructive criticism plays a vital role in growth.	4
Bosses who cultivate a diversity of approaches achieve success.	5
The best results from employees are gained by a hands-off management style.	6
Great bosses focus on maximising their employees' potential.	7
Overly controlling bosses stifle employee contribution.	8
Ardour for the job is essential in winning allegiance from employees.	9
Developing a unique relationship with each employee is key to success.	10

What Makes A Great Boss?

We asked some top professionals in the HR field just exactly what makes a boss exceptional. Here is what they had to say.

A Norma Schmidt, HR Manager LSN Hudson

It comes down to one simple concept: actions speak louder than words. Being positive and encouraging is all very nice but great bosses truly inspire through their actions. Many experts will pinpoint integrity as a vital quality of a great leader but only those who 'walk the talk' demonstrate integrity on a daily basis. Really exceptional bosses are transparent instead of secretively trying to hold on to their own power. Unlike typical bosses, they are unafraid to share information or enable authority. One of their main goals is to see their employees grow and become their best. They don't hesitate to give both positive and negative feedback along the way that cultivates a sense of cooperation and development.

B Carl Moss, CEO, RND Recruitment

Employees are not clones and a successful boss recognises this fundamental idea. Lumping people together and trying to motivate and foster potential in the same way is misguided leadership. Appreciating that different people have different abilities, needs and styles, an effective boss will work to figure out what these are by getting to know staff as individuals. Average bosses often make the mistake of not treating their staff as adults, believing that they need constant monitoring and supervision. They think their role is to set rules and prevent mistakes. Great bosses, on the other hand, treat employees as equals and trust in their decisions and capabilities. Like good coaches, they call the plays from the bench, guiding but not controlling their players. They are not afraid of mistakes and see them as learning opportunities.

C Janey Gillis, Career Forward Magazine

Nothing is more demotivating than a boss who looks bored with or lacks zeal for the job. Great leaders infect their followers with passion that makes them want to join in the quest. Not enough can be said for celebrating accomplishments and facing challenges with fervour. Of course, not all employees will react in the same way. Respecting that each employee is different and keeping an open mind to new ideas can reap benefits. Plus there is the added bonus that employees feel valued when acknowledged for their differences. Bosses who seek to align their employees' ideas with their own miss out on all kinds of possibilities. They are afraid of leaving their comfort zones. Top bosses seek out a variety of employees whose new ways of thinking push their companies ahead of the pack.

D Zak Miller, HR Manager Swildar Funds

'Do as you're told' is a motto for many mediocre bosses which basically yields minimal results and often attitudes from their employees. Bosses that instill fear and compliance in their employees will never get the most from them. Instead, these employees are only concerned with keeping in their bosses good books and not getting fired. They are never inspired or truly motivated by their work. Exceptional bosses, however, are visionary and invite change and experimentation. They lead fearlessly, not afraid of failure, and know that change often leads to growth. They have realised that not evolving is a death sentence for them and the company.

Language Knowledge 2

Word Formation

1 ★★ **For questions 1-8, read the text below. Use the word given in capitals at the end of some of the lines to form a word that fits in the space in the same line. There is an example at the beginning (0).**

Wonder Full Work!

Think of your dream job. Is it challenging? Does it involve travel or does	
it give you a certain level of **0)** *AUTHORITY*? Whatever aspects make it	**AUTHORISE**
ideal, most people are in agreement that although a big paycheck is	
a(n) **1)** .... attraction, it takes more than just that to make	**DENY**
a job worthy. In fact, many people with high salaries have reported	
feeling a sense of **2)** .... from their work.	**ATTACH**
Status, salary and **3)** .... don't matter as much as your	**SECURE**
interest level in your daily activities. Engaging work that draws you in	
and gives you a sense of **4)** .... is considerably more	**FILL**
satisfying. Having autonomy, **5)** .... of purpose and variety	**CLEAR**
of tasks as well as receiving constructive feedback are all factors that	
6) .... influence job satisfaction and are considered precise	**SIGN**
7) .... of whether a job will make you happy or not. Work	**PREDICT**
that involves helping others is often an ingredient for a(n)	
8) .... job. The right qualities can make the difference	**MEAN**
between putting a smile or a frown on your face while you work.	

Multiple choice cloze

2 ★★ **For questions 1-8, read the text below and decide which answer (A, B, C or D) best fits each gap. There is an example at the beginning (0).**

VR in the Classroom

We have seen it in films and some have even experienced it first 0) C. Virtual reality is not just a gimmick. It is **1)** .... the line between technology and daily life. VR has an experiential quality that **2)** .... your attention and allows you to interact with the on-screen world, which is extremely attractive to children. The question is, though, what role should VR **3)** .... in the classroom?

Besides overcoming the potential **4)** .... to incorporating VR into the classroom, it is necessary to discern how VR can be **5)** .... useful as an education tool. It is an appealing teaching method as many children respond better to seeing and experiencing things rather than having them explained verbally. Through VR, students are **6)** .... by the subject and they can, for example, examine the inside of a single-celled organism or discuss **7)** .... events with students around the world in VR social spaces. VR also **8)** .... a world of opportunities in the areas of product design, electronics and engineering. It's a virtual goldmine!

0	**A** opportunity	**B** look	**C** hand	**D** time
1	**A** blurring	**B** distorting	**C** clouding	**D** muddling
2	**A** squeezes	**B** clutches	**C** grabs	**D** conquers
3	**A** pose	**B** present	**C** provide	**D** play
4	**A** blocks	**B** blockades	**C** barriers	**D** barricades
5	**A** genuinely	**B** honestly	**C** hopefully	**D** purely
6	**A** encircled	**B** encased	**C** bordered	**D** surrounded
7	**A** current	**B** existing	**C** present	**D** modern
8	**A** brings up	**B** opens up	**C** sets up	**D** puts up

Key word transformations

3 ★★ **For questions 1-6, complete the second sentence so that it has a similar meaning to the first sentence, using the word given. Do not change the word given. You must use between three and eight words, including the word given.**

1 I was surprised at how challenging the job was. **EXPECTED**

I ....
.... so challenging.

2 Although I disagreed with the new company policy, I was forced to accept it. **CHOICE**

Despite my disagreement with the new company policy, I
....
.... it.

3 Only students with an access card can enter the microbiology labs. **RESTRICTED**

Entry to the microbiology labs
....
.... an access card.

4 My advisor said that, as far as she knows, the course has been cancelled. **BEST**

My advisor said that ....
....
the course has been cancelled.

5 Anyone at the college can attend the talk. **OPEN**

The talk ....
....
at the college.

6 Should a place on the course open up, we will contact you first. **OPENING**

We will contact you first ....
....
on the course.

Grammar

4 ★ Choose the correct item.

1 If it .... for the extra tutoring I did before, I would have failed the exam.
A weren't
B isn't
C hasn't been
D hadn't been

2 I prefer going to the library .... studying at home.
A to
B from
C than
D by

3 It is necessary for .... a sales report every Friday.
A you complete
B you to complete
C your completing
D completing

4 It's no use .... upset about not being hired for the job. There are many more you can apply for.
A to get
B you get
C at getting
D getting

5 The professor .... an extra research project this term.
A has her students to do
B has her students be doing
C is having her students do
D had her students been doing

6 The course was excellent. It was great .... something I really enjoyed for a change.
A I had studied
B to study
C study
D studying

7 Employees .... to take holiday leave must complete this form.
A are wishing
B wish
C who wishing
D who wish

8 The last staff meeting was ....
A before a month
B over a month
C a month before
D a month ago

9 Mr Barnes has worked .... director of communications at the university for over ten years.
A for
B like
C as
D to

10 Please hand in your assignments by Friday noon ....
A at the latest
B the later
C the latest
D latest

11 Under no circumstances .... this contract.
A she will sign
B will she sign
C won't she sign
D she signs

12 My boss proposed .... on this project in particular.
A I am working
B me to work
C my work
D that I work

Vocabulary

5 ★ Choose the correct item.

1 The research paper .... that certain peptides prevent premature aging.
A contends
B contracts
C contorts
D conflates

2 There is no point laying the .... on anyone; let's work together to solve the problem.
A blame
B liability
C guilt
D fault

3 The business partners used social media to .... their start up.
A project
B propel
C instigate
D launch

4 The new employee .... a lot of time in learning all the company's procedures.
A supplied
B furnished
C invested
D participated

5 He has made .... plans to visit the college in the spring.
A unsettled
B tentative
C transformative
D potential

6 There was a .... between the employment contracts so they issued a new one.
A disturbance
B difference
C discrepancy
D divergence

7 The job salary has little .... on whether I will accept it or not.
A bearing
B pertinence
C relation
D demeanor

8 The student was .... from the exam for incorrect use of the answer sheet.
A disgraced
B discredited
C disqualified
D disregarded

9 She was hired .... for her excellent mediation skills.
A substantially
B essentially
C respectively
D marginally

10 Her responsibilities go beyond the .... of most junior internships.
A scope
B scale
C arena
D realm

11 Ben was .... with guilt for cheating on his exam.
A exhumed
B consumed
C engulfed
D obsessed

12 The professor is a .... supporter of teaching research methods in the classroom.
A settled
B reliable
C steady
D staunch

3a Reading

Multiple choice

Preparing for the task

1 ★ **Read the passage below and answer the questions by choosing one of the words in bold from the passage.**

> Human beings have the **intrinsic** need to be affiliated with a group and belong. It is a **pressing** desire that we strive daily to satisfy. It's also of **paramount** importance in order to reach our potential and when left ignored and **unmet**, it can deeply affect our self-esteem, resulting in poor achievement, immune function and health.

A Which word emphasises the urgency of the need to belong?

B Which word conveys the idea that the need to belong is the number one factor for something?

C Which word describes when the need to belong is not fulfilled?

D Which word conveys that the need to belong is inherent?

Remember!

Remember to determine the meaning of specific words based on the context in which they are used in the text. When asked to choose the main idea of a text, the options may include statements that are true in the text but don't necessarily represent the overall idea of the text.

The Need to Belong

Humans, by nature, are social creatures. We live together, build communities together, raise families together and strive to shape our destinies together. As psychiatrist William Glasser famously said, 'we are driven by five genetic needs: survival, love and belonging, power, freedom and fun.' However, is there more to our desire for social connections than genetics and the practicalities of survival? Does this element of our psyche **run deeper**? Could belonging and connection be the universal sources of true well-being?

2 ★★ **For questions 1-5, read an article about the need to belong and decide which choice (A, B, C or D) best answers each question.**

1 In the first paragraph, what does the writer suggest about the need for social connections?
A They are a by-product of self-preservation.
B They are secondary to the continuation of the species.
C They are crucial to our overall physical and emotional welfare.
D They are impractical in some environments.

2 The word 'cultivated' in line 21 emphasises that social interaction
A develops over time.
B enriches us as people.
C needs to be nurtured.
D relies on the input of others.

3 What does 'this' in line 32 refer to?
A being a supporter
B joining a political party
C loving one's country
D starting a civic movement

4 Which phrase best describes the impact of a shared experience on fans?
A minor and inconsequential
B confusing and disorientating
C far-reaching and joyous
D soothing and refreshing

5 Why does the author believe that the desire to belong is so long lasting?
A It's culturally reinforced.
B It's an attractive option.
C It's entertaining for those involved.
D It's part of the human condition.

Many philosophers and theologians throughout history have certainly thought so. Aristotle once remarked that 'he who is unable to live in society, or has no need because he is sufficient for himself, must be either a beast or a god.' Over the centuries numerous others have come to the same conclusion: that the need to belong is the very thing that makes us human. This point was highlighted by social activist Dorothy Day when she said that 'we have all known the long loneliness, and we have found that the answer is community.' People have long known, then, that beyond a basic **primal** need, belonging helps us become cultivated on an emotional and spiritual level. Now, scientists and physiologists are able to see that social groups and communities can also help and change us on a biological and hormonal level too.

Take the tribal groupings of sports fans in the modern age, for example. Sports teams offer people a connection with more than just fellow fans and athletes. They also provide a sense of regional pride, further familial bonds and give membership to shared **aesthetic** preferences, such as a fondness for team colours. Research has shown that belonging to a group in this way is not only an expression of an individual's **sense of self**, but also benefits all aspects of life by providing a sense of **solidarity** and shared purpose. It lets people derive happiness from success and shared euphoria, even if that joy is something that passes.

While the benefits of belonging to such a group, such as higher self-esteem, lower levels of depression and reduced loneliness, are plentiful, they don't stop at **remedial** psychological aids. Amazingly, neuroscientists have also discovered that special cells called mirror neurons put spectators' brains **in sync** with the brains of those wearing their colours in the chaos on the field. Hormonal responses are also affected, with male fans' testosterone levels surging along with the athletes'. So when sports fans say that they are all one voice and a powerful **tangible** entity, they really are speaking quite literally!

So, it seems that both activity and the engagement in a said activity, be it sports, entertainment, politics or cultural events, can play a vital part in satisfying our need to connect with one another. Belonging is more than just simple affiliation and should be placed within a larger framework. As speaker and author Brian Solis reminds us, 'community is much more than belonging to something; it's about doing something together that makes belonging matter.' Belonging, and its enduring attraction, is part of our DNA and plays an essential role in our social and emotional makeup. It is why we, as a species, really are better together.

3 ★ **Choose the correct item.**

1 Ancient philosophers viewed the ability to live **in/with/at** society as essential.

2 Teams provide a connection **towards/with/after** more than just fellow fans.

3 Supporting a sports team offers a sense **of/for/to** regional pride and fellowship.

4 Social interaction benefits all aspects of life **via/by/through** providing happiness.

5 The players **on/at/in** the field have a duty to the fans and the city they represent.

4 ★★ **Fill in the verbs:** ***drive, connect, strive, derive*** **in the correct form.**

1 Humans have an essential need .... with one another.

2 Humanity is constantly .... to create a better world.

3 Psychologists believe we .... by five basic genetic needs.

4 It's common for people .... happiness from shared experiences.

5 ★★ **Match the words and phrases in bold in the text to their definitions below.**

A intended to improve sth that is inadequate
B to be more serious and strongly felt
C matched in timing, speed or intensity
D a feeling of support for others
E original or primitive
F the essential elements that form who somebody is as a person
G real and substantial
H related to the enjoyment of beauty

6 ★★ **Replace the underlined phrases in the text with their synonymous phrases below.**

- will go away
- reached a similar realisation
- viewed with a broader perspective
- to decide the direction of our future

3b Vocabulary

1 ★ **Choose the correct word.**

1 Artists take great pride **in/for/at** their creations.
2 Kim is notorious **of/for/in** her cruel sense of humour.
3 Jo came **across/against/round** to our point of view in the end.
4 Andy is very sensitive **over/to/in** other people's needs.
5 Her point really came **round/across/against** at the meeting.
6 She meant well but her comment came **off/over/out** as criticism.
7 She was too frightened to go **across/over/against** her parents' wishes.
8 He went **on/into/across** the contents of the email at great length.

2 ★★ **Replace the words/phrases in bold with their synonyms in the correct form.**

• wince • smirk • shrug • gape • snort • scowl

1 He **smiled with smugness** when he got all the answers to the quiz right.
2 She **had a look of resentment on her face** when she hung up the phone.
3 He **stood there staring** at the text message in shock after reading the bad news.
4 She **grunted** to show her impatience when the Internet went down.
5 He **moved his shoulders** to show his irritation and walked out of the room.
6 She **displayed discomfort** at the thought of using the difficult software program.

3 ★★ **Match the underlined idioms to their meaning.**

1 ☐	Her boss didn't mince words and told her that she was fired.	a	to not say something
2 ☐	Ann stood around making small talk about the weather.	b	to reveal a secret prematurely
3 ☐	Julie has to learn to hold her tongue and not upset people.	c	to say what you mean directly
4 ☐	Someone spilled the beans about her friend's surprise party.	d	to talk about things that are unimportant
5 ☐	Jack has the gift of the gab and could easily convince us that he was right.	e	to be able to persuade people

4 ★★ **Circle the odd one out.**

1 Tony has an **inhibited/impulsive/impetuous** nature and sometimes regrets things he's done.
2 Andy is such a(n) **amiable/stubborn/agreeable** and fun-loving person.
3 Kim's tone was **brusque/insolent/effusive** and hostile.
4 Henry made a series of **astute/shrewd/industrious** business decisions.
5 His point was so **strong-willed/explicit/clear** that we all understood why he said it.
6 Joe is so **obstinate/dogmatic/pertinent** that no one dares to argue with him.

5 ★★ **Fill in the correct word.**

• expressive • masterpieces • master • cool • renowned • twitching

Miming is a purely silent art where actors wear masks and perform scenes from life in a ridiculous and **1)** .... manner. They act out a story, through body motions without using words. The gestures and visual design clearly tell the story, which is usually humorous. One of the most **2)** .... moves done by mimes is 'The Lean' – leaning on an imaginary table. This may sound easy but is quite difficult to **3)** .... The actor has to bend his leg in close proximity to the imaginary table to give the illusion that he is resting on that object. He then has to be as **4)** .... as a cucumber and remain there without **5)** .... involuntarily. All these skills are vital in creating and performing amazing mime **6)** ....

Topic related vocabulary 3b

Fashion & Appearance

6 ★ **Choose the correct word.**

1 It's important to choose the right size; if clothes are too small, they can end up looking **puny/skimpy/scrawny/bony**.
2 Ted's got small hands with short **stocky/stubby/sturdy/burly** fingers.
3 Jenny's skin is youthful and **unblemished/unvarnished/untarnished/unimpaired**.
4 Judy's hair was so **grubby/shabby/tangled/scruffy** that she couldn't comb it.

Idioms *(related to clothes)*

7 ★★ **Fill in:** *pocket, hat, socks, belt, collar, glove.*

1 Sue buys extravagant clothes and jewels at a drop of a ....
2 Emma is a fashion blogger with several years' experience under her ....
3 These trousers fit me like a ....
4 Jackie got hot under the .... when I criticised her taste in clothes.
5 It's time he pulls his .... up and gets into shape.
6 Janet was out of .... after going on a shopping spree.

Prepositions/Phrasal verbs

8 ★ **Choose the correct item.**

1 There's been a rise **at/in/of** the number of people wearing sportswear to the office.
2 Tom's eyes glazed **about/off/over** at the thought of going shopping.
3 Janet gazed at the beautiful gown **in/on/at** awe.
4 Her fashion sense displays a lack **in/of/with** imagination.
5 Bell bottom trousers are **out/away/behind** of style.

Collocations

9 ★ **Match the words to make collocations. Then use them to make sentences of your own.**

1 ☐	short-lived	a	trend
2 ☐	blemish	b	flaws
3 ☐	skin	c	position
4 ☐	cosmetic	d	smile
5 ☐	hunched	e	enhancement
6 ☐	winning	f	free

10 ★★ **Fill in:** *shrink, coax, frowned, manipulations, enhance, distorted, photoshopped, reflections.*

Photo Editing

With advances in technology, magazine images of cover models now illustrate fictional portrayals rather than **1)** .... of reality. This is because most images, at least to some degree, are **2)** .... or airbrushed. Retouching software has made it easy to **3)** .... the appearance of models with lighting and exposure tricks which **4)** .... their waists and make them look thinner and more attractive. Such digital **5)** .... can create unrealistic and **6)** .... expectations of healthy weight and body image. While some of these photographs are considered skilful artwork, others are **7)** .... upon as unethical, especially when these models are used to **8)** .... the public into buying the products advertised.

Word formation

11 ★★ **Complete the sentences with words derived from the words in bold.**

1 He put much effort into the .... of his dream. **(REAL)**
2 For most people, losing weight is a(n) .... goal due to lack of willpower. **(ATTAIN)**
3 Pointed shoes are recently making a .... in fashion circles. **(COME)**
4 She uses persuasion and .... to get what she wants. **(FLATTER)**
5 She was a(n) .... who claimed to be a star. **(IMPOSE)**
6 The designer worked .... to organise the fashion show. **(RELENT)**
7 Mary was a(n) .... beautiful girl. **(STRIKE)**
8 Don't judge people just on their physical .... **(CHARACTER)**
9 Her creations .... haute couture fashion. **(EXAMPLE)**
10 The woman was .... after her cosmetic surgery. **(RECOGNISE)**

3c Grammar in use

Adjectives/Adverbs

1 ★ **Choose the correct sentence.**

1 a Anne and Jeff are such good-behaved children!
  b Anne and Jeff are such well-behaved children!
2 a Mark's chief concern is maintaining cordial relations with his neighbours.
  b Maintaining cordial relations with his neighbours is chief to Mark.
3 a The speaker is a well-known Canadian self-help coach.
  b The speaker is a Canadian well-known self-help coach.
4 a What's wrong with Jason? I've never seen him with such a stone face before.
  b What's wrong with Jason? I've never seen him with such a stony face before.
5 a It's wide understood that Paul's relationship with his brother is somewhat strained.
  b It's widely understood that Paul's relationship with his brother is somewhat strained.

2 ★★ **Replace the words in bold with an appropriate word/phrase.**

• perfectly • in a strict manner
• very soon • only just • clearly

1 Denise spoke to her children **firmly** to remind them how dangerous it is to cross the road without looking.
2 If you ask me, it's **abundantly** clear that Andy and Steve don't get on.
3 Andrea **explicitly** told Martin not to mention the problems with the project in front of Tony.
4 Larry had **barely** finished writing an email to Sandra when she called him on the telephone.
5 The company team-building workshop will start **shortly** in the atrium.

Intensifiers

3 ★ **Choose the correct item.**

1 Henry is **fully/greatly/simply** aware of the importance of making a good first impression in an interview.
2 The powers of observation that the body language expert has are **entirely/absolutely/deeply** brilliant!
3 Erica is a(n) **utterly/vitally/highly** motivated young woman; I've never seen someone so dedicated to her goals.
4 The way Clowie shouted at Nick was **downright/categorically/heartily** rude and so uncalled for!
5 I think the gift that we got for Erica was **surely/wholly/just** right; not too fancy but not too cheap either.
6 Anne is the total opposite of her brother Jack; he is **rather/pretty/fairly** a hardworking person.

Gradable & Non-gradable Adjectives

4 ★★ **Replace the words in bold with the non-gradable adjectives from the list below.**

• starving • aghast • superb • ajar • mortified

1 Miranda is **shocked** at the change in Peter; he's so much louder than he used to be.
....
2 The **very hungry** athletes ate their food quickly; they hadn't eaten anything all day!
....
3 Mr Vickers always left the door to his office **slightly open** so people knew they could come in and talk to him.
....
4 Karen felt **embarrassed** after her unfortunate faux pas at the party; she has no idea how she'll live it down.
....
5 This self-help guide that I'm reading at the moment is a **good** book! It's full of useful advice.
....

Comparisons – *Like/As*

5 ★★ **Use the prompts below and the words in bold in the correct form to write sentences using suitable comparative structures.**

1 Richard is/competitive/person/I have ever met. **FAR**
....
2 There is/nothing/go for a walk in the countryside. **LIKE**
....
3 The conference was/long/the event last year. **ALMOST AS**
....
4 Scott/meet friends in person/chat online. **WOULD SOONER**
....
5 Wendy's interpersonal skills/good/June's. **SLIGHTLY**
....

Grammar Revision 3c (Modules 1-3)

1 ★★ **Read the exchanges and put the verbs in brackets in the correct form.**

1 A: Here .... **(come)** trouble! Mark looks furious.
B: Nothing new there. He .... **(continually/complain)** about something or another!

2 A: I heard that you .... **(practise)** pilates these days, Jim.
B: That's right. I'm enjoying it, but to be honest it's the hardest thing I .... **(do)** in my life!

3 A: Mr Scott .... **(waffle)** on about teamwork for nearly an hour!
B: It is quite dull, isn't it? I wish I .... **(sign up)** for another seminar yesterday when I had the chance.

4 A: Look at this! It says here that Mark .... **(give)** a lecture about stress management at the civic centre tomorrow.
B: He's really done well for himself. I can't believe that by the end of the year he .... **(tour)** as a life coach for five years already.

5 A: They say that by the end of November they .... **(restore)** an ancient manuscript from a famous philosopher.
B: Ah, yes! I heard that also. It was the one he .... **(write)** just before he died.

2 ★★ **Read the sentences and correct the mistakes.**

1 William had been waiting in the station since several hours when I phoned him.

....

2 Ian is impressed greatly with the psychology seminar; the speaker is amazing!

....

3 It seems to be something bothering Sam; he's very upset.

....

4 The author's new lifestyle guide is ready to shipping to distributors.

....

5 I can't stand seeing people to be taken advantage of at work; it's very unfair.

....

6 Our train has a two hours delay due to the bad weather outside London.

....

7 Erica started her work placement the same year like Andrea.

....

Key word transformations

3 ★★ **For questions 1-5, complete the second sentence so that it has a similar meaning to the first sentence using the word given. Do not change the word given. You must use between three and eight words, including the word given.**

1 There is a rumour that the business lost more than half of its value during the financial crisis. **SUSTAINED**
The business is rumoured .... more than half of its value during the financial crisis.

2 It can be hard to make the right decision about something when there is not enough time to think. **REACH**
Not having enough time to think may .... decision.

3 Jon didn't try to talk to Janet about the situation until she had calmed down. **FOR**
Jon .... trying to talk to her about the situation.

4 Ellen came across badly but she doesn't intend to make the same mistake twice. **NO**
Ellen came across badly but she .... the same mistake twice.

5 Mark is an exceptionally good driver in hazardous conditions. **WELL**
Mark .... conditions.

Grammar in Focus

★★ **Read the sentences below and put the words in brackets in the correct form.**

1 When interacting with others it's not just what you say that .... **(matter)**, but also what you do.
2 The power of body language is known .... **(exploit)** by great communicators throughout history.
3 Well, ... **(tell)** you the truth, I don't have much time for self-help books.
4 Martin .... **(try)** hard all year to improve his relationship with his brother; it's not been easy but I think he's really making progress.
5 .... **(you/speak)** to Frank about the problems you have with Norman yet?
6 I .... **(be about/offer)** my help when the girls found a solution.
7 Emily .... **(smooth)** things over between the boys by now.
8 Mr Dickerson is not nearly .... **(organised)** as the other supervisors in the department.

3d Listening skills

Multiple choice

Preparing for the task

STUDY SKILLS

When attempting a multiple choice task, you should read the questions and options before you listen, but while you listen you should concentrate on the questions and their focus. Listen for the answer to the question in the recording and match what you hear to the appropriate option. REMEMBER the answer may be implied rather than stated explicitly.

1 **a) ★ Read the question. What is it asking for: opinion, gist or detail?**

What point does the speaker make about the language of children?

b) ★ Read the extract. Which of the underlined sections answers the question in Ex. 1a?

Many parents find it a struggle to communicate with their young ones. But, what many people don't realise is that, in the same way adults use words to communicate, children convey what they mean by way of sounds. Even from the cradle they develop their own language. The problem for new parents is they have to decipher what this language means.

c) ★ Read the options (A-D). Which option matches the answer in Ex. 1b?

A Parents cannot understand it.
B It is their own form of speech.
C It is difficult to translate.
D It is similar to that of adults.

d) ★ Is the answer in Ex. 1c stated explicitly or implied?

2 **★★ You will hear a radio interview in which a choreographer, Alice Reynolds, discusses a dance programme. For questions 1-5, choose the answer (A, B, C or D) which fits best according to what you hear.**

1 How is the programme designed to help youngsters?
A by getting them to talk about their feelings
B by encouraging them to loosen up
C by enabling them to convey their thoughts
D by giving them a way to entertain themselves

2 When talking about the nature of communication, Alice reveals that
A teenagers are quick to react to a number of emotions.
B people who learn to show how they feel can articulate better.
C shy youngsters find the programme more useful than others.
D young people have a lot of pent up negative emotions.

3 What aspect of the programme encourages teenagers to face their troubles?
A the social side of dance
B the freedom of the movement
C the obligation to interact
D the release of feelings

4 Alice contrasts professional and amateur dancers in order to
A highlight the usefulness of the programme.
B emphasise the use of emotions in dance.
C illustrate the difference between teaching styles.
D explain the ability to recognise feelings.

5 What point does Alice make about the study into a person's personality?
A It found that certain types of people dance better than others.
B Personality has a bearing on people's willingness to participate.
C Who people are can be recognised through their movements.
D It revealed that most people try to hide their true nature.

Speaking skills 3e

Expressing feelings/sympathy/regret

1 a) ★ Read the dialogue. Use phrases (a-f) to complete the dialogue.

a I'm sorry to hear that
b I was at the end of my tether
c Don't let it get to you
d I'm annoyed
e things will be alright
f I shouldn't have yelled at

Suzie: Hey Kimberly. What's the matter? You look upset.
Kimberly: **1)** .... with my sister. We had an argument this morning so I feel really down at the moment.
Suzie: **2)** .... We all have disagreements with our siblings from time to time.
Kimberly: I know but I'm partly to blame; **3)** .... her, but **4)** ....! She keeps taking my things without asking.
Suzie: **5)** ...., but it's probably a good idea to apologise to her when you get home.
Kimberly: Yes, I was planning to do that.
Suzie: Good. I'm sure **6)** ....
Kimberly: Thanks for your help.

b) ★ Replace the phrases (a-f) in Ex. 1 with the ones below.

• everything will work out • I'm irritated
• I was really frustrated • Cheer up • It's a pity
• I wish I had kept my cool with

c) ★ Which phrases in Exs 1a & b express feelings/sympathy/regret?

Feelings	1 ....
Sympathy	2 ....
Regret	3 ....

Expressing and justifying opinions

Remember!
When you are asked to comment on a set question with points, you need to consider the positive and negative aspects of each point and also give examples, either personal or general, to express your opinion.

2 ★ Look at the question and the bullet points below. Read the statements (a-e) and match them to the point each refers to. Then answer the questions. More than one answer may be possible.

How can people express their individuality?
• fashion choices
• music preferences
• leisure activities

a Many people say that a hobby provides a good way to showcase your personality.
b The main reason I believe this is that showing up in wrinkled clothes won't make a good impression.
c Personally, I enjoy listening to alternative songs even though they might not be popular with my peers.
d Facts suggest that women who feel uncomfortable with their bodies often prefer baggy clothes.
e Some people believe that youth who listen to violent lyrics often exhibit adverse personality traits.

Which of the statements:

refers to a positive aspect of the point?	1	
refers to a negative aspect of the point?	2	
gives an example with personal details?	3	
gives an example with general details?	4	
is expressing an opinion?	5	
is justifying an opinion?	6	

3 ★ Choose the correct item.

1 A: I don't feel so good.
B: **a** I know what you mean.
b I'm sorry to hear that.

2 A: Nothing is going right in my life.
B: **a** You must have been upset.
b Things can't be that bad.

3 A: I'm sorry about your dispute.
B: **a** If only I had been calmer.
b How terrible for you.

3f Writing Descriptive/Narrative/Discursive articles

1 ★ **Read the rubric and underline the key words. Then answer the questions.**

An international magazine is inviting readers to write an article about Internet slang. You decide to write an article describing your own use of Internet slang. You should also evaluate the positive and negative impacts of using this new form of communication. Write your **article** in 280-320 words.

1 What areas have you been asked to cover?
2 How much of your article should be descriptive; narrative; discursive?
3 What style of writing is appropriate for this article?
4 What outline would you use for this task?

2 a) ★ **Read the model. Has it covered the points in the rubric?**

Instant message slang
why do teens use it?

1) Do u no txt spk ? These days text speak, the shortening of common words into acronyms and abbreviations, is developing into a language of its own among teens on social media. This trendy text lingo has been welcomed by many teens, but why are they using it? And what effect does this have on the way we communicate?

On a personal note, I use instant message slang because it allows me to communicate with my friends in a quick, fun and interesting way. Using acronyms or abbreviations is easier and faster for me than typing everything out and gets the same point across. Some of the more common expressions I use are: LOL ('Laugh out loud') and CUL8R ('See you later'). **2)** Amusing as decoding language in this way may be for us teens, I can also understand those who wonder if this could also spill over to the real world and pose a threat to our writing skills.

3) On the positive side, using expressions particular to a group is part of developing a sense of identity. For instance, teens feel they belong to their peer groups when they express **4)** themselves with their own sayings. As a result, they can bond with other teens and build their self-confidence. **5)** What is more, as language is constantly evolving, it appears that the integration of text speak into popular usage is part of the natural process of this language evolution.

6) Nonetheless, there seems to be a major drawback to this new form of communication. Indeed, **7)** it can be said that the English language is becoming a casualty to Internet slang. **8)** An example of this is young people verbalising the word 'LOL' when they laugh and a host of acronyms slipping into their daily conversations and even appearing on school papers. As a result, teens might get so used to text speak that they may no longer realise there is a need for formal language.

All things considered, I believe that as language progresses teens can use slang to express themselves as long as it does not do injustice to their formal language skills. As a prominent linguist once said, **9)** 'Slang shows us how language is always changing.'

b) ★ **Read the model essay again and match the highlighted phrases to the formal style techniques below.**

A ☐	quote to summarise opinion
B ☐	hedging technique
C ☐	discourse marker to add a point
D ☐	highlighting exemplification
E ☐	fronting technique
F ☐	using referencing
G ☐	discourse marker introducing an argument
H ☐	question addressing the reader directly
I ☐	discourse marker presenting contrast

Your turn

3 ★ **Read the rubric and underline the key words. Then answer the questions that follow.**

The editor of an English-language magazine has invited readers to contribute to a series of articles entitled 'Communication in the Digital Age'. You decide to write an article describing the ways you communicate and commenting on how technology has changed communication. You should also evaluate the positive and negative impacts of these changes. Write your **article** in 280-320 words.

1 What areas have you been asked to cover?
2 How much of your article should be descriptive; narrative; discursive?
3 What outline would you use for this task?

4 ★ **Read the possible arguments and justifications for the rubric above. Match the arguments (1-4) to their justifications (a-d).**

1 ☐	overcoming impairments	a	threat to mental health and well-being
2 ☐	media addiction	b	lack of face-to-face interactions
3 ☐	diminishing interpersonal skills	c	keep in touch with contacts anywhere
4 ☐	no communication barriers	d	devices to help disabled to hear and speak

5 ★ **Use the model in Ex. 2, the ideas in Exs 3 & 4, your own ideas and the plan below to write your article.**

Plan

(Para 1)	*Introduction (state the topic)*
(Paras 2-4)	*Main body (presenting each new aspect in a separate paragraph with a clear topic sentence)*
(Para 5)	*Conclusion (summary of topic and opinion)*

Proudly Different

are subcultures a thing of the past?

Goths, punks, metallers, surfers, skaters. The 80s and 90s were dripping with youth tribes and it took a nanosecond to tell who belonged where. The boat-shoe-wearing wannabe yuppies, the pimply kid with the mohawk and tartan trousers. Box them up, give them a label, and off you go. Before social media, teen identity was played out through fierce musical allegiances and fashion. But fast-forward a few decades and normal is the new norm. Pennie Blair witnessed this first hand as a former programme manager at a local radio station. "I think the new kids on the block are visually subdued," she says. "But they are more openly vocal in their ideals and more accepting of people who are different." While they may not look as daring, Blair says the kids these days are actually a lot more sophisticated and open in their tastes and attitudes than the mohawked teens of the 1980s. So, who are today's Teen Tribes?

The Alties

She loves art and live bands. Lucia Taylor (17) doesn't consider herself "alternative" but others do.

'I had a friend over and she looked at my posters and my vinyl collections and said 'you're so altie!' It's weird, as I don't really see myself in that way.' Lucia has seen pictures of the Goths, punks, and new wavers of the 70s and 80s. And while she agrees that today's subcultures aren't as visible, they certainly exist. For Taylor, the need to stand out visually has been eroded by the development of a society that is more accepting of difference. She thinks the extreme style tribes of the past were a reaction to a more conformist and restrictive society. As we've become more open and accepting, the need for such rebellion has lessened. 'Most parents aren't judgmental and we don't have to prove anything. I think people are more confident with their identities and don't have the need to be so obviously different.'

The Performers

Mia Tayler has been singing since she was 4. While she still loves music, acting is her first love now.

She has a mighty singing voice, musical talent to burn, and loves trying on new personas in front of an audience. 'I'd do acting every day if I could,' says the 15-year-old. 'I really love it.' When Tayler started High School, she instantly gravitated to other actors. They are a tribe that's not restricted by age and she soon found friends among the older students. 'I've created a channel on a video sharing website with my friend. We film ourselves playing a lot of different roles, and I can really relate to how some actors play such a wide range of characters.'

The Gamers

Harrison Gerrard has been gaming since his dad bought him his first games console when he was 5.

Harrison (19) has always loved gaming for the sense of escape it offers, the way in which it can transport you away from the daily grind. Every tribe has its pariahs; in the PC gaming world they are console users. Then there are the stereotypes. Gerrard says that players of games such as *Skyrim* (an open-world action role-playing game) attracts the 'typical nerds' while *Counter Strike* (a shooter) is filled with males aged from mid-teens to early 20s. Even so, he says he's always surprised at how many people game – it's no longer the preserve of geeks and shut-ins. 'There are a lot more people than I expect. I'm often surprised by the people I meet who are really into it.'

So it seems that tribal lines are no longer drawn around the types of culture you consume anymore. Instead, subcultures have fractured with the development of the digital universe. Kids have the world at their fingertips (literally), and this is reflected in the ways they choose to express themselves.

Reading

1 **★★ For questions 1-5, read an article about teen tribes and decide which choice (A, B, C or D) best answers each question.**

1 In the first paragraph, what does the writer suggest about youth subculture in the past?
- **A** There was less of a variety than there is today.
- **B** They were more tolerant of diversity.
- **C** Their identity was tied to appearance only.
- **D** They were instantly recognisable.

2 According to Lucia, what has changed about teenagers today?
- **A** They don't feel the need to belong so much.
- **B** There is more pressure to conform to societal norms.
- **C** They express their tastes in a more nuanced fashion.
- **D** They are more accepting of family rules.

3 The phrase 'to burn' in line 25 emphasises that Mia's talent
- **A** is plentiful.
- **B** is beyond most people's.
- **C** is underdeveloped.
- **D** is refreshing.

4 The phrase 'daily grind' in line 35 is used to imply that life
- **A** is unimaginative.
- **B** is physically exhausting.
- **C** is lonely at times.
- **D** is dull and monotonous.

5 The overall impression of the text is of
- **A** an erosion of social interaction by technology.
- **B** a lack of originality in today's younger generations.
- **C** a rejection of society's established roles for teenagers.
- **D** a need for validation and praise for one's efforts.

Open cloze

1 ★★ **For questions 1-8, read the text below and think of the word which best fits each space. Use only one word for each space. There is an example at the beginning (0).**

Behind the Scenes

Technology has opened **0)** *up* a whole new world of social networking. It is now easier than **1)** .... to stay abreast of what's happening with friends and family any time, **2)** .... matter where they are in the world. But is that really a good thing? Take photo-sharing applications. They are a place **3)** .... people can share pictures and videos with like-minded individuals or, at **4)** .... , that's how they started out. Now, it would seem, they have mutated into something completely different. They have become online platforms for people to market themselves. The snaps uploaded **5)** .... appear spontaneous and innocuous but some take hours to plan and execute and they are taken for the **6)** .... purpose of getting exposure. But in **7)** .... to reach the heady heights of success through this means, users have to keep an unceasing vigil on their accounts, staying constantly on the **8)** .... for an opportunity. And the result of these picture-perfect images is a false reality that is available for all the world to see.

Multiple choice cloze

2 ★★ **For questions 1-8, read the text below and decide which answer (A, B, C or D) best fits each gap. There is an example at the beginning (0).**

Most Valuable Coach?

Most sports fans celebrate and praise their teams in the **0)** B way, by adoring the star players or the club's history and success. However, nowadays, the coaches of teams are getting **1)** .... bit as much attention as the superstars under their watch.

One factor that plays a huge part in the success of a coach is the strength of their communication skills. Successful coaches realise that they have to **2)** .... the trust of their players as well as their respect. **3)** .... to popular belief, good leadership isn't just about being tough. Smart coaches are under no **4)** .... about their responsibilities. They understand that reading the feelings of your players is a delicate skill that needs to be **5)** .... until it becomes second nature.

Successfully motivating athletes requires the ability to **6)** .... an influence on people in a positive way and has little to **7)** .... with intimidation. Encouragement, a kind word or sometimes even saying nothing at all can be the most effective way to **8)** .... a response from a person. Considering their need to be a drill instructor and a psychologist at the same time, maybe it's only fair that sports coaches are getting more credit after all!

	A	B	C	D
0	habitual	conventional	routine	common
1	every	each	all	any
2	achieve	beat	win	capture
3	Contrary	Against	Opposed	Adverse
4	impression	deception	misconception	illusion
5	refined	refreshed	redeemed	repurposed
6	utilise	exert	expel	apply
7	go	have	do	make
8	trigger	propel	sling	activate

Key word transformations

3 ★★ **For questions 1-6, complete the second sentence so that it has a similar meaning to the first sentence using the word given. Do not change the word given. You must use between three and eight words, including the word given.**

1. Carla was determined to be the leader of the group. **SET**
   Carla had ....
   ....
   the leader of the group.
2. Jim always goes out of his way to include everyone in the project. **POINT**
   Jim always ....
   ....
   everyone in the project.
3. Steve feels confident that we will agree on the issue. **UNDERSTANDING**
   Steve feels confident that an
   ....
   ....
   on the issue.
4. They agreed upon the deal in just a few hours. **MATTER**
   The deal ....
   ....
   hours to be agreed upon.
5. Alice really should get some feedback from the rest of the team. **TIME**
   It ....
   ....
   some feedback from the rest of the team.
6. Their relationship seems to have improved since they got help. **SIGNS**
   Their relationship ....
   ....
   since they got help.

Grammar

4 ★ **Choose the correct item.**

1 They .... be friends until they had a falling out.
A would C use to
B used to D got used to

2 If you have any problems ...., don't hesitate to call me.
A if ever C however
B whichever D whatsoever

3 Everyone on the team is committed .... a solution to the problem.
A they find C to find
B for finding D to finding

4 You should make a complaint .... you feel it's absolutely necessary.
A even though C only if
B unless D except

5 I was told .... discuss what happened in the meeting with anybody.
A not to C to not to
B don't D not

6 Janine is nowhere .... open-minded as she used to be.
A as near C nearly
B near as D next to

7 Your communication skills would improve if you .... this seminar.
A are to take
B had been taking
C were to take
D have taken

8 Many parents object .... their children spending too much time on social media.
A with C about
B at D to

9 Tina is actually .... she appears.
A more approachable than
B the most approachable than
C most approachable as
D more approachable as

10 It's vital that they .... this misunderstanding and move on.
A will sort out C sort out
B be sorting out D are going to sort out

11 It wasn't her fault. She wasn't ....
A at blame C to blame
B for blame D blamed

12 I felt as if I .... by her.
A were betrayed
B had been betrayed
C had betrayed
D would be betrayed

Vocabulary

5 ★ **Choose the correct item.**

1 His harsh tone .... he was still upset with everyone about what happened earlier.
A implied C disguised
B hinted D declared

2 There is a lot of discussion about the .... effects of the Internet on teenagers.
A opposing C contrary
B reversible D adverse

3 She tried to .... her excitement about meeting her idol.
A contain C tame
B enclose D soothe

4 Her .... behaviour made her the life of the party; everyone loved talking to her.
A exhaustive C exuberant
B fragrant D abundant

5 The .... use of social media in society is quite concerning.
A pervasive C enormous
B overwhelming D extravagant

6 The children are .... by this new app; they can't stop using it.
A revitalised C mesmerised
B hypnotised D capitalised

7 He uses a nickname to keep his .... online so that no one knows who he is.
A identity C personality
B anonymity D security

8 I have such a deep .... for all that he has done for us; I'm very grateful.
A gratification C admiration
B appreciation D recognition

9 Everyone was in .... of John representing the group.
A support C favour
B preference D approval

10 I'm .... in touch with my school friends anymore; we only speak about once a year.
A closely C nearly
B barely D sparsely

11 It .... me as odd that she left the party yesterday afternoon so abruptly.
A occurred C struck
B caught D hit

12 At no .... in the conversation did she make eye contact with me.
A instant C mark
B moment D point

4a Reading

Finding synonyms

Preparing for the task

Remember!

Remember to first determine the meaning of the word in bold in the context of the text. Then think of a word that means the same in that context and try it in place of the original word to see if it works.

1 ★ **Read the following sentences taken from the passage. Choose the correct meaning (a or b) of the words in bold. Then decide on the correct synonym (1 or 2).**

A Internet technology has changed our lives in numerous ways, and it is difficult to **keep track of** them all.

Definition: **a** to strictly oversee sth
b to know what is happening with sth

Synonym: **1** follow **2** control

B Computers, presentation programs and the Internet have given teaching an altogether different **dimension**.

Definition: **a** a way of considering sth
b a measurement of sth

Synonym: **1** width **2** quality

Summarising

Preparing for the task

Remember!

Remember to paraphrase the main ideas of the entire text in your summary and not mention only details.

2 ★ **Read the section taken from the passage. Match it to the correct summary statement (A-C).**

Whether you are a stay-at-home mum or an entrepreneur, the success of your business model can be guaranteed, to a large extent, if you're able to use the Internet to your advantage. Be they local shops, restaurants, shopping malls or retail stores, nearly all businesses have been boosted with the help of technological growth.

A Technology offers something for everyone.
B Success in technology means success in business.
C To benefit, businesses must use the Internet in a specific way.

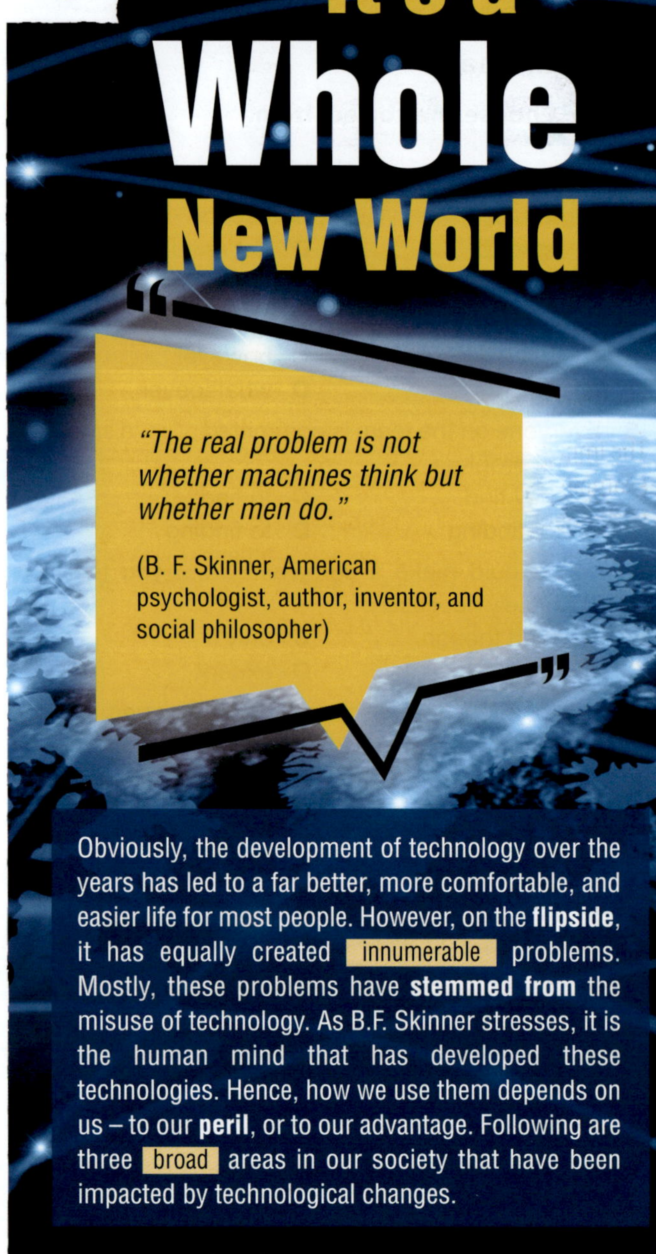

It's a Whole New World

"The real problem is not whether machines think but whether men do."

(B. F. Skinner, American psychologist, author, inventor, and social philosopher)

Obviously, the development of technology over the years has led to a far better, more comfortable, and easier life for most people. However, on the **flipside**, it has equally created [innumerable] problems. Mostly, these problems have **stemmed from** the misuse of technology. As B.F. Skinner stresses, it is the human mind that has developed these technologies. Hence, how we use them depends on us – to our **peril**, or to our advantage. Following are three [broad] areas in our society that have been impacted by technological changes.

3 a) ★★ **Replace the words or phrases in bold in the text with other words or phrases of your own so that the article still reads correctly, both grammatically and in the sense of what is said. There may be more than one way of answering; answer the way you think best.**

1 flipside: ....
2 stemmed from: ....
3 peril: ....
4 presence: ....
5 intricate: ....
6 the order of the day: ....
7 part and parcel of: ....
8 demerits: ....
9 regulate: ....
10 glued to: ....

4a

Business

Internet technology has changed our lives in numerous ways, and it is difficult to keep track of them all. Global trade and business has become faster, easier and more reliable in recent years. Banks and financial institutions also have introduced online systems that have made transactions effortless. Bill payment and account-related work are conveniently managed online. In today's world, it is basically impossible for any small or large business to thrive without a web **presence**. Whether you are a stay-at-home mum or an entrepreneur, the success of your business model can be guaranteed, to a large extent, if you're able to use the Internet to your advantage. Be they local shops, restaurants, shopping malls or retail stores, nearly all businesses have been boosted with the help of technological growth.

Business has become faster and more challenging, thereby increasing competition in every field. The impact of technology on business has been phenomenal, and in this era, information and knowledge have become commodities.

Education

The impact of technology on education is a classic example of the way our lives have changed. Our forefathers never had the opportunity to study in interactive classrooms with 3D images and projectors, nor did they have access to the Internet and various other technological facilities. Computers, presentation programs and the Internet have given teaching an altogether different dimension. Education has become computer-dominated in this era, going well beyond notebooks and blackboards. In recent years, online education and distance learning courses have changed the way we learn. Now, being physically present in classrooms to hear a lecture or discuss **intricate** concepts isn't even necessary. This doesn't mean that student-teacher interaction has been replaced by technological developments. Rather, students in different locations can easily access any lecture being conducted through video conferencing.

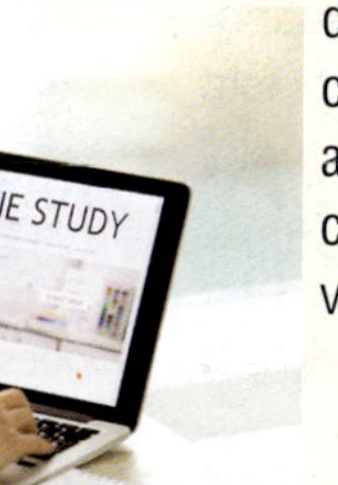

Communication

If you go through a list of the latest developments in technology, you will find that most of them have revolutionised the way we communicate in some way. Thanks to the Internet, communication has become amazingly fast. It has brought about innovations such as email, instant messaging and even video chatting. Social networking websites are **the order of the day**, and have given birth to the concept of social media marketing. From business networking to personal contact, communication has never been as fast and easy as it is now. The latest gadgets and gizmos have become **part and parcel of** life. No matter where we are, or what we're doing, we can contact our loved ones at any time of the day.

In seeking answers to the issue of technology's **demerits**, we need not look far. With the threat of Internet scams increasing every day, and cyber security becoming a global issue, governments everywhere are trying hard to **regulate** cyber access. Moreover, lifestyle habits have changed drastically. Nowadays, psychologists are frequently using the term 'Internet addiction' to address certain issues in the lives of people who are constantly **glued to** their screens.

How have we been affected by technology? The answer is that it has given us the power to make a difference in our lives, but only if we use it wisely. It all depends on us and what we do with it.

b) ★★ Summarise in no more than 150 words how technology has affected our lives, as described in the passage.

4 ★ Match the highlighted words in the text to their antonyms.

• insignificant • a little • local
• narrow • few • rarely

5 ★★ Fill in: *security, conferencing, transactions, threats, scams, commodities.*

1 More and more people are doing their banking .... online these days.
2 Content and information are precious .... exchanged on the Internet.
3 Internet .... software offers protection from hackers and cyber criminals.
4 Communicating through video .... has become popular with all ages.
5 Use caution when giving out personal details online in order to protect yourself against the .... of identity theft and hacking.
6 There are a variety of Internet .... that are attempts to trick people.

4b Vocabulary

1 ★ **Choose the correct item.**

1 Marketing forms the **predominant/contributing/compelling/obvious** part of his job and takes most of his time.
2 Technology offers **momentous/renowned/radical/resounding** new solutions to many issues in the field of medicine.
3 Exhaust emissions have caused **indispensable/irreversible/inevitable/endangered** damage to a number of historical sites; they will never be the same.
4 It's important for companies to be **fundamental/interactive/competitive/receptive** to technological change in order to keep up with competition.
5 The **prevailing/resounding/rewarding/wholesale** trend in communication is instant messaging.
6 With the new automated process, production costs are **menial/mundane/minimal/marked**.

2 ★★ **Fill in the correct word.**

1 **demolished/deteriorated**
   a The old factory was .... to make way for a solar farm.
   b The condition of the building has .... to such an extent that it needs to be torn down.
2 **comprise/compile**
   a We will .... the results of the focus group into a report to be submitted to the board.
   b The development team will .... two scientists and four research students.
3 **urges/provokes**
   a This app on my smartphone is great; it .... me on to achieve certain fitness targets.
   b Talk of fake news often .... a strong reaction from journalists.

3 ★★ **Fill in:** *in*, *after*, *up*, *of* **or** *to*.

1 We believe we are on the brink .... a breakthrough with our new application.
2 Marketing managers must be attuned .... the needs of consumers.
3 The design of the prototype is still .... its infancy.
4 I think production will more than double once the automated process is .... and running.
5 A solution to energy waste is highly sought ....

4 ★★ **Replace the words in bold with an idiom from the list.**

• roll off the tongue • break the mould
• changed his tune • set in stone
• been on the cards • turned over a new leaf

1 The timetable for the product development isn't **impossible to change** but it would be preferable to stick to it.
2 Alfred was against the idea of updating the computer system but he soon **had a different opinion** when he realised how efficient it would be.
3 We wanted to do something that would **be new and different** but most of our ideas were already out there.
4 A lot of the new buzzwords and application names **are easy to pronounce** especially for the younger generation.
5 After working for the power company for 30 years, Edmund **decided to be more responsible** about power usage and installed solar panels.
6 A merger between the tech giants has **been likely to happen** since they both started working in the same fields.

5 ★★ **Fill in the gaps with words from the list and choose the correct item.**

• discerning • contributing • blistering • power
• tangible

Go, go gadget free

Smartphones, tablets, laptops, e-books, the list goes on and on. With the **1)** .... pace of technological development, it's difficult to get away from all the gadgets. Technology nowadays is seen as a basic necessity of life. But even for the most **2)** .... user, these gadgets can take over. What is more, our overuse of technology is a **3)** .... factor in the problem of power consumption today, which is not very healthy for us or the planet. So, how easy a(n) **4) conclusion/implication/solution** would it be to give them up? Why not give it a go and put down all your gadgets for a week? Now this may **5) conjure/transfer/harness** up images of living in a wooden hut, cut off from civilisation, but I'm not talking about disconnecting yourself from the **6)** .... grid altogether. To begin with, it may require the **7) retention/attention/possession** of a strong will, but after a short while you will start to feel liberated and notice **8)** .... benefits. And who knows, maybe this little experiment will encourage some of you to **9) persist/account/hail** and go the whole hog, and eschew gadgets forever.

Topic related vocabulary

Technology – Technological change

6 ★ **Circle the odd one out.**

1 widespread – early – vague **adoption**
2 controversial – vigilant – industrial **application**
3 minimalist – objective – generic **design**
4 long-lasting – long-standing – long-winded **concept**

Prepositions & Phrasal verbs

7 ★ **Choose the correct item.**

1 The change in society was attributed **to/for/by** the government scheme.
2 The new computer system was issued **by/on/to** default as there were no other proposals.
3 Innovators are successful because they think **beyond/outside/above** the box.
4 It's amazing to think that the idea for the new invention came **about/across/around** by accident.
5 Thanks to the power of the Internet, young people nowadays have the world **on/at/by** their fingertips.
6 The old IT system that the company is using is really **behind/below/past** the times; it's so old-fashioned!

Idioms

8 ★★ **Fill in:** *get, bear, start, move, break, turn* **in the correct form.**

1 Sometimes Ann feels overwhelmed by the pace of modern life and wishes she could .... the clock back to a simpler time.
2 The new changes and social initiatives are finally starting to .... fruit.
3 It took a lot of investment and research to .... the new product off the ground.
4 The pioneering project is .... new ground in remarkable and unexpected ways.
5 After some discussion the R&D department decided to .... the ball rolling and begin their initial testing.
6 In today's fast-moving world you really must .... with the times or risk getting left behind.

9 ★★ **Choose the correct item.**

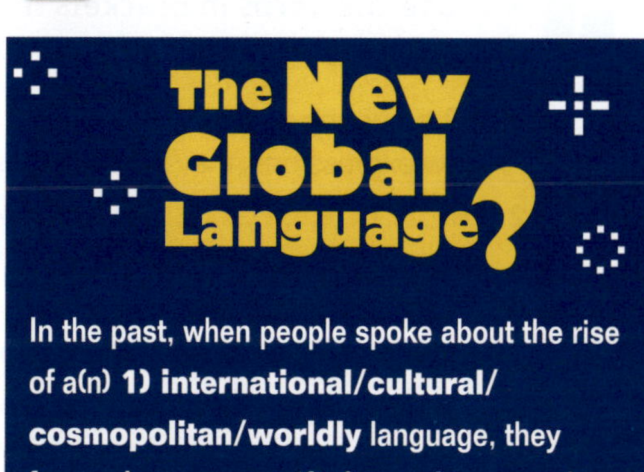

In the past, when people spoke about the rise of a(n) **1) international/cultural/cosmopolitan/worldly** language, they focused on one specific lingua franca such as English or Spanish. However, what if a new kind of language could **2) relocate/dislodge/budge/dislocate** these giants of the linguistic world: a language that **3) unveils/envisages/declares/depicts** social ideas in a way that anyone from any country could understand? This fascinating new means of communication is known as a meme, and is a virally-transmitted symbol, image or video that **4) conveys/divulges/exposes/validates** meaning. All one needs to understand a meme is a shared point of **5) reference/integration/intelligence/appreciation**, which is often provided by global youth culture, and some computer **6) articulacy/literacy/dexterity/efficiency**. Who knows, one day perhaps memes will replace language altogether!

Word formation

10 ★★ **Complete the sentences with words derived from the words in bold.**

1 Scientists believe that one day .... travel to distant stars might be possible. **(PLANET)**
2 Cafés nowadays have Wi-Fi .... **(HOT)**
3 Cultural .... helps to enrich us. **(DIVERSE)**
4 Young people take to new technology .... **(INSTINCT)**
5 In large cities where many different people live side by side, ... is the rule. **(CULTURAL)**
6 Many people buy new smartphones .... to keep up with their peers. **(SOLE)**
7 In electronics stores the .... are often very knowledgeable. **(EMPLOY)**
8 Lots of Sandra's friends and .... are interested in consumer technology. **(ACQUAINT)**
9 Mark didn't update his computer because it's .... powerful to play his games. **(SUFFICE)**

4c Grammar in use

Conditionals

1 ★★ **Use the verbs in brackets in the correct form.**

1 When young people .... **(invent)** new expressions, they spread across the Internet.
2 If I .... **(not/work)** last night, I could have signed up for the computing class.
3 If I were younger than I am, I .... **(use)** more fashionable slang words.
4 If you hadn't missed the special offer, you .... **(fly)** to Spain right now.
5 If you .... **(take)** a seat, I will tell Mr Erikson that you are here.
6 You won't be able to talk to Jeff online unless you .... **(sign up)** to an instant messaging service in advance.
7 If I were you, I .... **(study)** web design as it's a rapidly expanding field.
8 I don't know if Tom .... **(accept)** the delay to the project.

Other phrases with hypothetical meaning

2 ★ **Complete each pair of sentences with the options given.**

• even if • so long as

1 .... cryptocurrencies become more popular, people will still continue to use cash.
2 .... you make sure you log out when you're finished, your online account will remain perfectly secure.

• supposing that • assuming that

3 The company will stock more wearable tech .... customer demand remains the same.
4 Cashless transactions are very safe but what are the security features .... something goes wrong?

• given that • in case

5 .... the new language app is increasing its user base, we'll update its features.
6 We don't expect to see Mr King. However, ... he attends, do we have the proposals ready to present?

• what if • but for

7 .... the financial crisis, we would have increased our market share in the region.
8 .... we expand the business overseas?

Wishes

3 ★★ **Write wishes based on the words in bold in the sentences.**

1 **You didn't follow your friend's advice** and now you feel regretful about it.
....
2 **You want a friend to get the dream job** that they applied for.
....
3 A friend of yours is always rude and **you want them to be more polite**.
....
4 You're in a work meeting and **want to make a request** to your boss.
....
5 Someone you know is applying for a scholarship and **you want them to get it**.
....

Preferences/Unreal past

4 ★★ **What would you say in the following situations? Rewrite the sentences using a phrase from the list below.**

• It's high time • It would have been better if
• They would sooner have • I would rather
• We would just as soon • You would be better off
• You had better • Imagine you had

1 Buying a desktop computer would be preferable for them but their son wanted a laptop.
....
2 Please don't leave your games console on all night; it's a terrible waste of electricity.
....
3 It would have helped if you had given what you wanted to do at university more thought while you were applying for courses.
....
4 If you had accepted the internship, what options would it have offered you professionally?
....
5 Working while you are still studying would be better than searching for experience later.
....
6 Everyone would prefer to take the train to college together.
....
7 Paul really needs to be more responsible; I'm fed up with his reckless behaviour!
....
8 You need to type up this report or you will get in trouble.
....

Grammar Revision 4c (Modules 1-4)

1 ★ **Fill in the gaps. Use the appropriate form of the word in brackets when given.**

1 Upgrades to the system progressed .... **(fast)** than any of us .... expected.
2 Environmental experts are anxious that the government .... **(fall)** short of its carbon emission target.
3 It's high .... you .... **(complete)** your studies at college.
4 The team .... **(refine)** the product for several weeks when they realised that the order had been cancelled.
5 We .... **(see)** Jack this evening; would you like us to pass on your message?
6 Terry kept quiet because he was afraid of .... **(look)** silly for not knowing what his friends were talking about.
7 Before yesterday's meeting, Mrs Smith .... **(already/tell)** them that they could speak .... **(free)** about their concerns with the project.
8 If Frank .... stop by, tell him that I .... **(expect)** to see his report by tomorrow afternoon.
9 Mary and her husband enjoyed a beautiful .... **(candle/light)** dinner in a local restaurant.
10 Precious metals such .... gold and silver are often used to produce luxury jewellery.

2 ★★ **Choose the correct item.**

The New Approaches Group is proud **1) to announce/to be announcing/announcing** the Tech Innovators Award, a new initiative that **2) will aim/is going to aim/aims** to provide young inventors with a platform that offers a **3) very/much/lot** more powerful launching board than those currently available. New Approaches have spent the last three years **4) to develop/developing/develop** the Tech Innovators Award to produce something that is by far the **5) greatest/greater/most great** graduate level scheme in the industry. **6) Had we invested/Should we invest/Were we to invest** less there's no way that we would have created something so remarkable. If you visit our website, you **7) can judge/will judge/could judge** for yourself, and explore the many exciting opportunities available. So, take a moment and ask yourself one very important question. **8) Assuming/Supposing/Providing** you had the chance to pitch your ideas to the biggest names in tech, what would you say? Sign up to the Tech Innovators Award today for that chance, and the possibility of changing your life forever!

Key word transformations

3 ★★ **For questions 1-4, complete the second sentence so that is has a similar meaning to the first sentence, using the word given. Do not change the word given. You must use between three and eight words, including the word given.**

1 Maggie did not find it difficult to find solutions to the problems that arose during her project. **COMING**
Maggie had no .... the problems that arose during her project.
2 You won't face criticism providing that you admit that you made a mistake. **LONG**
You won't be .... to your mistake.
3 William is tired and wants us to leave him alone. **WE**
William is tired and would .... alone.
4 Jeff can't apply for the position because he isn't qualified enough. **COULD**
Were .... the position.

Grammar in Focus

★★ **Fill in the gaps with the correct word, put the words in brackets in the correct form or choose the correct word.**

- Once, driverless cars were so strange a concept that they seemed **1)** .... likely than flying cars! Nowadays, however, many people expect that they **2)** .... **(probably/be)** a common sight in the near future. In fact, the first models **3)** .... **(currently/undergo)** testing in the USA and the technology is on the verge **4)** .... being introduced onto our roads. If you **5) will find/find** yourself in California, you may see them on the road yourself!
- A recent wonder invention that **6)** .... **(become)** increasingly popular lately is the 3D printer. If you **7)** .... **(tell)** people twenty or thirty years ago that a printer could produce objects out of thin air, they would have thought you were mad. These days 3D printing is so widespread that people can even pursue it **8) as/like** a hobby! So forget about building models with glue and kit parts. Perhaps it's time you **9)** .... **(print)** them electronically instead on a 3D printer, **10) directly/direct** from your computer!

4d Listening skills

Listening for meaning and inference

Preparing for the task

STUDY SKILLS

In tasks where you are listening for opinions, these opinions may be stated by either or both of the speakers. It is therefore important to listen for language of agreement/disagreement to help you discern which speaker holds the opinion.

1 a) ★ **Put the phrases below in the correct column.**

• I'll go along with that • I don't think so either • you think so, do you? • me neither • I beg to differ • speak for yourself • I suppose so • I'm not convinced • you must be joking • you can say that again • that's not entirely accurate • you've got a point there • don't make me laugh • we'll agree to disagree • I couldn't have said it better myself • you're telling me

agreement	disagreement

b) ★ **Read the rubric and questions 1-3. Underline the key words.**

You will hear two friends talking about changing careers.

1 Job satisfaction is the most important aspect of work. ☐
2 Embarking on a new career is challenging. ☐
3 The unknown is part of the attraction. ☐

c) ★ 🎧 **Listen to part of a conversation and decide who states the opinions in Ex. 1b, Claire (*C*), Derek (*D*) or both (*B*). Mark your answers in the boxes in Ex. 1b.**

d) ★ 🎧 **Listen again. Which of the phrases in Ex. 1a were used in the conversation in Ex. 1c to indicate agreement/disagreement?**

agreement: ....

....

disagreement: ....

....

2 ★★ 🎧 **You will hear two colleagues discussing some new office software. For questions 1-5, decide whether the opinions are expressed by Catherine or Donald, or whether both speakers agree. Write: *B* if both speakers agree, *C* for Catherine or *D* for Donald.**

1 The existing software is fit for purpose. ☐
2 The new program is a waste of time and resources. ☐
3 Some modifications are done for the wrong reasons. ☐
4 The right software can be an asset to a business and its employees. ☐
5 Job security will soon be a thing of the past. ☐

Multiple choice – Short extracts

Remember!

In listening exercises the answers will be paraphrased or implied. It is therefore important to not only listen carefully to what is said, but also think about what is meant by the speakers.

3 ★★ 🎧 **You will hear two extracts from different conversations. After each there are 2 multiple-choice questions. For questions 1-4, choose the answer which fits best, according to what you hear.**

Extract one

You will hear a man talking about a smartphone.

1 Who is the man talking to?
A a friend **B** a colleague **C** a customer

2 What does he say about people's spending habits?
A They have changed little over the years.
B They don't have as much to spend these days.
C People are more wary of being impetuous.

Extract two

You will hear a woman talking to a friend about her hobby.

3 What hobby is she talking about?
A photography **B** drawing **C** painting

4 What point does she make about her hobby?
A She doesn't think she would enjoy it as a career.
B She uses professional equipment for better results.
C She has ambitions to have her work noticed.

Speaking skills 4e

Asking for/Expressing/Reacting to opinions

1 **a) ★ Read the dialogue. Use phrases (a-e) to complete the dialogue.**

a to my mind
b not really.
c Don't you agree
d If you ask me
e You may have a point

Aunt: What are you doing on your tablet?
Betty: I'm posting a selfie on my social media profile.
Aunt: Oh, I couldn't be bothered with all that. **1)** .... all this new technology is a huge distraction. **2)** ....?
Betty: Well no, **3)** .... My tablet is truly necessary. I can access the Internet, communicate with people all over the world, do my shopping and even pay my bills online.
Aunt: **4)** .... there. But I see youngsters diddling around with their gadgets all the time, even when they're with their friends. People don't communicate the same way anymore.
Betty: Yes, that may be so, but technology is advancing and we all need to get with the times.
Aunt: I guess so but **5)** .... , it's all a bit daunting.

b) ★ Replace the phrases (a-e) in Ex. 1 with the ones below.

• Isn't that so • You're right • I disagree
• Frankly, I think that • in my view

2 **★ Choose the correct item.**

1 A: How do you feel about having a social media detox?
B: **a** You're right. **b** That's a great idea.
2 A: This mobile learning app is easy to use.
B: **a** I'd suggest that. **b** My thoughts exactly.
3 A: What do you think about using gamification in the classroom?
B: **a** Frankly, I think that's interesting.
b Don't you agree that's interesting?

Paraphrasing

3 **a) ★ Look at Information Sheet A, about a possible improvement for a school library. Match the paraphrased sentences (1-7) to the points (A-G).**

Information Sheet A

Computer System Upgrade

A Latest software programs
B More computer stations available
C Online journal access
D Accessible to students, staff and alumni
E Connects to online catalogues of other libraries
F Books can be reserved or renewed from home
G Retraining required for staff and students

1 [ ] Articles could be obtained electronically.
2 [ ] Students would learn to use up-to-date operating systems.
3 [ ] Resources would be available for current and former students and teachers.
4 [ ] Material could be sourced from other establishments.
5 [ ] Investment of time would be needed to learn the new system.
6 [ ] It would offer more flexible borrowing arrangements.
7 [ ] There would be additional hardware for students.

b) ★ Look at Information Sheet B below. Match and expand the prompts (1-7) to form paraphrased sentences for the points (A-G).

Information Sheet B

New Reading Rooms

A Second-storey addition with large windows
B More cubical desks and tables for studying
C Electrical sockets for personal laptops
D New photocopiers and scanners
E Additional staff to assist students
F Security cameras for safety
G Library will be closed at least 6 months for renovations

1 [ ] comfortable/furniture/aid/schoolwork
2 [ ] create/bright/spacious/area/study
3 [ ] convenient/locations/plug in/own/devices
4 [ ] in-demand/equipment/provided/student/use
5 [ ] access/whole/building/restricted/some/time
6 [ ] installation/surveillance/system/keep/area/secure
7 [ ] recruit/personnel/give/advice/instructions

4f Writing Opinion essays

1 **a) ★ Read the rubric and underline the key words.**

Nowadays there is growing acceptance of the use of digital currencies for financial transactions. While some people welcome this new form of payment, claiming that it is an economic innovation, others raise concerns about its financial stability. Which side of this argument do you, personally, agree with, and why? Write your **essay** in approximately 300 words.

b) ★ Read the model. Fill in the correct linkers from the list.

- That being said
- That is because
- Secondly
- For all these reasons
- On the opposite side
- That is why

Have you ever considered using cryptocurrencies to purchase services and products online? Internet currencies are becoming increasingly popular all over the world. This has given rise to fears that they may lead to risky monetary transactions. Personally, however, I do not share these concerns. In my view, cryptocurrencies are competitive alternatives to regular currencies, despite their unstable nature.

Nowadays transacting in digital currencies is very convenient, instantaneous and cheap. **1)** .... they operate independently from any central bank. As a result, transactions only take a few minutes since they do not have to wait for approvals from third parties. Moreover, they have extremely low transaction costs compared to other electronic payment methods. **2)** .... many small businesses prefer them, as they do not have to account for added expenses, which means lower prices for the customer.

3) .... , digital currencies are less prone to fraud. This is due to the fact that they use advanced encryption techniques to perform financial transactions. This means that there are rarely instances of identity theft and forged passwords, making private transactions secure. Consequently, this added security eliminates some of the fraud issues that banks have.

4) .... , cryptocurrencies are volatile and subject to market fluctuations. For instance, the values of most digital currencies can change wildly in a short amount of time. This means that people who invest in them can make a lot of money when their price escalates and can lose as much when the price crashes. **5)** .... , as digital currencies increase in popularity this volatility will likely level out, making them more stable currencies.

6) .... , I am of the firm belief that cryptocurrencies will not be nearly as volatile as some people fear. In fact, it is possible that all other currencies will be incorporated into the digital world in the very near future.

c) ★ Read the model again. What techniques have been used to begin and end the essay?

Your turn

2 **★ Read the rubric and underline the key words. Then answer the questions.**

Nowadays there is a growing shift towards the use of cashless transactions. While some people argue in support of a cashless society, claiming that it is beneficial to citizens, others raise concerns about security. Which side of this argument do you, personally, agree with, and why? Write your **essay** in approximately 300 words.

1. Which side of this issue do you agree with?
2. How will you present your opinion in the introduction?
3. What will you include in the conclusion?
4. What outline will you follow?

3 **★★ Look at the rubric in Ex. 2 and the prompts below. Match the viewpoints to the supporting details and put them in the right box.**

Viewpoints	Supporting details
• security and convenience	• limit on parallel economy/ prevent money laundering, tax evasion, cyber crime
• lower transaction costs	• governments track all transactions/invade privacy/vulnerable to identity theft
• records of transactions useful in the fight against crime	• lower banking fees/ customers save money
• transactions are recorded by third parties	• no need to carry cash/ instant access to funds

Viewpoint 1	**Supporting details**
Viewpoint 2	**Supporting details**
Opposing viewpoint and argument against it	**Supporting details**
	Supporting details

4 **★★ Use the ideas in Ex. 3 and/or your own ideas to write the essay.**

Languages The secret extinction

516 languages are critically endangered and up to two a month are lost for good, but few people are even aware of their disappearance.

Imagine how **eerie**, isolating and plain terrifying it must be to be the only person alive speaking your native tongue. Cristina Calderón doesn't have to imagine: since her sister-in-law died in 2005, she is probably the last remaining native speaker of Yagan, a language now only spoken on Chile's Navarino Island in Tierra del Fuego.

Calderón's **plight** is tragic, but not unusual. When William Sutherland, a professor of conservation biology, researched the comparative disappearance of languages, birds and mammals in 2003, he identified 46 languages that were down to their last speaker and found 357 spoken by fewer than 50 people. 'Languages are becoming extinct at a far greater rate than species of birds or mammals,' he says.

Unnatural selection

For some, the demise of an Australian Aboriginal language here, a Native American language there, is only cause for casual regret. For others, this is Darwinian natural selection at work. Mark Abley, author of *Spoken Here: Travels Among Threatened Languages*, doesn't agree: 'Languages have always lived and died, just like species in the natural world. But what we're seeing today is entirely, hideously unnatural. Just 10% of languages may be effectively alive by the end of this century. To call that 'natural selection' would have Darwin **spinning in his grave**.' The mass extinction is, he insists, a truly global phenomenon. 'In my own country, Canada, there are about 55 **indigenous** languages but only four or five are in good health.' Other examples of languages **clinging on** for dear life by a fingertip or two are Livonian, a Uralic Finnic language spoken by around 20 people, most of whom live in eight Latvian coastal villages, and Ainu, the native language of Japan's indigenous people – spoken by just 15 of the 150,000 Ainu who now live in Japan.

Linguistic genocide

Official oppression of languages is thankfully now very rare, yet languages are still dying, probably at an even faster rate than before. Why is this? 'Today, the causes are more likely to involve economic difficulty that leads to migration from a traditional homeland to a major city, or the cultural loss of confidence that comes when speakers of a minority language are exposed to mass media in a powerful language such as English. The economic and environmental pressures facing indigenous peoples have worsened,' says Abley.

English for all

The global **allure** of successful languages isn't helping matters. 'There is evidence that language **latches onto** technology,' says Sutherland. 'The Indo-European languages spread to Europe from the Near East with agriculture, replacing most, if not all, of the native languages. Today, English is the language of the Internet and multinational corporations, so many ambitious young people want to learn it.' But when people adopt a more 'successful' foreign language, the sum of human knowledge is reduced. 'You find in Mexico, for example, that when some races adopted Spanish, they lost the native terms for the plants they used in their everyday lives,' says Sutherland. 'Over time, they forgot how they'd used those plants.'

Lose a language, lose your brain

If the human race is to accept multiculturalism – and that is, at this precise point in the history of our species, **the mother of all** ifs – then it must remain multilingual. The death of a language marks the death of a culture, the point at which a nation loses its heart or, as some linguists put it, the ability of its people to express their collective genius. Exactly how we learn language is still the focus of **abstruse** intellectual debate, but the most common theory is that our brains are naturally **hard-wired** to learn languages. A world where everyone speaks Mandarin, Spanish and English wouldn't just be a poorer, less diverse place, it would be a world where parts of our brains grow rusty or just shut down. Scary prospect, isn't it?

Reading

1 **a) ★★ Replace the words or phrases in bold in the text with other words or phrases of your own so that the article still reads correctly, both grammatically and in the sense of what is said. There may be more than one way of answering; answer the way you think best.**

1 eerie: ....
2 plight: ....
3 spinning in his grave: ....
4 indigenous: ....
5 clinging on: ....
6 allure: ....
7 latches onto: ....
8 the mother of all: ....
9 abstruse: ....
10 hard-wired: ....

b) ★★ Summarise in no more than 150 words why some languages are facing extinction and what the consequences of this are as described in the article.

Word Formation

1 ★★ **For question 1-8, read the text below. Use the word given in capitals at the end of some of the lines to form a word that fits in the space in the same line. There is an example at the beginning (0).**

The Always-On Generation

From the very **0)** *outset* of its existence, social media as a means of	SET
communication has **1)** .... revolutionised the way we	DOUBT
interact with each other. This is particularly true with the advent of the	
smartphone, allowing **2)** .... access. As a result, we now	LIMIT
have a generation permanently switched on and plugged in. But have	
technology and global **3)** .... helped us or hindered us?	CONNECT
Telecoms companies may claim that their services encourage a	
4) .... of social barriers by bringing us closer together.	BREAK
However, a negative side-effect is emerging. Fear of missing out	
(FOMO), the **5)** .... that one is being left out of wonderful	PERCEIVE
experiences, is causing people to constantly and almost	VOLUNTARY
6) .... check their social media accounts. This compulsive	
behaviour is a surprisingly common **7)** .... and a worrying	OCCUR
by-product of the **8)** .... process of online communities.	EVOLVE

Key word transformations

2 ★★ **Write a new sentence which is as close to the meaning of the given sentence as possible, using the word or phrase given. You may not change the word or phrase in any way.**

1 Computers are becoming more and more affordable these days. **(costing)**

....

2 This agreement has nothing to do with you. **(business)**

....

3 Watch the new computer programmer carefully in case he needs help. **(eye)**

....

4 I haven't got a clue how Photoshop works. **(whatsoever)**

....

5 The teacher will not tolerate the use of mobile phones in the classroom. **(put)**

....

6 There is no need to tell you that technological change is inevitable. **(saying)**

....

7 It has taken Shelly a long time to learn programming. **(picked)**

....

8 I don't care which laptop we buy as long as it's affordable. **(matter)**

....

9 I was really fascinated by the talk about new business methods. **(found)**

....

10 I never find time to back up my files. **(round)**

....

3 ★★ **For questions 1-6, complete the second sentence so that it has a similar meaning to the first sentence, using the word given. Do not change the word given. You must use between three and eight words, including the word given.**

1 Tina is much better at web design than Mike.
NEARLY
Mike ....
....
Tina at web design.

2 Everyone is criticising the company for releasing private data about their clients.
CRITICISM
The company ....
....
releasing private data about their clients.

3 Was it your idea to promote the company on social media?
CAME
Was it ....
....
the idea to promote the company on social media?

4 I'm certain that the video will go viral.
DOUBT
There ....
....
mind that the video will go viral.

5 As soon as we arrived at the hotel, the kids started playing video games.
SOONER
No ....
....
the kids started playing video games.

6 I ought to have had the computer repaired this week.
BETTER
It ....
.... the computer repaired this week.

Grammar

4 ★ **Choose the correct item.**

1 I'm still not convinced .... this firewall will protect my computer from attacks by hackers.
A to using C that using
B by using D if I use

2 The professor was thrilled that a student of .... won the Young Innovators Award.
A her C herself
B hers D she

3 The app .... the amount of exercise you do, it also suggests new exercise programmes.
A doesn't monitor only C only monitors
B doesn't monitor D not only monitors

4 .... what went wrong, Jason immediately made corrections to the program.
A By understanding C Since understanding
B Having understood D Had he understood

5 Video content .... more and more popular online these days.
A becomes C is becoming
B has become D has been becoming

6 Make sure to upload the documents as soon as you .... at the office.
A will arrive C arrived
B will have arrived D arrive

7 The latest home technology covers everything .... security systems to voice-controlled devices.
A to C from
B through D in

8 I'm sure he would have reported the problem .... hackers had gotten into the main server.
A had he known C would he have known
B he had known D he would have known

9 The game isn't available to you .... you sign up as a member on the website.
A in case of C otherwise
B on the condition that D unless

10 I'd rather Steve .... my laptop while I was gone.
A didn't use C hadn't used
B doesn't use D wouldn't use

11 She was late .... her application and missed the deadline.
A uploading C in uploading
B to upload D for upload

12 There is still a lot more work .... with nanotechnology before it's ready for the marketplace.
A of being done C to have been done
B to be done D having been done

Vocabulary

5 ★ **Choose the correct item.**

1 People .... the power of social media at first; no one expected it to become so influential.
A miscalculated C underestimated
B misconstrued D undermined

2 Heavy fines are .... by online companies that break privacy laws.
A imposed C earned
B incurred D gained

3 The online fundraising campaign has received .... support across the world.
A excessive C widespread
B outspread D sweeping

4 Every parent has their own .... on their child's use of the Internet.
A stance C manner
B point D bearing

5 After appearing at the technology conference, the computer expert has been .... with requests for help.
A invaded C inundated
B impeded D immersed

6 The evidence .... the hacker in several cases of identity theft.
A implanted C implemented
B consumed D implicated

7 You can .... the size of the fonts by pressing here.
A tune C adapt
B turn D adjust

8 The school has a .... tolerance policy on the use of mobile phones during school hours.
A never C zero
B none D nil

9 DVDs are slowly becoming .... with the popularity of online streaming.
A old-fashioned C obsolete
B primitive D archaic

10 The dog became an Internet .... when his video went viral.
A marvel C miracle
B sensation D wonder

11 The robotics developer .... a long-term contract with a major healthcare provider.
A consulted C negotiated
B instigated D intersected

12 This tiny chip holds .... amounts of information.
A vast C virtual
B voluminous D visual

5a Reading

1 ★★ **You are going to read an article. Seven paragraphs have been removed from the article. Choose from the paragraphs A-H the one that fits each gap (1-7). There is one extra paragraph which you do not need to use.**

Remember!

Gapped text

Remember to read through the gapped text and think about the content of the paragraphs before and after each gap. Highlight discourse makers in both the text and missing paragraphs and check for agreement before making your choice. Finally, read through the text again with the chosen paragraphs to check for cohesion.

COACH CARTER:
Having the Courage to Make a Stand

"Our deepest fear is not that we are inadequate, our deepest fear is that we are powerful beyond measure. It is our light not our darkness that most frightens us."
(Marianne Williamson)

This powerful message from author Marianne Williamson rings true in an incredible story about a group of young men and their struggle against adversity. It is a story so astonishing that it seems like it should come straight from a Hollywood film. In this case, however, it was a series of remarkable real life events that provided the story for the Hollywood blockbuster *Coach Carter*.

1 ☐

The reason, while unorthodox, was simple enough. Although the team were having huge success on the court, they weren't having the same level of success off the court academically. In a bold move at the start of the season, Ken Carter had taken the unusual decision to make his players sign a contract, one which set them clear targets for improvement in their studies, for their behaviour in and out of class, and for meeting their obligations as role models to other students.

2 ☐

To Coach Carter there was more to life than trophies or medals. Being a graduate of Richmond High School himself, and coming from a poor family of nine, he knew first-hand the difficulties and social inequalities faced by young people in the area: crime, delinquency, low income and a troubling lack of opportunities for higher education. Ken Carter understood that he had a duty to help these young men break through those socio-economic barriers, and so he set an ambitious goal for his players to play sports at college.

3 ☐

It was against this backdrop of opposition and fear, a fear of taking a stand and saying no, a fear of reaching out and seizing one's inner potential and realizing one's power, that Coach Carter fought for the sake of his students. Never giving up, never writing them off, and never ceasing to believe in them and their ability to better themselves, despite the objections and outcry.

4 ☐

What's more, despite the initial hostility, Carter found himself flooded by notes and letters of support, from all over the country, for his courageous act, congratulating him for his youth mentoring, advocacy and social work. News networks also rushed to Richmond High. Requests came for interviews from magazines and newspapers such as *Sports Illustrated*, *People* magazine, the *Los Angeles Times* and *USA Today*. And most incredibly, permission was sought to turn the team's story into a major motion picture starring actor Samuel L Jackson.

5 ☐

People took to heart that success in life depends on academic and social success and not just sporting skill alone. This was especially true for students at Richmond High, whose success was solid proof of Carter's methods. During his time as coach from 1997 to 2002, every single one of his athletes graduated, with many going on to college.

6 ☐

This approach to mentoring unquestionably helped change his students' lives, and his methods and charisma are perfectly portrayed by Jackson, who plays his part on the silver screen to perfection. Ultimately however, it is Ken Carter the real person who makes the story so powerful and moving.

7 ☐

Coach Carter's inspirational character traits are an example to us all. His story is a reminder to never give up in the face of overwhelming odds, to always stand by our convictions, and to never lose faith in the goodness of people and their ability to break free from the restrictions that circumstance places on them.

A Carter never anticipated so much publicity from his stance, and was quick to point out that things were about his students and not himself. The power of his message, that young people have to take responsibility for their actions and shape their own place in society, struck a chord across the nation, however.

B Ken Carter was just an ordinary basketball coach trying to help students in his local high school, Richmond High, when one single action turned his life upside down and made him and his players the focus of national media attention. That act was his decision to pull chains across the doors of the school gym and lock out his team of young sports stars. The lockout came as a total shock to the boys, who were undefeated. Why would their coach cancel training on the cusp of such great success?

C And they were significant. Not only did he face verbal abuse and threats, he also risked losing his job as coach when parents rallied against him and demanded he be replaced. On top of this, his decision cost the team two forfeits and the chance for an unbeaten season. Yet, Coach Carter's athletes stood by him, fueled by the desire to break social stereotypes and get away from their inner-city lives. Together the boys made the decision to take responsibility for themselves and devote the time that they needed to their studies so that they could have a brighter future.

D The catalyst for Carter denying access to the gym was discovering that 15 of his 45 athletes were not honouring these contracts, which they had signed in good faith. Carter knew full well that his rules were strict and was under no illusions. In fact many of the school's best athletes refused to play for him as a result. However, that didn't faze Ken Carter, or make him back down from his principles one bit.

E His clarity of purpose, tenacity and compassion made him a true hero. One who ceaselessly campaigned for more and refused to write anyone off. Few other people could have been as good a custodian for these troubled young men as Ken Carter was.

F In order to do so however, they would have to become student athletes and earn the grades needed for a sports scholarship. Here, the brave sports coach faced unexpected opposition when his actions prompted resistance not only from reluctant students, but also from a faculty that had seemingly given up and a body of parents who didn't believe their kids could go professional and were furious with his decision to take high school sport away from their boys.

G When asked about the secret to his success, Carter explained his belief in three crucial elements that are required to change a person for the better. He motivated students by putting a contract in their hand, providing knowledge to expand their mind and connecting with them emotionally. These simple things he believes can change peoples' way of thinking and alter their vision of the world forever.

H Following the lockout college scouts attended the state championship to watch Richmond High. Many stated that while the Richmond story was remarkable, the really amazing thing was the respect and affection that the players held for their coach.

2 ★ **Replace the word(s) in bold in the sentences with the verbs below in the correct form.**

• prompt • flood • motivate • anticipate • struggle

1 The coach's lockout **triggered** a great deal of opposition from parents and the school. ....
2 The young men had to **fight** against adversity and hardship. ....
3 Coach Carter never **expected** such a huge public interest in his actions. ....
4 Students **were inspired** by their coach's methods and heartfelt approach. ....
5 Shortly after the lockout, the coach **was inundated** with letters of support. ....

3 ★★ **Fill in:** *for, of, from, down, on, by.*

1 The social challenges faced .... young people in the area were significant.
2 Despite all the pressure from the community, the coach refused to back .... from what he knew was right.
3 Richmond High unexpectedly became the focus .... national media attention.
4 Student contracts set targets .... improvement in exam results and behaviour.
5 The athletes' amazing story sounded like something straight .... a film.
6 Carter realised that success in life depends .... success at school.

4 ★★ **Fill in:** *struck, locked, outcry, access, vision, honoured.*

When high school basketball coach Carter discovered that his players had not **1)** .... their contract with the school to keep good grades and attend class, he knew he had to take action and get them to take their education more seriously. He **2)** .... out his players from the school gym, denying them **3)** .... so they could focus more on their studies. His actions caused a(n) **4)** .... from parents and the community due to the team's undefeated record. Despite the initial opposition, Carter's message of the importance of education for athletes **5)** .... a chord with America and he was soon seen as a hero for inner-city kids. Carter believes that through encouragement and commitment one can change a person's **6)** .... on the world forever. He definitely did something right as every one of Carter's players went on to graduate.

5b Vocabulary

1 ★★ **Rewrite the following sentences replacing the words in bold with idioms from the list.**

• take the law into your own hands • throw the book at • on the run • bury your head in the sand • live and let live • lay down the law

1 At the trial, the judge decided to **severely punish** the defendant by giving him a life sentence.
2 It's easier to get on with people if you just **accept the way other people behave**.
3 You shouldn't feel angry, the new manager wasn't trying to **force us to do the work the way he wants**, he was just voicing his opinion.
4 The burglar was **trying to avoid being captured** for six weeks before police finally caught up with him.
5 It's better to let the authorities deal with criminals instead of trying to **punish them in your own way**.
6 It's no use thinking you can **ignore the unpleasant reality** over the recent allegation of corruption.

2 ★★ **Fill in:** *up, away, of, at, against, down, for, on, with, to.*

1 The issues we face today boil .... to a lack of government investment.
2 When James went to university, he fell in .... an unusual bunch of people.
3 We all have to be .... to speed when the new manager arrives.
4 It's important to stand up .... bullies.
5 The committee ran up .... a problem when they tried to get extra funding.
6 Does the prevalence .... joblessness in the area contribute to the high crime rate?
7 The new legislation places considerable constraints .... small businesses.
8 Unresolved issues can gnaw .... at you until they are dealt with.
9 It's wrong to try to get back .... someone just because they did something bad to you.
10 George tried to remain upbeat after the accident .... the sake of his family.

3 ★★ **Fill in the gaps with the correct word.**

1 **verdict/sentence**
   a After much deliberation, the jury delivered a .... of innocent.
   b The judge passed .... on the arsonist after the jury found him guilty.

2 **profoundly/incredibly**
   a The defendants were .... lucky to get away with just a fine.
   b The demographic of the area has changed .... over the years.

3 **scheme/initiative**
   a A community .... to allow residents to take an active role in the refurbishment of the area has been launched by the council.
   b The new pension .... should allow employees to plan for the future.

4 ★★ **Fill in the gaps with the correct word.**

• undermined • deprived • persecuted

1 It's wrong for any group of people to be .... of their civil liberties.
2 No one should feel they are being .... simply because of their beliefs.
3 The minister was embarrassed when he was .... by his colleague at the meeting.

• advocate • avail • afford

4 I don't .... civil unrest, but I do understand it.
5 The company decided to .... themselves of the latest guidelines concerning disability allowance.
6 This scheme will .... young people a route into local government.

5 ★★ **Fill in:** *repeat, prime, deprived, drastic, redeeming, suspended, progressive.*

A pilot scheme in the North of England is taking **1)** .... action in the hope of revolutionising the justice system by employing offenders to help construct housing developments and improve disabled facilities in **2)** .... areas to help the community. This remarkable situation has come about in an effort to reduce prison numbers with **3)** .... offenders being the **4)** .... target of the initiative. Instead of serving a jail term, offenders will receive a(n) **5)** .... sentence and community service on one of the many projects designed not only to improve the area but also to give them a chance to demonstrate **6)** .... qualities. This **7)** .... project has the backing of local residents and looks set to be the future of judicial punishment in the area.

Topic related vocabulary

Freedom & Independence

6 ★ **Choose the correct item.**

1 The economic, social and political **extrication/ emancipation** of women was a gradual process.
2 The politician warmly **condoned/embraced** his party's new stance on the social issue.
3 Civil rights charities **intervene/revoke** in cases where people are unfairly prosecuted.
4 After a mammoth session of parliament, MPs managed to **testify/ratify** the bill of rights.
5 The political stage in the country is **dominated/ intimidated** by two main parties who monopolise national discourse.

Collocations

7 ★ **Fill in:** *elbow, will, vassal, conflict, country, crisis, freedom, power.*

1 In modern Britain, monarchs no longer wield .... ; they only act as head of state in a symbolic capacity.
2 The nature of the bill allowed the new president plenty of .... room to do as he wished.
3 In a democracy, certain principles, such as .... of the press, are seen as essential to a just society.
4 The depth of the scandal triggered a constitutional .... that brought the government to its knees.
5 International diplomacy is seen as vital to .... resolution between opposing sides.
6 During elections, citizens must be allowed to exercise their free .... without fear of reprisal.
7 The small island nation is a .... state that is forced to do as its neighbour wishes.
8 Injustice is rife in the war-torn .... ; there's been a total breakdown of law and order.

Prepositions & Phrasal verbs

8 ★ **Fill in:** *to, on, out (x2), about, down.*

1 Campaigners have kept .... protesting despite all the difficulties.
2 His critics suspect that the minister has been getting up .... no good.
3 There are concerns that the new policy singles .... certain people unfairly.
4 During the interview the mayor refused to back .... over the issue.
5 Lawyers hope the new ruling will finally bring .... change.
6 We mustn't rule .... the possibility that voters will change their minds.

9 ★★ **Choose the correct item.**

1 In Britain major decisions are made in the **aisles/ corridors/hallways/landings** of power in Westminster.
2 Regional parliaments allow **self-government/self-sufficiency/self-regulation/self-support** for remote parts of the country or islands far from the capital.
3 The system of checks and balances ensures that no one individual has **scope/latitude/carte blanche/franchise** to do as they please.
4 Although citizen-centred schemes involve residents in debates full political **autonomy/autarchy/autocracy/ authority** is kept by local councillors and MPs.

Word formation

10 ★★ **Complete the sentences with words derived from the words in bold.**

1 People show .... in a society by following certain social norms. **(CONFORM)**
2 The doctor became a famous .... in his field of healthcare. **(REVOLVE)**
3 After the civil war, ... of the country became a paramount concern. **(UNIFY)**
4 He is running for office despite his lack of a political .... **(BACK)**
5 The development cleaned up the neighbourhood and .... it brought new jobs. **(ADD)**
6 The .... state had complete control over all aspects of life. **(TOTAL)**
7 MPs are their constituents' political .... in parliament. **(PRESENT)**
8 The politician is a(n) .... who opposes reform. **(REACT)**
9 Political .... is not one of Tim's strong points; he's quite blunt. **(SENSE)**
10 A certain level of .... is often found in some politicians. **(ECCENTRIC)**

5c Grammar in use

The passive

1 ★ **The following sentences contain mistakes. Find them and correct them.**

1 She was volunteered in Morocco last summer. ....
2 The donations were been distributed by the charity. ....
3 Amazing opportunities may be arisen at any time while on an internship. ....
4 The crowdfunding website was filled by supportive comments. ....
5 Supplies are sent rural communities by aid agencies every month. ....

2 ★★ **Fill in the gaps using the verbs in the list in the correct active or passive form.**

• say • renovate • report • threaten • deal • find

Pro-Pro Bono!

The path to true happiness is said **1)** .... in helping others. One group of kind local volunteers certainly agrees! Community group One For All love offering their services to those in need and they **2)** .... Pro Bono work is transforming lives in Edgeford. One For All provide support for problems that couldn't **3)** .... with by the local authority. Just last week a local playground **4)** .... with help from All For One. And in one case they even provided legal assistance to a family that **5)** .... with eviction from their home. All For One are definitely taking being a good Samaritan to a whole new level, and it **6)** .... by the press that they also plan to expand their services to healthcare as well!

Causative Form

3 ★★ **Use the words in bold in the correct causative form.**

volunteers/collect
1 The orphanage .... donations for the new nursery every two months.

leaflets/print
2 Tom .... for the work programme at school at the moment.

the offender/perform
3 The judge .... one hundred hours of community service.

sports coaches/provide
4 The council .... training sessions to teens next summer.

Reflexive/Emphatic pronouns

4 ★★ **Fill in with the correct reflexive/emphatic pronoun where necessary.**

1 A: I'm exhausted!
B: You did a great job, though! Why don't you sit down and rest ....!
2 A: What's wrong with Helen? She doesn't seem .... today.
B: She's upset; she just heard the community centre is closing.
3 A: The transformation in the school is incredible!
B: Absolutely! And what's even more incredible is that the students fixed it up entirely by ....!
4 A: I still can't believe that Johnny Depp .... visited the children's hospital!
B: I know! Wasn't it amazing? What a great guy!

Substitution/Ellipsis

5 ★★ **Rewrite the sentences using ellipsis and substitution.**

1 He seems happy and he seems relieved that the charity scheme was such a huge success.
....
2 We're going to the event at the community centre tomorrow. Will you be at the community centre?
....
3 I'm sorry for knocking over your fundraising banner; I didn't mean to knock over your fundraising banner.
....
4 Someone should unlock the meeting room by 2 o'clock; if someone does not unlock the meeting room, I will unlock the meeting room at half past two.
....
5 He's not attending the neighbourhood watch meeting and his parents are not attending the neighbourhood watch meeting.
....
6 'Are they going to have an alarm installed at their cottage?' 'They have already had an alarm installed at their cottage.'
....
7 'Do you think the judge is fair?' 'Yes, I think the judge is fair.'
....

Grammar Revision 5c (Modules 1-5)

1 ★ **Choose the correct item.**

1 Promoting social initiatives online **is getting/has got/gets/has been getting** more and more popular every year.
2 Jamie was keen **to have found out/finding out/to find out/to be finding out** how much money he had raised for his sponsored run.
3 When Sandra took the placement in Gambia, she couldn't imagine that she **was to have remained/would have remained/was remaining/was to remain** there for fifteen years.
4 Social media campaigns are **just about as effective as/not nearly as effective as/the most effective as/not so much effective as** TV advertisements; both reach equally large audiences.
5 Our fundraising target isn't realistic, there's no way we **will raise/will have raised/are going to raise/will have been raising** that amount by the end of the week.
6 The situation in deprived urban areas is **abundantly/bitterly/fully/gravely** serious; people need immediate access to improved healthcare.
7 If I **had been knowing/had known/was knowing/have known** about the outreach programme, I would have offered to help.
8 The offenders **were picking up/were made to be picking up/were made to pick up/were to pick up** litter by the police.

2 ★★ **Fill in the gaps. Use the appropriate form of the word in brackets when given.**

1 Tom .... **(believe)** that it's everyone's responsibility .... **(contribute)** in some way to society.
2 I .... **(work)** at the community garden all day and I feel very proud of .... for all the good work I .... **(achieve)**.
3 Excuse me, ... **(you/hope)** to attend the charity performance by any chance? We have some tickets left if .... **(you/be)** interested.
4 I wish there .... **(be)** more that I could have done when I worked at the soup kitchen. I hate .... **(feel)** like I could have made more of a difference.
5 If I .... you, I .... **(pursue)** additional options for the sports centre funding in case the government grant .... **(fall)** through.

Key word transformations

3 ★★ **For questions 1-4, complete the second sentence so that it has a similar meaning to the first sentence, using the word given. Do not change the word given. You must use between three and eight words, including the word given.**

1 Your crowdfunding page isn't working properly. I think you should get someone to look into it. **SEEN**
Your crowdfunding page isn't working properly. I'd .... I were you.
2 The project has been approved by the UN, so we can start work. **MET**
The project ....
so we can start work.
3 You need support from three signatories to file for a grant. **UNLESS**
You had ....
have support from three signatories.
4 The committee had been reviewing the aid project proposal for several weeks when their initiative was cancelled. **REVIEW**
Their aid project .... for several weeks when their initiative was cancelled.

Grammar in Focus

★★ **Fill in the gaps with the correct word, put the words in brackets in the correct form or choose the correct word.**

- Most of us are lucky **1)** .... to have parents or other close relatives in our lives who support and care for us. However, evidence shows that it's becoming **2)** .... **(abundant)** clear that if you don't have such adults during your teens, you **3)** .... **(struggle)** to find the help you need. Action groups and youth workers realise that responsible adults are vital to a young person's development and that **4) –/they** play a large part in a youth's personal and social growth.
- Bearing this in mind, youth mentoring schemes aim **5)** .... **(link)** teens with an unrelated adult who can act **6)** .... a role model and guide them both socially and academically. Lots of former participants in youth mentoring schemes **7)** .... **(speak)** glowingly about the positive effects that it had on their lives. Many are happy to admit just how crucial that was, stating that **8)** .... for their mentor helping them, they would never have made it into college or found a decent job. So, if you wish **9)** .... **(offer)** a young person more than a handout or a kind word, sign up as a youth mentor and help make a real difference that **10) changed/will change** a life forever!

5d Listening skills

Multiple choice

Remember!
In multiple choice tasks the answers to the questions will either be paraphrased or implied. It is therefore necessary to listen carefully to what is said as well as what is meant by the speakers. It is also important to take the time allowed to read all the questions and possible answers in order to be prepared for what you are going to hear.

1 a) ★ **You will listen to the first section of a radio programme in which a presenter talks to Gemma Aitkens, a teacher and guidance counsellor, about an intergenerational project in her school. Before you listen, check these words in the Word List.**

• intergenerational • tap into • wealth • all walks of life • respectful • notion • pilot • font of knowledge • retiree • while away the hours • rejuvenate • two-way street • excursion • dubious • echo • sentiment • envision

b) ★★ **Listen, and for questions 1-5, choose the correct answer A, B or C.**

1 According to Gemma, the people that sign up to the initiative
   A already have a relationship with the school.
   B come from varied backgrounds.
   C interact with the pupils socially.

2 Gemma implies that the retirees on the programme
   A appreciate the opportunity it affords.
   B take a while to adjust to it.
   C are satisfied by what the children know.

3 Gemma feels that the volunteers
   A understand enough about the younger generation to make it work.
   B believe that their knowledge is sufficient to teach the children.
   C are getting a new lease of life from participating in the programme.

4 According to Gemma, the emphasis this year is on
   A raising funds for new schemes.
   B widening the scope of the programme.
   C encouraging a wider diversity of volunteers.

5 Gemma regards the continued success of the programme as
   A doubtful. **B** problematic. **C** assured.

c) ★ **You will listen to the second section of a radio programme in which the presenter talks to Iain Crawley about taking part in an intergenerational programme. Before you listen, check these words in the Word List.**

• inception • at a loose end • magnanimous • engage • take a back seat • keep your hand in • mix things up • eye-opener • daunting • prospect • apprehension • settle in • anecdote • gratifying

d) ★★ **Listen, and for questions 1-5, choose the correct answer A, B or C.**

1 Iain says that his decision to join the programme was
   A guided by financial concerns.
   B taken due to a lack of other options.
   C made in order to repay his good fortune.

2 Iain feels that retirees
   A are often sidelined when they finish working.
   B enjoy learning new and interesting things.
   C forget what it is like to be young.

3 Iain believes that education
   A shouldn't stand still.
   B should return to the way it was.
   C should be surprising.

4 According to Iain, how will new participants find the experience overall?
   A daunting **B** amusing **C** gratifying

5 Iain implies that he
   A wishes he were still working.
   B is relieved to leave work behind.
   C still has a lot to appreciate in life.

2 ★★ **Use words/phrases from Exs 1a & c in the correct form to complete the summary about the programme discussed in the listenings.**

The **1)** .... programme pairs year 8 children with **2)** .... who have volunteered from all **3)** .... to pass on their wisdom to the younger generation. The children **4)** .... with their partner to complete projects. It can be **5)** .... for the volunteers but the process is a(n) **6)** .... and offers them an understanding of the younger generation. They also get satisfaction from seeing the children learning and becoming more **7)** .... to the older generation. It is a(n) **8)** .... experience for all involved.

Speaking skills  5e

Discussing causes/results – Offering solutions

1 **a) ★ Read the dialogue between two city council members. Use the phrases (a-d) to complete the dialogue.**

a has a knock-on effect
b a great deal can be achieved
c I consider the lack of
d have a much more powerful impact

A: There seems to be a rise in the number of home burglaries lately.
B: Yes, I know. The problem seems to be accelerating. Why do you think that is?
A: Well, **1)** .... policing to be a crucial factor. I think it **2)** .... on the levels of crime.
B: I agree, but how could burglaries be reduced?
A: Well, **3)** .... by increasing police patrols in the area.
B: It would certainly be useful. But the police can't always be present. I believe effective neighbourhood watch programmes would **4)** ....
A: That's true. I think I'm going to mention that at the next city council meeting.
B: Good idea.

b) ★ Which phrases (a-d) in Ex. 1a introduce:

1 a cause? ....
2 a result? ....
3 a solution? ....

2 **★ Choose the correct item.**

1 A: **a** I believe that more surveillance cameras will deter criminals.
b I consider crime to be a huge social problem.
B: As I see it, that's only part of the solution.

2 A: What do you think about the increase in vandalism?
B: **a** It's a terrible problem.
b It's strongly impacted.

3 A: I think I will discuss that issue with other community members.
B: **a** You're absolutely right.
b I'd definitely second that motion.

3 **★ Read the information sheet below, which is about Mr Irving, who has been selected for promotion. Then read the text explaining the decision for the promotion based on the reasons given and fill in the gaps with:** *The main reason, therefore, to begin with, Another reason, As far as I am concerned, As we all.*

Promotion of an employee to vice president of the philanthropic foundation

Richard Irving
- 56 years old
- 6 years' experience with the foundation
- Master's degree in Finance
- Has successfully managed various funding projects
- Wrote a book on the management of charities
- Strong-willed, authoritative personality
- Unable to travel due to family obligations

Well, **1)** .... , I believe that Richard Irving is the best employee for the promotion to vice president. **2)** .... for this is that he has been with the foundation for the past six years and during that time he has proven to be a valuable employee. Also, he understands the workings of the foundation, and **3)** .... , would be able to transfer this experience to his new position. **4)** .... why I support Mr Irving is because he has previous experience raising money for various causes. **5)** .... know, there are social duties that are associated with fundraising like maintaining good relations with donors. Over the years Mr Irving has become well-networked in the community and these connections will assist him in his new position. So these are the main reasons that I would like to recommend that you choose Mr Irving for the promotion.

6) .... , he is perfect for the position of vice president.

4 **★ The head of the hiring committee has expressed concerns about the employee chosen in Ex. 3 so the person making the suggestion has to defend their decision. Read the prompts and expand the sentences to complete their exchange.**

Concerns
- you/present/interesting/points
- however/some/associates/have/negative/opinion/consider/bossy
- unsure/ability/manage/employees

Defence
- may/come across/somewhat/assertive
- this/be/quality/needed/in/management field
- this/way/ensure/employee/respect
- also/past work/managing funding projects/demonstrate/suitable/interpersonal skills

5f Writing An essay based on written input

1 ★ **Read the rubric and underline the key words. Then answer the questions.**

Read the two texts below. Write an **essay** summarising and evaluating the key points from both texts. Use your own words throughout as far as possible, and include your own ideas in your answers. Write your answer in 240-280 words.

1 What type of writing task is it?
2 What skills should be used to analyse the material?
3 How should the information in the text be presented?

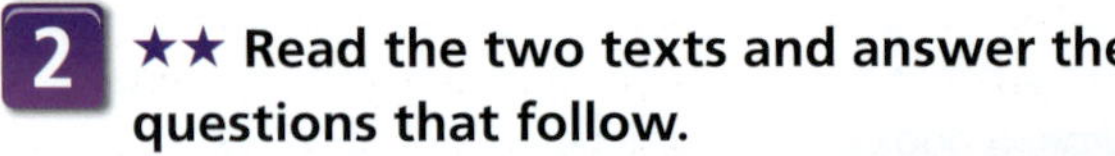

2 ★★ **Read the two texts and answer the questions that follow.**

Text 1

Collective action

The idea behind community development is simple: residents come together to generate solutions to common problems. Engagement in community service generates a participatory energy that makes people feel integrated and involved. This sense of community brings out the best in people, and inspires them to do more for themselves and their communities. In working together they not only improve the quality of their lives but also of those that need it the most as they address social issues related to poverty, crime and health which has a positive impact on society at large.

Text 2

Social work

The role of a community development worker depends on the needs of the people they serve. Their main objective is to generate community involvement programmes that allow local citizens to contribute to their community's development plans. Some administer programmes designed to help specific groups as well as assess community needs on a larger scale. As counselors, they have an important role in helping communities overcome grave social issues by providing the energy that empowers residents to use their knowledge and resources to make a difference in their communities by volunteering for social causes.

1 What are the key points of each text? Underline them.
2 Are the key points in the set of texts opposing or complementary?
3 How many paragraphs will the essay contain?
4 What would you include in the introduction to the essay?
5 Do you need to evaluate the points raised?

3 ★★ **Read the sentences. Which correctly paraphrase the key points in texts 1 and 2?**

Text 1

Point 1

a Citizens will definitely volunteer in community projects when they see other members taking part.

b Citizens feel like important members of a group when they play a meaningful role in community projects, and this improves their well-being.

Point 2

a Community participation helps to resolve challenging social problems, which benefits the whole community.

b The effect of community development is primarily significant in communities that suffer from economic and social problems.

Text 2

Point 1

a The community development worker is responsible for creating effective ways to engage communities in development projects.

b The community development worker is responsible for raising awareness of community problems.

Point 2

a Community development workers aim to assemble more volunteers for community campaigns.

b Community development workers support residents and help them to develop mental strength to work towards solutions.

Remember!

In essays you need to add your own ideas to enhance your opinion.

4 ★★ **Read the prompts that express additional ideas to those in the texts in Ex. 2 and expand them into sentences.**

1 solutions/reached/by/community/more likely/persist/individuals/understand/value/them
2 community development workers/guide/process/conflict resolution/help/residents/reach/agreements/best/way/forward

Your turn

5 ★ **Use the rubric in Ex. 1 and your answers in Exs 2, 3 & 4 and one of the plans on. p. 12 to write your essay.**

It's all in the GAME

This month we try our hand at the World Peace Game, and discover it's a lot more than kids' stuff.

I've barely started and already I'm sweating and feeling the stress! A nine-year-old student next to me notices my obvious discomfort and smiles, assuring me that disaster, for the moment at least, has been averted! It's 2 pm on a rainy Wednesday afternoon, and a tense round of negotiations has just ended regarding a border dispute between the poor underdeveloped nation of Soolar and the oil-rich nation of Opuland. The countries are, of course, fictional; part of an amazing game that aims to introduce real-world social issues and international politics to school children in an innovative way.

1 ☐

When I raise my point the teacher laughs and concedes that I'm not wrong. The game, he adds, is unpredictable and chaotic just like the real world. This, however, is all part of its appeal and purpose. Its aim being to throw young people into often hazardous or controversial issues and encourage them to reach a mutually beneficial peaceful outcome.

2 ☐

After many years of successful use in his classroom, a documentary film was made about the game grabbing the attention of educational professionals, the media and even world leaders around the globe! Hunter and his students were even invited to the Pentagon to play the game there and discuss it with generals and policymakers.

3 ☐

To make the situations more realistic and obviously more complicated there is a World Bank handling payments between countries as well as a United Nations overseeing disputes and agreements. There are even arms dealers and a secret saboteur whose goal is to undermine pretty much everything with misinformation and ambiguity.

4 ☐

All is not lost however; the students brainstorm to find a solution to our dilemma and avoid conflict, and I am pleased to see them collaborating and engaging in critical thinking skills. They work in ways not seen in a typical classroom environment, they take chances, evaluate consequences, all the time learning how not to do the wrong thing.

5 ☐

The game is still in play when it's time for me to leave. I thank the students for allowing me to participate although I really didn't have much to offer. My fellow countrymen seem far more attuned to the issues, leaving me feeling rather inadequate but content knowing that someday these players will add true value to whatever they take on.

Reading

1 ★★ **You are going to read an article. Five paragraphs have been removed from the article. Choose from the paragraphs A-F the one which fits each gap (1-5). There is one extra paragraph which you do not need to use.**

A The brainchild of American teacher John Hunter, who wanted a novel way to spark children's interest in current affairs, the game works by challenging students to come up with their own solutions to global problems. Hunter designed the game to tap into students' interests while driving learning through problem solving.

B All this unpredictability results in countless outcomes and consequences. And while the students for the most part deal with things in an admirably mature way, there are often moments of friction and times when players become frustrated. I feel the frustration myself as Soolar faces a crisis with another neighbouring nation over a chemical spill and who is responsible for the clean-up. Tensions in the room elevate.

C It's not called the World Peace Game for nothing; it's truly engaging and strategic as Hunter intended it to be-all with the goal of peace in mind. Hopes are it will proliferate to other areas beyond the classroom.

D It's my first glimpse into the World Peace Game and it's certainly not your average classroom exercise. Students play out various scenarios, often with global doom or prosperity weighing in the balance. My role is the minister of defense of Soolar and upon arrival, I'm told by the students' teacher to expect a hands-on political simulation that addresses a wide range of interlocking global problems. The role of the teacher, as he explains to me, is that of facilitator only guiding the game. The fate of the world is in the students' hands, it seems to me!

E After playing a few rounds of the game, such interest in it does not come as a surprise. It really pushes players and situations naturally arise that even a seasoned politician or policymaker would find formidable. In fact I find myself amazed that a group of fourth-graders solve their issues and ratify deals so easily!

F I see the minds of future leaders at work. It's somehow comforting and reassuring as I come to realise by playing the game these youngsters are being equipped with the skills they will need to face the ever expanding challenges on the global front.

Open Cloze

1 ★★ **For questions 1-8, read the text below and think of the word which best fits each space. Use only one word for each space. There is an example at the beginning (0).**

A Helping Hand

Many people talk of how they want to help society **0)** *but* how many of them actually do it? Well, one man decided to put his **1)** .... where his mouth is and started a social enterprise **2)** .... aims to give young people a way **3)** .... of crime. It may sound like a(n) **4)** .... order, but it's one that Josh Babarinde believed in. After working as a volunteer youth worker, he created a company which hires unemployed people, and those at **5)** .... of committing crimes, to repair smartphones. Josh hopes that being trained in a skill will steer these young people **6)** .... a better future. And it seems to be working. Of the youngsters that have worked for the company, two thirds have made good **7)** .... of their time and have gone on to study or have found jobs. And around 80% of troubled teens have kept their noses **8)** .... and given themselves a chance at a better life.

Idiom Completion

2 ★★ **Read the following sentences and write ONE word in each gap.**

1 If you're thinking of signing up as a volunteer, there's no .... like the present.
2 At the end of the .... , you only get out of something as much as you are willing to put into it.
3 Harry always goes the extra .... to help those in need.
4 If you break the law, you should be prepared to pay the ....
5 Even though Gary was a bit wet behind the .... , he soon picked up how things worked around the office.
6 It's important to take .... of your life every now and then and reappraise where you are going.
7 Having some volunteer work on your CV can be a real feather in your .... when it comes to applying to university.
8 Jeff's mother read him the riot .... when he got into trouble at school.
9 Carol is involved with a lot of charities but she doesn't seem like the sort of person that would put herself out for others; I guess you can't judge a .... by its cover.
10 Hearing stories about endangered animals really brings a .... to your throat.

Key word transformations

3 ★★ **For questions 1-5, complete the second sentence so that is has a similar meaning to the first sentence, using the word given. Do not change the word given. You must use between three and eight words, including the word given.**

1 Don't be afraid to say what you really think about the regeneration project in the meeting. **SPEAK**
Please ....
.... the regeneration project in the meeting.

2 We can't ignore this issue any longer; it needs our attention. **HIGH**
It's ....
.... attention to this issue.

3 He rarely participates in community events. **OCCASIONS**
Only ....
.... in community events.

4 I didn't know what to say when I saw the incredible results of the food drive. **WORDS**
I ....
.... when I saw the incredible results of the food drive.

5 Once we handed in our proposal, the only thing we could do was wait for an answer from the committee. **NOTHING**
Once we handed in our proposal, there ....
.... for an answer from the committee.

Grammar

4 ★ **Choose the correct item.**

1 We won't know the results of the election until all the votes .... by tellers later this evening.
A were counted **C** having counted
B are being counted **D** have been counted

2 The strike will happen .... the company agree to workers' terms regarding improved pension plans.
A provided **C** if
B unless **D** so long as

3 This youth mentoring programme is considered .... the best in the country; it's had fantastic results.
A being **B** to be **C** to being **D** as to be

4 There is no point .... for the scheme unless you have sufficient time to devote to the cause.
A in your volunteering **C** on your volunteering
B you to volunteer **D** for you volunteering

5 Having been a victim of burglary in the past, I plan .... joining the neighbourhood watch programme.
A to **B** on **C** for **D** at

6 The exact reason why .... the recycling programme is unknown, although it is believed that the high maintenance costs of the equipment played a part.
A did they stop **C** they stopped
B was it stopped **D** it was stopped

7 I didn't see Jane at the final talk of the conference; she .... early for some reason.
A may leave **C** ought to have left
B should have left **D** must have left

8 We weren't .... surprised by the success of the community programme; everyone had expected it to be very popular with young people.
A the least bit **C** the most
B a lot **D** too much

9 As soon as .... a sponsor for his research project, he will start recruiting volunteers to take part.
A he will find **C** he finds
B his finding **D** he is to find

10 On his way out of the courtroom, the lawyer .... questions from reporters about the trial.
A stopped to answer
B stopped answering
C had stopped answering
D was stopping to answer

11 The activists seem .... they are unsure about working with government officials.
A like as **C** though
B to be **D** as though

12 He didn't write his speech to the general assembly; he .... by a professional writer.
A did it **C** had it done
B had done it **D** had to do it

Vocabulary

5 ★ **Choose the correct item.**

1 How do you .... for the sudden drop in support for this cause?
A answer **C** justify
B clarify **D** account

2 .... of banning all plastic shopping bags claim that it will drastically reduce plastic pollution.
A Activists **C** Promoters
B Advocates **D** Sponsors

3 The conservation group is very close to .... its goal of securing protection status for the wetlands.
A receiving **C** undertaking
B accomplishing **D** succeeding

4 One of the .... of the negative press about the company's employment practices has been a drop in sales.
A concerns **C** complaints
B conditions **D** consequences

5 Unless we intervene immediately, the extinction of the snow leopard is ....
A invariable **C** inevitable
B inflexible **D** inexcusable

6 The Red Cross works to .... suffering in war-torn areas around the world.
A alleviate **C** placate
B diminish **D** temper

7 You can donate via the website to help .... hunger in third world countries.
A contend **C** challenge
B combat **D** contest

8 There is .... concern regarding the rapid spread of disease in poverty stricken countries.
A broad **C** thorough
B overall **D** widespread

9 The high levels of air pollution is .... a result of local factory emissions.
A plainly **C** distinctly
B abruptly **D** markedly

10 Thankfully the vandalism of the park statue seems to be an isolated ....; no further problems have been reported.
A circumstance **C** incident
B sequence **D** instance

11 The vote on the anti-bullying policy was .... and it will be put into effect immediately at the school.
A unanimous **C** undoubted
B united **D** undivided

12 The campaign focuses on supporting animals on the .... of extinction.
A limit **C** verge
B hem **D** margin

6a Reading

Motivational Posters

Do they actually work?

Every social media site, every trendy office, every form of public communication seems compelled to include as many motivational images and messages as possible. But do these have any effect on people? Or are they just one step up from wallpaper?

Obviously it's impossible to know for certain. There hasn't been any reliable research that has asked people whether their motivation and later-life success was due to a well-placed poster (how would you ever go about confirming such a thing even if it were the case?), but we can theorise as to how they could work. To look at whether a poster could be classed as motivational, it's important to clarify what this actually means. What is motivation?

Broadly, motivation can be characterised as either an internal or external drive that helps a person to remain interested and/or undertake a project, goal,

Multiple choice

Preparing for the task

Remember!

Some multiple choice questions focus on implication and what the author is implying or suggesting. This means the writer is communicating an idea or feeling without directly saying it. Writers often use questions, example and reference in order to imply or suggest an idea.

1 **a) ★ Read the extract below, paying attention to the underlined words. What is the writer implying?**

Pitting one employee against another is a common motivational strategy. But does it really work? Unlike positive feedback, it sends the wrong message. Often interpreted as an insult, such a strategy can even diminish performance.

b) ★ Now read the question and possible answers, paying attention to the underlined words. Which answer reflects what the writer is implying in Ex. 1a?

The writer implies that employees

A are highly productive under competition.
B do not respond positively to competition.
C prefer encouragement over competition.

2 **★★ Read the text about motivational sayings. For questions 1-8, choose the correct answer A, B, C or D.**

1 The author suggests that the effectiveness of motivational messages
A depends on the context of where they appear.
B tend to manifest much later on in life.
C cannot be precisely measured.
D was predicted by existing research.

2 The author describes motivation as
A an interaction between personal and impersonal factors.
B something arising from either inner desires or outside reinforcements.
C determined primarily by one's internal state.
D as the particular goals we set for ourselves.

3 According to the text, the 'ought' self
A is primarily driven by motivational sayings.
B acts independently of the ideal self with no regard for it.
C operates with the attainment of the ideal self in mind.
D is unaffected by most motivational sayings.

4 **Impetus** in paragraph 4 is best replaced by
A ambition. **C** urge.
B encouragement. **D** impulse.

etc. The internal and external emphasis is an interesting one. People can be motivated by intrinsic factors (e.g. studying hard for your exams because you are genuinely interested in medicine) or extrinsic factors (e.g. studying hard for your exams because it will please your parents and help ensure well-paid work later in life).

Now, let's focus on the original question: do these motivational posters actually work? The actual mechanism by which they could work is almost certainly intrinsic; there is no obvious external reward offered by looking at a poster. The psychologist Higgins argued that people have three types of self: the 'ideal' self, which is what we hope to become; the 'ought' self, which is how we think we should behave to achieve the ideal self; and the actual self, which is the extent to which we actually possess these desired attributes. The 'ideal' self encourages us to do things that take our actual self closer to that state (e.g. dressing smarter at work to seem more professional), the 'ought' self stops us doing things that lead our actual self away from it (e.g. avoiding fatty foods because we want to be healthier). In either case, it usually takes effort and motivation, so could a well-placed reminder that our efforts aren't necessarily futile provide the necessary **impetus** we need? A well-phrased quote emphasising the things a person can achieve could boost our ideal self, or one reassuring us that hard work is normal and necessary may shore up our ought self.

It's easy to scoff at the corporate use of motivational posters like these. It often seems like a company trying to get more from employees without actually paying them any more money, but this is to overlook the importance of intrinsic motivation, as exemplified by the 'overjustification effect'. This effect suggests that if you reward people for something they already like doing, they'll actually lose the motivation for doing it. This has led to the agency theory of motivation, where it is argued that autonomy is better than financial reward for motivating people, as the reward is an external factor, beyond their control and could be taken away at any time, whereas giving someone autonomy means they have control and so a sense of achievement. You can sort of see how a well-placed quote could provide a nugget of confidence, particularly if paired with a stunning image. But it's impossible to say where or when such a thing would be most helpful, so the only solution is to flood the environment with them wherever possible. Except, this is likely to undermine the impact of motivational posters, not increase it. We are likely to ignore them due to oversaturation (my own favourite example of this was finding a motivational message on a bag of French fries).

But all is not lost for the motivational poster. Thanks to social networking, people can now make or share motivational images to their heart's content. Doing this suggests that you are a wise and thoughtful person. It's fine if you want to share something that's helped you, but some seem to take it too far. It's as if they want to be seen as more wise and in touch with their feelings than anyone else, and thus share as many motivational images as possible, as often as possible. This must take a lot of effort, and so it seems that, in some cases, motivational posters do work after all. Although, probably not in the way intended.

5 The corporate use of motivational posters is
- **A** often interpreted negatively by many.
- **B** overrated and relatively ineffective.
- **C** not based on how rewards work.
- **D** connected to external motivators.

6 According to the agency theory the best motivation is
- **A** recognition and encouragement by others.
- **B** small incentives along the way.
- **C** financial reward or bonuses.
- **D** an internal sense for accomplishment.

7 The writer suggests that motivational posters today are largely ineffective because
- **A** most people find them annoying.
- **B** their spectacular images distract from the message.
- **C** they have become too commonplace.
- **D** they aren't placed in enough appropriate places.

8 The writer implies that, on social media, motivational posters
- **A** are most effective when used regularly.
- **B** are shared for reasons other than motivating others.
- **C** appear more genuine thus attracting more people.
- **D** are targeted at the most receptive audience.

3 ★ Match the highlighted words in the text to their synonyms.

• put together • a bit • connected • pointless • honestly • independence

4 ★★ Choose the correct word.

1 There are certain criteria used to **compel/class/clarify** a behaviour as instinctual.

2 The plethora of motivational quotes everywhere **overlooks/undertakes/undermines** their effectiveness.

3 Constant praise is relatively ineffective as **exemplified/emphasised/encouraged** by the overjustification effect.

4 Motivational posters attempt to create a **mechanism/drive/state** within us to achieve our goals.

5 Our 'ought' self works to **scoff/shore/sort** up our ideal self.

6 There are many extrinsic **factors/efforts/attributes** that play a role in motivation.

5 ★★ Match the underlined phrases from the text to their meaning below.

- **A** to fill an entire area or place with a large quantity of sth
- **B** to continue to do sth beyond reasonable limits
- **C** to mock sth without second thoughts
- **D** as much as sb wants
- **E** to be only a little better than sth

6b Vocabulary

1 ★ **Choose the correct item.**

1 Messages are **formed/circulated/built/transmitted** along nerves from the brain to the muscles.
2 The local surgery hired a **physician/practitioner/locum/provider** to cover the practice while the doctor was on leave.
3 Scientists are experimenting with **manipulating/handling/triggering/provoking** DNA to halt the aging process.
4 You have to be careful when working around chemicals because some of them can give off **contagious/infectious/noxious/inflammatory** gases.
5 The clinic provides access to **conventional/complementary/superficial/conformist** therapies like aromatherapy and yoga.

2 ★ **Choose A or B according to the meaning of the words in bold.**

1 Doctors and nurses need to **have a strong stomach** to deal with everything they see on a daily basis.
   A be able to eat hot, spicy food
   B not feel ill from experiencing unpleasant things
2 Losing weight gave Jeremy **a new lease of life** and he hasn't looked back since.
   A a larger period of time to be active
   B more energy and ability to be active
3 I'm going to do well in Biology this year; I just **feel it in my bones**.
   A believe sth even though it can't be explained
   B begin to start understanding sth
4 The doctor gave Bobby **a clean bill of health** after his illness so he can now start training again.
   A the news that he is healthy
   B an itemised account of the cost of treatment
5 The students' suggestions for a new healthy menu gave us a lot of **food for thought**.
   A things to seriously think about
   B ideas of what to cook

3 ★★ **Fill in:** *to, with, through, off.*

1 The doctors are confident that Simon will pull .... despite his high fever.
2 Extreme sports are fraught .... danger and injuries are commonplace.
3 My mum swears by drinking a glass of orange juice every day to ward .... a cold.
4 Doctors and scientists are concerned about what will happen when infectious diseases become resistant .... antibiotics.

4 ★★ **Use the words in the list to complete the sentences.**

• surge • whirlwind • outpouring • flash

1 There was a(n) .... of support in the community when the village hospital was threatened with closure.
2 Casey felt a(n) .... of emotions when her son took his first steps.
3 Tina had a(n) .... of inspiration and used her scarf as a makeshift sling for Rex's arm when he fell and hurt his wrist.
4 There was a(n) .... of activity as the doctors treated the man that was injured in the accident.

5 ★★ **Fill in the gaps with a word from the list and choose the correct word.**

• miraculous • mental • inner • anxiety

Mind over Matter

The brain is a complex organ and its **1)** .... workings are not yet fully understood by the medical community. A **2) treatment/case/condition** in point is the placebo effect. It is rumoured that a doctor in World War II gave his patients a placebo when pain medication was in short supply. He was able to operate on them successfully and the patients went on to make a(n) **3)** .... recovery. From this, the doctor deduced that the positive **4)** .... outlook that taking a placebo can give patients, can prove extremely powerful in treating them. The mere action of **5) admitting/permitting/ingesting** a pill or getting an injection seems to reduce **6)** .... levels and allows the brain to release its own painkilling chemicals. Placebos cannot **7) dissipate/acknowledge/modify** a disease themselves, but they can assist the body in healing itself. Even though the **8) propensity/correlation/mechanism** behind it is not yet fully understood, it could be a powerful tool that can go a long way in the care of patients.

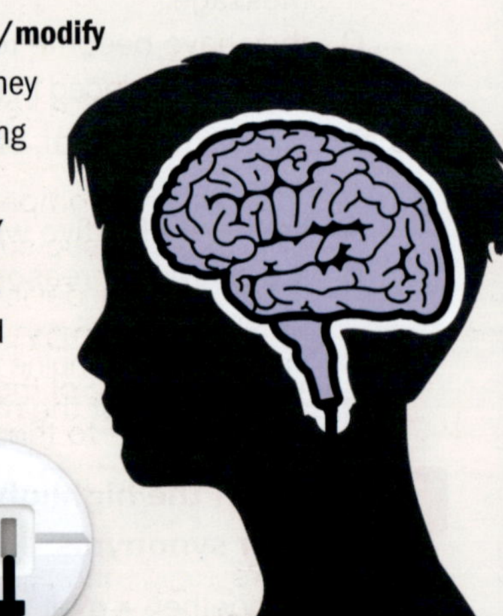

Topic related vocabulary 6b

Science & Genetics

Phrasal verbs

6 ★ **Choose the correct item.**

1 Geoffrey bounced **back/down/up** incredibly well after his operation and returned to work in a matter of days.
2 Did you know that all blue-eyed people are descended **with/to/from** one person who lived more than 6,000 years ago?
3 After the fervour surrounding the discovery of the gene that caused the disease died **back/down/off**, scientists concentrated on learning more about it.
4 Parents hand **over/back/down** more than just possessions to their offspring; they also give them their physical characteristics.
5 Angela lived **through/between/across** a terrible accident only to be struck **back/down/out** with a degenerative illness two years later.

7 ★★ **Fill in the noun formed from the verbs in the list.**

• convalesce • implicate • presume • diagnose • absorb • vary

1 This new drug boasts rapid .... which means quicker pain relief for sufferers.
2 From what was stated in the report, the .... was that the research had been inadequate.
3 The article was about the .... of techniques that can be employed in research.
4 After an illness, a period of .... is necessary in order to make a full recovery.
5 After examining Mike's test result, the doctors agreed on a ....
6 Making a(n) .... has no place in scientific research; we work with certainties.

8 ★★ **Complete the sentences with a word from the list.**

• observable • acute • calculable • chronic

1 There are always .... risks when testing a new drug but the potential benefits tend to outweigh them.
2 In tests, there was no .... difference between the drugs that could be perceived.
3 .... conditions have symptoms that come on suddenly.
4 Homeopathic therapies are often employed to relieve .... pain over long periods.

9 ★★ **Fill in the gaps with a word from the list and choose the correct item.**

• unintended • health • hostile • informed • hereditary

A Costly Inheritance

Genetic testing has been around for some time now but in the past it was often met with a(n) **1)** .... reception from a sceptical public. There was also a fear that the results would affect the **2)** .... insurance of those tested resulting in the **3)** .... consequence of higher premiums **4) irrespective/irresponsible/irrelevant** of whether they developed the **5)** .... illness they were being tested for. However, society seems to have caught up with science and we are now able to have a(n) **6)** .... debate over the legitimacy of genetic testing. So much so, that legislation has been introduced in the USA to **7) adjust/regulate/trigger** the insurance companies, preventing them from **8) discrediting/disputing/disqualifying** applicants on the basis of a positive result. As a result, individuals can now look into their genes without fear of reprisal.

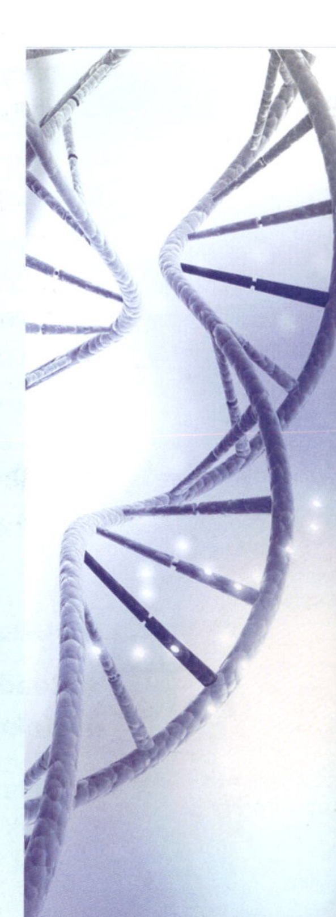

Word formation

10 ★★ **Complete the sentences with words derived from the words in bold.**

1 The patient was completely .... after his facial plastic surgery. **(RECOGNISE)**
2 The latest medical devices .... new improvements. **(BODY)**
3 Some .... of the project are to provide health care and support to the less privileged. **(OBJECT)**
4 The scientist's .... was in engineering. **(BACK)**
5 Society's .... on healthcare technology is increasing. **(RELY)**
6 The rumours will do .... damage to his reputation. **(TELL)**
7 Personal trainers help to .... the benefits of fitness programmes. **(MAXIMUM)**
8 .... neck glands may signal an infection. **(LARGE)**
9 Many people suffer from sleep .... due to long work hours. **(DEPRIVE)**
10 Facial exercises help to retain the skin's .... **(ELASTIC)**

6c Grammar in use

Modals

1 ★★ Rewrite the sentences using the modals in the list. Make any necessary changes.

• must be • would you like • needn't
• must • might • ought to have • have got to
• needn't have

1 Don't forget that you need to collect your prescription later today.
....
2 It isn't necessary for you to get more plasters; I have some in our first aid kit.
....
3 It's likely we'll go to the life coaching seminar tonight; want to join us?
....
4 You are required to take the patient's test results to Dr Jones.
....
5 Do you want another appointment with your personal trainer?
....
6 It wasn't necessary for you to worry; the aerobics class has lots of spaces left.
....
7 It would have been better if you had spoken to the pharmacist before buying the medicine.
....
8 I'm almost sure that Jim is training at the gym at the moment.
....

Nouns

2 ★ Read the sentences and correct the mistakes.

1 Lots of researches shows that it's important to look after your healths by having a balanced diet.
....
2 The statistics is eye opening; I never realised that obesity were such a widespread issue.
....
3 His family prefers different types of leisure activities in order to relax.
....
4 One hundred pound were the total cost for the health club membership.
....
5 The doctor told Sue that there wasn't much damages done to her ankle due to her fall.
....

Compound nouns

3 ★★ Replace the underlined words with a compound noun.

1 Jane likes to drink herbal tea from her favourite <u>cup for drinking tea</u>. ....
2 Bill was offered the position of the <u>chief of the editors</u> at the wellness magazine. ....
3 In Angela's office <u>the time for coffee</u> is usually at midday. ....
4 There's nothing better than stopping to enjoy the <u>rising of the sun</u> while on holiday. ....
5 Ellen was enjoying a <u>dream during the day</u> about her plans for the weekend. ....

Nominalisation

4 ★★ Complete the sentences using nominalisation so that it has a similar meaning to the first one. Make any necessary changes.

1 It has been suggested that we offer more Pilates classes throughout the week.
A .... to offer more Pilates classes throughout the week.
2 Helen looked quickly around the room for her heart rate monitor.
Helen had a .... around the room for her heart rate monitor.
3 Positive user reviews have risen significantly since the new fitness app update was released.
There .... positive user reviews since the release of the fitness app update.
4 They didn't explain why the gym was closed.
They didn't .... for why the gym was closed.

Quantifiers

5 ★ Read the sentence and choose the meaning (A or B) that best matches it.

1 Few healthcare professionals in the NHS have embraced alternative therapies.
A Enough healthcare professionals have accepted it.
B Hardly any healthcare professionals have accepted it.
2 Each stage of a consultation must be explained to a patient.
A All individual stages must be explained.
B All of the stages as a group must be explained.
3 Some life coach is giving a talk at the conference centre tomorrow.
A An amazing life coach is giving a talk.
B A life coach that I don't know is giving a talk.

Grammar Revision 6c (Modules 1-6)

1 ★ **Choose the correct item.**

1 By the end of the month the community medical clinic **will have been running/will be running/shall be running/is going to be running** for two years.
2 Call a life coach if you **are needing/will need/will be needing/need** help with reaching your goals.
3 I heard Jim **discuss/discussing/to discuss/having discussed** the motivational seminar before he left the room.
4 Mandy **is wanting/does want/do want/will want** to come to the gym with us but she might not be able to.
5 Paul **rather/quite/absolutely/barely** hates self-help books; he can't stand them.
6 **If you will go on/Should you go on/If you happen to go on/If you should happen to go on** interrupting the speaker, I'll be forced to ask you to leave the auditorium.
7 The therapy **was proven/will be proven/is being proven/is having to be proven** to be completely effective at the conclusion of the study.
8 Nurses in a team rely on **every other/another/the other one/each other** to provide patient care on the entire ward.

2 ★★ **Fill in the gaps. Use the appropriate form of the word in brackets when given.**

1 Critics of homeopathy claim that prices are becoming .... **(expensive)** and that the industry operates without .... **(receive)** sufficient regulation.
2 Jim had his medical condition .... **(diagnose)** by a GP who is .... his local area.
3 I .... ever exercised when I was younger but one day I .... **(listen)** to a podcast about yoga and decided to give it a try. I haven't looked back since!
4 If we .... **(have)** a fitness studio in the neighbourhood, I'd definitely learn how .... Tai Chi.
5 I dread .... **(imagine)** how much money the new spa is going to charge for .... of its different beauty treatments.
6 I .... **(exercise)** at the gym when someone .... **(set)** the fire alarm off.

Key word transformations

3 ★★ **For questions 1-4, complete the second sentence so that it has a similar meaning to the first sentence, using the word given. Do not change the word given. You must use between three and eight words, including the word given.**

1 I think Jane paid too much for her insurance policy. **GOT**
I think Jane ....
.... cheaply.
2 I was surprised at how strongly he reacted to the diagnosis. **STRENGTH**
The ....
.... me by surprise.
3 On no account would I use that sports centre again. **LIKELIHOOD**
The ....
.... is non-existent.
4 Martin was not used to doing such intensive exercise. **HABIT**
Martin was not ....
.... intensively.

Grammar in Focus

★★ **Fill in the gaps with the correct word, the correct form of the word in brackets or choose the correct word.**

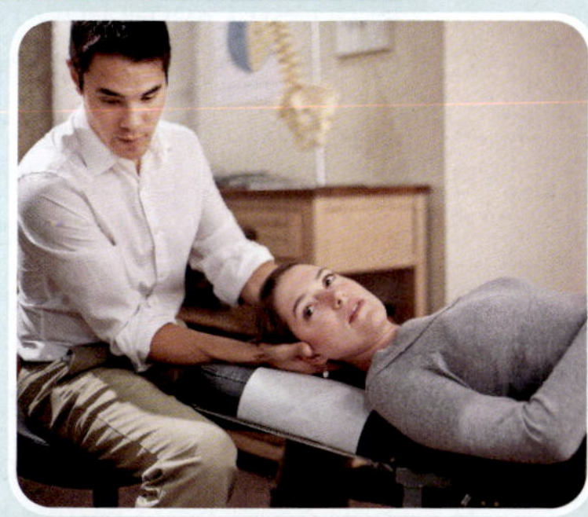

Clickety-clack!

To some people, osteopathic treatment **1)** .... **(seem)** more like a form of torture **2)** .... a therapy. However, it isn't **3) as painful as/more painful than** you'd think! In fact, although it can come across as harsh it isn't distressing at all. Many patients who **4)** .... **(use)** osteopaths for years swear by their skills and, as a result, the proponents of this complementary therapy are becoming **5)** .... **(abundant)** every year. Osteopathy includes **6)** .... of manual work on the limbs and spine; not only techniques such as massage and stretching but **7)** .... bone manipulation. There are lots of benefits as it's **8) free of drugs/drug-free** and can also help strengthen the musculoskeletal framework of the body. So, if you find yourself suffering from back pains or sports injuries you **9) ought to/must** give osteopathy a try. You might just be **10)** .... **(surprised/surprising)** at how helpful it is!

6d Listening skills

Multiple choice

Remember!

You should always read the answer choices before you listen to prepare yourself for what you will hear. While listening, it is important to listen to what is being said as well as the way it is said. This is especially important when the information is implied by the speaker.

1 ★★ **You will hear short conversations. Listen and from the three answer choices, select the answer which means about the same thing as what you hear, or is true based on what you hear.**

1 **A** They are going shopping.
B He is making dessert.
C She needs some ingredients.

2 **A** He is worried the restaurant may be full.
B He will call the restaurant for her.
C The restaurant doesn't have a table big enough.

3 **A** They are meeting at his house.
B They are going cycling together.
C It is the weekend.

4 **A** He thinks Kenny will keep to the regime.
B He doesn't know how Kenny is doing.
C He believes Kenny has given up.

5 **A** They are joining the gym.
B He prefers exercising outdoors.
C She doesn't understand his attitude.

6 **A** They are having a lesson.
B They are eating eggs.
C They are having a meal.

7 **A** They are shopping for dinner.
B They don't have much time.
C They want something quick to cook.

8 **A** He caught a virus from a colleague.
B She is worried about him.
C He has to go back to work.

9 **A** He has been working for 40 years.
B They wish they were younger.
C She is on a diet.

10 **A** He is unhappy.
B He is getting ill.
C He is hungry.

11 **A** The team needs more practice.
B He is confident about their abilities.
C She can't make the game.

12 **A** There's not enough funding for both locations.
B They go to the city for treatment.
C The clinic has shut down.

13 **A** She will eat for free.
B She doesn't have time to eat.
C She will eat at home.

14 **A** Monica is responding to treatment.
B He is worried Monica won't pull through.
C Monica is making a speedy recovery.

15 **A** He had to have an operation.
B He badly fractured his foot.
C He is going to be laid up for over a month.

Listening for meaning and inference

2 a) ★ **You will hear two friends discussing studying for exams. Before you listen, check these words in the Word List.**

• keep sth straight • regurgitate
• need your head examined • gauge • genius
• go overboard • burn the candle at both ends
• grab • function • detrimental • wholesome
• having a laugh • energise • hit the books

b) ★★ **Listen, and for questions 1-5, decide whether the opinions are expressed by Catherine, Donald or whether both speakers agree. Write:** *B* **if both speakers agree,** *C* **for Catherine,** *D* **for Donald.**

1 Exams are an ineffective method for assessing knowledge. ☐
2 Exams can hinder even the brightest minds. ☐
3 Rest and recuperation aid one's long-term memory. ☐
4 Proper nutrition can boost cognitive ability. ☐
5 Physical activity is good for dealing with anxieties. ☐

Speaking skills 6e

Asking for/Reacting to/Giving advice

1 **a) ★ Read the dialogue. Use phrases (a-f) to complete the dialogue.**

a maybe you're right
b What do you think I should do
c have you thought about
d maybe you could
e I appreciate
f I'm not sure

Nancy: What's wrong James? You look like you're in pain.
James: I am. My sciatica is playing up again. I went to the chiropractor but my lower back still hurts. **1)** ....?
Nancy: Well, **2)** .... trying some home remedies?
James: **3)** .... ; do they actually work?
Nancy: I think so. I mean you can always go online and do some research. I'm sure you'll find a good remedy. For instance, **4)** .... do a home routine of stretches.
James: How can they help?
Nancy: Well, by stretching your abdominal muscles and lower back you might relieve the pain.
James: Yes, **5)** .... I think I'll give it a go. **6)** .... the advice.
Nancy: Anytime!

b) ★ Replace the phrases (a-f) in Ex. 1 with the ones below.

• have you considered • I don't know
• What advice can you give • if I were you, I would
• Thanks for • all right

c) ★★ Which phrases in Exs 1a & b ask for/ react to/give advice? Complete the table.

Ask	....
React	....
Give	....

2 **★ Choose the correct item.**

1 A: Have you ever thought of trying acupuncture?
B: **a** That's not a bad idea.
b Yes, all right.

2 A: What do you think I should do for my back problem?
B: **a** Have you got any advice?
b Why don't you go to a chiropractor?

3 A: If I were you, I would try alternative therapies.

Commenting on/Reacting to an article

3 **a) ★ Read the notes based on an article on leisure sickness. Then read the sample answer. Complete the text with the phrases (A-E) in the list.**

A Evidence suggests
B It's obvious
C concludes by
D I think
E The reason given

Leisure Sickness

• lately many people are plagued by feeling ill during weekends or while on holiday
• one study discovered illness more common in men (3%) than in women (2%)
• stress related symptoms include headaches, fatigue, aching joints, melancholy and anxiety
• according to studies stress causes the body to release adrenaline, which gives energy and boosts the immune system
• once work slows down and the stress decreases – the adrenaline stops and the body produces cortisol which weakens the immune system
• this leaves a person susceptible to illness
• one study reveals that there is a way to reverse the illness with a change of attitude towards life in general

Personally, **1)** .... this article offers some very surprising facts about leisure sickness. It mentions that a growing number of people cannot enjoy their weekend or holiday time anymore. **2)** .... that 1 percent more men than women are affected, which is not a huge difference. This is a syndrome where people develop various physical symptoms such as exhaustion, body pain and depression. **3)** .... to me that our psychological state affects our physiological condition. **4)** .... for this illness is that changes in the production of hormones between times of stress and relaxation can wreak havoc on the immune system. The article **5)** .... pointing out the possibility of combating the syndrome by having a more positive outlook on life, which seems like an entirely logical notion.

b) ★ Which of the phrases (A-E) comment on the article or react to the article by giving examples or justifying?

6f Writing Reports

1 ★ **Read the rubric and underline the key words. Then read the model report. Have all the points in the rubric been covered?**

You are student president at your college. The college authorities have asked you to write a report on the most pressing health problems faced by students today. You should briefly describe two or three serious problems. Your report should also recommend ways of dealing with these problems and explain how this would benefit students. Write your **report** (approximately 280-320 words).

To:	Dr Mary Collins, Senior Health Advisor
From:	John Harper, Student Union President
Subject:	Student health issues
Date:	10th June, 2018

A ....

The aim of this report is to **1)** .... some of the health issues that affect students at this institution and to make suggestions on how to address them outlining the benefits of these suggestions for students. I hope that it may be instrumental in contributing to a common policy on student health concerns at this college.

B ....

To begin with, the most common issue to affect **2)** .... of students is anxiety. Students often feel depressed and anxious as a result of having intense pressure to obtain high grades **3)** .... their career aspirations. These emotions begin to interfere with their day-to-day life and negatively impact their academic performance. An initial step for countering the effects of stress is for the college to set up a stress workshop prior to the exam period which would teach students techniques to manage and overcome it.

C ....

The lack of physical exercise is another major factor that affects students overall. During college years most students do not have the time or the energy to work out and become more sedentary due to heavy workloads. **4)** .... , their physical activity levels decrease which may cause health problems **5)** .... weight gain and obesity. One way to get students more active is by forming more college fitness clubs or group exercise classes that students can join and participate in which would get them into shape.

D ....

Today's students are well aware of the link between bad health and bad diet but tend to ignore the dangers of poor nutrition. **6)** .... the constraints of their sedentary lifestyles and limited time available, most students fail to maintain nutritional diets **7)** .... fast food and ready-made meals instead. Consequently, they develop unhealthy eating habits. I would suggest commissioning a survey to find the extent of the problem and then form nutritional programmes based around the results of the survey to further educate students.

E ....

8) .... , this report highlights the need for greater awareness of students' health concerns. I strongly believe that the combined actions of the stress workshop, the additional activity and nutritional programmes will be meaningful contributions to addressing student health issues at this college. My recommendation would be to implement these suggestions so that students can maintain healthier lifestyles.

2 a) ★ **Fill in the missing word in the phrases below, as in the example.**

• as • light • for • with • this • vast • to • whole

1 for *this* reason
2 shed .... on
3 in connection ....
4 such ....
5 the .... majority
6 due ....
7 opting ....
8 On the ....

b) ★ **Read the model again and fill in the appropriate phrases from Ex. 2a.**

3 ★★ **Look at the model again and use the headings in the list to complete the report.**

• Mental health • Purpose • Conclusion • Nourishment • Physical activity

Your turn

4 ★★ **Read the rubric. Then read the notes (1-6) and list them under the correct subheadings.**

You work at a five star hotel with a health spa. Your manager has asked you to write a report on how to attract more visitors to the health spa facilities. You should briefly describe the facilities that are currently available. Your report should also recommend two or three improvements that would enhance the health spa further and explain why these would attract even more visitors. Write your **report** (approximately 280-320 words).

1 With spa-replicated thalassotherapy more visitors will come for treatment instead of going to the ocean.
2 Health spa offers visitors massage therapy sessions.
3 Create additional programmes for meditation run by celebrity instructors or coaches.
4 Visitors take part in a wellness programme which includes yoga.
5 Add therapeutic bathing with additional large pool filled with heated seawater.
6 Visitors will value additional instruction and will sign up for classes.

Current facilities	Improvements	Effects
....	....	....

5 ★★ **Use the notes in Ex. 4 and your own ideas to write your report.**

What Exactly is Life Coaching?

I HIRED A COACH TO FIND OUT!

My life coach's name is Hailey Jordan Yatros. She's 21. I'm 29. Yatros is a natural encourager; it's one of her gifts. I know this because she told me so the first time we talked.

When I searched 'life coaches' online, Yatros came up on the first page. At 21, she was one of the youngest coaches I found, but she had a professional-looking website with positive endorsements, and she'd published a book. I was a writer, and nearly 30, and I didn't have those things. But what hooked me was her splash photo: a close-up of her youthful face with an expression of happiness so intense it bordered on insanity. I wanted that expression – and that shade of lipstick.

Also, I wanted advice. I'd recently moved back to New York as a freelance writer. I was underemployed but overworked, with friends who seemed to exist only as green dots on my chat screen. Time management seemed like an equation I could never solve. Basically, I'd lie awake at night unable to shake the feeling that I was doing everything wrong.

Online sessions are the norm for most life coaches, so it didn't matter that I lived in Brooklyn and Yatros lived in a suburb of Detroit. I hired her for a month – four sessions once a week. Before our first session, she asked me to fill out a questionnaire about my short-term and long-term goals and my general happiness. These were questions I hadn't asked myself in a while; I felt like I was making progress already.

Search 'how to cure anxiety' and you'll get around 39 million results. A life coach is a shot of humanity in this crush of data. Hiring one isn't like calling a taxi on an app or listening to a self-help podcast. It's an old-school **leap of faith** that requires blocking out the din of the digital age and looking someone in the, uh, laptop camera's eye.

That said, our first session got off to a bumpy start. I had a bad Internet connection, so our voices were out of sync, and she looked more like a glitchy monster than a beaming, clear-eyed truth teller. We spent maybe three minutes talking about my family. 'I just like to get a little snippet,' she said. Then, we got into my questionnaire. She asked me how I was at self-care. I told her I went to the gym, but in general I had a hard time relaxing. 'Every millennial feels this way,' Yatros said. She told me the Internet was to blame. 'I love technology, but it's what's made us want things now. We want to be the CEO, but we don't know how to be the janitor first.' My homework was to try meditating for 20 minutes a day until our next session and set reminders on my phone to ask myself how I was feeling. She also told me to complete an online test about myself.

In the following session, we both seemed more at ease. I'd taken the online test earlier in the week and sent her the results. I'd put an alert on my phone to remind me to ask myself how I was feeling. Usually I was feeling annoyed that my phone was going off. I hadn't meditated once. When I admitted as much to Yatros, she waved me away saying it was no problem. She told me I had a 'perfect personality' based on my test results, which showed that I worked well alone but also with people, was good at collecting information but also taking action. 'I think they're amazing,' said Yatros about these core strengths, as she called them.

My biggest problem, she said, was that I was stressing out about trying to use all my strengths at the same time. Guilt and shame were the anchors holding my bird down. The universe would open doors for me if I stayed true to who I was in each moment.

Between our sessions, I'd get emails full of praise and encouragement which I kind of liked. Maybe I'm just another millennial wanting a trophy for being me, but it felt good to have a personal cheerleader on call. Her optimism never faltered; she had words of encouragement for every issue I raised. On dealing with difficult people: 'Treat everybody like they have a broken heart.' On worrying about being too old or too young: 'Forget your age and live.' The clichés were relentless, but surprisingly comforting.

In the months since I finished my sessions with Yatros, my career has stabilized and I'm finding time to see my friends. I'm calmer and happier than I've been since I can remember. It's probably just that I'm getting older. But also, well, I'm meditating. Not every day, never for more than ten minutes, but it's a start!

Reading

1 ★★ **Read the text about Life Coaching. For questions 1-6, choose the correct answer A, B, C or D.**

1 The main reason that the writer hired Yatros as a life coach was
- A her sophisticated web presence.
- B the positive recommendations from others.
- C her impressive accomplishments for her age.
- D her apparent positive disposition.

2 The writer states she sought out the help of a life coach because
- A she was spending too much time on the Internet.
- B she really felt her life wasn't going right.
- C she was miserable with her career choice.
- D she wanted to find more free time in her schedule.

3 The phrase 'leap of faith' in paragraph 5 suggests that life coaching requires one to
- A offer your unbridled attention to your coach.
- B surrender all logic and just relax and enjoy it.
- C trust it even though you are not sure what it's about.
- D focus on the spiritual self and leave behind everyday issues.

4 Yatros suggests that the Internet
- A has made young people impatient and stressed.
- B has caused people to ignore important needs.
- C is partly responsible for the lack of initiative today.
- D puts a lot of pressure on youth to overachieve.

5 Yatros' main advice to the writer is to
- A use all her strengths at one time.
- B be herself and at all times.
- C ignore the negative feelings that keep her down.
- D focus on improving her strengths.

6 Yatros' constant optimism and encouragement made the writer
- A feel self-conscious and embarrassed.
- B annoyed by the onslaught of silly clichés.
- C rethink her whole outlook on life.
- D more positive and relaxed about herself.

Language Knowledge 6

Multiple Choice Cloze

1 ★★ **For questions 1-8, read the text below and decide which answer (A, B, C or D) best fits each gap. There is an example at the beginning (0).**

IS THERE AN ATHLETIC ***GENE?***

How is it that some athletes appear to be naturals? Can their incredible talent be **0)** B back to their DNA? The idea that athletic performance is **1)** .... encoded in our genetic material, just as intelligence and disease, is being **2)** .... examined by genetic researchers. They are trying to **3)** .... specific genetic material that is associated with **4)** .... athletic performance. For example, a gene called ACTN3 has been **5)** .... to speed. Researchers found that a certain variant of the gene was present in the DNA of all world-record-holding runners as opposed to control groups that did not **6)** .... this specific gene variation. If performance is indeed genetically determined then it could have massive **7)** .... for our understanding of sport. Recruitment methods could also be revolutionised with the introduction of genetic **8)** .... for athletic genes as part of the scouting process.

	A		B		C		D	
0	**A**	drawn	**B**	traced	**C**	outlined	**D**	placed
1	**A**	implicitly	**B**	internally	**C**	inherently	**D**	intimately
2	**A**	solemnly	**B**	soberly	**C**	sedately	**D**	seriously
3	**A**	pinpoint	**B**	circle	**C**	indicate	**D**	mark
4	**A**	enriched	**B**	enhanced	**C**	enlarged	**D**	embellished
5	**A**	connected	**B**	combined	**C**	linked	**D**	affiliated
6	**A**	convey	**B**	carry	**C**	express	**D**	harbour
7	**A**	allegations	**B**	insinuations	**C**	implications	**D**	associations
8	**A**	selection	**B**	manipulation	**C**	screening	**D**	programming

2 ★★ **For questions 1-8, read the text below and think of a word which best fits each gap. There is an example at the beginning (0).**

Energy Management: recharge your life

These days, a great deal of emphasis is 0) placed on developing time management skills in 1) .... to achieve much more in even 2) .... time. However, there is an underlying problem with focusing on time as a linear measurement to increase productivity, as it is finite in nature and not flexible 3) .... to modify extensively. Energy, on the other hand, is 4) .... renewable and sustainable. The key to getting more 5) .... your day is identifying energy depleting behaviour thus 6) .... yourself the ability to manage and renew your energy throughout a twenty-four hour period. The good news is that this is easier than it sounds. 7) .... simple actions like taking a revitalising walk at lunch time or meditating for a few minutes after work could make the difference between feeling burnt 8) .... or recharged and ready for action!

Key word transformations

3 ★★ **For questions 1-6, complete the second sentence so that it has a similar meaning to the first sentence, using the word given. Do not change the word given. You must use between three and eight words including the word given.**

1 I immediately liked my new coach.
LIKING
I ....
.... my new coach.

2 She regretted the fact that she had to attend the meeting.
RATHER
She ....
.... the meeting.

3 You can use the gym to work out whenever you want.
DISPOSAL
The gym ....
.... work out whenever you want.

4 The patient didn't seem distressed even though her test results were not good.
SIGN
The patient ....
.... even though her test results were not good.

5 The self-help programme did nothing to help Karen with her problems.
INEFFECTIVE
The self-help programme ....
....
Karen with her problems.

6 Jim's outburst was completely inexcusable.
EXCUSE
There ....
.... Jim acted.

Grammar

4 ★ Choose the correct item.

1 It's not unusual for yoga students .... uncomfortable the first time they meditate.
A feeling
B to feel
C having felt
D to have felt

2 This exercise programme is definitely .... difficult of the two.
A more
B the more
C most
D the most

3 Carl is .... the most health conscious person I've ever met.
A no doubt
B without a doubt
C not to doubt
D not in doubt

4 The serenity of the place .... everyone was able to relax immediately.
A was such that
B were so that
C were that
D was that

5 It was disappointing that .... showed up for the fitness challenge.
A almost anybody
B almost none
C hardly anybody
D scarcely nobody

6 When I was young I .... hours walking in the forest near my home.
A was spending
B would spend
C used to be spending
D was used to spending

7 She basically lives .... a diet of fruits and vegetables.
A by
B for
C on
D with

8 To become a psychologist would have meant .... for another four years.
A to study
B study
C studying
D to studying

9 He may be a good doctor, but his views on alternative therapy are far too negative ....
A for me liking it
B for my liking
C for his liking
D for my having liked

10 "How was your meeting with the therapist?"
"It wasn't .... difficult as I had thought it would be."
A nearly as
B as nearly
C as nearly as
D as near as

11 It seems .... she's afraid to talk about her problems.
A though as
B to be
C as though
D as like

12 Her medical history .... available to the doctor yet.
A hasn't been made
B has been made
C haven't been made
D hasn't made

Vocabulary

5 ★ Choose the correct item.

1 Current opinion has .... in support of many self-help therapies.
A reached
B swung
C wavered
D motioned

2 Sue was asked to keep a diary of her day to see if there was a(n) .... in her behaviour.
A pattern
B outline
C programme
D path

3 As a last .... I turned to meditation to help reduce my stress.
A surrogate
B recourse
C resort
D stopgap

4 Jack's trainer .... his concern about the dangers of his overtraining.
A told
B presented
C voiced
D complained

5 The article talks about how a very high fat diet puts people at .... of heart disease.
A danger
B risk
C threat
D fear

6 After the treatment, extra care is required as the patient is highly .... to infections.
A sceptical
B subjectable
C susceptible
D suggestible

7 The motivational speaker .... all my expectations with his very impressive talk about positive thinking.
A receded
B succeeded
C exceeded
D proceeded

8 She has written more than 30 self-help books and continues to .... books to this day.
A stir up
B work up
C move out
D churn out

9 Over the years, homeopathic medicine has received a great deal of academic criticism; .... , it has become accepted as an ineffective form of treatment.
A obviously
B respectively
C consequently
D correspondingly

10 Pet-assisted therapy is primarily .... with assisting in recovery through interaction with a trained animal.
A concerned
B understood
C involved
D regarded

11 My therapist asked me to put .... some free time each evening to reflect upon the events of the day.
A across
B away
C aside
D apart

12 I was completely .... of the possible side effects of the drug.
A unfamiliar
B unaccustomed
C unacquainted
D unaware

7a Reading

Remember!

Matching headings to short texts
Remember to read the headlines carefully focusing on their meanings (some may have hidden meanings as in the case of idioms). Read the texts paying attention to their overall meanings and match them to the headline that best represents their meaning.

1 ★★ **There are fifteen headlines below and ten short news stories. Match the headlines to the news stories that fit best. There are five headlines you do not need.**

1 THE SKY'S THE LIMIT ACCORDING TO AMBITIOUS DEVELOPER

2 COUNCIL REJECTS DEVELOPMENT APPLICATION

3 NEW SCHEME EMPOWERS YOUNG PEOPLE

4 YOUNG NOMADS RUN RISK OF FALLING FOUL OF LAW

5 ACTION GROUP TAKES A STAND OVER HEALTH & SAFETY

6 UNUSUAL HOUSING BANNED BY GOVERNMENT

7 MILLENNIALS QUESTIONED AFTER ILLEGALLY HOUSE SHARING

8 A NOVEL SOLUTION FROM AN UNLIKELY SOURCE

9 THE HIGH LIFE UNDER THE LENS

10 SAFETY OF NEW SKYSCRAPER CALLED INTO DOUBT

11 LACK OF QUALIFIED TRADESPEOPLE A GROWING PROBLEM

12 POLITICIAN STANDS BY CONTROVERSIAL POLICY

13 COMMUNAL LIVING SEES A SUBSTANTIAL RISE

14 RESIDENTS FEELING THE SQUEEZE IN MORE WAYS THAN ONE

15 DIY TAKEN TO TOTALLY NEW HEIGHTS

URBAN REALITIES

A ☐ Hong Kong has once again made real-estate headlines with its pint-sized solutions to the city's housing crisis. The newest project by a local property developer features micro-housing at just 11 square metres, residences roughly the size of a small car! With rents starting at 800 USD/month, this development is another reflection of the growing housing crisis facing not just Hong Kong but other major metropolises around the world.

B ☐ Hong Kong's secretary for housing had come under harsh criticism for the continued support of the building and rental of cage homes. Consisting of a bunk bed surrounded by a metal cage, these homes service the city's poorest. The secretary stands behind the territory's long history of micro-housing as the best way to cope with the surging demand. Community leaders are demanding an end to this inhumane system.

C ☐ With housing costs skyrocketing in the San Francisco Bay Area, some millennials are turning to some rather unorthodox housing solutions. Tired of seeing their income disappear on rent, Heather Stewart and Luke Iseman decided to purchase a shipping container and convert it into a pocket-sized home on a small parking lot. Realising there were other like-minded individuals out there, they started Boxouse – a community where people can come and make their own homes in these unusual structures.

D ☐ A young man was arrested in a van parked in a local supermarket parking lot just after 1 am this morning and taken into custody. Upon investigation police discovered the man had been living in the van and attends a local college. Van dwelling appears to be on the rise with desperate millennials who see it as a more affordable and freer way of living than renting and traditional options. Care however is needed, as although not illegal, there are laws restricting overnight parking in various public areas.

E Community build schemes are offering fresh hope to young people and providing new solutions that tackle the housing crisis. By building new housing themselves, millennials are learning essential skills and trades while also increasing housing options for charities and young people in need. These community homes are often even rented out to the same people who helped build them!

F The US Census Bureau released its annual report on Wednesday. Of particular interest is the significant increase in co-living arrangements in urban centres; specifically millennials who rent rooms in shared large homes and apartments. The prevalence of communal living offers the perks of shared living expenses and a sense of community and camaraderie between tenants. However, it's essential to make sure that you aren't subletting illegally.

G Most of us have made our own furniture from flat-packs, but what if we could 'flat-pack' our entire homes? TV celebrity and Architect Kevin McCloud, a major proponent of the flat-pack home movement, encourages millennials to do exactly that! In particular, he focuses on the environmental and monetary benefits of small but sustainable homes for the community, and how they can help young people desperate to get onto the housing ladder.

H A petition demanding more regulation of subcontracted work on council housing was presented to the mayor by community groups last night. Signed by over 2000 homeowners from around London, the petition draws attention to the dangers and risks of cutting costs on electrical work and plumbing and calls for more stringent checks. According to resident groups fears over both the suitability of selected contractors and the quality of work carried out have been widely ignored by councils.

I Maselbow Properties unveiled plans for their latest addition to a series of residential skyscrapers in the city centre yesterday. At 20 storeys and with 700 units, the building will offer a new benchmark for high-rise accommodation. The tower's wide range of amenities include pools, gyms, retail spaces, full concierge service and a day-care centre. 'Our goal from the beginning was to provide affordable housing with a sense of community right in the heart of the city' explained project manager Jeena Harsling.

J With high-rise development in urban centres at an all-time high, a new book, *Vertical Dreams or Nightmares* by Vera Monto, has renewed debate amongst architects, designers, and politicians about skyscraper and apartment block living. Monto explores the benefits and disadvantages for residents, social, financial and emotional. Risks from accidents, social isolation and depression are all areas explored in detail in the book.

7a

2 ★ Match the columns to form collocations and phrases.

1	housing	a	individuals
2	monetary	b	room
3	social	c	crisis
4	like-minded	d	benefits
5	latest	e	centres
6	retail	f	housing
7	affordable	g	space
8	living	h	addition
9	spare	i	isolation
10	urban	j	expenses

3 ★ Fill in: *under, of, out, for, on.*

1 Protesters insist .... an end to further development in the river valley.

2 The politician has come .... criticism for his negative comments on the low income housing project.

3 Community housing in the area is rented .... to young families.

4 The luxury apartments aim to set a new benchmark .... urban living.

5 The tower consists .... two storeys of retail space.

4 ★★ Replace the word(s) in bold in the sentences with the highlighted words from the text in the correct form.

1 Residents **demand** changes to government legislation.

2 The mayor hopes to **deal with** the city's housing demand by providing more public housing.

3 There are numerous **advantages** to living with a roommate.

4 There is a serious housing shortage **confronting** the city.

5 They **revealed** their new project at the press conference.

6 The rents in this area have **dramatically risen** this past year.

7 The community **fully backs** the new housing development.

8 The report **reopened** discussion over the building of a new subdivision.

9 George is a big **supporter** of sustainable living.

10 He lives in a rather unusual **residence** in the mountains.

7b Vocabulary

1 ★ Choose the correct item.

1 Tropical rainforests mainly consist **in/of** trees and vegetation.
2 Charity organisers are trying to weed **out/away** ineffective aid schemes.
3 Environmentalists are studying how the world is coping **about/with** the effects of climate change.
4 It is hoped that governments will actively invest **on/in** renewable energy sources.
5 New housing developments are springing **on/up** due to the growing urban sprawl.
6 Most non-profit organisations have to rely **in/on** public donations for funding.
7 Many environmental problems stem **off/from** human activities.
8 It is predicted that many endangered species will be wiped **out/off** in the future.

2 ★★ Fill in: *arid*, *rampant*, *relentless*, *receding*, *compressed*.

1 Energy efficient vehicles will run on .... air instead of fuel in the future.
2 The rich soil in the tropical rainforest is infested with weeds and .... vegetation.
3 The .... heat of the desert can wreak havoc on existing plant life.
4 In the .... wasteland the landscape is brown and dusty.
5 Rising sea levels and .... shorelines are linked to global warming.

3 ★★ Complete the idioms with: *roots*, *woods*, *landscape*, *field*, *tree*.

1 She was barking up the wrong .... when she accused my dog of ravaging her flowers.
2 The scientist had to put down .... in Antarctica in order to study melting ice caps.
3 The initiative has helped to reduce pollution levels but we're not out of the .... yet.
4 The new power plant is an ugly blot on the ....
5 The media had a .... day when they discovered the politician was getting kickbacks from the oil company.

4 ★★ Complete the sentences with a word from the box.

• degeneration • dehydration • declination

1 The overuse of pesticides has caused the rapid .... of nutrient levels in the soil.
2 Uncontrolled tourism in the area has led to the .... of vital ecosystems.
3 Plants that are resilient to .... flourish in arid conditions.

• diversification • reparation • reclamation

4 The government has agreed to pay .... to growers who lost their harvest in the hailstorm.
5 The woodlands will be used for a land .... project to build new housing settlements.
6 The farmer planned the .... of his crops to improve the sustainability of his agricultural production.

5 ★★ Fill in: *industrial*, *irreversible*, *sustainable*, *severe*, *ecological*, *atmospheric*, *insufficient*, *detrimental*.

Oceans at risk

Ocean acidification is one of the top environmental issues today. It is a(n) **1)** .... disaster as oceans are becoming more acidic due to the increase of carbon dioxide in the air which also affects ocean waters. Undeniably, this **2)** .... pollution is a direct result of an excessive production of fumes from **3)** .... activity and transportation. **4)** .... oxygen in our oceans threatens some large marine animals and poses **5)** .... problems. The high levels of acidity in oceans is also starting to have **6)** .... effects on shellfish and coral reefs and the damage may become **7)** .... unless action is taken immediately. Now is the time to switch to renewable energy sources and start buying **8)** .... products in order to reverse the cycle and save our oceans.

Topic related vocabulary

The Natural World

Prepositions

6 ★ **Choose the correct item.**

1 Many species of animals have colourful markings to ward **off/against** predators.
2 A number of people think it should be illegal to experiment **with/on** animals.
3 Nature reserves were set up to protect vulnerable animals **by/from** poaching.
4 We are headed **for/out** a planet-wide ecological disaster unless we tackle climate change now.
5 The conservation group has been criticised **for/by** some of the methods they employ.

Fixed phrases and Idioms

7 ★★ **Rewrite the sentences replacing the word(s) in bold with a fixed phrase/idiom containing *turn* or *wear* and the word in brackets.**

1 If we are not careful, we will lose much of the planet's flora and fauna by the **end of 2099**. **(CENTURY)**

....

2 The charity is not looking to **earn money**, they just want to raise enough funds to finance the work they do. **(PROFIT)**

....

3 People's excuses for not committing to recycling their waste are **getting tiresome**. **(THIN)**

....

4 The company's recent decision to donate their year-end profits to an animal sanctuary was a surprising **development**. **(EVENTS)**

....

5 The plight of the red squirrel **deteriorated dramatically** after the North American grey squirrel was introduced in the 19th century. **(WORSE)**

....

Words often confused

8 ★★ **Fill in the correct word.**

1 **equilibrium/stability**
 a An interruption in the food chain can affect the .... of an ecosystem.
 b The .... between man and animals on the island is dependent on little interference from the mainland.

2 **organic/natural**
 a Composting is the process of breaking down .... material using earthworms.
 b A volcanic stream is the source of this .... mineral water.

3 **corrosion/erosion**
 a The .... of a vast number of the shipwrecks in our oceans poses a severe threat to sea life.
 b The recent landslide was a direct result of soil .... caused by tree-felling.

9 ★★ **Fill in the gaps with a noun formed from the verbs in the list.**

• jeopardise • endure • survive • disrupt
• colonise • evolve

When Nature Strikes Back

The encroachment of mankind can have a negative impact on fragile ecosystems and place them in **1)** .... , but nature has a way of safeguarding its **2)** .... Through **3)** .... and the ability to adapt, the natural world has thrived in the most unlikely of situations.
The **4)** .... of sponges, tunicates and anemones adorning the surfaces of shipwrecks that lie striken on the seabed is just one example which proves the **5)** .... of nature. It shows that no matter the level of **6)** .... man causes, Mother Nature will always strike back.

Word formation

10 ★★ **Complete the sentences with words derived from the words in bold.**

1 The .... of some indigenous species have made them difficult to study. **(ELUDE)**
2 The charity .... estimated that they would reach a total of £100,000 at the auction when, in reality, they tripled that figure. **(CONSERVE)**
3 The damage done to the car by the animals on the safari was .... exaggerated when really it only sustained a few scratches. **(WILD)**
4 The Arctic Fox has adapted to the harsh environment of the tundra which it .... **(HABIT)**
5 CO_2 emissions have long been established as a(n) .... factor in global warming. **(CAUSE)**
6 The new security measures that have been put in place should prevent a(n) .... of the illegal dumping on the site. **(OCCUR)**
7 This species of rose has .... beautiful lilac flowers. **(STRIKE)**
8 The problems faced by the environment may seem .... but there is always something we can do. **(MOUNT)**

7c Grammar in use

Reported Speech

1 ★★ **Read the news report and complete it using a verb from the list in the correct form. Some verbs can be changed into a noun.**

• abandon • announce • start • receive • react • reiterate • do • lack

Theatre lovers were ecstatic at the news last night that the historic Kingview Theatre will be saved from demolition. When we spoke to Save the King! campaign manager Mark Thompson, he **1)** .... by praising the diligent efforts of his team. With a wry smile, he **2)** .... that nobody expected them to block the property developer's plans to tear down the theatre and how lots of people advised them **3)** .... their campaign. He added that despite the constant reminders by others that the campaign **4)** .... resources, the group had continued their efforts to convince the city council of the historical significance of the theatre. Thompson also made a(n) **5)** .... that for some time now the group **6)** .... letters of support from a famous actor praising their efforts. When asked for his **7)** .... to the news that developers may appeal the council decision, Thompson promised that his group **8)** .... whatever it takes to protect this beloved testimony to our city's history.

2 ★★ **Find and correct the mistakes.**

1 The letter from the landlord says he would do the inspection of our apartment the following week!
....

2 He wanted to know what was the decision of the town planners the previous day.
....

3 He asked me should he bring the contacts to the meeting with the developers.
....

4 The caretaker says he wanted the communal areas to be kept clear at all times.
....

5 The police officer asked to me to leave the area immediately due to an emergency.
....

6 She begged the landlord to not raise her rent.
....

Reporting nouns instead of verbs

3 ★★ **Complete the sentences using a noun phrase instead of the verb in bold.**

1 She highly **recommended** buying a home in this area of the city.
She .... that they buy a home in this area of the city.

2 She **threatened** to report Luke for destroying public property.
She ....
against Luke for destroying public property.

3 He **explained** the cause of the changing face of the high street to the visitors.
He .... for the changing face of the high street to the visitors.

4 I totally **deny** that I built this extension without the proper planning permission!
He ....
building the extension without the proper planning permission.

Special introductory verbs

4 ★★ **Fill in the gaps with the verbs in the list in the correct form.**

• boast • insist • admit • inform

1 The parking attendant .... us that the lot was full.

2 She .... on presenting her proposal for a fountain park to the building committee.

3 The energy secretary .... about how advanced his city was in the field of sustainability.

4 The building manager .... to not following some of the safety regulations required by law.

Subjunctive

5 ★★ **Complete the sentences with the verbs in brackets in the correct subjunctive form.**

1 The head of the retailers' association proposed that a meeting .... **(hold)** later in the month to discuss changes to the high street.

2 It is imperative that restrictions on certain vehicles .... **(enforce)** during peak traffic times.

3 It is necessary that all volunteers .... **(arrive)** a half hour early for a brief orientation about the programme.

4 The landlord insisted that two months' rent .... **(pay)** in advance.

Grammar Revision

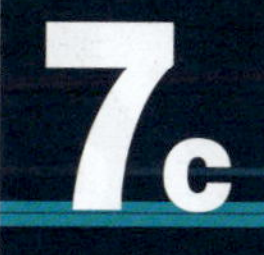

7c (Modules 1-7)

1 ★ **Choose the correct item.**

1 I'd rather you **not attend/haven't attended/didn't attend/hadn't attended** the meeting; it was a waste of time.
2 The environmental protest was **slightly/barely/fairly/partially** peaceful without any incidents.
3 If we leave for dinner at 7:30, rush hour traffic **finishes/will be finished/will have finished/will finish** by then.
4 The city **couldn't/shouldn't/mustn't/can't** have allowed the factory to open near parkland; it's had a terrible impact on the environment.
5 The members of the committee regard **itself/themselves/each other/ourselves** as the authority on all historic buildings in the city.
6 I still can't believe that by this time next month our ecological group **will have been operating/is to be operating/will be operating/is going to be operating** for five years!

2 ★★ **Complete the text with the correct form of the verbs in brackets.**

London Belongs to the Nightwalkers

Tim Tolner shares an experience that changed his view of the city forever…

London is a great city. I **1)** .... **(live)** here for the past 6 years and I absolutely love it. When I first moved to the city, however, that wasn't the case. At the time, I **2)** .... **(work)** every night at a busy restaurant. One day at the end of my shift I had a terrible headache as I 3) .... **(take)** orders and dealing with difficult customers all night. Unfortunately, I ended up finishing late and by the time I clocked out, the underground **4)** .... **(stop)** running! My only option was to take the night bus which only made me **5)** .... **(feel)** worse. This trend continued, so one night I decided **6)** .... **(walk)** to my flat to get some fresh air despite it being an hour away. That's when I **7)** .... **(discover)** the quieter side of London. The city **8)** .... **(transform)** by the night, with sleeping skyscrapers, peaceful parks and shining street lamps. Had I known how truly wonderful the city was after dark, I **9)** .... **(start)** my night walks earlier. I now have a day job, but I still appreciate **10)** .... **(go)** on my nightly strolls. Over the past few years, they **11)** .... **(become)** the perfect remedy for the stress of London life. I love exploring, and I hope that in the very near future I **12)** .... **(see)** all of this incredible city by night!

Key word transformations

3 ★★ **For questions 1-5, complete the second sentence so that it has a similar meaning to the first sentence, using the word given. You must use between three and eight words, including the word given.**

1 Uncle Peter gets someone to take his rubbish to the recycling centre. **TAKEN**
Uncle Peter ....
.... to the recycling centre.

2 "I do not want my building inspected by the housing authority" the man said. **OBJECTED**
The man ....
.... inspected by the housing authority.

3 Due to a protest in the city centre, they rescheduled the meeting for next week. **PUT**
Due to a protest in the city centre, the meeting
.... next week.

4 Fiona started her studies into forestry three years ago. **HAS**
Fiona ....
.... three years.

5 Initially the city warned the factory to stop dumping waste into the river. **WARNING**
The factory ....
.... dumping waste into the river.

Grammar in Focus

★★ **Complete the gaps with the correct word. Then put the words in brackets into the correct form or choose the correct word.**

- If we all just read the Sunday newspaper online **1)** .... of a printed copy, we **2)** .... **(save)** half a million trees.
- Landfills **3)** .... **(compose)** of 35% packaging material that **4)** .... **(be)** otherwise recycled.
- If everyone in the USA recycled just one aluminium can, **5)** .... would save energy equivalent **6)** .... 80 000 barrels of oil.
- A plastic grocery bag takes 500-1000 years to degrade. Only **7) between/among** 1 and 3% of all plastic waste is recycled. Globally, we throw away 5 trillion plastic bags **8)** .... year. 10 % of plastic waste ends **9)** .... in the oceans. **10) If/Unless** we continue like this, the oceans **11)** .... **(contain)** more plastic than fish by weight.

7d Listening skills

Sentence completion

Remember!

In some listening tasks you will have to listen for specific vocabulary to fill a gap in a sentence. It is important to pay attention to what appears before and after the gap. You may also hear a number of options in the audio that might fit, but only one will complete the sentence grammatically and lexically. You must write the word(s) as they appear in the audio.

1 ★★ **You will hear a student, Sophie Reece, giving a short talk about a conservation project. For questions 1-9, complete the sentences with a word or short phrase.**

The state of the planet is the result of people's need to make 1) ....
Sophie doesn't want to delve into the subject of 2) ....
The volunteers offer the group whatever 3) .... they can spare.
The generosity of the public allows the group to take care of their 4) ....
Recently the group have been working on a(n) 5) .... involving local businesses.
The group discovered that 6) .... in the way companies conduct themselves can cut down on their environmental impact.
After the group left, the publishing company were almost a(n) 7) ....
Volunteering to help the environment can help alleviate one's 8) ....
Sophie believes everyone's 9) .... is to do something positive.

Understanding questions

Preparing for the task

STUDY SKILLS

In listening tasks it is important to understand the function of question words in order to recognise what the question relates to. While you listen, remember that native English speakers use contractions such as 'What'll ya do' instead of 'What will you do' in everyday speech.

2 a) ★ **Read the answer choices 1-10 below and match them to the function they refer to (a-j).**

1 ☐	At 2.
2 ☐	It's scheduled for 2 hours.
3 ☐	Cleaning up the park.
4 ☐	In the conference room at City Hall.
5 ☐	About 50.
6 ☐	They put posters up around town.
7 ☐	Discuss what each of us can contribute.
8 ☐	The mayor.
9 ☐	This is only the second time.
10 ☐	About £500 for the afternoon.

a number
b time
c duration
d frequency
e cost
f place
g people/person
h activity
i manner
j reason

b) ★ **Listen to questions A-J and match them to the answer choices 1-10 in Ex. 2a.**

A	B	C	D	E	F	G	H	I	J

3 ★★ **You will hear a question. From the three answer choices given, choose the one that best answers the question.**

1 **A** They'll have enough time.
B They'll decide next week.
C They'll consider them carefully.

2 **A** He said he'd call before he arrived.
B The rally starts at 10 o'clock.
C He wants to know how we're getting there.

3 **A** No, I don't think I need help tidying.
B No, I'm afraid I'm busy.
C No, I'm free all day.

4 **A** Adding a picture might help.
B It was just printed.
C We could print a prototype.

5 **A** Yes, they're moving to a bigger office.
B Yes, they wanted to be rent free.
C Yes, they just received a sizeable donation.

6 **A** I thought I might donate them to good will.
B They're OK, they don't need mending.
C I wear all of them a lot.

7 **A** Yes, he rarely talks about them.
B Yes, he's already managed a lot.
C Yes, he mentioned them repeatedly.

8 **A** No, he wasn't thirsty.
B No, he didn't like it.
C No, he wasn't in his office.

9 **A** Sure, the group is meeting this Friday.
B Sure, I'm doing gardening this weekend.
C Sure, and I know the perfect location.

10 **A** You have to sort your recycling into different bins.
B The different coloured bins confuse me.
C The blue bin is picked up Thursday morning.

Speaking skills

Convincing; Expressing interest/ uncertainty

1 a) ★ Read the dialogue. Then use phrases (a-f) to complete it.

a	I'm not convinced	**d**	the best thing about
b	Is that so	**e**	I don't think that's
c	Just think about	**f**	interests me,

Sophie: The new solar park outside of my town is totally amazing!

Eric: **1)** ....? Personally, I think all those panels on the ground are an eyesore!

Sophie: Well, using renewable resources is important for the environment. **2)** .... how these panels convert sunlight directly to electricity for the whole area.

Eric: **3)** .... I mean, it's good that they provide electricity when it's sunny. But do they work in cloudy weather?

Sophie: Of course. You see **4)** .... them is that they can generate power even when light is blocked by clouds.

Eric: Well, protecting the environment **5)** .... but installing a solar park in my area... **6)** .... possible at the moment. I'm not sure people in the community would go for it.

Sophie: I see.

Eric: Perhaps it's something to consider when we all get our next electricity bill!

b) ★ Which phrases in Ex. 1a convince, express interest/uncertainty? Complete the table.

Convincing	1 ....
Interest	2 ....
Uncertainty	3 ....

2 ★ Choose the correct item.

1 A: Is it worth investing in energy saving devices?
B: **a** Yes, the best thing is that they cut your energy bills.
b Yes, I'm sure that's possible.

2 A: I think you should install solar panels on your roof.
B: **a** If I were you, I would.
b It's something I'll consider.

3 A: I'm interested in that green gadget.
B: **a** Really? **b** What do you think?

Exchanging views

3 a) ★★ Read the questions and the prompts (1-8) about the natural world. Match the prompts to the ideas (A-H).

- How important are each of the following for protecting the natural world?
- What are the most effective measures people can take to protect the natural world?

1	pesticide reduction	**6**	create urban green spaces
2	strict environmental laws	**7**	solid waste reduction
3	energy conservation	**8**	buy sustainable products
4	environmental activism		
5	environmental education		

A ☐ • support/local/farmer's market • purchase/recycled products • invest/energy-efficient appliances • reduce/carbon emissions **(In my view/By doing this)**

B ☐ • stop/use/chemicals • create/safe/conditions/farm/workers • ensure/healthier/food/crops • beneficial/use/insects/control pest/population/instead **(I nevertheless think that/In particular)**

C ☐ • prevent/pollution • decrease/energy/consumption associated/manufacture/new/materials • conserve/space/existing/landfills **(The main reason is/Consequently)**

D ☐ • best/way/protect/environment • teach/people/issues/impact/planet • come up/solutions improve/natural world **(Looking at it from another point of view/so that)**

E ☐ • bring/issues/light • protests/force/factories/stop/polluting • fear/activist backlash • prevent/environmental/damage **(Another important reason is/Therefore)**

F ☐ • improve/city/areas • plant/more/trees/shrubs • remove/pollutants/air • provide/shade/lower/temperature • help/reduce/flooding **(On the other hand/In fact)**

G ☐ • protect/health/humans/environment • prohibits/emissions/pollutants/dumping/waste/without permits • increase/environmentally-friendly technology **(I feel that/As a result)**

H ☐ • reduce/amount/electricity • adopt/energy-saving habits • recycle • use/renewable energy • benefit/environment/conserve/natural resources **(To my mind/As a matter of fact)**

b) ★★ Expand the ideas in Ex. 3a to form sentences using the useful language phrases in bold.

Writing Essays (Reasons and solutions)

General introduction

Reasons and solutions essays ask for two tasks to be carried out: discuss the causes of a particular problem and then propose solutions. The development of ideas throughout the whole essay is important and the causes should be closely related to the solutions. Pay attention to the linking of ideas and general coherence of the essay as a whole.

General outline for reasons and solutions essays

Para 1 ► a clear statement of the topic
Para 2 ► reason 1 & example/explanation
Para 3 ► reason 2 & example/explanation
Para 4 ► Solutions
Para 5 ► restatement of the topic & your opinion

1 a) ★ **Read the rubric and underline the key words.**

One of the greatest problems faced by humanity today is dealing with the effects of an unstable and changing climate. In your opinion, what are the main reasons behind climate change? What can be done to slow down or reverse this process? Discuss your ideas, with examples. Write your **essay** (approximately 350 words).

b) ★ **Read the model. Fill in with the correct phrases.**

• One reason • As far as • However • This is • Another solution
• Equally • Even though • It is high time • In conclusion

Climate change is one of the most pressing problems the world is currently facing. Its impacts are being felt across the globe as temperatures rise and extreme weather becomes more common. There are two serious reasons for the deteriorating climate: the burning of fossil fuels and deforestation. **1)** .... measures were implemented to ameliorate the effects of climate change.

2) .... for climate change is the burning of fossil fuels for transportation and industry, which results in gases being released into the air that contribute to global warming. **3)** .... vehicles today produce fewer pollutants and there are more environmental regulations on industrial emissions, the number of vehicles on the roads and factories in operation is constantly increasing. **4)** .... a daunting challenge as citizens of developed nations literally eat, wear and use the products made from the burning of fossil fuels.

5) .... devastating for the climate is the issue of deforestation. Forests are being cleared at an unprecedented rate to make way for agricultural expansion or new settlements. This negatively impacts the climate because plants and trees not only remove CO_2 from air to create the oxygen we breathe, but also store CO_2 which is released back into the atmosphere when the forests are destroyed. They also regulate the water cycle, and their destruction can exacerbate warming and drought.

Once the roots of climate change are understood, it is possible to propose a number of solutions. **6)** .... fossil fuels are concerned, we need to increase the use of public transport, promote the use of electric vehicles and introduce stricter laws limiting factory emissions. **7)** .... is to start investing in renewable energies such as wind and solar power. As for deforestation, better farming methods along with paper recycling and managing development could help to solve the problem.

8) .... , climate change is a complicated problem. **9)** .... , I believe that the effects can be counterbalanced if we redesign our transport system, impose stricter industry regulations, invest in renewable energy technologies and improve agricultural practices and forest management. After all, if we do not take steps to reduce climate change now, who will?

Your turn

2 a) ★ **Read the rubric and underline the key words. Then answer the questions.**

Contemporary society is generating an increasing amount of household waste. Existing landfills will soon reach capacity if waste production continues at the present rate. In your opinion, what are the two most serious reasons for this phenomenon? How can it be dealt with? Discuss your ideas with examples. Write your **essay** (approximately 350 words).

1 What type of essay is it?
2 What question does this rubric ask you to answer?
3 Which causes might contribute to the issue?

b) ★ **Read the points (a-f). Are they causes or solutions?**

a widespread use of plastics
b educate people, make facilities available
c avoid packaging and synthetic materials
d modern consumer lifestyle
e buy less and use it longer
f inadequate recycling

c) ★★ **Match the ideas (1-6) below to the causes or solutions (a-f) in Ex. 3b. Then expand the prompts to write sentences.**

1 [ ] society/bombarded/adverts/result/excessive/shopping
2 [ ] purchase/only/necessities/repair/reuse/ products/rather/replace
3 [ ] not/enough/recycling/bins/little/public/participation
4 [ ] used/packaging/products/manufacturing/never/decompose
5 [ ] raise/awareness/recycling/practices/ increase/citizen/participation/add/more/bins
6 [ ] buy/unpackaged/produce/carry/cloth bags/choose/natural materials/responsibly/produced

3 ★★ **Use the ideas in Ex. 2b & c and your own ideas to write the essay.**

Reading

1 ★★ **There are ten headlines below and seven short news stories. Match the headlines to the news stories that fit best. There are three headlines you do not need.**

1 TOLLS LAUDED FOR TRANSFORMATIVE POWERS
2 NEW TECHNOLOGY KEEPS MAJOR ROADS MOVING
3 PUBLIC TRANSPORT GIVEN A HELPING HAND
4 CONGESTION CHARGING SCHEME FAILS TO HELP ENVIRONMENT
5 AMAZING THINGS DO COME IN SMALL PACKAGES
6 NEW SYSTEM OFFERS MOTORISTS DATA IN REAL-TIME VIA SMARTPHONES
7 CUTTING-EDGE INITIATIVES SPELL END OF TRADITIONAL CAR PARKS
8 THE TRANSPORT OPTION THAT'S CLEAN, QUICK AND CONVENIENT
9 ROBOT TRAFFIC CONDUCTOR DIRECTS TRAFFIC AT BUSY JUNCTION
10 BIG BROTHER REALLY IS WATCHING YOU

Navigating the Urban Jungle

A ☐ A groundbreaking new invention is being used in Canadian cities to help ease the burden of heavy traffic and congestion. Canada's new transit signal priority system (TSP) uses on-board computers, Wi-Fi, and automatic smart traffic lights to keep a clear travel path for buses through the city. Unlike traditional TSPs that control only traffic lights, the new system knows in real time the exact location of a bus and cross checks this with the timetable, changing traffic lights only if a service is late.

B ☐ Reports released today confirm that Stockholm's electronic road charging scheme has been a massive success. Launched to divert traffic away from the city centre and reduce congestion, the scheme has had a startling impact. An amazing one million vehicles a day have been removed from city streets and daily revenues have reached hundreds of thousands of Euros. Officials are ecstatic and have hailed it as a triumph for transport, the environment, and the city.

C ☐ No one likes being stuck in a traffic jam on a motorway. Luckily, an ingenious system in England hopes to make jams on motorways a thing of the past. The active traffic management (ATM) system uses variable speed limits to control the flow of vehicles to combat congestion at peak times or as a response to unexpected problems like traffic accidents or crashes. It can also allow the opening of new lanes and send notifications via electronic signs to motorists in advance.

D ☐ Ever found it difficult to find a parking space? Well, that could be a thing of the past thanks to a revolutionary invention from Japan. Designed by Kunio Okawara, the amazing robotic car folds in order to fit into the smallest of parking spaces. When interviewed by the press Okawara explained that he took his inspiration from transformers the shape changing robots of cartoons and film. Don't expect to see many of these on the road soon however; they have huge price tags!

E ☐ Barcelona, like many world cities, has streets jammed with parked cars. Finding a parking space can often be extremely difficult and time consuming. Authorities, however, are keen to tackle this problem with the latest smart technology. Parking sensors and video analytics provide up-to-date information on parking availability and transmit this via a Wi-Fi network directly to users through their mobile devices.

F ☐ Urban centres are always looking for new ways to combat the problem of parking. One solution is not to build more large sprawling parking lots, but to offer parking spaces above or underground. With car stacking, rows of cars can be stored and 'stacked' one on top of the other in multiple columns or levels vertically. These mechanical systems can provide huge vaults and take parked cars off the street once and for all!

G ☐ Bike sharing schemes are making waves all over the world. Popular in major cities such as Paris and London, they allow people to rent bicycles for short periods. With collection and drop off points all over cities, it's easy to find a bike station for that next quick trip around town. The benefits are numerous, they help the environment, get cars off the road, and also improve health. So hop on, for a ride to remember!

Open Cloze

1 ★★ **For questions 1-8, read the text below and think of a word which best fits each gap. There is an example at the beginning (0).**

Biophilic Cities:
More than just greenery

There is a lot of talk **0)** *these* days about sustainable cities with plenty of green spaces. Some urban planners are taking this idea one step **1)** .... by putting nature at the very core **2)** .... their designs and planning. Known as 'biophilic cities', these urban areas, **3)** .... the name suggests, recognise our love for nature and our intrinsic human need to connect with it. In biophilic cities, nature is integrated **4)** .... every part of the city. It can be found **5)** .... around residents and not just by walking to a green space ten minutes **6)** .... Biophilic urban planners don't just want people to be near parks, they want people to feel like they are actually living in them! Their designs include, **7)** .... from vertical gardens, community farms and green belt trails to butterfly parks, fish ponds and bird sanctuaries. As a **8)** .... of cohabiting with nature, urbanites thrive, feeling both physically and mentally healthier, something every city needs!

Word Formation

2 ★★ **For questions 1-8, read the text below. Use the word given in capitals at the end of some of the lines to form a word that fits in the space in the same line. There is an example at the beginning (0).**

Welcome to Kamikatsu:
the waste-free town!

Recycling is on the minds of most conscientious **0)** *citizens* today with **CITY**
municipalities implementing aggressive **1)** .... to **INITIATE**
drastically reduce waste. But is it possible to achieve zero-waste? It may seem **2)** .... but one town in **IMAGINE**
Japan is very close to this target with a(n) **3)** .... **PRECEDE**
80% of total waste currently recycled. After years of incinerating their waste, the town of Kamikatsu realised the dire **4)** .... of greenhouse gas emissions **SEQUENCE**
on the environment and embarked on a rigorous recycling programme. Residents have to sort through their waste separating it into 34 different categories. Initially, residents had difficulty adjusting with the **5)** .... of it being rather time-consuming. **SIDE**
With encouragement from the town's Zero Waste Academy, residents eventually **6)** .... **BRACE**
the programme and now take pride in their achievements. **7)** .... , the Zero Waste **ADD**
Academy has set up composting and a swap shop for the reuse of **8)** .... items. This is one **WANT**
community working together for a better tomorrow!

Key word transformations

3 ★★ **Write a new sentence which is as close to the meaning of the given sentence as possible, using the word or phrase given. You may not change the word or phrase in any way.**

1 After carrying all the recycling boxes to the centre, I could barely breathe. **BREATH**

....

2 Everyone was opposed to the building of a factory along the river. **OUTRIGHT**

....

3 Nancy offered to let us stay the night at her beach house when we finish the beach clean-up. **UP**

....

4 The property developer claimed to have no involvement in the housing scandal. **DISTANCED**

....

5 Everyone needs to support this new recycling programme. **BEHIND**

....

6 When it comes to the issue of air pollution, the factory tends to blame everyone else. **BUCK**

....

7 Her car is in very bad condition. **BETTER DAYS**

....

8 The organisation is very reliable in handling all citizen complaints. **COUNT**

....

9 The volunteer programme wasn't as good as I expected. **LIVE UP**

....

10 Tim is very proud of his conservation work. **PRIDE**

....

Grammar

4 ★ **Choose the correct item.**

1 The recycling workshop starts at 8 am but we should be there by 7:30 .... for registration.
A no later
C the later
B at the latest
D no latest

2 We have not seen any improvement in .... of the two areas we targeted despite our best efforts.
A neither B either C both D none

3 By the time the redevelopment is completed, many local businesses ....
A have relocated.
C will have relocated.
B will relocate
D may relocate.

4 The nature reserve contains grasslands and woodland .... a large fresh water lake.
A furthermore
C besides
B moreover
D in addition to

5 The newly developed computer algorithms were recommended .... traffic congestion.
A to help cities reduce
B for help to reduce cities
C in helping reduce cities
D to helping reducing cities

6 The appliances are very energy efficient .... that were produced after 2012.
A that is particularly for them
B them particularly
C they are particularly
D particularly those

7 The entire community regeneration project was funded .... an online crowdfunding platform.
A throughout B via C during D in

8 "When will the reforestation be completed?"
"The commissioner said .... about 5 years."
A they take
C it takes
B to be taking
D it would take

9 The inspectors will be checking the factory's emissions .... waste disposal practices.
A together B and C along with D as well

10 Consumers are trying to reduce their consumption of packaging .... the severity of damage to ocean life caused by plastic waste.
A on account B given C due D in light

11 The CEO believes the technology .... at the moment will clean up water pollutants by 70 percent.
A his company develops
B being developed by his company
C is developed by his company
D by his company is being developed

12 The wildlife fund remains dedicated to saving endangered animals despite .... official funding.
A it was losing
C its loss of
B losing it's
D its losses

Vocabulary

5 ★ **Choose the correct item.**

1 Urban planners must .... to public safety codes and regulations.
A follow
C adhere
B observe
D obey

2 Recent climate data shows the .... of the problem of global warming.
A magnitude
C weight
B bulk
D matter

3 Vehicle emissions have risen .... over the past decade forcing engineers to seek alternative forms of transport and energy.
A accordingly
C essentially
B adversely
D significantly

4 The city council is under .... pressure to designate the land as a nature reserve.
A rigorous
C drastic
B intense
D harsh

5 The energy proposal has created a great deal of .... regarding its actual effectiveness.
A controversy
C altercation
B embroilment
D anticipation

6 The mayor .... the idea of turning the city centre into a no car zone.
A generated
C dismissed
B discharged
D terminated

7 Traffic congestion is .... in most large cities.
A paramount
C established
B prevalent
D conventional

8 The animal rights activists .... the practices of the local hunting society.
A condemned
C condoned
B convicted
D confounded

9 An increase in industrial pollution could have serious .... for the local ecosystem.
A backlash
C repercussions
B aftermath
D outcomes

10 There's growing .... over the rise of pollution-related diseases in large cities.
A concern
C reference
B awareness
D regard

11 The extinction of the Javan Rhinoceros is expected .... unless drastic measures are taken to save the species.
A impulsively
C imminently
B urgently
D impertinently

12 The .... of volunteering a year abroad seems like an incredible experience.
A outlook
C impression
B purpose
D prospect

8a Reading

Finding synonyms

Preparing for the task

Remember!

Remember that questions focusing on the main idea of a text ask you to identify the idea the author is presenting throughout the text and not just true statements that appear in the text.

1 ★ **Read the passage below. Answer the questions (A-C).**

Within the growing trend of reality TV programming, talent shows have taken viewer ratings by storm. With their combination of stirring reality drama and the excitement of quiz show competitiveness, there seems to be no end to viewers' fascination with finding a star. Although the format has been around for some time, TV audiences are still eagerly tuning in each week to see who will be eliminated and who will come one step closer to getting the opportunity of a lifetime.

1 Tick (✓) the topic of the passage.
- **A** TV Drama ☐
- **B** Quiz Shows ☐
- **C** Reality TV ☐

2 Tick (✓) the main idea of the passage.
- **A** Talent shows have the highest ratings for reality programming. ☐
- **B** Many TV viewers are captivated with the process of becoming a star. ☐

3 Tick (✓) the appropriate title for this passage.
- **A** REALITY TV LEADS THE WAY ☐
- **B** THE NEXT BIG THING ☐

2 ★★ **Read the article. For questions 1-5 choose the answer (A, B, C or D) which you think fits best according to the text.**

1 What is the main purpose of this passage?
- **A** to discuss the lack of ticket sales at cinemas
- **B** to examine the impact of streaming on new films
- **C** to explain the reasons film executives target teens
- **D** to show how entertainment is changing

2 According to the passage, what is true of televised drama nowadays?
- **A** It's increasingly attractive to high profile artists.
- **B** Attitudes towards television remain dismissive.
- **C** Actors are reluctant to commit to a project long-term.
- **D** Ratings are placed above innovative ideas.

3 What does the author think about film adaptations?
- **A** They devalue their original source material.
- **B** They offer incredible new creative opportunities.
- **C** They are unable to match the production standards of film.
- **D** They win more awards than their cinematic equivalents.

4 In the third sentence of paragraph 5, what is meant by behemoth?
- **A** an organisation that shows little regard for the industry
- **B** an organisation with a large size but limited influence
- **C** an organisation formed from lots of smaller companies
- **D** an organisation with massive power in the industry

5 According to the passage, what is remarkable about the current trend?
- **A** It's driven by a single key factor and isn't affected by anything else.
- **B** It's developed new technology in totally unexpected ways.
- **C** It presents a dual evolution that affects both the industry and consumers.
- **D** It's steered by audience feedback and online reviews.

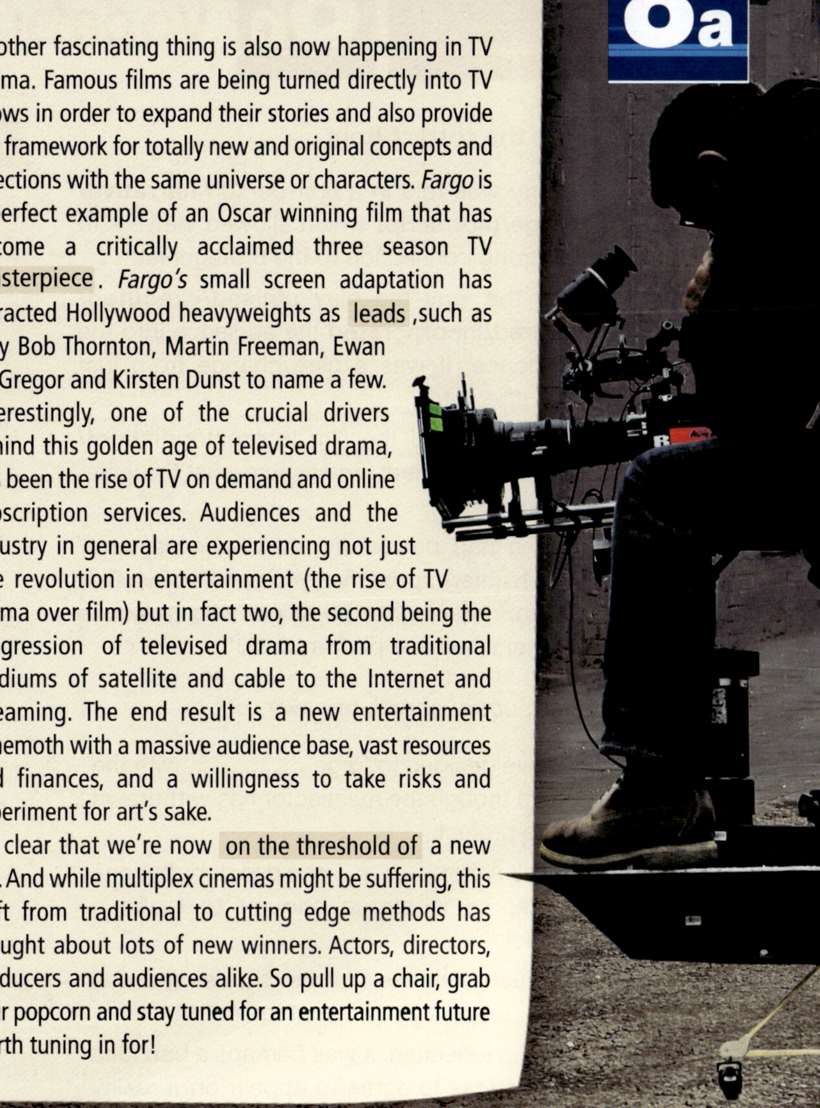

The trailer opens to a lavish scene of England in the 1920s, detailed sets, intricate period costumes and an all-star cast featuring Hollywood actors such as Cillian Murphy, Tom Hardy and Adrien Brody. This might sound like the latest cinema blockbuster, but it isn't, it's actually the fourth season of a popular BBC TV show *Peaky Blinders*!

Programmes such as *Peaky Blinders* are a great example of a rising trend nowadays that would have been unthinkable even ten years ago. More and more actors and directors are swapping the glamour and prestige of the silver screen for the small screen. But, why is this the case, especially when television was looked down upon as the poor cousin of film?

One of the main attractions to big-name film stars and directors is the creative freedom that television now offers. Television has massive scope for pursuing different genres, from period gangster projects such as Peaky Blinders and Martin Scorsese's *Boardwalk Empire*, to science fiction such as the Duffer Brothers' *Stranger Things*. Television has a range unlike cinema, which is increasingly narrowing its target demographic to young teenagers and adults and focusing mostly on action and superhero projects. Television also allows directors, writers and actors to really explore a character and story arc in much greater length and detail than a single ninety minute film. Even a short series of six episodes typically allows six hours for an actor to really breathe life into their part and give a multifaceted performance.

Another fascinating thing is also now happening in TV drama. Famous films are being turned directly into TV shows in order to expand their stories and also provide the framework for totally new and original concepts and directions with the same universe or characters. *Fargo* is a perfect example of an Oscar winning film that has become a critically acclaimed three season TV masterpiece. *Fargo's* small screen adaptation has attracted Hollywood heavyweights as leads ,such as Billy Bob Thornton, Martin Freeman, Ewan McGregor and Kirsten Dunst to name a few. Interestingly, one of the crucial drivers behind this golden age of televised drama, has been the rise of TV on demand and online subscription services. Audiences and the industry in general are experiencing not just one revolution in entertainment (the rise of TV drama over film) but in fact two, the second being the progression of televised drama from traditional mediums of satellite and cable to the Internet and streaming. The end result is a new entertainment behemoth with a massive audience base, vast resources and finances, and a willingness to take risks and experiment for art's sake.

It's clear that we're now on the threshold of a new era. And while multiplex cinemas might be suffering, this shift from traditional to cutting edge methods has brought about lots of new winners. Actors, directors, producers and audiences alike. So pull up a chair, grab your popcorn and stay tuned for an entertainment future worth tuning in for!

3 ★ **Match the highlighted words and phrases from the text to their correct meaning based on the context of their use.**

1 **lavish**
  - **a** very expensive and impressive
  - **b** very generous

2 **scope**
  - **a** a varied range of subjects or topics
  - **b** an opportunity for doing sth

3 **masterpiece**
  - **a** a programme or film made with great skill
  - **b** an impressive example of sth (masterpiece of)

4 **lead**
  - **a** a vital piece of information
  - **b** the main role in a television or film production

5 **on the threshold of sth**
  - **a** on the level that sth starts to occur
  - **b** at the start of an important new period

4 ★★ **Fill in:** ***unthinkable, demographic, prestige, intricate, acclaimed.***

The **1)** .... level of detail found in both costumes and props in television dramas nowadays is breathtaking and would have been **2)** .... in the recent past. Nowadays, however, thanks to record levels of new investment and a wide **3)** .... , TV dramas are overtaking film in numerous ways. More and more **4)** .... directors and actors are eagerly flocking to TV as it's offering a new level of **5)** .... and greater creative freedom than ever before!

Vocabulary

1 ★ Choose the correct item.

1 The story was told in a first-person **narrative/message/plot/script** which allowed viewers to feel a strong connection to the protagonist.

2 I loved the way the play **utilised/executed/structured/incorporated** the audience into the performance; it was a nice change from just being a spectator.

3 I'm afraid I found the film **internal/indistinct/incoherent/inhibited**; I'm not sure what the writer was trying to say.

4 The song had powerfully **enigmatic/earnest/impenetrable/expressive** lyrics and it obviously had great meaning to the singer who got quite emotional when she performed it.

2 ★★ Fill in: *upon, ahead, up, over, off.*

1 They have decided to forge .... with the film even though the main actor has withdrawn from the project.

2 I wouldn't write .... the director after one bad film; he is strong enough to make a comeback.

3 It was such a shame that the actress messed .... her lines on her stage debut.

4 .... reflection, it was perhaps a bad idea for the actress to agree to appear on a reality show.

5 Many artists face an internal struggle .... whether to compromise their integrity to make money.

3 ★★ Choose whether A or B best completes the sentence containing the idiomatic expression in bold.

1 The film memorabilia **went for a song** at the auction
   A and included the original theme music.
   B but still raised some money for charity.

2 With this play the audience must **read between the lines** to see
   A the subtle messages the director wanted to express.
   B what each of the characters are saying.

3 Alexander didn't want to **play second fiddle** anymore so he
   A bought a more expensive violin.
   B started auditioning for lead roles.

4 It's important to **take note of** what the director says because
   A he has a vision for the whole film.
   B the music is important for the feel of the film.

4 ★★ Complete the sentences with a word from the box.

• perspective • portrayal • performance

1 The actress gave a sublime .... that left the audience in tears.

2 The story was told from the unique .... of two of the supporting characters.

3 The actor's .... of the character was different to previous versions that have graced our screens.

• implement • augment • supplement

4 A lot of budding actors have to .... their income with menial jobs until they get their big break.

5 The cinematographer used a special lens to .... the colours in the scene to make them stand out.

6 The director decided not to .... the producer's changes to the script and shot the scene the way the writer intended.

• moving • transparent • mesmerising

7 All the actors gave .... performances that had the audience laughing and crying in droves.

8 The actor's motives were completely ....; it was obvious that he wanted the part.

9 The actor has a .... presence which leaves people spell-bound.

5 ★★ Fill in: *reviews, humour, audience, perspective, audition, vocalist.*

Sample the Stage

Some people have a distorted 1) .... when it comes to courses in the dramatic arts. It's not all fun and games like it is on TV. These courses are in-depth and hard work. For a taster you can join a summer school at one of the many drama institutions around the country. As well as developing your skills, they will teach you how to give a flawless 2) .... and how to perform in front of a demanding 3) .... to ensure that your performance will receive rave 4) .... Be you a budding actor, a graceful dancer, an accomplished 5) .... or even a comedian with a wry sense of 6) .... there is a course for you and it is a great way to get a taste of what to expect should you want to pursue a career in the performing arts.

Topic related vocabulary

8b

Media & Advertising

Phrasal verbs

6 ★ **Choose the correct item.**

1 When the reporter was questioned by her editor she blurted **over/up/out** the name of her informant.
2 The story quickly got **around/on/away** and it was soon old news.
3 The editor has come **on/in/up** for a lot of criticism over his handling of the leaked information.
4 When the conversation between his guests dried **out/up/off**, the host was forced to go to an ad break.

Words often confused

7 ★★ **Fill in the correct word.**

1 **discreet/discrete**
  a This article deals with a set of .... issues that would perhaps be better dealt with individually.
  b A lot of actors are .... about their personal life when interviewed and don't like to talk about private matters.

2 **feasible/credible**
  a The reporter was unable to back up his story with any .... evidence or witness accounts.
  b A .... solution to the problems the newspaper is experiencing with their drop in readership numbers is to increase their online presence.

3 **cited/quoted**
  a The actress was .... as saying she had never worked with a director who was so involved in every aspect of the production before.
  b The director .... previous work by his mentor as his inspiration for the new film.

4 **slander/libel**
  a The actress threatened to sue the magazine for .... after they published false information about her.
  b The statement the politician made during his speech was considered .... and he had to apologise for it.

Phrases & Idioms

8 ★★ **Fill in:** *proof, tune, views, statement.*

1 The director often uses improvisational techniques to get his actors in .... with their characters.
2 The actor was forced to issue a .... to put to bed the rumours of his illness.
3 The public were asked to call in to air their .... on the matter of the politician's apology.
4 Whether or not he can write, the .... is in the pudding: we'll just have to read his article.

9 ★★ **Fill in:** *defamation, conduct, muckraking, extent, impartiality, scoop, arbiter, tabloids.*

The Ethics of Media

Many journalists, working for the **1)** ...., dream of getting a major **2)** .... about somebody in the public eye. However, the **3)** .... to which they are willing to go has to have its limits. Media ethics are an important code of **4)** .... that ensures we read the truth and reporters are less likely to indulge in **5)** .... to obtain their stories. Reporters must adhere to these ethics but ultimately, the publication's editor must be the **6)** .... of taste and be answerable for any claims made against them for **7)** .... of character. This way we can rely on the **8)** .... of the news to inform us of the facts and not scurrilous rumours.

FAKE / FACT

Word formation

10 ★★ **Complete the sentences with words derived from the words in bold.**

1 Protecting the .... of sources is an important part of being a journalist. **(ANONYMOUS)**
2 The actor claimed that the story was a(n) .... of the facts. **(DISTORT)**
3 Many people attribute the .... of anti-social behaviour among youngsters to violent computer games and films. **(PREVAIL)**
4 The journalist uncovered proof that the government had .... the public about the source of the funding. **(LEAD)**
5 The headline on the magazine cover promised .... about the infighting on the set of the new sci-fi film. **(REVEAL)**
6 Some in the entertainment industry might say that the .... to being in the public eye is the lack of privacy. **(SIDE)**
7 There is no need for films to show .... violence or use bad language. **(EXCEED)**
8 The actress's joy was .... upon receiving the award. **(DENY)**

8c Grammar in use

Relative clauses

1 ★★ **Join the sentences using the correct relative pronoun or adverb.**

1 The film was fully booked. I didn't get to see it.

....

2 Denis Villeneuve is a director. He made *Blade Runner 2049* and *Arrival*.

....

3 The author wrote three books. They are set in Victorian England.

....

4 This is my studio. I paint my commission pieces here.

....

5 That's the reason. We don't use traditional rolls of film anymore.

....

Other clauses

2 ★★ **Use the conjunctions to complete the sentences.**

• as soon as • as if • whilst • given that
• in order that

1 The supporting actor walks around the set .... he were the big star!

2 Erica is a painter .... her husband works as an art dealer.

3 The film will be distributed .... the post production work is finalised.

4 Jason decided to study creative writing .... he might further develop his skills.

5 .... online streaming is so popular nowadays I doubt DVD sales will continue for much longer.

Participle clauses

3 ★★ **Use the words in brackets to rewrite the sentences making any necessary changes.**

1 Ian was given the wrong book and then returned it to the library. **(having)**

....

2 If you use a HD television, the film looks stunning! **(watched)**

....

3 Paula organised her CDs. She had nothing else to do till Steve got back from work. **(waiting)**

....

4 Because she had spoken to Jack, she didn't need to leave a note for him. **(having)**

....

Cleft sentences

4 ★★ **Use the words in bold to complete the sentences.**

1 The cameraman himself doesn't want to risk filming in this location. **WHO**
It .... doesn't want to risk filming in this location.

2 Harrison Ford is the film star promoting the new product. **IS**
It .... the film star promoting the new product.

3 Did they meet the famous singer while they were on holiday? **THEM**
Was .... while they were on holiday?

4 My brother only watches TV shows online all day long! **DOES**
All .... watch TV shows online all day long!

Inversion

5 ★★ **Rewrite the sentences using the words/phrases from the list below. Make any necessary changes to form inversion.**

• Only by • Rarely • Under no circumstances
• Never before

1 It was the first time a concert had brought me to tears.

....

2 The only way they can finance their project is through crowdfunding online.

....

3 It's not often that you see an author's debut novel being so successful.

....

4 You are absolutely forbidden to go backstage during the performance.

....

Fronting

6 ★★ **Use the words in bold to rewrite the sentences using fronting.**

1 The genre he enjoys most is **crime**.

....

2 The poet's words are **even more relevant** today than they were in his lifetime.

....

3 The type of programme she likes the least is **reality TV.**

....

4 Though she was **exhausted**, the dancer practised the routine one more time.

....

Grammar Revision 8c (Modules 1-8)

1 ★ Choose the correct item.

1 The exquisite statue was sculpted .... a local artisan.
A by B with C from D of

2 .... the famous actor being cast, the film wouldn't have been successful at all.
A Given that C Provided
B But for D Supposing

3 The executives agreed that it was .... clear that the show would have to be cancelled; sadly, it just wasn't profitable enough.
A deeply C highly
B abundantly D fully

4 Being a mature gentleman, Mark's literature tutor has a lifetime of .... in the field.
A the experience C experience
B experiences D an experience

5 Roger says that he .... it big in show business one day; you certainly can't fault his ambition!
A is going to make C will be making
B will make D will have made

6 'I want to go to the recital tonight but I'm not sure if I'll be able to ....'
A go to the recital C go to this
B go to D –

7 You really .... in your requisition form for a video camera last week.
A ought to have handed C might have handed
B had to hand D would have handed

2 ★★ Choose the correct item.

Watch It Now!

In the past, in order to watch a **1) released newly/new released/newly released** film at home you had to buy or rent the video or DVD. This aspect of home entertainment however is about **2) being consigned/to be consigned/will be consigned** to history thanks to online streaming services. For a subscription fee, viewers can choose from a diverse library of **3) each/both/every** classic films and the latest blockbusters to watch **4) whenever/while/the sooner** they want. Such companies are not only obtaining films at a **5) much/by far/so** faster rate than ever before they are also offering a(n) **6) wholly/ very/extremely** revolutionary approach to media consumption. **7) Even though/As if/Despite** this is great news for viewers, it's definitely not for DVD rental stores as it has cost **8) them/ themselves/itself** billions of dollars in lost revenue. In an ever changing world however, how relevant are DVDs anymore anyway?

Key word transformations

3 ★★ For questions 1-4, complete the second sentence so that it has a similar meaning to the first sentence, using the word given. Do not change the word given. You must use between three and eight words, including the word given.

1 The actress learned her lines after hours of rehearsing. **DID**
Only .... her lines.

2 Most people don't understand how to make a film. **INVOLVED**
Most people don't understand ....
.... a film.

3 It may be difficult to believe, but actor Johnny Depp never went to acting school. **SEEM**
Unlikely .... ,
actor Johnny Depp never went to acting school.

4 She didn't spend enough time preparing for the audition. **SPENT**
She ought ....
preparing for the audition.

Grammar in Focus

★★ Fill in the gaps with the correct word, put the words in brackets in the correct form or choose the correct word.

- When author RL Stine was nine years old, he came **1)** .... an old typewriter at home and began to write amusing stories and jokes. After **2)** .... **(graduate)** from college, he wrote humourous books but with **3) few/little** success. Feeling frustrated, Stine hoped he **4)** .... **(have)** better luck by switching to the horror genre. His move paid off and he **5)** .... **(throw)** into the limelight with his bestselling *Goosebumps* series **6) aimed/aiming** at young readers.
- As a young girl Margaret Mitchell loved reading adventure novels and writing. Remarkably, by age 11 she **7)** .... **(already/produce)** hundreds of her own short stories. Later, after college, she worked as a journalist until she broke her ankle in an accident. **8) In order to/So that** avoid boredom while recovering, she proceeded **9)** .... **(write)** a ground breaking novel **10)** .... heroine, Scarlett, would become one of the best known of all time. Mitchell's *Gone With The Wind* even earned **11)** .... a Pulitzer Prize to add to her resume. **12) Tragically/Tragic**, she died soon after in an accident. *Gone With The Wind* remains her only published novel.

8d Listening skills

Multiple matching

Remember!

It's important with listening tasks to read the rubric and the options before you listen to give yourself an idea of what you will be listening for. Once you have read all the options, you must listen carefully as the speakers will say words and phrases that allude to one or more of the options and are designed to distract you but only one option is correct.

1 ★★ **You will hear five short extracts in which people are talking about an art exhibition they went to. While you listen, you must complete both tasks.**

TASK ONE

For questions 1-5, choose from the list (A-H) the reason each speaker attended the exhibition.

A a friendship with the artist
B a familial connection
C a recommendation from a friend
D a chance encounter
E the lack of an alternative
F the provision of disabled access
G a company trip
H a positive review

Speaker		
Speaker 1		1
Speaker 2		2
Speaker 3		3
Speaker 4		4
Speaker 5		5

TASK TWO

For questions 6-10, choose from the list (A-H) what each speaker found most remarkable about the experience.

A the intricacy of the pieces
B the scale of the attractions
C the use of the space
D the variety of pieces
E the allure of the artwork
F the ability to interact with the exhibits
G the imagination of the artist
H the service of the attendants

Speaker		
Speaker 1		6
Speaker 2		7
Speaker 3		8
Speaker 4		9
Speaker 5		10

Multiple choice

2 ★★ **You will hear short conversations. Listen and from the three answer choices, select the answer which means about the same thing as what you hear, or is true based on what you hear.**

1 **A** Tours take half an hour.
B She will have lunch at the museum.
C She is going on the morning specialist tour.

2 **A** He will speak to the decorator.
B He will call the newspaper.
C They are inviting the press.

3 **A** She is training to be an actress.
B They are in a lesson.
C They are attending a play.

4 **A** She is annoyed at his actions.
B He was rude to her.
C He can't decide what to do.

5 **A** He didn't like the pictures.
B She only enjoyed the shots of marine life.
C The exhibition was of her work.

6 **A** She wants him to return a book.
B She wants to borrow a book from him.
C She has lost her book.

7 **A** They will go to the cinema.
B The old cinema accommodated events.
C The cinema will be demolished.

8 **A** His favourite actor always makes him laugh.
B She is laughing at his expense.
C She is annoyed by his reaction.

9 **A** They will buy tickets at the door.
B They have tickets for good seats.
C The online tickets were sold out.

10 **A** She got stage fright.
B He went to the concert.
C She lost her voice.

11 **A** She is not happy with her writing.
B She is stuck for ideas.
C She has spoken to the teacher.

12 **A** He is no longer clumsy.
B He has joined a gym.
C He is an incredible dancer.

13 **A** The book is still in its infancy.
B She is a first time author.
C She has reached a tricky stage in the book.

14 **A** Her granddaughter is an artist.
B He believes she is being unjust.
C She doesn't agree with studying art.

15 **A** Her brother is a comedian.
B Her brother downloaded a new app.
C Her brother has similar features to her uncle.

Speaking skills 8e

Asking about/Describing an experience/Recommending

1 **a) ★ Read the dialogue. Use the phrases (a-e) to complete the dialogue.**

a It's reasonably priced
b How was it
c What about the service
d It's well worth
e it was so tasty

Julia: So, have you been to that new Italian restaurant in town yet?
Carmen: Yes, I went there last week for dinner.
Julia: Really? **1)** ....?
Carmen: It was great! I loved the food. They only serve basic Italian dishes like pasta and pizza but they use fresh ingredients so it's a lot like home-cooking.
Julia: What did you have?
Carmen: I ordered the traditional lasagna dish and **2)** ....
Julia: **3)** ....?
Carmen: Well, to be honest it was a bit slow because it was busy but I didn't mind because the waiters were really friendly.
Julia: So, you'd recommend it?
Carmen: Definitely. **4)** .... and the food is delicious.
Julia: Sounds good. I love Italian cuisine. I can't wait to give it a try.
Carmen: You should. **5)** .... it!

b) ★ Which phrases in Ex. 1a ask about / describe/recommend an experience? Complete the table.

Ask	....
Describe	....
Recommend	....

2 **★ Choose the correct item.**

1 A: Did you enjoy the show?
B: **a** It was highly recommended.
b It was the best I've ever seen.

2 A: What was so special about it?
B: **a** The special effects were great.
b It was worth seeing.

3 A: Should I give it a try?
B: **a** Definitely. You won't regret it!
b Interesting. That sounds good!

Narration/Supported opinion

3 **★ Read the question and the speaker's answer below. Then use the information in the text to complete the *wh*-questions.**

Can you describe your favourite comedy show and your favourite character from that show?

My favourite comedy show is *The Big Bang Theory*. It's a hilarious sitcom about a group of nerdy friends going through the trials and tribulations of life. I love watching everybody on the show and particularly Dr Sheldon Cooper, a theoretical physicist, who is known for his brilliant mind and quirky behaviour. I find him intriguing because he is extremely narcissistic and a know-it-all on every subject which makes him obnoxious to everyone around him. What I love most about him is that his self obsession and complete unawareness of sarcasm actually makes him quite funny and charming without meaning to be.

1 What is the name of the show? ....
2 What is the plot of the show? ....
3 Who is the speaker's favourite character? ....
4 What is he/she like? ....
5 Why does the speaker like him/her? ....

4 **★ Read the question below and the reasons and examples that support the answer. Then match the reasons to the examples and expand the prompts into sentences.**

Why is laughter important in life?

Reasons	Examples
1 ☐ social benefits	**A** help/create/positive/ emotion/ optimism/cope/struggles/life
2 ☐ mental benefits	**B** release/physical/tension/stress/ leave/muscle/relax/body/more/ resistant/infection
3 ☐ health benefits	**C** foster/better/communication/ appear/friendlier/people/be/ more/popular

8f Writing Reviews

1 **a) ★ Read the rubric and underline the key words.**

An international magazine is inviting readers to submit reviews of a practical travel app. You decide to send a review recommending an app that you have found useful, describing how it works and explaining the reasons it is useful. Write your **review** in 280-320 words.

b) ★ Read the model and put the paragraphs in the right order.

A ☐ Overall, the app that I downloaded is excellent as it helps you discover new places and provides testimonials from other users while keeping track of places you have been to or want to go. For me, it has completely changed the way I manage my outings. I would highly recommend it to anyone looking to find an amazing city guide as it really does make finding hotspots easier.

B ☐ There are a number of reasons why such apps are useful. To start with, they allow users to generate a list of favourite places, spots and restaurants. They use these preferences along with your check-in history and their own data to provide recommendations just for you. What is more, you can read customer reviews and see uploaded pictures to determine whether unfamiliar locations are worth spending your time to visit.

C ☐ I enjoy hitting the town and am constantly looking for new hotspots to discover. A while ago, a friend of mine convinced me to try a popular city guide app to find new places of interest. I downloaded it out of curiosity and after discovering a few awesome restaurants I was immediately hooked.

D ☐ The app's innovative features work together to assist you to discover and share information about businesses and attractions around you. To use it, simply download the app on your mobile phone. Then tap 'explore' and choose the categories to find a place nearby that fits your taste criteria. At any time, you can edit or add to your tastes, by tapping the icon at the top. If you find an attraction but are unable to attend, you can add it to your 'to do' list to check back later.

Your turn

2 **★ Read the rubric and underline the key words. Then answer the questions.**

An international magazine is inviting readers to submit reviews of their favourite music streaming service. You decide to send a review recommending a service that you enjoy using, describing how it works and explaining the reasons it is useful. Write your **review** in 280-320 words.

1 What do you have to review?
2 Who is the target reader?
3 What style should you write in?
4 What information should you include in the introduction?
5 What information do you need in the main body?

Brainstorming

3 **★ Think of a music streaming service that you enjoy using. Complete the sentences below with relevant information.**

Name of service

1 One of the most striking things about this service is ....
2 Its function lies in ....
3 It is compatible with the vast majority of ....
4 The cost of this service is ....
5 In conclusion, it is ....

4 **a) ★ Read the rubric in Ex. 2 and the prompts below and fill in the plan.**

- recommendation
- main features of the service
- which app/reason for using it
- value of the service

Plan

Introduction
(Para 1) ....
Main body
(Para 2) ....
(Para 3) ....
Conclusion
(Para 4) ....

b) ★ Use your ideas in Exs 2 & 3 and the plan to write your review.

Off Script
and Out of this world ...

Certain moments in cinema grab hold of us and stick in our minds forever: iconic characters, interesting actions, or captivating dialogue that excite, enthral or move us in ways we'd never have imagined. These special scenes that cast a spell on us are often the difference between a good film and a truly amazing one and, thanks to phenomenal actors, have a truly lasting power.

Surely one would think that these iconic elements were meticulously planned by the director or heavily scripted by the screenwriter. Yet, what if such moments of classic cinematic history were never meant to be in the films originally at all and were nothing more than random chance or improvisation?

In the case of many great performances that have elevated good films to greater heights this is often exactly the case. They can range from gestures and physical performance, such as the Joker's emblematic slow sarcastic applause in *The Dark Knight*, to dialogue like Roy Scheider's famous 'You're gonna need a bigger boat' line in *Jaws* or Han Solo's laconic 'I know' response to Leia's declaration of love in *The Empire Strikes Back*. In each of these cases actors were given the freedom to express themselves by deviating from the script in spontaneous ways. Such actions require trust from a director and an open mind, however the impact of the end results are unquestionable. Could you imagine, for example, Ridley Scott's Science Fiction masterpiece *Blade Runner*, without its powerful 'tears in rain' monologue from actor Rutger Hauer, or Martin Scorsese's *Taxi Driver* without Robert De Niro's 'you talkin' to me?' soliloquy?

How these moments of magic occur vary from actor to actor. For example, they can be the result of a choice that the actor feels best for their character, such as Hauer's monologue. In this case instead of merely adding a single line, the entirety of this famous 'tears in rain' speech was completely improvised by Hauer. Or, alternatively they can be born from necessity and a lack of clarity on a script, as was the case with De Niro's performance where the script merely said 'Travis talks to himself in the mirror.'

Whatever the reason for their genesis, scenes such as these plunge the observer into the world and feelings of a character in a unique way because their spontaneity makes them seem sincere in a way that a scripted word or moment could never match. Taking risks, as we can see, can lead to extraordinary creativity. So the next time you quote your favourite movie line, stop and think; it might just have been a beautiful accident that was never meant to exist!

Reading

1 ★★ **Read the article. For questions 1-5 choose the answer (A, B, C or D) which you think fits best according to the text.**

1 What is the passage mainly about?
- **A** the cultural significance of classic films
- **B** the power talented performances have over an audience
- **C** the importance of good direction during a shoot
- **D** the benefits of giving actors free reign

2 In the second sentence of paragraph 3, why does the author use the word *emblematic*?
- **A** to illustrate how representative the act became of the character
- **B** to give an example of how other actors had influenced the gesture
- **C** to demonstrate how widely copied the scene has become
- **D** to explain how the mannerisms of the character were derived from comics

3 According to the passage, what is undeniable about flexibility on set?
- **A** It builds respect between members of the cast and crew.
- **B** It occurs mostly as a result of unavoidable problems.
- **C** It produces moments of remarkable power and significance.
- **D** It's the prerogative of the director, who has final say.

4 In paragraph 4, what does the author compare?
- **A** the differing reasons why a performer might need to be inventive
- **B** the outcomes of different kinds of film scripts
- **C** how two actors respond to confusion and stress on set
- **D** how an actor's understanding of a character's motivation differs to a director's.

5 What does the author think about improvisation?
- **A** It's a creative gamble that is best avoided.
- **B** It can't match the quality of scripted dialogue.
- **C** It offers something organic that written words can't.
- **D** It's the last resort of a weak actor who's forgotten the line.

Language Knowledge 8

Multiple choice cloze

1 ★★ **For questions 1-8, read the text below and decide which answer (A, B, C or D) best fits each gap. There is an example at the beginning (0).**

The right pitch?

Many cinematic classics of **0)** *A* cultural significance owe their existence to favours, connections, or the director simply being in the right place at the **1)** .... time. This traditional system for movie financing **2)** .... in privilege is not only unfair, it also has the serious **3)** .... of overlooking new and unknown talent.

Now, with the growth of crowdfunding, it's becoming the **4)** .... to pursue funding via the Internet. Through crowdfunding, directors and writers can pitch their ideas straight to audiences who can then choose a project and donate money **5)** .... Experts and media commentators have **6)** .... crowdfunding's success to an audience's natural ability to **7)** .... if an idea will be a hit or not. **8)** .... , there's no guarantee that a crowdfunded film will become a blockbuster, but one thing is for sure: involving audiences in the process can only be a good thing!

	A	B	C	D
0	enduring	lingering	unabating	unceasing
1	suitable	right	correct	desirable
2	entrenched	embedded	rooted	implanted
3	snag	fault	flaw	blemish
4	standard	benchmark	exemplar	norm
5	proportionately	correspondingly	accordingly	respectively
6	attributed	assigned	accounted	applied
7	reason	sense	notice	read
8	Admittedly	Conceivably	Assuredly	Inexorably

Open cloze

2 ★★ **For questions 1-8, read the text below and think of a word which best fits each gap. There is an example at the beginning (0).**

Brand Journalism: a change for the better?

Most of us would agree that the importance **0)** *of* impartiality in journalism is, **1)** .... a doubt, essential. Yet, this view is now being called into question by the rise of a new breed of journalism derived **2)** .... marketing known as Brand Journalism.

Strictly **3)** .... , these writers only focus on producing journalistic style stories about companies, however many people can't help **4)** .... wonder just how appropriate this is as almost **5)** .... the content will have corporate interests at heart. Even more concerning, could ethics end **6)** .... taking a back seat as a result of a firm directly steering public discourse? Indeed **7)** .... could.

While our ideas about the nature of news might be changing, it shouldn't be too difficult to distinguish fact from fiction **8)** .... enough vigilance and a critical mind.

Key word transformations

3 ★★ **For questions 1-6, complete the second sentence so that it has a similar meaning to the first sentence, using the word given. Use between three and eight words including the word given.**

1 The actor is unlikely to join the cast for a reunion episode.
DOUBTFUL
It is ....
....
the cast for a reunion episode.

2 It's necessary to wear 3D glasses throughout the film.
DURATION
3D glasses ....
....
of the film.

3 The actor tried to convince the director that it would be better if he did his stunts himself.
REALISE
The actor tried ....
....
it would be better if he did his stunts himself.

4 I really don't remember watching this film.
RECOLLECTION
I really ....
....
watching this film.

5 It's a shame that Peter missed the opening night.
MADE
If only ....
....
the opening night.

6 The actress has been late for media appearances before.
TIME
It's ....
....
has been late for a media appearance.

Grammar

4 ★ **Choose the correct item.**

1 Only by practicing hard .... her goals as a dancer.
A she achieved C achieved she
B did she achieve D she did achieve

2 You'd better get your act together, James! Your .... unacceptable on set.
A behaviour is C behaviours are
B behaviours is D behaviour are

3 The director will support the leading man .... he suggests we try.
A whenever C however
B wherever D whatever

4 There's a lot of demand for tickets this week, so I recommend .... sooner than you normally would.
A you book C to book
B you to book D you're booking

5 The woman .... in the lobby is the new record producer.
A is waiting C who waiting
B waiting D she is waiting

6 When .... the actor play Hamlet on stage?
A were you seen C were you seeing
B you saw D was it that you saw

7 The film studio was never able to determine .... leaked the film on the Internet.
A who it was that C that it was
B was it that D who was it that

8 You should turn that song off. It ....
A sounds awful C sounds awfully
B is sounding awful D is sounding awfully

9 I'd sooner .... the music festival, but I had to work at the weekend so I had no choice.
A didn't miss C not have missed
B hadn't missed D not miss

10 The famous actress is said .... with her agent.
A to fall out C she has fallen out
B to have fallen out D that she has fallen out

11 Before a concert, the musicians are usually asked to attend rehearsals .... day.
A every other C another
B the other D each other

12 Annoyed .... Jess was at the price of the album, she bought it to complete her collection.
A although C yet
B still D though

Vocabulary

5 ★ **Choose the correct item.**

1 Most films that are made today are digitally .... to make them more impressive.
A reinforced C boosted
B improved D enhanced

2 The film's .... to cinemas was delayed as a result of problems in post-production.
A placement C circulation
B distribution D inclination

3 It is hardly .... that the studio would refuse to finance the director's next project after he just won an Oscar.
A plausible C precise
B plain D predictable

4 She is a .... theatre actress with over 15 years of experience on Broadway.
A well-rehearsed C well-schooled
B well-prepared D well-seasoned

5 Everyone is eagerly awaiting the film .... of the book.
A adaptation C adjustment
B amendment D alteration

6 The book is a .... reminder of the struggle of women in the late 19th century.
A pungent C poignant
B pathetic D pervasive

7 She looked absolutely .... in that Victorian costume; it's so beautiful!
A startling C shocking
B stunning D staggering

8 Teenagers like to .... the behaviour and images they see on social media.
A simulate C impose
B emulate D impress

9 The Italian countryside was the perfect .... for the love story.
A scenery C backdrop
B view D property

10 .... half of all social media users are under the age of 25.
A Ultimately C Roughly
B Particularly D Predominantly

11 The music festival will .... some local bands as well.
A entail C emphasise
B feature D accentuate

12 This news site cannot be trusted as it does not rely on .... sources.
A excusable C pardonable
B tenable D credible

Prepositions & Phrasal Verbs Revision

★ **Choose the correct item.**

1 After a slow start, the rookie began to gain **from/on/off** the race leader.

2 Jeremy is always complaining about something, he never lets **out/off/up**.

3 We could tell **at/in/on** a glance that something was wrong because Emily had gone white as a sheet.

4 I wish people would wake **on/up/of** to the fact that we are all responsible for climate change.

5 A number of people thought George wouldn't amount **to/by/at** anything but he proved them all wrong when he got the job at the law firm.

6 Charles obviously isn't hungry, he's just picking **through/over/at** his dinner.

7 There's been a high demand **of/from/for** durable shopping bags since the government introduced the charge for plastic bags.

8 Parents should discourage their children **for/from/of** watching too much television.

9 I don't know why some directors insist **to/on/in** including gratuitous violence in their films, it's not necessary.

10 It's a good idea to put something **by/in/off** each month in case of emergencies.

11 Did you know that shopping **by/of/on** an empty stomach makes you spend more money?

12 Members of the board have called **for/out/at** the CEO's resignation so he doesn't have much choice now.

13 The subject **beyond/over/under** discussion at today's meeting is the proposed take-over bid.

14 You don't need to dress **up/off/down** for the party, just wear something casual.

15 The author dedicated his book **over/at/to** his childhood friend who had inspired the story.

16 We're going to have to take **over/out/up** a loan to finance the extension to the building.

17 Some children love the end of the holidays so they can go **over/through/back** to school and see all their friends.

18 Roger is capable **with/to/of** getting better marks if he puts in the hard work.

19 I was just leafing **through/over/around** this magazine when I spotted a story about my favourite actor.

20 Jimmie fell **aside/behind/out** with his school work when he was laid up with the flu.

21 The band are **on/of/in** great demand and have added four new dates to their latest tour.

22 The football team returned to a hero's welcome after they triumphed **over/into/with** their biggest rivals.

23 Leaving **beyond/behind/aside** the question of cost, how many people will we need to accommodate at the event?

24 After years of lying empty the old house fell **back/for/into** a bad state and had to be torn down.

25 You'll never guess who rung me **up/down/over** yesterday out of the blue; Dave, I haven't heard from him in years!

26 People in the know say that the market will sort itself **into/under/out** in the long run.

27 The rain this afternoon will turn **on/away/into** snow overnight when temperatures drop.

28 There is no cure **by/for/over** the common cold, you just have to let your body's defences do their job.

29 We'll leave the lawyers to see **in/off/to** the finer points of the deal but I think we've covered all the basics.

30 My brother and I take it **by/in/to** turns doing the washing up after dinner.

31 Siblings often compete **with/over/about** each other for their parents' affection.

32 Families with young children have been done out **for/to/of** thousands of pounds thanks to the recent changes to benefits.

33 The team were proud of their old strip and didn't want to part **with/off/for** it but their new sponsor insisted.

34 The meeting was brought **through/around/forward** because the head of the marketing department had to leave at lunchtime.

35 The restaurant is **under/out of/in** favour with young people in the town since it put up its prices.

36 Nobody picked up **from/on/of** the mistake in the story until it went to print so the paper had to print a retraction.

37 An architect drew **out/in/up** the plans for the new office building and they look great.

38 The teacher threatened Susie **over/with/to** detention if she didn't stop talking in class.

39 The economy is improving **by/at/in** degrees but it will take some time before it is back to its pre-recession days.

40 Carly improved **on/to/over** her personal best by a staggering 10 seconds.

Grammar Bank

Module 1

Present Simple and Present Continuous

We use the **present simple**:

- for facts and permanent states. *Laura **lives** in Barcelona.*
- for general truths and laws of nature. *Approximately 20 inches of rain **fall** annually.*
- for habits and routines (with ***always***, ***usually***, etc). *We usually **travel** to the seaside for our holidays.*
- for timetables and programmes (with future reference). *The train to Manchester **departs** at 11:00 am.*
- to give instructions or directions (instead of the imperative). *First you **check** your baggage and then you **make** your way to the departure gate.* (Instead of: *First **check** your baggage and then **make** your way to the departure gate.*)
- in narrating stories and plots, telling jokes, writing summaries and reviews, and broadcasting commentaries. *'And all of a sudden, as we **approach** the summit, I begin to feel a sense of euphoria.'*

Note: We use the **present continuous** together with the **present simple** to bring the reader closer to the events in a **narration**. The continuous form comes first to establish the background while the simple form narrates the main events that make up the rest of the narrative. *A woman **is sailing** to France when she **sees** a ship in the distance.*

- in sayings and proverbs. *Fortune **favours** the bold.*
- for feelings and emotions. *Nick **misses** his family now that he is away at university.*
- in exclamatory sentences beginning with '***Here***' or '***There***'. *Here **comes** the parade! There **goes** our ferry!*
- in oral speech, to introduce phrases or sentences, with verbs such as: ***admit***, ***agree***, ***believe***, ***bet***, ***gather***, ***insist***, ***know***, ***promise***, ***regret***, ***suppose***, ***swear***, ***understand***, etc. *I **gather** you've met before.*
- in type 1 conditional sentences. *If you **go** to the waterfall, you will need to wear waterproof clothing.*

Note: In order to express emphasis, we use the form: **subject + *do* + verb**. ***I do want** to visit the museum; let's go there first!*

In the 3rd person singular we use: **subject + *does* + verb**. ***Jasmine does want** to come camping but she might have to work that weekend.*

> **The time words/phrases we use with the *present simple* are:** usually, often, always, every day/week/month/year etc, in the morning/afternoon/evening, at night/the weekend, on Fridays, etc.

We use the **present continuous** (***to be*** + verb ***-ing***):

- for actions taking place at or around the time of speaking. *My cousins **are hiking** in the national park right now.*
- for temporary situations. *They **are staying** with us these days.*
- to make requests and statements sound less definite or formal. *I'**m hoping** to find accommodation when I arrive.* (less definite than 'I hope'), *I'**m looking** forward to meeting everyone when I arrive on Tuesday.* (less formal than 'I look')
- for picture/photo descriptions. *In this photo, a group of tourists **are shopping** in a bazaar.*
- for fixed arrangements in the near future. *He **is attending** a lecture on the Trans-Siberian Railway tomorrow afternoon.*
- for currently changing and developing situations. *Permission to travel in certain regions **is becoming** more and more difficult to obtain.*
- with '***always***', '***constantly***' and '***continually***' to express anger or irritation at a repeated action. *They **are** always **bragging** on social media about their extravagant lifestyle.*

> **The time words/phrases we use with the *present continuous* are:** now, at the moment, at present, these days, nowadays, still, today, tonight, etc.

Stative Verbs

Stative verbs are verbs which describe a state rather than an action, and so do not usually have continuous tenses. These verbs are:

- verbs of the senses (***see***, ***think***, ***hear***, ***smell***, ***taste***, ***feel***, ***look***, ***sound***, ***seem***, ***appear***, etc). *The food in Thailand **tastes** like nothing Jim has ever eaten before.*
- verbs of perception (***know***, ***believe***, ***understand***, ***realise***, ***remember***, ***forget***, etc). *Jessica **believes** that studying abroad is an essential part of the course.*
- verbs which express feelings and emotions (***like***, ***love***, ***feel***, ***hate***, ***prefer***, ***detest***, ***desire***, ***want***, ***desire***, ***loathe***, etc). *He **detests** having his suitcase opened and checked at airports.*
- some other verbs (***be***, ***contain***, ***include***, ***belong***, ***fit***, ***need***, ***matter***, ***cost***, ***own***, ***want***, ***weigh***, ***wish***, ***have***, ***keep***, ***return***, etc). *That small suitcase **contains** everything he owns.*

Some of these verbs can be used in continuous tenses, but with a difference in meaning.

Present Simple	Present Continuous
THINK *I **think** you need to get some vaccinations before you travel to Central America.* (= believe)	*They **are thinking** of emigrating to Buenos Aires.* (= are considering)

Present Simple	Present Continuous
HAVE *Lawrence **has** a British passport.* (= own, possess)	*She **is having** doubts about the accommodation she booked.* (= is experiencing) *The child **is having** a nap.* (= is taking) *They **are having** dinner on the flight.* (= are eating)
SEE *You can **see** for miles from this lookout if the weather is clear.* (= have a view) *Do you **see** what I mean now about the crowds?* (= understand)	*I'**m seeing** the Joneses this evening; they're coming around for a meal.* (= am meeting)
TASTE *Alan thinks that broccoli **tastes** disgusting.* (= has a specific type of flavour)	*Bea **is tasting** the curry to see if it is spicy enough.* (= is testing for flavour)
SMELL *This tree has flowers that **smell** like vanilla.* (= have a specific type of aroma)	*Tina **is smelling** the strawberries to see if they are ripe.* (= is sniffing)
APPEAR *The passengers **appear** to be enjoying their cruise.* (= seem)	*My favourite band **is appearing** at several music festivals this summer.* (= is performing)
FIT *Her walking shoes **fit** well so they won't hurt her feet.* (= are the right size)	*Jason **is fitting** a new sink and countertop in his caravan.* (= is installing)
LOOK *Free climbing **looks** extremely difficult.* (= appears to be)	*She **is looking** at the photos we took in Nepal.* (= is taking a look)
FEEL *This coat **feels** like it is made of wool.* (= it has a specific type of texture)	*She **is feeling** the fabrics in order to judge their quality.* (= is touching)
BE *He **is** an easy-going travelling companion.* (character – permanent state)	*He **is being** irritable today because he didn't get enough sleep.* (behaviour – temporary state)

Notes:

- Although some verbs, such as ***cherish*** and ***enjoy*** express a feeling, they do not function as stative verbs and can also be used in continuous tenses. *They **enjoy** wild camping. They **are enjoying** camping in Denali National Park.*
- The verbs ***look*** (when we refer to a person's appearance), ***feel*** (to experience a particular emotion), ***hurt*** and ***ache*** can be used in simple or continuous tenses with no difference in meaning. *She **is feeling** seasick. She **feels** seasick.*

Adverbs of Frequency

These include: ***always***, ***frequently***, ***often***, ***once***, ***twice***, ***sometimes***, ***never***, ***usually***, ***ever***, ***hardly ever***, ***rarely***, ***seldom***, ***occasionally***, etc.

- Adverbs of frequency are normally placed before the main verb. *They **hardly ever** stay in expensive hotels. He **frequently** sleeps on overnight trains.*
- However, they are placed after the verb ***be*** and after the **auxiliary/modal verbs**. If there is more than one modal/auxiliary verb, the adverb is generally placed after the first. *The queues outside this museum are **often** very long. He would **never** photograph someone without asking permission. I have **never** been invited to a wedding.*
- In short answers, they are placed before the auxiliary verbs. *'Buses **are usually** late here, aren't they?' 'Yes, they **usually are**.'*
- Time phrases such as ***every day***, ***once/twice a week/ month***, ***most mornings/evenings***, etc are placed at the beginning or the end of a sentence. For emphasis, ***usually***, ***often***, ***sometimes***, ***normally*** and ***occasionally*** can also be placed at the beginning or the end of a sentence. *We travel to Stockholm **twice a year**. **Normally**, I take the month of July off. She travels without planning anything in advance **occasionally**.*
- The adverbs ***never***, ***seldom*** and ***rarely*** have a negative meaning and are never used with the word 'not'. *I **rarely** go abroad.* (NOT: ~~I rarely don't go~~ …)

Present Perfect

We use the **present perfect** (***have*** **+ past participle**):

- for an action that happened at an unstated time in the past. The emphasis is on the action. The time when it happened is unimportant or unknown. *Matt **has climbed** most of the world's highest mountains. They **have booked** their flight.*
- for an action which started in the past and continues up to the present, especially with stative verbs. *The Browns **have known** the Smiths for years.*
- for a recently completed action. *Jenny **has just finished** her ecotourism course.*
- for personal experiences or changes. *He **has become** extremely tanned.*
- for an action which happened within a specific time period which is not over at the time of speaking (with time words/phrases such as: *today, this week/ morning/evening/month/year*, etc). *They **have visited** three continents **this year**.* (the year is not over yet)
- to announce a piece of news. In this case, we can use the past simple or past continuous to give more details

about it. *The authorities **have evacuated** the train station due to a security threat. The police **found** a suspicious package.*

- to put emphasis on the number of things that have happened up till now. *They **have visited** four Caribbean islands **so far**.*
- with present structures containing the superlative degree (hardest, best, etc) and ordinal numbers (first, second, etc) *This is **the most difficult** hike I **have ever attempted**. It is the **first** time Anna **has travelled** abroad.*

Notes:

- *She **has been to** Soho.* (= she has gone and come back)
  *She **has been in** London for two years now.* (= she lives there)
  *She **has gone to** New York.* (= she hasn't come back yet)
- In American English, the present perfect is often replaced by the past simple. US: ***Did** you **stroll** through Central Park yet?* UK: ***Have** you **strolled** through Central Park yet?* US: *I already **did** that.* UK: *I **have** already **done** that.*

The time words/phrases we use with the *present perfect* are: for, since, already, always, just, ever, never, so far, today, this week/month, etc, How long ...?, lately, recently, still (in negations), etc.

Present Perfect Continuous

We use the **present perfect continuous** (***have been*** + verb ***-ing***):

- to put emphasis on the duration of an action which started in the past and continues up to the present. *We **have been walking** for five hours already.*
- for an action which started in the past and lasted for some time. It may still be continuing or may have finished recently, but its result is visible in the present. *Paul knows exactly what he wants to see in Paris because he **has been reading** guidebooks for months.*
- to express anger, irritation or annoyance. *Jack **has been lying** on the beach ignoring us for hours.*
- for repeated actions in the past continuing up to the present. *My parents **have been taking** me to the same place on holiday for years!*

Notes:

- With the verbs ***live***, ***work***, ***teach*** and ***feel*** we can use the present perfect or the present perfect continuous with no difference in meaning. *She **has taught/has been teaching** History for the last thirty years.*
- We use the present perfect continuous to put emphasis on the duration of the action, and the present perfect to put emphasis on the number of things that have happened up till now. *They **have been volunteering** at organic farms all summer. They **have volunteered** at four farms so far.*

The time words/phrases we use with the *present perfect continuous* are: for, since, How long ...?, all day/morning/month, etc, lately, recently, etc.

Past Simple

We use the **past simple**:

- for an action that happened at a definite time (stated or implied) in the past. *I **renewed** my passport last April.*
- for actions that happened immediately one after the other in the past. *He **placed** his luggage in the compartment above his seat and **sat** down.*
- to talk about the main events in a story. *A stranger **arrived** in the village last week. He **took** a room at the only guesthouse. Then, he **disappeared**.*
- for habits, states and repeated actions in the past which do not happen any more. *Tom often **travelled** for competitions when he was on a sports team at university.*
- to talk about actions which were performed by people who are no longer alive, even if the time is not stated. *William Shakespeare **wrote** 'Romeo and Juliet'.*
- in type 2 conditional sentences and wishes when we refer to the present or future (unreal past). *If I **had** unlimited funds, I would never stop travelling. I **wish** I still **lived** in Ireland.*

Note: In order to express emphasis we use the form: **subject + *did* + verb.** *Their plane **did arrive** on time.*

The time words/phrases we use with the *past simple* are: yesterday, then, when, How long ago ...?, last night/week/month/year/Friday/October etc, three days/weeks etc ago, in 1999, etc.

Past Continuous

We use the **past continuous** (***was/were*** + verb ***-ing***):

- for an action which was in progress when another action interrupted it. We use the **past continuous** for the action in progress (longer action) and the **past simple** for the action which interrupted it (shorter action). *They **were staying** in Miami when the hurricane **hit**.*
- for two or more simultaneous actions in the past. *Pat **was packing** while Eliza **was checking** the bus schedule online.*
- for an action which was in progress at a stated time in the past. We don't mention when the action started or finished. *On the tenth of August, he **was camping** by a lake.*
- to describe the atmosphere, setting, etc and to give background information about a story. *The sun **was beating** down on the dry vegetation and cicadas **were chirping** as we started off along the trail.*
- in type 2 conditional sentences and wishes when we refer to the present or future (unreal past). *If I **was going** that way, I'd take you. I wish I **was lying** on a sandy beach right now.*
- for polite enquiries and offers. *I **was considering** renting a bicycle; are there any available? – Excuse me, **were you looking** for accommodation by any chance?*

- with '***always***', '***constantly***' and '***continually***' to describe repeated unpleasant and irritating actions in the past. *When we were on holiday, people **were** constantly **leaving** towels out overnight on the best sunbeds.*
- to describe plans and intentions that didn't come true. *He **was planning** to go to Vietnam but he couldn't get a visa.*

Notes:

- When there are two past continuous forms in a sentence with the same subject, we can avoid repetition by using the present participle (-***ing*** form) and leave out the subject and the verb ***was/were*** of the second verb form. ***They were fishing** by the lake and **they were enjoying** themselves. = They were fishing by the lake and **enjoying** themselves.*
- Although the past simple is used for past repeated actions, we can use the past continuous for such actions if they provide background information about what we say. *Tom **was** often **travelling** for competitions in the year before he quit the sports team.*

> **The time words/phrases we use with the *past continuous* are:** while, when, as, all morning/evening/day/week, etc.

Past Perfect

We use the **past perfect** (***had*** + **past participle**):

- for an action which happened before another past action or before a stated time in the past. *Lisa **had attended** a workshop in Chennai the year before she started teaching yoga. The train **had** already **left** by three o'clock.*
- for an action which finished in the past and whose result was visible at a later point in the past. *He was thrilled; he **had passed** all his exams with high marks.*
- with past structures containing the superlative degree (hardest, best, etc) or ordinal numbers (first, second, etc). *That was **the coldest** place they **had** ever **camped**. It was the **first** time he **had visited** a non-English-speaking country.*
- to describe hopes and wishes that were never realised. *She **had hoped** to see the northern lights but it was overcast every night.*
- in type 3 conditional sentences. *If I **had known** how expensive it was, I would have gone somewhere else.*
- in reported speech to report a past action. The reporting verb must be in the past. *She **said** that she **hadn't been able** to attend the meeting because she was away on business.*
- after the following expressions referring to the past: ***as if***, ***as though***, ***I would rather he/she** ...*, ***I wish/If only*** (expressing regrets). *The town looked **as if** it **had not changed** for a hundred years. **I'd rather** she **had told** me she was allergic to mosquitoes before we went to the Amazon Rainforest. **I wish** I **had gone** to San Francisco while I was in California. **If only** I **had left** earlier, I wouldn't have missed my flight.*

Notes:

- Verbs of knowing and understanding are not normally used in past perfect, unless they are followed by '***for***'. *I didn't **understand** how upset she was until I'd read her letter. After they **had known** each other **for** a few months, they decided to go on a road trip together.*
- In oral speech, we can use the past perfect or the past simple with ***before*** or ***after*** without any difference in meaning. *She went to university after she **spent/had spent** a year teaching English in Spain.*
- The past perfect is the past equivalent of the present perfect. *The city **had renovated** the seafront and it looked completely unfamiliar.* (The action 'had renovated' happened in the past. The result 'looked completely unfamiliar' was also visible in the past.) *The city **has renovated** the seafront and it looks completely unfamiliar.* (The action 'has renovated' happened in the past. The result 'looks completely unfamiliar' is still visible in the present.)
- We can use the past simple, past continuous or past perfect without any difference in meaning with verbs such as ***think***, ***hope***, ***mean***, ***expect***, etc for actions we hoped or wished to do, but we didn't. *I **meant/was meaning/had meant** to visit the Louvre but I didn't have time.*

> **The time words/phrases we use with the *past perfect* are:** before, after, already, just, for, since, till/until, when, by the time, never, How long ...?, etc.

Past Perfect Continuous

We use the **past perfect continuous** (***had been*** + verb ***-ing***):

- to put emphasis on the duration of an action which started and finished in the past, before another action or stated time in the past, usually with ***for*** or ***since***. *He **had been walking** in the forest **for** several hours when he realised he was lost.*
- for an action which lasted for some time in the past and whose result was visible in the past. *They **had been swimming** so they were dripping wet.*

Note: The past perfect continuous is the past equivalent of the present perfect continuous.

a) *I had been travelling for twenty-four hours, so I felt exhausted.* (The action 'had been travelling' lasted for some time in the past. The result 'felt exhausted' was also visible in the past.)

b) *I have been travelling for twenty-four hours, so I feel exhausted.* (The action 'have been travelling' started in the past. The result 'feel exhausted' is still visible in the present.)

> **The time words/phrases we use with the *past perfect continuous* are:** for, since, How long ...?, before, until, etc.

used to – *would* – Past Simple – *be/get used to*

- We use ***used to/would*/past simple** to talk about habits, routines and repeated actions in the past that no longer happen. *We **used to swim/would swim/swam** here before the hotel was built.* (We don't any more.)
- We use ***used to*/past simple** (NOT 'would') for past states. ***Would*** cannot be used with stative verbs. *She **used to have/had** a student railcard before she graduated.* (NOT: ~~*She would have a student railcard before she graduated*~~.)
- We use only the **past simple** (NOT 'used to/would') for an action that happened at a definite time in the past. *I **stayed** in an eco-lodge last night.* (NOT: ~~*I used to/would stay in an eco-lodge last night*~~.)
- We use only the **past simple** (NOT 'used to/would') to say how many times an action happened at a definite period of time in the past. *He **drove** to Edinburgh twice last week.* (NOT: ~~*He used to drive to Edinburgh twice last week*~~.)
- We use ***be used to*** + **noun/pronoun/*-ing* form** to talk about habits (= be accustomed to/be in the habit of). *They **are used to sleeping** in noisy hostel dormitories.*
- We can also use ***get used to*** + **noun/pronoun/*-ing* form** to talk about habits (= become accustomed to). *You will soon **get used to sleeping** on a camping mat.*

Time words to talk about the past:

ago (= back in time from now) is used with the past simple. *We arrived about an hour **ago**.*

since (= from a starting point in the past) is used with the present and past perfect (simple and continuous). *He hasn't been to London **since** the 1990s.*

for (= over a period of time) is used with the present and past perfect (simple and continuous). *They had been waiting in the queue **for** hours.*

already (=before now) is used in statements and questions in the present and past perfect to show surprise. *I've **already** booked our tickets. Have you **already** printed out the boarding pass?*

yet (at this time, so far) is used with the present and past perfect in questions and negations. *Have you posted any photos onto social media **yet**? The waiter hasn't brought our food **yet**.*

Present & Past tenses

1 ★ **Match the sentences to their uses.**

1 ☐ Accommodation **is** expensive during peak season.
2 ☐ They **have stayed** in three luxury resorts so far.
3 ☐ The company **does offer** tours to archeological sites.
4 ☐ We **have been waiting** for our plane to leave for two hours!
5 ☐ At four o'clock yesterday, they **were speaking** to their travel agent.
6 ☐ The ferry to the island **leaves** at 1 pm.
7 ☐ The quality of service on the cruise **is getting** less and less acceptable.
8 ☐ Kevin **reserved** his seat online and **paid** with his card.
9 ☐ The restaurant **had closed** by the time we returned to Paris.
10 ☐ They **had been lying** in the sun for hours and got a sunburn.
11 ☐ Jack was very happy; he **had been** to all the museums in London that he wanted to visit.
12 ☐ Emily **posted** her holiday pictures online last week.
13 ☐ Excuse me, **were** you **looking** for accommodation this evening by any chance?

A an action that happened at a definite time in the past
B to put emphasis on the duration of an action which started in the past and continues up to the present
C a currently changing and developing situation
D to put emphasis on the number of things that have happened up till now
E an action which happened before another past action
F a timetable (with future reference)
G actions that happened immediately one after the other in the past
H a general truth
I an action which finished in the past and whose result was visible at a later point in the past
J an action which lasted for some time in the past and whose result was visible in the past
K for polite enquiries and offers
L an action which was in progress at a stated time in the past
M to express emphasis in the present

2 ★ **Underline the correct item.**

1 The other passengers looked bored so Brian decided to tell a joke. 'So, a chicken **walks/is walking/has walked/has been walking** into a shop ...' he began.
2 After Matt and Paul **have known/had known/had been knowing/were knowing** each other for a few months, they decided to go on holiday together.
3 When she asked her dad why he didn't want to travel anymore, he said, 'He who **travels/has travelled/is travelling/has been travelling** becomes wise; he who is wise stays home.'
4 In this photo, our tour group **cooks/is cooking/was cooking/had cooked** local dishes in Portugal.
5 As Tim looked at the posters in the travel agent's, he thought, 'I really wish we **were lying/had lain/have been lying/are lying** on the beach in Spain.'
6 They **expected/had expected/were expecting/had been expecting** to meet other travellers in the hostel, but as it was winter they were the only guests.
7 Karen **has gone to/has been in/has gone in/has been to** Beijing and won't be back for another two weeks.
8 He **was just paying/just paid/had just been paying/has just paid** for the hotel when he saw a cheaper deal online.

3 ★★ **Fill in the gaps using the correct present tense of the verbs in the list.**

• plan • love • usually/stay • continually/complain • fly • know

1 Henry .... meeting new people while travelling overseas.
2 My friends .... about package tours, but I quite like them!
3 Emily .... in youth hostels to save money.
4 The Smiths .... the hotel owner for the last six years.
5 We .... to find somewhere to stay once we get to Glasgow.
6 I .... for thirteen hours already; I can't wait to get off this plane.

4 ★★ **Put the verbs in brackets in the correct past tense.**

1 Scott regularly .... **(deal)** with difficult customers when he worked as a holiday rep.
2 Our tour bus .... **(constantly/break down)** while we were in Spain.
3 The remote village in Vietnam looked as if it .... **(remain)** untouched by time.
4 I was staying in Florida when the hurricane .... **(hit)**.
5 We .... **(hike)** for many hours, so we felt extremely grateful for a break.
6 Finland was the coldest country they .... **(ever/visit)**.

5 ★★ **Fill in the gaps with a suitable time word/phrase:** ***nowadays, often, since, for, how long, at the moment, already, yet.***

1 A: .... have you been working as a travel agent?
B: .... around five years.
2 A: Have you booked our train tickets to Paris?
B: I've .... noted down some train times, but I haven't finalised our reservations ....
3 A: You're such an amazing cook, Julie. Have you been doing this for long?
B: Thank you! Actually, I haven't made these local dishes .... I was a child!
4 A: Overcrowding and litter is becoming a real problem. The tourist board really need to take action.
B: Yes, you're right. It's getting worse now as more and more people are visiting the island .... than ever before.
5 A: I'm having a wonderful time ....; the views here are amazing!
B: Yes, it's my favourite place to relax. I .... come here to unwind and get away from it all.

used to – would – be/get used to

6 ★★ **Fill in each gap with the correct form of *be/get used to, used to* or *would*.**

1 Peter .... own a car rental company when he lived in Spain.
2 Tom .... sharing a kitchen in a youth hostel.
3 Angela .... walk to work every day when she was a receptionist at the beach resort.
4 Running a hotel didn't .... be so difficult; there's a lot more competition now.
5 At first, I didn't really like sleeping on a camping mat but now I am trying to .... it.
6 Maggie hated flying long distance, but now she .... it.
7 It takes a little time, but you'll .... hot desking with other people in the travel agency.

Revision of Present & Past tenses

7 ★★ **Put the verbs in brackets in the correct present or past tense.**

1 You've really got to seize the moment; as my old manager at Travel World used to say, 'time and tide .... **(wait)** for no man!"
2 The ferry tickets .... **(sell out)** by the time we went to the ticket office.
3 Picture this: it is a quiet spring morning. The family are driving through the safari park when they suddenly .... **(notice)** a lion in the distance.
4 I can't believe we .... **(sightsee)** for the last two hours!
5 Eric .... **(cycle)** along the coast since twelve o'clock so he was extremely sore.
6 The wind .... **(blow)** and the long grass .... **(sway)** in the breeze as I walked through the field on my way to the villa.
7 The tourist board .... **(renovate)** the visitor centre and it looked much more modern.
8 Mike .... **(write)** his review of the hotel and .... **(post)** it online.
9 The folk singer .... **(appear)** at the cultural show near our hotel tomorrow.
10 Martin .... **(become)** much more open minded since he started travelling.

8 ★★ **Find and correct the mistake(s) in each sentence.**

1 Martin and I was enjoying the view when Henry suddenly had walked onto the balcony to lecture us about it.
2 We were being both busy yesterday morning at eight o'clock; Barry packed his suitcase while I was printing our boarding passes.
3 Maria had walked to the beach, as she usually was doing on holiday, when she came across a couple of tourists who was looking for their hotel.
4 Karen has certainly travelled a lot recently; she is visiting five different islands in Greece this year.
5 Andy is knowing so much about the history of the region; he has hoped to have his book about the area ready soon; he has written it for two years already.
6 Although Donald had a map of the town in his hotel room and he was thinking he remembered the route well enough, it wasn't until he had walked for nearly an hour that he was realising he was lost.

9 ★★ **Fill in the gaps using the verbs in brackets in a suitable tense.**

A While it's true that package holidays **1)** .... **(remain)** popular, mainly as people **2)** .... **(use)** travel agents for years, we can now see a paradigm shift in the way people **3)** .... **(approach)** travel due to the rise of bespoke options online.

B My enduring passion for travel all **1)** .... **(start)** when as a child I first **2)** .... **(open)** a holiday brochure that my mother **3)** .... **(leave)** on the dining room table some days before.

C Mitch **1)** .... **(save up)** to go to Italy for months; normally he **2)** .... **(put)** twenty pounds a week aside for the trip but he **3)** .... **(become)** rather complacent and is unlikely to reach his goal by the end of the year.

D Reports **1)** .... **(come)** in all morning that the authorities **2)** .... **(cancel)** all flights from Gatwick since they **3)** .... **(discover)** a suspicious item inside the airport terminal.

10 ★ **Choose the correct item.**

1 Jack .... for his ferry tickets yet.
A didn't pay C hadn't paid
B hasn't paid D has paid

2 '........ Jane .... life in China?'
'I'm not sure. I haven't spoken to her for weeks.'
A Did, enjoy C Is, enjoying
B Has, enjoyed D Had, enjoyed

3 'James is struggling to keep up with things.'
'Yes, I guess he .... to travelling so much for business.'
A isn't getting used C isn't used
B didn't use D hasn't been used

4 Jen .... to London three times this week.
A used to drive C was driving
B would drive D drove

5 'I can't believe that ferries were cancelled today.'
'Actually, a few .... for the mainland this morning.'
A did leave C had left
B were leaving D do leave

6 Stuart .... travel websites for his next holiday since lunchtime.
A is browsing C has been browsing
B has browsed D browses

7 Ben .... Prague twice this week on business.
A has been to C has gone to
B has been in D has gone in

8 Julia .... checking in at the airport; the queues are always terrible!
A is detesting C has detested
B detests D has been detesting

9 'Wasn't cancelling the tour rather unexpected on the company's part?'
'Not really; they .... clients that it was a possibility several times already.'
A had been informing C had informed
B were informing D would inform

10 This is the first time Fiona .... Mexico; she loves it!
A is visiting C visits
B has visited D has been visiting

11 Rick .... to take the sleeper train to Edinburgh but couldn't get tickets.
A planned C was planning
B has been planning D used to plan

12 The price of the package deal .... food and board at a five star hotel.
A has included C has been including
B is including D includes

11 ★★ **Read the text and put the verbs in brackets into the correct present or past tense.**

SURF'S UP!

Imagine the scene, you **1)** .... **(swim)** through the shallow waves on holiday in California when you **2)** .... **(notice)** something strange in the distance. The surfing instructor by the shore **3)** .... **(teach)** a private class, to... a dog! Although you probably **4)** .... **(never/see)** this before, surfing instructor Teevan McManus **5)** .... **(actually/do)** this since 2005. It all started when one day, while he **6)** .... **(surf)** his dog 'Murphy' ran out to sea after him. Murphy **7)** .... **(follow)** his owner for weeks before Teevan finally **8)** .... **(stop)** and put the dog on the board. To his amazement, Murphy loved it! Teevan **9)** .... **(coach)** visitors and their canine friends ever since! If you find Teevan's special classes odd, remember, it **10)** .... **(take)** all kinds to make a world!

Key word transformations

12 ★★ **For questions 1-5, complete the second sentence so that it has a similar meaning to the first sentence, using the word given. Do not change the word given. You must use between three and eight words, including the word given.**

1 More and more visitors are staying in beach villas on the island. **GROWTH**
There ....
visitors staying in beach villas on the island.

2 When did you open your guesthouse on the coast? **AGO**
How .... when you opened your guesthouse on the coast?

3 Milo's hasn't received an award for its food for years. **TIME**
It's ....
an award for its food.

4 Mary had never felt so happy before she achieved her goal! **EVER**
It ....
happy when she achieved her goal.

5 The climber said he no longer thought that his expedition would ever reach the summit. **HOPE**
The climber said he ....
.... ever reaching the summit.

Module 2

Infinitive

	Tenses of the infinitive	
	Active voice	**Passive voice**
present	(to) break	(to) be broken
present continuous	(to) be breaking	
perfect	(to) have broken	(to) have been broken
perfect continuous	(to) have been breaking	

Tenses of the infinitive corresponding to verb tenses
present simple/future simple → **present infinitive**
present continuous/future continuous → **present continuous infinitive**
past simple/present perfect/past perfect/future perfect → **perfect infinitive**
past continuous/present perfect continuous/ past perfect continuous/future perfect continuous → **perfect continuous infinitive**

- When the subject of the main clause is the same as the subject of the infinitive, then the latter is omitted. ***He managed to pass** all his exams.*
- When the subjects of the main clause and of the infinitive are not the same, then we put the latter before the infinitive as an object pronoun, a noun or a name. *His colleagues don't like **him to chew** gum loudly. I would prefer **her/the sound engineer/Nora** to check the quality of the recording.*
- Also, the subject of the infinitive can be used after the preposition ***for***. *Toby arranged **for the economist** to give a lecture to the students. It is unusual **for Emily** to be so argumentative. Their suggestion was **for the artists** to take turns working in the gallery.*

The ***to*-infinitive** is used:

- to express purpose. *We use this computer **to print** shipping labels.*
- after certain verbs (***agree***, ***appear***, ***decide***, ***encourage***, ***expect***, ***hope***, ***plan***, ***pretend***, ***proceed***, ***promise***, ***refuse***, ***seem***, ***tend***, etc). *Alan **tends to work** better when he has written out a detailed schedule.*
- after ***would like***, ***would prefer*** and ***would love*** to express a specific preference. *They **would prefer to attend** the second workshop on Friday.*
- after adjectives which describe feelings/emotions (***happy***, ***sad***, ***glad***, etc), express willingness/unwillingness (***willing***, ***eager***, ***reluctant***, etc), refer to a person's character (***clever***, ***kind***, etc) and the adjectives ***lucky*** and ***fortunate***. *Tina has not used this software before but she is **eager to learn**.*
  Note: With adjectives that refer to character, we can also use an impersonal construction. ***It was kind of Jim to bring** sandwiches when everyone was so busy.*
- with ***it*** + ***be*** + **adjective/noun**. ***It is important to get** there on time. **It is her ambition to open** her own shop.*
- after ***too/enough***. *It is **too** noisy **to think** in this office! This printer is good **enough to do** the job.*
- to talk about an unexpected event, usually with ***only***. *She took a taxi in order to be on time, **only to find** that the meeting had been postponed.*
- after **certain nouns** and **pronouns**, such as ***advantage***, ***anyone***, ***decision***, ***demand***, ***disadvantage***, ***idea***, ***mistake***, ***need***, ***nightmare***, ***nothing***, ***nuisance***, ***pleasure***, ***somebody***, ***something***, ***wish***, etc. *It was a good **idea to promote** our brand using social media. It is my **pleasure to make** your acquaintance. Tom doesn't have **anyone to assist** him with the inventory.*
- to replace a relative clause after the phrases ***the first***, ***the second***, ***the third***, etc., ***the last***, ***the only***, and sometimes after **superlatives**. *He works long hours; he is always **the first to arrive** and **the last to go**.* (The first who arrives and the last who goes.) *Michael is **the youngest** person **to hold** the position of artistic director.*
- in newspaper headlines referring to the future. *FUNDING FOR SMALL BUSINESSES **TO GO UP** IN 2018*
- to avoid repeating an infinitive clause. *I've never visited Africa, but I'd like **to (visit)**.* (to visit Africa)
- after the expressions ***so kind as/so silly as***, etc. *Would you be **so kind as to bring** some more paper for the printer, please?*
- Certain adjectives, such as ***difficult***, ***easy***, ***good***, ***hard***, ***important***, ***impossible***, ***interesting***, ***ready***, etc, are followed by infinitives in the active form when the subject of the main clause is the object of the infinitive. *The fax machine is **ready to use**. The project is **impossible to complete** in a week. Calculus is **difficult to understand**.*
  This structure is not possible when the subjects of the main clause and of the infinitive are the same. *People have difficulty understanding calculus.* (NOT: ~~*People are difficult to understand calculus.*~~)
- after verbs such as ***ask***, ***decide***, ***explain***, ***find out***, ***learn***, ***want to know***, etc when they are followed by a question word ***(who, whom, which, what, when, where, how)***. *Has Mr Williamson decided **when to launch** the new product?*
  Note: ***why*** is followed by **subject** + **verb**, NOT an infinitive. *I wonder **why he talks** so loudly all the time.*
- in the expressions ***to tell you the truth***, ***to be honest***, ***to sum up***, ***to begin with***, etc. ***To begin with**, we need to increase productivity.*
  Note: If two ***to*-infinitives** are linked by ***and*** or ***or***, the ***to*** of the second infinitive can be omitted. *He asked Nathan **to check** the inventory or **get** somebody else to do it.*

The **infinitive without *to*** is used:

- with ***need*** (as modal verb). *You **needn't book** your ferry ticket in advance.* (**BUT** *You **don't need to book** your ferry ticket in advance.*)
- after modal verbs. *David **can fix** the scanner.*

- after the verbs **make**, **see**, **hear**, **notice**, **see**, **watch** and **let**. *They **made** everyone **go** outside.* **BUT** we use the ***to*-infinitive** after **be made**, **be heard**, **be noticed** and **be seen** and **be watched** (passive form). *Everyone **was made to go** outside.*
  Note: When **see**, **hear** and **watch** are followed by an ***-ing*** form, there is no change in the passive. *We **saw** him **entering** the room. He **was seen entering** the room.*
- after **had better**, **would rather** and **would sooner**. *She **would rather walk** to work than take the bus.*
  Note: *help* can be followed by either the ***to*-infinitive** or the **infinitive without *to***. *Emily **helped** me **(to) build** the website.*
- after ***do*** + ***everything/anything/nothing*** + ***except/but***. *He **did nothing but send** emails all day.*
- after ***why (not)*** to make suggestions. *Why **not put** the information into a spreadsheet?*

Notes:

- ***dare*** expressing **courage** or **lack of courage** can be followed by ***to*-infinitive** or **infinitive without *to***. *They don't **dare (to) point** out his mistake. She **dared (to) raise** a dissenting opinion.*
- ***dare*** expressing **threats**, **warning**, **anger**, etc is followed by **infinitive without *to***. *Don't you **dare go** to Paris without me! How **dare** you **accuse** me of taking your diary!*
- ***dare*** expressing **challenge** is followed by ***to*-infinitive**. *I **dare** you **to** come bungee jumping with me tomorrow.*

Gerund (*-ing* form)

	Tenses of the *-ing* form	
	Active voice	**Passive voice**
present	buying	being bought
perfect	having bought	having been bought

The subject of the ***-ing* form** is omitted when it is the same as the subject of the main verb.
When it is different, however, it is not omitted. The **subject** of the ***-ing* form** can be an object pronoun, a possessive adjective, a name or a possessive case. *A colleague's absence resulted in **him speaking** at the seminar.* (less formal) *A colleague's absence resulted in **his speaking** at the seminar.* (very formal) *I remember **Freda performing** for the first time.* (less formal) *I remember **Freda's performing** for the first time.* (very formal)

The ***-ing*** form is used:

- as a noun. ***Starting** your own business is usually a lot of hard work.*
- after certain verbs: ***admit***, ***appreciate***, ***avoid***, ***confess***, ***deny***, ***fancy***, ***go*** (for activities), ***consider***, ***delay***, ***excuse***, ***forgive***, ***imagine***, ***involve***, ***keep***, ***mean***, ***mind***, ***miss***, ***pardon***, ***postpone***, ***practise***, ***prevent***, ***quit***, ***recall***, ***recollect***, ***risk***, ***save***, ***shirk***, ***suggest***, ***understand***, etc. *I **recollect reading** something about this topic last week.*
- after ***enjoy***, ***detest***, ***dislike***, ***hate***, ***like***, ***loathe***, ***love***, ***prefer*** and ***resent*** to express general preference. *Terry **prefers working** in a lively team setting.* **BUT** for a specific preference (***would like/would prefer/would love***) we use a **to-infinitive**. *I **would prefer to finish** this project before starting another.*
- after expressions such as ***be busy***, ***it's no use***, ***it's (no) good***, ***it's (not) worth***, ***feel like***, ***can't help***, ***there's no point in***, ***can't stand***, ***have difficulty (in)***, ***have trouble***, etc. ***It's no use waiting** any longer to start the meeting; I don't think they are coming.*
- after ***spend***, ***waste*** and ***lose*** (**time** and **money**). *They **spent** a lot of money **upgrading** the workstations.*
- after the preposition ***to*** with verbs and expressions such as ***look forward to***, ***be used to***, ***in addition to***, ***get round to***, ***object to***, ***prefer*** **(doing)** sth ***to*** **(doing)** sth else, etc. ***In addition to advertising** on TV, they also make use of social media.*
- after all the other prepositions. *Olivia is thinking **of sailing** around the Caribbean.*
- after the verbs ***hear***, ***listen to***, ***notice***, ***see***, ***watch*** and ***feel*** to describe an incomplete action. *I **saw** Sophie **shutting down** her computer as I walked by the office.* (I only saw part of the action.)
  BUT we use the **infinitive without *to*** with ***hear***, ***listen to***, ***notice***, ***see***, ***watch*** and ***feel*** to describe a complete action. *I **saw** Sophie **shut down** her computer before she left the office.* (I saw the whole action.)

Difference in meaning between the *to*-infinitive and the *-ing* form

Some verbs can take either the ***to*-infinitive** or the ***-ing* form** with a change in meaning:

- ***forget*** + ***to*-infinitive** = to not remember to do sth – *Margaret **forgot to order** more ink for the printer.*
  forget + ***-ing* form** = to not recall doing sth – *How could he possibly **forget winning** the design award?*
- ***remember*** + ***to*-infinitive** = to not forget to do sth – *Did you **remember to take** the packages to the post office?*
  remember + ***-ing* form** = to recall doing sth – *I will always **remember going** to my first job interview.*
- ***mean*** + ***to*-infinitive** = to intend to do sth – *They **meant to take** a month off in July but they were too busy.*
  mean + ***-ing* form** = to involve – *They realised that opening a new branch **meant taking on** more staff.*
- ***regret*** + ***to*-infinitive** = to be sorry for what you are going to do (normally used in the present simple with verbs such as ***say***, ***tell*** and ***inform***) – *We **regret to tell** you that the position has already been filled.*
  regret + ***-ing* form** = to feel sorry for doing sth in the past – *Bill **regretted agreeing** to translate the book when he realised how long it would take.*
- ***try*** + ***to*-infinitive** = to do my best, to attempt – *Everyone **tried to find** a solution to the problem.*
  try + ***-ing* form** = to do sth as an experiment – *Have you **tried doing** the hardest task first thing in the morning?*
- ***stop*** + ***to*-infinitive** = to stop doing sth temporarily in order to do sth else – *After working for five hours, they **stopped to have** lunch.*

stop + *-ing* **form** = to finish doing sth – *At ten o'clock in the morning, all the computers **stopped working**.*

- ***go on*** + ***to*-infinitive** = to do sth else after an activity stated previously – *Once the chef had prepared the main course, he **went on to make** the salad.*
  go on + ***-ing* form** = to continue an activity stated previously – *The earthquake was minor and everyone **went on working** as usual.*
- ***like*** + ***to*-infinitive** = to find sth good to do – *Jan **likes to work** from home rather than commute.*
  like + ***-ing* form** = to enjoy – *George **likes walking** to work.*
  would like + ***to*-infinitive** – *She **would like to go** to the gym on her way home from work today.* (specific)
- ***propose*** + ***to*-infinitive** = to intend – *'I **propose to have finished** the novel by April,' the writer told his agent.*
  propose + ***-ing* form** = to suggest – *The members of the think tank **proposed implementing** a new strategy.*
- ***be understood*** + ***to*-infinitive** = to give the impression – *They **are understood to support** the same political party.*
  understand + ***-ing* form** = to understand sb's feelings or actions – *I can **understand** his **refusing** to talk about politics.*
- ***want*** + ***to*-infinitive** – *He **wants to reorganise** his work space.*
  sth wants + ***-ing* form** – *The office is quite dusty; it **wants cleaning**.*
- ***dread*** + ***to*-infinitive** = to be afraid to do sth (specific) – *I **dread to imagine** how much time this is going to take.*
  dread + ***-ing* form** = to fear greatly (general) – *She **dreads doing** her taxes each year.*
- ***be sorry*** + ***to*-infinitive** = to apologise for what you are going to do, or for current events – *I **am sorry to interrupt** you now but I need your help.*
  be sorry for + ***-ing* form** = to express regret for what has happened – *I **am sorry for interrupting** you yesterday when you were so busy.* (ALSO: I am sorry to have interrupted you.)
- ***be afraid*** + ***to*-infinitive** (the subject is too frightened to do sth) – *He **was afraid to try** to fix the printer because he didn't want to break it.*
  be afraid of + ***-ing* form** (the subject fears that the action expressed by the gerund may happen) – *He **was afraid of breaking** the printer if he tried to fix it.*
- ***be ashamed*** + ***to*-infinitive** (the infinitive refers to a subsequent action) – *She **is ashamed to ask** for help with the assignment; that's why she is putting it off.*
  be ashamed of + ***-ing* form** (the gerund refers to a present or previous action) – *She's **ashamed of deeply offending** her colleague in the plenary session.*
- ***would prefer*** + ***to*-infinitive** (specific preference) – *She **would prefer to review** her notes before the meeting.*
  prefer + ***-ing* form** (general) – *He **prefers taking** notes on a tablet.*
  prefer + ***to*-infinitive** (general) – *He **prefers to take** notes on a tablet.*
- ***can't/couldn't bear*** + ***to*-infinitive** (specific) – *The artist **can't bear to sell** that painting because it's his favourite.*
  can't/couldn't bear + ***-ing* form** (general) – *The sculptor **can't bear selling** works she's not satisfied with.*

Verbs taking infinitive or *-ing* form without a change in meaning

- The verbs ***begin***, ***start***, ***continue***, ***cease***, ***commence*** and ***omit*** can be followed by either a ***to*-infinitive** or an ***-ing* form** without any change in meaning. We normally use the infinitive after the continuous forms of the above verbs. *He **continued writing/to write** the proposal. The lecture theatre **is starting to get** crowded.* (NOT: ~~The lecture theatre is starting getting crowded.~~) *After much study, the mathematician **began understanding/to understand** the theorem.*
- The verbs ***advise***, ***allow***, ***permit*** and ***recommend*** take the ***to*-infinitive** when they are followed by an object or when they are in the passive form. They take the ***-ing* form** when they are not followed by an object. *They advised **us to attend** the conference. We **were advised to attend** the conference. They advise **attending** the conference.*
- The phrase ***sth needs/requires/wants*** is followed by an ***-ing* form** or by a **passive infinitive** in order to show that something is necessary to be done. *This order still **needs completing/to be completed**.*

Infinitive – Gerund (*-ing* form)

1 ★ **Choose the correct item.**

1 Mary had expected the report **to have been completed/to be completing/having been completed** by the end of the week.

2 John denied **being contradicted/having contradicted/to have contradicted** his boss's instructions.

3 I seem **to leave/to having left/to have left** the filing cabinet unlocked by mistake.

4 After **have been bought/having bought/having been bought** by a multinational firm, the company moved its headquarters.

5 Sally confessed to **be having/having/have had** more staff on her project than she needed.

6 I would prefer **being told/having been told/to be told** the whole truth about the new scheme.

7 It's important **liaising/to liaise/to be liaising** with the rest of the team before developing a new product.

8 There's no point **struggling/to be struggling/to struggle** to finish the report if the deadline is too tight; ask for an extension.

2 ★★ **Put the verbs in brackets into the correct infinitive or *-ing* form.**

1 The way I see it, if your job is too far from where you live, you will end up .... **(feel)** exhausted all the time.

2 .... **(invest)** in staff is one way to improve the efficiency of the company, he explained.

3 Duties for the team are .... **(delegate)** by Thomas.

4 We have fallen behind in our payments. In fact, they were to .... **(pay)** several months ago.

5 You are encouraged .... **(provide)** feedback of your user experience to the IT department.

6 Most employees would rather .... **(devote)** their time to further professional development than settle for their current position.

7 .... **(contact)** by competitors already, Terry was aware of the demand for his skills.

8 The injection of capital meant the company avoided .... **(buy)** out by investors.

3 ★★ **Match column A with column B to make correct sentences and put the verbs in brackets into the correct infinitive or *-ing* form.**

A		B	
1 [ ]	Brian had had a lot of errands to run so he really appreciated	a	.... **(accept)** the transfer to the Paris office as he wanted to stay in London.
2 [ ]	Our boss wants help in the office. However, the firm would rather	b	.... **(train)** existing staff than hire new people.
3 [ ]	The assistant manager received many applications after	c	.... **(put)** them into practice so as not to encounter issues again.
4 [ ]	Ellen generally likes to deal with things in person so she can't stand	d	.... **(discuss)** problems in writing over email.
5 [ ]	Once we had written down all the possible solutions, we went on	e	.... **(send)** the information about the vacancy to the recruitment agency.
6 [ ]	I'm afraid Bob is unlikely	f	.... **(have)** the morning off work yesterday.

4 ★★ **Put the verbs in brackets into the correct infinitive or *-ing* form.**

1 A: I regret not .... **(try)** harder on my essay.
B: .... **(be honest)**, I think you could have got an A with a little more effort.

2 A: Mark is anxious after .... **(give)** feedback on his project by his administrator this morning.
B: Well, I'm not surprised. He seems .... **(ignore)** all the advice that he was offered at the start of his project.

3 A: Sorry, Jim, but I left work without .... **(ask)** whether you got that promotion or not.
B: It's OK, and yes, I did! Although it seems that out of all the other candidates I was the last .... **(tell)**!

4 A: Don't stop .... **(call)** the suppliers until they answer.
B: OK, certainly. I'm sorry that I forgot .... **(contact)** them yesterday.

5 A: Make sure that students don't start reading the question paper before .... **(receive)** their answer sheets.
B: Yes, of course. They sometimes find it difficult .... **(resist)** taking a peek!

6 A: Have you finished .... **(distribute)** the minutes from the meeting yesterday?
B: Not yet. I was meant .... **(hand)** them out this afternoon, but I got pulled into an important video conference.

7 A: Will you be so kind as .... **(stay)** a little longer in order to make the corrections I told you about?
B: Of course. I'll make sure I get round to .... **(look)** at them later on.

8 A: Without a university degree the likelihood of him .... **(offer)** a job in marketing is slim.
B: Possibly. Although he appears .... **(have)** lots of experience in sales over the years, so this will definitely work in his favour.

9 A: Has James decided where .... **(go)** to university yet?
B: No, I don't know why he keeps .... **(avoid)** the issue all the time.

5 ★★ Rephrase the sentences using the appropriate form of the infinitive.

1 The courier has been trying to deliver the items for a few weeks now.
The courier seems ....
....

2 Tom's lecturer expects the class to complete their dissertations by Friday.
Their dissertations are expected ....
....

3 The assistant manager is worrying about sales and has asked for more stock.
The assistant manager appears ....
....

4 It was understood that the new IT system was operating very well.
The new IT system was understood ....
....

5 He promised that we will have finished off the design by the end of the day.
The design was promised ....
....

6 They say the project was cancelled by the CEO.
The project is said ....
....

6 ★★ Read the short texts below and put the verbs in brackets into the correct infinitive or *-ing* form.

A The new software update has proved **1)** .... **(be)** even more efficient that the last one. I suggest **2)** .... **(speak)** to the marketing team. Try **3)** .... **(make)** sure they highlight that claim.

B It was very kind of Ian **4)** .... **(provide)** me with an opportunity **5)** .... **(attend)** a work experience seminar. I'm really looking forward to **6)** .... **(take)** part in it!

C **7)** .... **(generate)** interest in new products can be difficult. However, I believe that **8)** .... **(face)** challenges and **9)** .... **(overcome)** them is a very rewarding part of the job.

7 ★★ Rephrase the following sentences making any necessary changes, as in the example.

1 Ann usually comes to the office a few minutes early on Fridays. **(habit)**
Ann is in the habit of coming to the office a few minutes early on Fridays.

2 Advertisers find it very difficult to pitch niche products to the mass market. **(difficulty)**
....

3 John would never imagine being absent from work! **(dare)**
....

4 He needs to sort out the files as soon as possible. **(need)**
....

5 It wasn't my intention to interrupt you while you were working. **(mean)**
....

8 ★★ Put the verbs in brackets into the correct infinitive or *-ing* form.

1 a When the examination starts, you can begin .... **(read)**, but you are not allowed to ask any questions.
b The sales representative's confidence is gradually beginning .... **(improve)**.

2 a The management team proposed .... **(expand)** the business by opening two more stores.
b We propose .... **(finalise)** the blueprints by August.

3 a We were advised .... **(report)** any errors we detected while proofreading the documents.
b I strongly advise .... **(start)** your own family business.

4 a The store is continuing .... **(trade)** during the holiday season.
b The outlet continued .... **(offer)** discounts after regular sales finished.

5 a She dreads .... **(not/be able)** to find a job after university, but I'm sure she'll be fine.
b I would dread .... **(think)** what would happen if my boss were to leave the company.

6 a I understand your .... **(refuse)** to work overtime again tonight; you need some rest.
b The project manager is understood .... **(support)** the new proposals.

9 ★★ Find and correct the mistakes in each sentence.

1 The shop owner is thinking of install security cameras in the store to prevent further thefts.
....
2 It is important being here for the presentation.
....
3 Can you imagine to be offered a job on the other side of the world!
....
4 My boss constantly objects to my wear my casual shirts at work.
....
5 I walked into the station only find that the trains to my office were on strike.
....
6 Jenny is ashamed asking for guidance on her new duties.
....
7 She managed she to finish all her reports in time.
....
8 The discussion was a waste of time; we did nothing but to go over the same things again and again.
....

10 ★ Choose the correct item.

1 The financial advisor admitted .... in favour of the business merger.
A being C to be
B to have been D having been

2 .... an incentive, the employees worked hard to raise productivity levels.
A Being given C Having been given
B To have been given D To be given

3 The traffic is really heavy, so there's no chance of .... on time for the meeting.
A us to arrive C us to be arriving
B our arriving D our being arrived

4 Mark regrets .... more efficiently to get a promotion.
A not to have worked C for not to have worked
B not having worked D not have worked

5 Frankly, I have no time to eat lunch, let alone .... the client!
A to contact C contact
B contacting D to have contacted

6 In the event of fire, workers are advised .... through the fire escapes which can be found on each floor.
A to exiting C exit
B exiting D to exit

11 ★★ Read the text and put the verbs in brackets into the correct infinitive or *-ing* form.

EASY PEASY!

For many people, **1)** .... **(feel)** overwhelmed before an exam is very common. Lately, however, students are lucky enough **2)** .... **(provide)** with a wide variety of hi-tech learning aids, most of which can **3)** .... **(download)** onto a mobile phone or tablet computer. When using these revision apps, study notes must **4)** .... **(enter)** into the software by a student in order to create personalised flashcards. This allows those who have difficulty in **5)** .... **(remember)** key facts to get information in bite sized chunks throughout the day. **6)** .... **(develop)** for many types of modern learners, revision apps also feature mind map and spider gram functions for those who dislike **7)** .... **(rely)** on flashcards alone. Combining different mediums in this way offers students the chance **8)** .... **(tailor)** their approach to their own individual needs. So the next time an exam is round the corner, don't feel lost or postpone **9)** .... **(tackle)** your revision out of fear. **10)** .... **(install)** yourself a study app and take the first step to success!

Key word transformations

12 ★★ For questions 1-4, complete the second sentence so that it has a similar meaning to the first sentence, using the word given. Do not change the word given. You must use between three and eight words, including the word given.

1 I really don't remember saying that James could lead the contract negotiations.
RECOLLECTION
I really ....
allowing James to lead the contract negotiations.

2 It is believed that the two companies have agreed to the deal. **THROUGH**
The two companies ....
.... with the deal.

3 I bet Laura wouldn't take on such a demanding task. **DARE**
I don't ....
such a demanding task.

4 Would you please keep your mobile phone switched off during work hours? **MIND**
Would you ....
.... you are at work?

it

We can use *it*:

- to replace an **infinitive phrase.** ***It***'s *easy to install this software.* (= To install this software is easy.)
- in certain set expressions: ***It seems that***, ***It appears that***, ***It looks like***, ***It is said that***, ***It doesn't matter***, ***It's (high/about) time; It's a shame/pity***, ***It's pointless/It's no good/It's no fun*** + ***-ing*** **form.**
  It's no fun having *impossible deadlines.*
- for emphasis (***It is/It was*** + subject + ***that/who*** ...).
  Although Ann made the suggestion to management, ***it was*** *Lisa* ***who*** *first came up with the idea.*
- as the **preparatory 'it'** after verbs such as ***find***, ***hate***, ***like***, ***love***, ***think***, ***would appreciate***, ***would love***, etc.
  He ***finds it*** *hard to be indoors when the sun is shining. We* ***think it*** *wise to back up the computer system.*
  I ***would appreciate it*** *if you could proofread my essay.*
- for **distance**, **temperature**, **time** and **weather**.
  I can't believe ***it****'s nearly five o'clock!*
  It*'s rather gusty during this period of the year.*
- **to identify people**, especially in informal English.
  *"Who's that?" "****It****'s Irene."*
  "Hello, ***it****'s William here. May I speak to Beth?"*
  Note: In order to say how much money, time or energy is necessary for someone to do an action, we use: ***It takes/took someone*** + ***to*-infinitive**. *It* ***took him*** *two hours* ***to finish*** *the report.*

there

- ***There*** + ***be*** is used for something mentioned for the first time, or to say that someone or something exists.
  There are *twenty emails in my inbox.*
- **Personal pronoun** + ***be*****/other verb** is used to give more details about something or someone already mentioned. ***There is*** *a technician on the factory floor;* ***he is inspecting*** *the machines.*
- Expressions with ***there***: ***there's no point in, there's no need to, there's no reason to, there's no choice but to,*** etc.
  Note: In formal English, especially in literature, ***there*** is used as a subject to verbs such as: ***appear***, ***arise***, ***arrive***, ***come***, ***develop***, ***emerge***, ***enter***, ***exist***, ***follow***, ***grow***, ***happen***, ***lie***, ***live***, ***occur***, ***remain***, ***seem***, ***stand***, etc. *As soon as she looked out at the golden pyramids, there arose inside her a feeling of awe.*

Study the structural conversions:

- It seems that there's something wrong. → *There seems to be something wrong.*
- It's possible there are still free rooms. → *There may still be free rooms.*
- It's certain there'll be somebody to help you. → *There must be someone to help you.*

Future Simple

We use the **future simple** (***will*** + **bare infinitive**):

- for decisions made at the moment of speaking.
  The phone's ringing; ***I'll pick*** *it up.*
- for **predictions** based on what we think, believe or imagine, with the verbs ***think***, ***believe***, ***expect*** etc, the expressions ***be sure***, ***be afraid*** etc, and the adverbs ***probably***, ***certainly***, ***perhaps*** etc.
  Sandra ***will probably get*** *the promotion.*
- for **promises**, **threats**, **warnings**, **requests**, **hopes** and **offers.** *I hope you* ***will forgive*** *me for losing your camera.*
- for actions, events and situations which will definitely happen in the future and which **we can't control**.
  It ***will be*** *winter soon.*
- to express **insistence** and **determination.** *I* ***will keep*** *calling until they answer the phone. He* ***won't come*** *to the meeting.* (He refuses to, he insists on not coming) *No matter how hard they may try, he* ***won't agree*** *with them.*
- in **formal announcements**, often in **news reports** and **weather forecasts.** *The Prime Minister* ***will meet*** *with other European leaders during his state visit.* (But in conversations we would say: *The Prime Minister* ***is going to meet/is meeting*** *other European leaders this afternoon.*) *The rain* ***will persist*** *throughout the weekend.*

Notes:

- ***Will*** is used in all persons.
- We use ***shall we*** to form question tags after structures with ***let's***. *Let's get something to eat,* ***shall we****?*
- We also use ***shall I/shall we*** to ask for advice and instructions, to make offers and suggestions. ***Shall I*** *seek the opinion of an expert?* (asking for advice) – *What* ***shall we*** *do with these papers?* (asking for instructions) – ***Shall I*** *get some sandwiches from the bakery?* (offer) – ***Shall we*** *book a flight before they sell out?* (suggestion)
- The future simple is **never** used after specific time words (***when***, ***as soon as***, ***until***, ***before***, ***after***, ***the moment that***, etc) and after the conditional '***if***' and '***in case***'. Instead, we can use the **present simple** or **present perfect**.

be going to

We use ***be going to***:

- for **plans**, **intentions** or **ambitions.** *Miles says he* ***is going to study*** *law at university.*
- for actions that **we have already decided to do** in the near future. *They* ***are going to have*** *a meeting at eleven o'clock.*
- for **predictions based on what we can see or what we know**, especially when there is evidence that something will happen. *We****'re going to be*** *late; look at all this traffic blocking the road!*

Notes:

- We normally use ***be going to*** to talk about something we intend to do, and ***will*** to give details or make comments about what we have already mentioned.
  *"I****'m going to clean*** *off my desk this morning. I****'ll recycle*** *all my old papers." "That****'ll be*** *good."*
- We normally use the present continuous, rather than ***be going to***, with verbs which express movement, especially the verbs ***go*** and ***come***. *Joyce* ***is going*** *to the stock room in a few minutes. Sienna* ***is coming*** *to the product launch this afternoon.*

The time words/phrases we use with the *future simple* and *be going to* are: tomorrow, the day after tomorrow, tonight, soon, next week/month/year/summer, etc, in a week/month, etc.

Present Simple/Present Continuous (future meaning)

- We can use the **present simple** for future actions when we refer to programmes, timetables, etc. *The train **arrives** in Birmingham at 9:30.*
- We can use the **present continuous** for actions that we have decided and arranged to do in the near future. *I**'m flying** to London on Friday morning.*

Future Continuous

We use the **future continuous** (***will be*** + verb ***-ing***):

- for actions which will be in progress at a stated future time. *This time next week Maya **will be starting** her internship in Berlin.*
- for actions which will definitely happen in the future as a result of a routine or arrangement. *The new advertisement **will be showing** on TV next weekend.*
- when we ask politely about someone's plans for the near future. ***Will** you **be needing** any more help today, sir?*
- for logical assumptions about sb's actions in the present. *He **will be travelling** to the office now.* (It's 8:30 in the morning.)
- for previously planned actions (instead of present continuous). *I**'ll be seeing** Michael this afternoon; would you like me to tell him our plan?*

Future Perfect (*will have* + past participle)

- We use the **future perfect** for actions that will have finished before a stated time in the future. *She **will have finished** writing the report by 6:00.*
- We can also use the **future perfect** to express logical assumptions about the past; that is, to talk about things which we suppose must already have happened. *It's almost 9 o'clock; she**'ll have left** for work by now.* (= I suppose she has left for work.)

  Note: ***Until/till*** are only used in negative sentences. *She **will have submitted** the proposal by tomorrow.* (NOT: … ~~until/till tomorrow~~.) *She **won't have submitted** the proposal **until/till** 2 o'clock.*

The time words/phrases we use with the *future perfect* are: before, by, by then, by the time, until/till (only in negative sentences), etc.

Future Perfect Continuous (*will have been* + verb *-ing*)

We use the **future perfect continuous** to emphasise the duration of an action up to a certain time in the future. The future perfect continuous is used with ***by … for***. ***By** the end of the year, she **will have been working** as a nurse **for** several months.*

Note: We can use the **future simple**, **future continuous** or the **future perfect** to make **predictions** about the present or past, to say what we believe may be happening or have happened.
Study the following examples:

a) *"There's somebody on the phone for you."*
"That will be my mother."
b) *Don't call her now – she'll be sleeping.*
c) *It's seven o' clock; Dad will have left the office by now.*

Time clauses with future reference

We use the **present simple** or **present perfect**, but NOT future forms, with words and expressions such as ***while***, ***before***, ***after***, ***until/till***, ***as***, ***when***, ***whenever***, ***once***, ***as soon as***, ***as long as***, ***by the time***, etc to introduce time clauses. ***By the time** we **finish** lunch, they will have repaired the computers.* (NOT: ~~By the time we will finish~~ …)
We also use the **present simple** or **present perfect**, but NOT future forms, after words and expressions such as ***unless***, ***if***, ***suppose/supposing***, ***in case***, etc. *Call an accountant **if** you **need** help with your taxes.* (NOT: …~~if you will need help with your taxes~~.)
We use **future forms** with:

- ***when*** when it is used as a question word. ***When will** they **be hiring** a new laboratory technician?*
- ***if/whether*** after expressions which show uncertainty/ignorance, etc, such as ***I don't know***, ***I doubt***, ***I wonder***, ***I'm not sure***, etc. *I **doubt if** these jewellery designs **will be** popular with customers.*

Other future forms

be + ***to*-infinitive** is used to express:

- formal arrangements/scheduled events. *Marissa **is to join** the graphic design department in May.*
- instructions/orders. *You **are to turn off** all the lights and lock up before you leave.*
- prohibitions (in negations). *You **are not to eat** or drink in the meeting room.*

Notes:

- ***Be*** + ***to*-infinitive** is used to express plans and agreements in a formal way, especially in news reports. *The Queen **is to open** the new university library next week.*
- ***Be*** + ***to*-infinitive** can replace the present/past simple in the ***if*-clauses** of type 1/2 conditionals. ***If** we **are to get** there on time, we must take the car. Tina knew well that **if** she **was to pass** the exam, she would have to read everything on the reading list.*

be due to + **infinitive** is used to express something that is expected to happen at a particular time. It is often used with timetables. *The Smiths **are due to arrive** in half an hour. The train to Manchester **is due to depart** at 6:15.*

be about to + **infinitive/*be on the point of/be on the verge of*** + ***-ing*** **form** are used to talk about actions that will take place in the immediate future. *The video conference **is about to be cancelled**. The video conference **is on the verge / on the point of being cancelled**.*

***be bound to/be sure to/be certain to* + infinitive** are used to talk about actions which are almost certain to happen in the future. *They **are bound/sure/certain to win** the contest because they have been working really hard.*

The future in the past

We use the following patterns to talk about things which we intended to do, or plans we had for the future, but which didn't happen.

a) ***was to/was going to/was about to/was due to* + infinitive** *He **was going to go** to medical school, but he didn't get a scholarship.* (So he didn't go.)

Notes:

- ***was to*** can also be followed by a **perfect infinitive.** *He **was to have visited** his uncle but he was taken ill.*
- ***was to* + infinitive** can also describe actions which were destined to happen. *When she decided to take the job in Germany, she couldn't imagine that she **was to remain** there for a decade.*

b) ***was on the point of* + *-ing* form** *He **was on the point of accepting** the job offer when he received a better one.* (So he didn't accept it.)

It/There

13 ★ **Fill in:** *there* **or** *it***.**

1 .... is a note on the table for you. It's from Patricia.
2 .... is time you stopped acting so irresponsibly in the workplace!
3 .... is no need to do an internship while studying if you haven't decided what field of work you want to follow.
4 As soon as he saw the firm's new skyscraper, ... arose inside him a feeling of awe.
5 In fact, ... was Karen who invited us to the trade fair.
6 Surely .... must be someone who can help you with your workload.
7 I would appreciate .... if you could present the latest initiative to our staff.
8 .... seems to be a misunderstanding. I haven't received an email on this subject.
9 I'm afraid .... is no choice but to announce the date of the conference before we've confirmed the speakers.
10 .... is time we got rid of all these old pamphlets in the office.
11 .... is no point in installing the software update; our current version works absolutely fine.
12 .... appears that the printers haven't produced enough delegate packs for the conference yet.

Future tenses

14 ★ **Underline the correct future forms.**

1 It's past midday, so I assume Tony **will probably have arrived/will probably arrive/is probably arriving** at the venue by now.
2 Make sure you speak to Mr Johnson before he **will have started/will start/starts** his meeting.
3 This time next year, a lot of new graduates **will have applied/will have been applying/will be applying** for jobs.
4 What time **will you be leaving/will you leave/will you have left** for the office? I was wondering if I could get a lift.
5 This time next month, Jo **will have been working/will work/will be working** in the sales department for almost a year.
6 I'm sure that the bank **shall reply/will reply/is going to reply** to your request shortly.
7 It's worth asking Mr Jones for help, in case he **will have/is having/has** some free time later this afternoon.
8 It was agreed that Mrs Stevens **will take over/is going to take over/is taking over** as senior manager.
9 Jen **is holding/will hold/will have held** interviews for a new assistant on Tuesday morning.
10 I doubt whether our professor **will allow/will be allowing/is allowing** us to leave early today.

15 ★★ **Choose the correct item and put the verbs in brackets into the correct future form.**

1 I promise I .... **(call)** you **after/as long as** I reach the office.
2 He .... **(make)** his decision to apply for the job **as soon as/while** he has read through all the other vacancies on the website.
3 You can't enter the building **unless/as long as** they .... **(give)** you permission.
4 You .... **(get)** a pay rise **provided/supposing** that you work harder.
5 The nurse .... **(call out)** your name **while/when** the interview panel is ready to see you.
6 My colleagues .... **(leave)** the office **by the time/until** I arrive at work.
7 **If/Unless** you need assistance .... **(not/hesitate)** to call technical support.
8 I **doubt/suppose** if he .... **(manage)** to get into work on time; the trains are badly delayed.

16 ★★ **For each pair of sentences choose the verb that fits best in each gap. Then put it in the correct future form.**

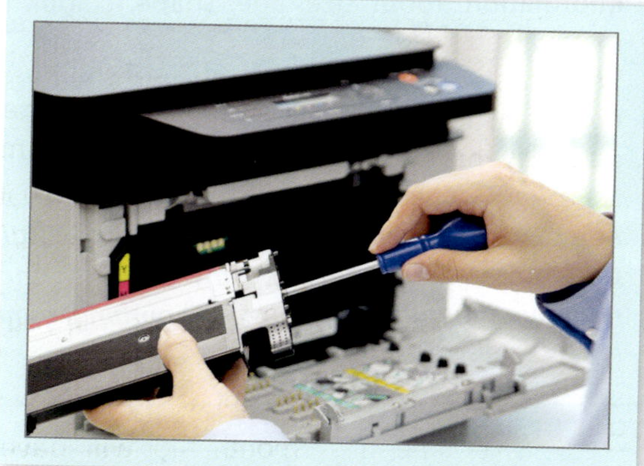

1 **remove/install**
  a The IT department .... all the old printers by Saturday.
  b Don .... the latest version of the software on Friday afternoon.
2 **qualify/meet**
  a The auditor .... with the company's representatives at 4 pm tomorrow.
  b By the time Mr Jones has completed his business degree, he .... as a financial advisor.
3 **start/apply**
  a All students must be at the exam centre not later than 8:30 as the exam .... at 9:00.
  b When I graduate I .... for an internship at the local hospital.

Other future forms / The future in the past

17 ★★ **Underline the correct future form.**

1 Laura **was on the point of/was due to** changing courses at university when her tutor persuaded her not to.
2 Newspapers report that universities in the area **are to/are certain to** offer more courses next term.
3 Ever since he left school Mark knew he **was bound to/was to** spend the rest of his life in academia.
4 The company **is on the verge of/is about to** being taken over by a foreign investor.
5 Helen **was sure to/was going to** apply for the research grant, but missed the deadline for submissions.

18 ★★ **Read the email and choose the correct item.**

REPLY MAIL

Hi Peter,

I seem to be having problems with my project and I don't know how to proceed. **1) Shall I seek/Will I seek/Should I have been seeking** the opinion of one of our supervisors? Or do you think I **2) am going to end up/will end up/am ending up** looking rather foolish? I'm just worried that everyone **3) will have given/will have been given/will be giving** Mr Hendrix their proposals before me, and this is my big chance to make a good impression. Maybe I worry too much, but by the end of the week I **4) will prepare/will have prepared/will have been preparing** this project for nearly two months, and I'm no closer to a solution. I **5) 'll be going over/go over/'ll have been going over** the figures with Ted again at five o'clock but I'm not confident that he understands the issues either. As they reminded us in the meeting today, phase one **6) was to end/is to end/is bound to end** this July as scheduled... so time is really running out! What do you think? Should I swallow my pride and ask for help?

Please get back to me as soon as you can,
Jackie

Key word transformations

19 ★★ **For questions 1-4, complete the second sentence so that it has a similar meaning to the first sentence, using the word given. Do not change the word given. You must use between three and eight words, including the word given.**

1 I was just about to post the meeting papers when Mr Erikson asked for an amendment.
POINT
I was ....
when Mr Erikson asked for an amendment.

2 It was very kind of you to let us know about the change in meeting room.
APPRECIATE
We ....
about the change in meeting room.

3 This team is certain to make a lot of sales.
DOUBT
There ....
a lot of sales.

4 The company wants to break into the European market so they are sending reps to Berlin and Paris. **VIEW**
The company is sending reps to Berlin and Paris ....
the European market.

Adjectives

Adjectives describe nouns. They have the same form in the singular and plural. They go before nouns (e.g. *a **small** house*) but after the verbs ***be***, ***look***, ***smell***, ***sound***, ***feel***, ***taste***, ***seem***, ***appear***, ***become***, ***get***, ***stay***, etc. *She had a talk with the rebellious students about their behaviour.*
The vessel appeared seaworthy for the journey.

- Most common adjectives (***large***, ***long***, ***heavy***, ***late***, etc) do not have a particular ending. However, there are certain endings (suffixes) for adjectives which are formed from nouns and verbs. These are:
  -able (predictable), ***-al*** (practical), ***-an*** (republican), ***-ant*** (observant), ***-ar*** (polar), ***-ary*** (honorary), ***-ate*** (passionate), ***-en*** (wooden), ***-ent*** (dependent), ***-eous*** (courteous), ***-ese*** (Chinese), ***-ful*** (remorseful), ***-fold*** (twofold), ***-ial*** (racial), ***-ian*** (Darwinian), ***-ible*** (sensible), ***-ic*** (dramatic), ***-ical*** (economical), ***-(i)ous*** (dangerous, vicious), ***-ish*** (selfish), ***-ite*** (socialite), ***-ive*** (reactive), ***-less*** (mindless), ***-like*** (man-like), ***-ly*** (homely), ***-proof*** (waterproof), ***-some*** (lonesome), ***-uble*** (soluble), ***-ward*** (homeward), ***-worthy*** (noteworthy), ***-y*** (funny), etc.
  *The actor received an **honorary** degree from the university in acknowledgment of his work for equal rights.*
  *Sandra is a very **observant** woman who never misses anything that happens around her.*
- The prefixes used to form adjectives are:
  a- (asocial), ***ab-*** (abnormal), ***ante-*** (antenatal), ***anti-*** (anticlockwise), ***be-*** (bejewelled), ***bi-*** (bilingual), ***co-*** (cooperative), ***col-*** (collateral), ***con-*** (contextual), ***cor-*** (correlative), ***counter-*** (counterproductive), ***dis-*** (discontent), ***eco-*** (eco-friendly), ***extra-*** (extraterrestrial), ***geo-*** (geometric), ***hyper-*** (hypersensitive), ***il-*** (illegal), ***im-*** (impossible), ***in-*** (incredible), ***inter-*** (international), ***ir-*** (irrational), ***mal-*** (malnourished), ***mid-*** (midway), ***mono-*** (monolingual), ***multi-*** (multicultural), ***neo-*** (neolithic), ***non-*** (non-violent), ***omni-*** (omnipotent), ***over-*** (overexcited), ***out-*** (outlandish), ***pan-*** (pan-American), ***photo-*** (photosensitive), ***poly-*** (polysyllabic), ***post-*** (postnatal), ***pre-*** (prepacked), ***pro-*** (pro-government), ***pseudo-*** (pseudointellectual), ***quasi-*** (quasi-scientific), ***retro-*** (retrograde), ***self-*** (self-catering), ***semi-*** (semi-precious), ***sub-*** (subterranean), ***super-*** (superconfident), ***sur-*** (surrealistic), ***trans-*** (transatlantic), ***ultra-*** (ultrasonic), ***un-*** (unappreciated), ***under-*** (underprivileged), ***uni-*** (unilateral), ***up-*** (uplifting), etc.
  *His document was **irretrievable** so we created a new one.*
  *We will have to change all **prearranged** meetings for another date.*
- There are also **compound adjectives** which are formed with: a) ***present participles*** e.g. *a never-ending journey*, b) **past participles** e.g. *brightly-coloured garments*, c) **cardinal numbers + nouns** e.g. *a three-hour delay* (NOT ~~a three hours delay~~) d) ***well/badly/ill/poorly*** **+ past participle** e.g. *well-behaved children, badly-made furniture, an ill-equipped army*
- There are **opinion adjectives** and **fact adjectives**. Opinion adjectives (*a mediocre performance*, etc) show what a person thinks of somebody or something. Fact adjectives (*an ancient relic*, etc) give us factual information about size, age, shape, colour, origin, material, etc.
- We can also use **nouns as adjectives** before other nouns. When nouns are used as adjectives, they generally have no plural form. *college students, a television programme*
- Adjectives are always placed after the indefinite pronouns ***someone/body***, ***anyone/body***, ***no-one/nobody***, ***something***, ***anything*** and ***nothing***. *something larger, someone neutral*

Order of adjectives

When there are two or more adjectives in a sentence, they normally go in the following order:

	OPINION	FACT							
		size	age	shape	colour	origin	material	used for/ be about	noun
It's a	lovely	big	new	square	brown	Swiss	plastic	alarm	clock.

- We do not usually use a long list of adjectives before a single noun. A noun is usually described by one, two or three adjectives at the most. *He is a **well-known American horror** author.*
- Ordinal numbers (***first***, ***second***, ***third***, etc) go before cardinal numbers (***one***, ***two***, ***three***, etc). *the **first five** days*
- The adjectives ***ablaze***, ***afloat***, ***afraid***, ***aghast***, ***ajar***, ***alight***, ***alike***, ***alive***, ***alone***, ***aloof***, ***ashamed***, ***asleep***, ***averse***, ***awake***, ***aware***, ***content***, ***fond***, ***glad***, ***ill***, ***involved***, ***pleased***, ***sure***, etc are never followed by a noun. *The CEO was **absent** from the meeting.*
- The adjectives ***chief***, ***eastern***, ***elder***, ***eldest***, ***former***, ***indoor***, ***inner***, ***lower***, ***main***, ***northern***, ***only***, ***outdoor***, ***outer***, ***principal***, ***southern***, ***western***, ***upper*** etc are always followed by nouns. *His **inner circle** consisted of **former politicians** and activists.*
- Certain adjectives take a slightly different sense when they precede or follow the noun they modify: **the visible stars** (= all the stars that can be seen), **the stars visible** (= the stars seen at a specific time), **the present students** (= all those who have enrolled for the current academic year), **the students present** (= those who are attending a lecture now)
  *The **man concerned*** (= involved/affected) *is my father.*
  *A **concerned*** (= worried) *father asked about student safety on campus.*
  However, there are some standardised phrases where the adjectives follow the nouns: ***attorney general***, ***body politic***, ***court martial***, ***God Almighty***, ***heir apparent***, ***notary public***, ***poet laureate***, ***secretary general***, ***the president elect***.
- Certain adjectives are used with ***the*** as nouns to refer to groups of people in general. These are: ***blind***, ***dead***, ***deaf***, ***disabled***, ***elderly***, ***homeless***, ***hungry***, ***living***,

middle-aged*, *old*, *poor*, *rich*, *sick*, *strong*, *unemployed*, *weak*, *young, etc. *The building is equipped with facilities for **the disabled**.*

Notes:

- **Present** and **past participles** can be used as **adjectives**. Present participles describe the quality of a noun. *annoying behaviour* (What kind of behaviour? Annoying.) Past participles describe how the subject feels. *an annoyed teacher* (How does the teacher feel? Annoyed.)
- Nouns describing **materials, substances, purpose, use** and **origin** can be used as adjectives, but they **do not have comparative** or **superlative forms** and **cannot be modified** by ***very***. *a cotton shirt, a silver brooch, a stone wall, a gold necklace, a summer dress, a chopping board* (**BUT** *a wooden table* [NOT ~~*wood table*~~]), *a woollen hat* [NOT ~~*wool hat*~~], *a London accent*
  However, if an adjective of origin refers to behaviour, it can be modified by ***very***. *Lucio is **very Italian**.*
  Also, there are adjectives which are derived from nouns describing materials (*silk, stone, gold, feather, metal*, etc). These **adjectives** can be used metaphorically: *silky skin* (= skin that is smooth and soft, like silk), **BUT** *a silk shirt* (= a shirt made of silk); *a stony face* (= a cold, emotionless face), **BUT** *a stone fence* (= a fence made of stone); *golden hair* (= hair the colour of gold), **BUT** *a gold ring* (= a ring made of gold); *feathery leaves* (= leaves that are soft and delicate), **BUT** *a feather pillow* (= a pillow made with feathers); *a metallic colour* (= a colour which looks like metal), **BUT** *a metal gate* (= a gate made of metal).
- There are certain adverbs, such as ***above***, ***downstairs***, ***inside***, ***outside***, ***upstairs***, etc which can be used as adjectives. *an upstairs room, the downstairs bathroom, the above rule, the inside page*
- Commas are only used to separate adjectives which convey similar information; they are never used between the final adjective and the noun it modifies. *a brilliant, eccentric, French writer* (NOT ~~*a brilliant, eccentric, French, writer*~~) *a long(,) distinguished career – a rare(,) colourful bird*

Adjectives

1 ★ **Write the adjectives made from the following words.**

1 observe ....
2 rust ....
3 honour ....
4 depend ....
5 access ....
6 economy ....
7 mind ....

2 ★★ **Make compound adjectives to describe the following.**

1 A journey that seems like it doesn't end.
A .... journey.
2 A teacher with good qualifications.
A .... teacher.
3 A drive of five hours duration.
A .... drive.
4 A product that has been made badly.
A .... product.
5 An article with five pages.
A .... article.

3 ★★ **Fill in the gaps with the items in the correct order.**

1 Jessica is going to a(n) .... **(autumn/fantastic/annual)** festival on Saturday.
2 William's car is a(n) .... **(Italian/red/classic)** Ferrari from the late 80s.
3 The .... **(three/first)** days of the conference were the most interesting.
4 Ian's proposal covered all the .... **(areas/main)** of discussion.
5 The .... **(present/students)** in the seminar room were involved in a discussion about social issues.

4 ★★ **Choose the correct item(s).**

1 Helen runs therapy sessions at the shelter for **the homeless/homeless**.
2 Your food is outside on the **wood/wooden** table in the garden.
3 Angela's youngest son has long **gold/golden** blonde hair.
4 This is such a **badly-produced/bad-produced** report; revise it and resubmit it.
5 The **concerned man/man concerned** lives at number ten Downston Avenue.
6 **The building is ablaze/The ablaze building is**; I don't think the fire brigade will be able to save it.
7 The actress was wearing a stunning long **silky/silk** dress.
8 The lake looked magnificent in the **gold/golden** sunlight.
9 These **vibrantly-coloured/vibrantly-colour** fabrics are amazing! They're so beautiful!
10 Jenny visited her cousins in their **summery/summer** house in Majorca.

Adverbs

- **Adverbs** describe verbs, past participles, adjectives or other adverbs. *Susan was **extremely** pleased with her exam results.*
- An **adverb** can be one word *(She described the process **explicitly**.)*, two words (an adverbial phrase) *(She described the process **this morning**.)* or a prepositional phrase which functions as an adverb in a sentence *(She described the process **at the meeting**.)* Adverbs can express manner (***how***), place (***where***), time (***when***), frequency (***how often***), degree (***to what extent***), etc.
- **Adverbs** can also function as linking words, especially at the beginning of sentences e.g. ***firstly***, ***secondly***, ***moreover***, etc.

Formation of adverbs

- We usually form an adverb by adding ***-ly*** to the adjective. *effectively*
- Adjectives ending in ***-le*** drop the ***-e*** and take ***-y***. *reasonably*
- Adjectives ending in a consonant + ***-y*** drop the ***-y*** and take ***-ily***. *noisily*
- Adjectives ending in ***-l*** take ***-ly***. *bashfully*
- Adjectives ending in ***-ic*** usually take ***-ally***. *dramatic – dramatically* **BUT** *public – publicly*
- The adjectives ending in ***-ly*** (*deadly, elderly, friendly, likely, lively, lonely, lovely, silly, ugly,* etc) form their adverbs with the phrase ***in a ... way/manner/fashion***. *She speaks to all employees **in a friendly manner**.*
- There are certain adverbs which have the same form as their adjectives: ***best, better, big, cheap*****, ***clean, clear*****, ***close, cold, daily, dead, dear*****, ***dirty, early, extra, far, fast, fine*****, ***further, hourly, inside, kindly, long, loud*****, ***low, monthly, past, quick*****, ***quiet*****, ***right, slow, straight, sure, thin*****, ***thick, tight, weekly, well, yearly***, etc. *She was an **early** riser. She woke up **early**.* The adverbs with the asterisk (*) can also occur with the ***-ly*** suffix without a difference in meaning, but then they are more formal. *I bought it **cheap**.* (informal) *I bought it **cheaply**.* (formal)

The adverbs below have two forms, each with a different meaning:

- **deep** = a long way down *She dived **deep** into the sea.*
  deeply = greatly *She **deeply** regretted telling her secret to him.*
- **direct** = by the shortest route *The airline flies **direct** to New York.*
  directly = immediately *The meeting starts **directly** after school.*
- **easy** = gently and slowly *After the accident, Mike took it **easy** for a while.*
  easily = without difficulty *He will **easily** find a job with all his experience.*
- **free** = without cost *At this restaurant children under seven can eat **free**.*
  freely = willingly *The witness spoke **freely** about the accident.*
- **full** = definitely, very *He knew **full** well what had happened but didn't say anything.*
  fully = completely *He **fully** explained the problem to us.*
- **hard** = with much effort/force *He fell **hard** onto the ground.*
  hardly = scarcely *He **hardly** spoke to anyone because he was so upset.*
- **high** = at/to a high level *The boxes were stacked **high** to the ceiling.*
  highly = very much *Mr Keller is **highly** skilled.*
- **last** = after all others *He finished **last** in the race.*
  lastly = finally ***Lastly**, we spoke about how to improve sales.*
- **late** = not early *We arrived **late** at the opera.*
  lately = recently *We have had some problems **lately** with our computer.*
- **near** = close *I always walk to work as it's quite **near**.*
  nearly = almost *I **nearly** missed the bus.*
- **short** = without reaching sth *The plane came down **short** of the runway, landing on the grass first.*
  shortly = soon *The presentation will start **shortly**.*
- **pretty** = fairly *I'm **pretty** sure that I turned off the lights when I left, but I'm not certain.*
  prettily = in a pretty way *Everyone noticed the **prettily** dressed woman across the room.*
- **wide** = off-target *The footballer's shot went **wide** and missed the goal.*
  widely = to a large extent *It is **widely** known that the economy is in trouble.*
- **wrong** = incorrectly *He tied the knot **wrong** and was asked to redo it.*
  wrongly = unjustly (before verbs and past participles) *He was **wrongly** accused of the crime.*

Order of adverbs

Adverbs can be placed at the front, in the middle or at the end of a sentence (or clause).

When they are placed in the middle of the sentence:

- they go between the subject and the main verb. ***They frequently attend** meetings. Do **they frequently attend** meetings?*
- But when the main verb is 'be', the adverb is placed after it (except in cases of emphasis). *Our manager **is frequently** in meetings. (Our manager **frequently is** in meetings.)*
- If there is more than one verb, adverbs go after the first auxiliary or modal verb. *We **don't frequently** attend meetings. We **must frequently** be informed of progress.*

Adverbs of frequency (***occasionally***, ***rarely***, ***scarcely***, ***never***, ***always***, ***hardly ever***, etc) are usually (but not always) placed in the middle of the sentence. *He **rarely argues**.*
Adverbs of manner (***carefully***, ***quickly***, ***impatiently***, etc), **place** (***down***, ***inside***, ***there***, ***in the park***, etc) and **time** (***now***, ***then***, ***today***, ***this month***, etc) are usually (but not always) placed after the object (if there is one) or at the end of a sentence or clause. Sometimes they are placed in the middle if the object is very long, or at the beginning for emphasis.

*The teacher spoke to the children **firmly**.*
*The teacher spoke to the children **firmly** even though she was not angry.*
*The teacher **firmly** spoke to the children who had broken the window.*
*She argued with her brother **yesterday**. **Yesterday**, she argued with her brother.*
Note: if an adverb is modifying an adjective or other adverb, it is placed in front of the word it is modifying.

When there are two or more adverbs in the same sentence,
- they usually go in the following order: manner – place – time. *The children waited **impatiently at the bus stop after school**.*
- if there is a verb of movement, such as ***go***, ***come*** and ***leave***, in the sentence, the adverbs usually go in the following order: place-manner-time. *I **went there quickly this morning**.*

Intensifiers

Intensifiers are adverbs or adverbial phrases which are used to further modify adjectives, adverbs, verbs or clauses.
The most common intensifier is ***very***. We can use it before adjectives, adjective + noun and adverbs.

We can also repeat it for extra emphasis. *The film was **very very** bad.* **BUT** we don't use ***very*** with strong adjectives, such as ***enormous***, ***furious***, ***disgusting***, etc. *He was **furious** with me.* (NOT: ~~He was very furious with me.~~)
We can also use some adjectives (***absolute***, ***utter***, ***total***, ***complete***, ***perfect***, ***real***) as intensifiers with nouns. *That is **utter** nonsense!*

Intensifiers fall into three categories:
- **emphasisers** put general emphasis on the item they modify: *actually, certainly, clearly, definitely, frankly, for certain, for sure, honestly, indeed, just, literally, obviously, of course, plainly, really, simply, surely.*
  *We were **simply** amazed by his performance.*
- **amplifiers** increase the intensity of the modified item: *absolutely, a good/great deal, a lot, altogether, awfully, badly, by far, categorically, completely, deeply, entirely, extremely, fully, greatly, heartily, in all respects, particularly, perfectly, quite, so terribly, thoroughly, totally, utterly, (very) much, most, violently, vitally, well.*
  *He **thoroughly** examined the evidence.*
- **downtoners** decrease the intensity of the modified item: *a bit, a little, a little bit, all but, almost, as good as (= almost), at all, barely, conceivably, fairly, hardly, in part, in the least, more or less, nearly, not much, partly, possibly, practically, pretty, quite, rather, scarcely, slightly, somewhat, to some extent, virtually.*
  *We understood **to some extent** what he was saying.*

Certain **intensifier-adjective combinations** have become collocations:

absolutely	brilliant/fantastic/fed up/marvellous/ ridiculous
deeply	ashamed/depressed/disappointed/ disturbed/hurt/involved/moving/worried
abundantly	clear
completely	empty/full/lost/new/open/unreasonable/ wrong
utterly	hopeless/ludicrous/useless
greatly	changed/impressed/mistaken
downright	rude
fully	aware/conscious
just	perfect/right
wholly	inadequate
highly	motivated

The most common intensifiers are ranked below in order of intensity:

	very (+++)	rather (++)	a little (+)
with adjectives, adverbs and verbs	absolutely, awfully, just, really, terribly, totally, simply *Kate **absolutely** hates romance films.*	quite, rather *It's **quite** warm outside.*	a bit, a little *The soup is **a little** cold.*
with adjectives and adverbs	very, extremely *Mr Brown is a **really** kind person.*	fairly, pretty *She can speak Spanish **fairly** well.*	slightly *Turn the camera **slightly** to the left.*
with verbs and the comparative degree	much, a lot *Tom's house is **a lot** smaller than mine.*	rather *The test was **rather** easier than what we had expected.*	not much *They do **not** go out **much** at the weekends.*

Quite – Rather – Fairly/Pretty

- ***Quite*** (= fairly, to some degree) is used in favourable comments. *He's **quite** good at tennis.* It is placed before '***a/an***'. *He's **quite a** successful businessman.*
  Quite (= completely, totally) is used with strong and non-gradable adjectives such as: ***alone***, ***amazing***, ***brilliant***, ***certain***, ***different***, ***dreadful***, ***exhausted***, ***extraordinary***, ***false***, ***horrible***, ***impossible***, ***perfect***, ***ridiculous***, ***right***, ***sure***, ***true***, ***useless***, etc.
  *It's **quite certain** he's committed the crime. I'm **quite sure** he hasn't told us the truth.*
- ***Rather*** is used: **a)** in unfavourable comments. *She's **rather** bad at Maths.* **b)** in favourable comments meaning 'to an unusual degree'. *The meeting was **rather** interesting.* (= it was more interesting than what we had expected), and **c)** with the comparative degree. *She's **rather taller** than me.* ***Rather*** is placed before or after '***a/an***'. *It's **a rather cold day/rather a cold day**.* (= more than usual, more than wanted, expected, etc)
- ***Fairly*** and ***pretty*** are synonymous with ***quite*** and ***rather***. They are placed after '***a***'. *She's **a fairly/pretty** hardworking person.*

Adverbs

5 ★★ Fill in each gap with an adverb formed from the words in brackets.

1 This new app works more .... than the last one. **(effective)**
2 Denise has been speaking .... about her experiences for some time. **(public)**
3 The girls argue so .... when they fall out. **(noise)**
4 Kelly looked at Karen .... when she mentioned they might go out. **(hopeful)**
5 Kevin always interacts with people .... fashion. **(lively)**
6 Ian spoke .... about Martin when he heard we were his parents. **(kind)**
7 You can't .... expect Steve to drop everything whenever you ask. **(reasonable)**
8 Julie was .... grumpy after missing her train. **(awful)**

6 ★★ Complete each sentence using an adverb from the list.

• near • wrongly • high • wrong • fully • highly • full • nearly • direct • directly

1 I .... forgot about Jeff's birthday! Thank you for reminding me.
2 Larry set up his website .... and had to get someone to fix it.
3 If we park .... the shops, we won't have to walk.
4 Ben was .... perceived as aloof when he was just very shy.
5 The company needs .... skilled workers for the new factory.
6 Paul knew .... well that he should have bought the bus ticket in advance.
7 The lecture in the main hall started .... after lunch.
8 Bob had some difficulty .... understanding what Jim wanted.
9 The folders that you want are stored .... on the shelf.
10 That train goes .... to the city centre.

Order of adverbs

7 ★ Underline and identify the types of adverbs in each sentence.

1 Mark scarcely talks to Tim anymore; they've really grown apart. ....
2 Victor stormed off impatiently when he didn't get what he wanted. ....
3 Fiona met her friends for a coffee and a chat yesterday. ....
4 Sensing the tension, Rob chose his words carefully. ....
5 I don't walk to work often, just occasionally. ....
6 Jason hardly ever works at weekends; this Saturday is a one off. ....
7 We rarely see students in the office outside of work experience. ....
8 Are you visiting your relatives in New York this month? ....

8 ★★ Put the adverbs in brackets in the sentences in the correct order.

1 People who take the time to relax have a better quality of life than those that don't.
(usually/unsurprisingly/regularly)
....
2 Martin consoled Margaret.
(at home/last night/late)
....
3 I left work when Nicky called me to ask for my help.
(this afternoon/politely/quickly)
....
4 Bill raised his concerns to Jack following the meeting.
(last night/discreetly/in the café)
....
5 The company will refurbish the office facilities.
(this year/at our head office/entirely)
....
6 Rather than run, we decided to wait for the next bus.
(at the bus stop/patiently/after school).
....
7 Maria explained the situation to the rest of the team.
(before lunch/in the seminar room/calmly)
....

Intensifiers

9 a) ★ **Match the columns to form collocations.**

1	just	a	rude
2	fully	b	clear
3	wholly	c	perfect
4	downright	d	conscious
5	abundantly	e	inadequate

b) ★★ **Use the collocations from Ex. 9a to complete the sentences.**

1 He's the ideal candidate; he's .... for the position that we have available.
2 What you said was ....; I suggest that you apologise.
3 Mark rapidly became .... after the sedative wore off following his treatment.
4 Mina doesn't mince words; if she disagrees with you, it will be ....
5 I'm sorry, but your solution is ....; and doesn't address my concerns at all!

Quite – Rather – Fairly/Pretty

10 ★ **Choose the correct item.**

1 Karen is **fairly/a fairly/fairly a** successful public speaker.
2 I felt **rather/fairly/quite** alone when I lived overseas; I was extremely homesick.
3 The seminar was **rather/quite/very** eye-opening; I didn't expect it to be so good.
4 Excuse me, but what you just said is **rather/quite/fairly** ridiculous! That's totally wrong!
5 James is **rather/quiet/pretty** better at managing difficult customers than Jude.
6 This book is **quite/quite an/a quite** interesting; it has a lot of novel ideas.
7 Mediating in disputes can be **a quite/a pretty/pretty a** stressful job.
8 This is **quite a/quite/a quite** useless invention; it hardly even works!
9 Mark talks **fairly/pretty/rather** too much.
10 This task was **very/quite/rather** impossible.

11 ★★ **Read the text and use the adverbs in the list to fill in the gaps.**

• courageously • badly • quickly • direct
• this day • quite • highly • entirely

A miracle that led to an incredible friendship

The 20th of December 1943 would be a day that would stay in young pilot Charles Brown's memory forever. On **1)** ...., Brown and his crew experienced a remarkable act of kindness from a young German fighter pilot that defies belief. With his plane **2)** .... damaged and unaccompanied, the American was **3)** .... sure that his opponent would move in for the kill. However, when Franz Stigler locked eyes with Brown, the American saw compassion not anger. Instead of attacking, Stigler nodded and set a **4)** .... course alongside the wounded plane. Stigler **5)** .... escorted the Americans through German territory so that his own forces would not attack. As they reached the North Sea, the young German pilot saluted Brown and **6)** .... left at once for Germany. This **7)** .... unusual story doesn't end there. Nearly 50 years later the two men met face to face to share their amazing memories and forge **8)** .... an extraordinary friendship that would last for the rest of their lives.

Key word transformations

12 ★★ **For questions 1-5, complete the second sentence so that is has a similar meaning to the first sentence, using the word given. Do not change the word given. You must use between three and eight words, including the word given.**

1 Martin was behaving very generously with his money. **WAY**
Martin was behaving ....
.... with his money.
2 Erica couldn't understand the reason for Janet's strange reaction to what was said at the meeting yesterday. **WHY**
Erica couldn't understand ....
...... to what was said at the meeting yesterday.
3 He performs well and the crowd loves him. **RATHER**
He's ....
and the crowd loves him.
4 Natalie visits the local cultural centre frequently. **FREQUENT**
Natalie is ....
local cultural centre.
5 'It doesn't take a moment to consider other people's feelings,' said Jack kindly. **HARDLY**
'Considering other people's feelings ....
.... all,' said Jack kindly.

Gradable & Non-gradable adjectives

The majority of adjectives can either be **gradable** or **non-gradable**, depending on the meaning they have. **Gradable adjectives** are those that we can grade in some way on a scale of differing degree.

Note: Native speakers frequently treat non-gradable adjectives as if they are gradable:

- either because the adjective has acquired a second weaker meaning ('unique' means there is only one – non-gradable – *Every human being is unique;* or it can also mean 'unusual' which becomes gradable *Nina was wearing **the most unique** shoes I have ever seen.*)
- or because they are breaking the rules for effect, irony or as a literary device. *All animals are equal but some are **more equal** than others.*

In formal contexts, however, using non-gradable adjectives as gradable should be avoided.

Non-gradable adjectives are the following:

- those describing **materials**, **substances**, **purpose**, **use** and **origin** (see p. GR11).
- those describing **qualities**, such as ***absolute***, ***correct***, ***equal***, ***left***, ***right***, ***single***, etc. *The calculations were correct.* (NOT: ~~The calculations were most correct~~.)
- the adverbs used as adjectives (see p. GR12).
- the adjectives ***afraid***, ***alike***, ***alive***, ***alone***, etc (see p. GR11).
- the adjectives ***chief***, ***indoor***, ***northern***, etc (see p. GR11).

These adjectives can be modified by intensifiers (see p. GR13).

Comparisons

We use the **comparative** to compare one person or thing with another. We use the **superlative** to compare one person or thing with more than one person or thing of the same group. We also use it to show that one person or thing is the best of their type. We often use ***than*** after a comparative and ***the*** before a superlative. *This offer is **more competitive than** the other. She is **the most competitive** in the team.*

Formation of comparatives and superlatives of adjectives and adverbs:

- to one-syllable adjectives we add ***-e(r)*** to form the comparative and ***-e(st)*** to form the superlative. *older, oldest*

Note: In one-syllable adjectives ending in **a vowel + a consonant**, we double the consonant. *thinner, thinnest*

- to two-syllable adjectives ending in ***-ly***, ***-y***, ***-w*** we also add ***-er***/***-est***. *shallower, shallowest*

Note: In adjectives ending in **a consonant + *y***, we replace the ***-y*** with an ***-i***. *luckier, luckiest*

- other two-syllable adjectives, or adjectives with more than two syllables, form comparatives and superlatives with ***more/most***. *more serious, most serious*
- to adverbs that have the same form as their adjectives we add ***-er***/***-est***. *harder, hardest*
- two-syllable or compound adverbs take ***more/most***. *more quickly, most quickly*

Notes:

- The adjectives ***clever***, ***common***, ***cruel***, ***gentle***, ***pleasant***, ***polite***, ***quiet***, ***stupid***, etc can form their comparatives and superlatives either with ***-er***/***-est*** or with ***more/most***. *more polite/politer, most quiet/quietest*
- **Irregular forms:** good/well – better – best; bad/badly – worse – worst; much – more – most; little – less – least; far – farther/further – farthest/furthest; much/many/a lot of – more – most
  *She received **less** money than she had calculated.*
  *It was **the least** amount of money she had ever received for her work.*

Types of comparisons using *as*

- ***as*** **+ adjective (+ *a(n)* + singular noun) +** ***as*** (to show that two people or things are similar or different in some way). In negative sentences we can use ***not as/so ... as***.
  *This book has **as detailed an explanation as** the other.*
  *This book is **not so humorous as** the first book in the series.*

To further modify this comparison, we can use the following structures:

- ***just as*** **+ adjective +** ***as*** *She is **just as friendly as** her sister.*
- ***just about as*** **+ adjective +** ***as*** *This box is **just about as heavy as** that one.*
- ***almost as*** **+ adjective +** ***as*** *The first presentation was **almost as long as** the second.*
- ***not quite/nearly as*** **+ adjective +** ***as*** *Ms Thomas is **not nearly as strict as** the other teachers.*
- ***not so much*** **+ adjective +** ***as*** *He **isn't so much sad as** angry.*
- ***not such a*** **+ adjective + singular noun +** ***as*** *Tim is **not such a talented singer as** his father.*
- ***nowhere near as*** **+ adjective +** ***as*** *This proposal was **nowhere near as competitive as** the others.*
- ***half/twice/three times as*** **+ adjective +** ***as*** *This car model is **twice as expensive as** the previous models we saw.*

Other types of structures with adjectives/adverbs and comparisons

- ***less*** **+ adjective +** ***than*** (the opposite of ***more ... than***). *Delivery from this website is **less reliable than** others.*
- ***the*** **least + adjective +** ***of/in*** (the opposite of ***the most ... of/in***). *This beach is **the least crowded in** the area.*
- ***no/not any*** **anyone/anything/anywhere + comparative** *That computer is **no more expensive than** the other one. There **isn't anywhere cheaper** to eat **than** the restaurant we ate at yesterday.*
- ***too*** **+ adjective/adverb +** ***to*****-infinitive** *The child was **too shy to speak**.*
- ***too*** **+ adjective +** ***a(n)*** **+ singular noun +** ***to*****-infinitive** (to show that something is more than necessary, or at a higher degree than possible). *It's **too complicated an issue to solve** quickly.*
- **adjective/adverb +** ***enough*** **+** ***to*****-infinitive** (to show that there is as much of something as needed, or at the necessary degree). *She studied **hard enough to pass** with merit.*

- *a bit/a little/a little bit/a lot/even/far/much/slightly* + **comparative** (to modify the comparative degree). *The film was **slightly better received than** its prequel.*
- *by far* + *the* + **superlative** (to modify the superlative degree). *This holiday is **by far the most exciting** we have ever had.*
- **comparative** + *and* + **comparative** (to show that something is increasing or decreasing gradually). *The strange noise became **louder and louder** as we approached the house.*
- *the* + **comparative ...**, *the* + **comparative** (to show that two things gradually change together, or that one thing depends on another thing). ***The faster** he wrote, **the more illegible** his writing became.*
- *fairly/pretty/quite/rather/very* + **adjective/adverb** *Jane is a **very hardworking** person.*
- *there* + *be* + *no comparison between* (to compare two very different things). ***There was no comparison between** this hotel and the last one.*
- *most* + **adjective/adverb** (= very) *She was waiting **most patiently** to see the doctor.*
- *prefer* + **gerund/noun** + *to* + **gerund/noun** (general preference) *I **prefer dancing to singing**. I **prefer vegetables to meat**.*
- *prefer* + *to*-**infinitive** + *rather than* + **bare infinitive** (general preference) *I **prefer to eat** out **rather than stay** in at weekends.*
- *would prefer* + *to*-**infinitive** + *rather than* + **bare infinitive** (specific preference) *I **would prefer to go** swimming **rather than watch** television this afternoon.*
- *would rather/sooner* + **bare infinitive** + *than* + **bare infinitive** *I'**d rather/sooner walk than drive**.*
- **clause** + *but/whereas/while* + **clause** (comparison by contrast) *This book says the battle was fought in 1066, **whereas** that book says it was in 1166.*

like – as

- *like* (for similarities): *Jane makes clothes **like** a professional fashion designer.* (she isn't a professional designer)
- **negative clause** + *like* + **noun/pronoun/-*ing* form** (comparison): *There's no place **like home**. There's nothing **like swimming**.*
- *as* (for what sb/sth really is): *June works **as** a shop manager.* (she is a manager)
- *as* + *always/much/usual*: *Frank is wearing a suit **as always**.* (In informal speech, you may also hear ***like always***.)
- *such as* (to introduce examples): *Precious stones **such as** jade and amethyst are used to make jewellery.*
- *the same* + **noun** + *as* *I graduated **the same year as** Helen.*
- *accept/be known/describe/refer to/regard/use* + **sb/sth** + *as* *People **refer to** Milan **as** the centre of the fashion industry in Europe.*
- *feel/look/smell/sound/taste/act* + *like* *This material **feels like** real wool.*

Gradable & Non-gradable adjectives

13 ★ **Look at the adjectives below and mark which are gradable (*G*) and which are non-gradable (*NG*).**

1	huge	....	**6**	enormous	....
2	freezing	....	**7**	overjoyed	....
3	amazing	....	**8**	attractive	....
4	sick	....	**9**	cold	....
5	dead	....	**10**	correct	....

14 ★ **Choose the correct word.**

1 Ian was **very/absolutely/heartily** happy with what was agreed at the meeting.
2 Janet was **wholly/totally/abundantly** devastated when she heard the bad news.
3 Everyone was **extremely/completely/utterly** alarmed to hear that Eric had resigned.
4 It was **absolutely/entirely/categorically** marvellous to see Steve again after so many years!
5 Mr Jackson was **totally/fully/very much** furious that Ben hadn't spoken to the client.
6 Although it may not seem like it, I can speak Spanish **completely/fairly/fully** well.

15 ★★ **Fill in the gaps with the correct item.**

• simple • fairly simple

1 The .... fact of the matter is that Sean should have been kinder to Paul.
2 The solution to your problem really is .... to solve if you think about it.

• absolutely crucial • crucial

3 Staffing levels are a(n) .... factor in the ongoing success of the company.
4 It is .... that you make regular backups of your work to be safe.

• novel • very novel

5 A .... feature of the software is its interactive user interface.
6 Peter's ideas present a .... approach to issues that we are discussing.

• virtually indispensable • indispensable

7 Trust is a(n) .... part of any successful friendship; it forms the essential foundation of any relationship.
8 The Internet is .... for most businesses today; nearly everyone uses it.

Comparisons

16 ★ **Put the adjectives or adverbs in brackets into the correct form, adding any necessary words.**

1 As a delegator, Lewis is far .... **(competent)** than Michael.

2 Dennis feels much .... **(good)**.

3 Seeing his daughter for the first time was .... **(happy)** moment of Jack's life.

4 This restaurant doesn't produce dishes .... **(skilful)** the one in my area.

5 This is by far .... **(bad)** book on conflict management that I have ever read!

6 Andrew has been a public speaker for a little .... **(long)** than I have.

7 Can we move a bit .... **(fast)** please? I have an appointment to get to.

8 Of all the self-help guides I've used, this one is .... **(clear)**.

17 ★★ **Put the adjectives or adverbs in brackets into the correct form, adding any necessary words.**

1 A: I hated that film, personally; the original was definitely .... **(good)**.

B: I think you're being a bit harsh, Jack. OK, it wasn't prefect, but it was almost as .... **(good)** the first one.

2 A: I don't see the point in this new computer upgrade. It's no .... **(effective)** than the ones currently on the market.

B: I agree. I definitely wouldn't buy it myself.

3 A: I was shocked that Anna didn't get that promotion.

B: Absolutely! She totally works .... **(hard)** to get a position as senior as that.

4 A: Having met him yesterday, what do you think of Dermot?

B: Honestly. He's by far .... **(friendly)** person I've ever met!

5 A: Why didn't you come by to say hello yesterday?

B: I'm sorry, but I was running .... **(late)** to stop for a chat.

18 ★ **Circle the correct item.**

1 To tell you the truth, I'm not so much angry as disappointed.

A I should be annoyed but I feel more let down than anything else.

B I feel much more annoyed than anything else.

2 It's too complex a problem to remedy easily.

A The severity of the issue is of a greater level than is required.

B The severity of the issue is of a higher degree than a quick fix allows.

3 I would prefer to meet tomorrow rather than join you tonight.

A My preference would be to go out at another time.

B I don't have any preference for when we decide to go out.

4 The more he considered it, the more he resisted doing what Jane suggested.

A Jane's suggestion became more and more appealing.

B Jane's suggestion became more and more unappealing.

5 This must have been the hardest decision that you have ever had to make.

A You've never made such a difficult decision ever before.

B You've had much harder decisions to make before.

19 ★★ **Fill in the gaps with the correct form of the words in the list. Add any necessary words.**

• sweet • full • old • serious • dull • lovely • cheap • innovative

1 Jon is a .... person than his cousin Laura; she's very laidback.

2 I've seen something like this before; it's not such a(n) .... design as the last concept.

3 Take that bottle; it's just about .... this one.

4 The phones in that shop are nowhere near .... the ones here.

5 Mike finds Sci-Fi films less .... dramas.

6 Emma's garden gets .... and lovelier every year!

7 We need more stock for the library; these books are twice .... the new items.

8 Karen always behaves most ....

like – as

20 ★ **Fill in *like* or *as*.**

1 Terry works .... a youth councillor for the local council.
2 Although this bracelet looks .... gold it's actually coloured steel.
3 Mary is chatting with her friends again on the phone .... usual.
4 There's nothing .... spending time with good friends.
5 People refer to Saville Row .... the home of fine tailoring.
6 Eric is working .... a man possessed; I've never seen him so enthusiastic!
7 I studied in the same university .... my brother Scott.
8 He is regarded .... an authority on Physics.

Revision

21 ★ **Choose the correct item.**

1 It's difficult to **say exactly/exact say/say exact/ exactly say** when the book will be finished.
2 I'm finding work easier now; I seem to be making **least/fewest/fewer/little** mistakes.
3 Even though Tim is an amateur, he writes **as/like/just as/just about** a professional.
4 Unfortunately the bank near my house is closed until **farther/furthest/far/further** notice.
5 This cover is **by far the best/by far good/the best by far/good by far** version of the song.
6 I worry about Sandra, she was behaving in a very **strangely manner/strange manner/more strange manner/strangest manner** last night.
7 Hannah is a(n) **absolutely/deeply/abundantly/ greatly** lovely young woman.
8 The food Scott cooked last night **wonderfully tasty/tasted wonderful/wonderful taste/ wonderfully tasted**.
9 Tim likes to read in a **well-lit/lit-well/lit-good/ good-lit** room in the evening.
10 Wendy is **high/highly/much high/very high** experienced in her field.
11 The screenplay was written by a(n) **brilliant, eccentric, French/French, brilliant, eccentric/ eccentric, French, brilliant** writer.
12 She was **very much furious/much furious/ most furious/too furious** with me.

22 ★★ **Fill the gaps with the correct word. Then put the words in brackets into the correct comparative/superlative form or use them to form adverbs.**

WORDS HAVE POWER

Communication plays a vital part in our lives, and nothing is 1) .... important as language. But what's in the words that we say? As it turns out, 2) .... a lot actually. Few things are 3) .... (**powerful**) than the phrases or vocabulary that we choose. While body language and gestures can express a certain amount, words offer 4) .... (**great**) clarity and impact. With enough thought, they can be used 5) .... a shield, a tool or a weapon, and can mask meaning 6) .... (**subtle**) or parade it proudly to the world. So as our world gets closer and 7) .... (**close**) to being completely digital and the written word especially becomes by far 8) .... (**important**) thing we possess, remember the importance of a diverse and rich vocabulary!

Key word transformations

23 ★★ **For questions 1-5, complete the second sentence so that it has a similar meaning to the first sentence using the word given. Do not change the word given. You must use between three and eight words, including the word given.**

1 We got to the conference late and didn't hear the talk. **SOON**
We wanted to hear the talk but we .... to catch it.
2 It was the most well-written book I had ever read. **MORE**
Never .... well-written book.
3 In my country, only a few people have heard of that director. **ENTIRELY**
That director is .... in my country.
4 In the whole area Paul's the best cook of all. **AS**
No one else .... in the whole area.
5 Is that the highest score you can get in the game? **THAN**
Can't you .... that in the game?

Module 4

Conditionals

Type 0 conditionals are used to express a general truth or a scientific fact. In this type of conditionals, we can use ***when*** instead of ***if***.

If-clause		Main clause
If/When **+ present simple**	→	**present simple**
*If/When it **rains**, the grass **gets** wet.*		

Type 1 conditionals are used to express a real or very probable situation in the present or future.

If-clause		Main clause
If **+ any present form (present simple/present continuous/ present perfect)/*should* + present bare infinitive**	→	**future simple/ imperative/*can/must/ may* etc + present bare infinitive**
*If we **arrive** at the show early, we **will/can have** a snack in the lounge.*		

When the hypothesis (*if*-clause) comes before the main clause, we separate them with a comma. When the main clause comes before the *if*-clause, then we do not use a comma to separate them.

Note: In **type 1 conditionals** we can use ***unless*** **+ affirmative verb** (= *if* + negative verb). *He won't be able to meet with you **unless** you **book** an appointment in advance.* (= **if** you **do not book**)

Type 2 conditionals (unreal present) are used to express imaginary situations, which are contrary to facts in the present and, therefore, are unlikely to happen in the present or future. We can use ***were*** for all persons in the ***if*-clause**. We can also use '***If I were you***' to give advice.

If-clause		Main clause
If **+ past simple/ past continuous**	→	***would/could/might/should*** **+ present bare infinitive**
*If they **had** access to the Internet, they **would/could book** tickets online.* *If we **were designing** the website, we **would include** a review section.* ***If I were you**, I **might sign up** for the course.*		

Type 3 conditionals (unreal past) are used to express imaginary situations, which are contrary to facts in the past. They are also used to express regrets or criticism.

If-clause		Main clause
If **+ past perfect/past perfect continuous**	→	***would/could/might/should*** **+ perfect bare infinitive**
*If you **had told** me about his accident, I **would have gone** to the hospital.* *If I **hadn't been working** yesterday, I **could have attended** the conference.*		

Mixed Conditionals

We can form mixed conditionals, if the context permits it, by combining an ***if*-clause** from one type with a main clause from another.

If-clause	Main clause
Type 1 *If he **is** as clever as they say,*	**Type 3** *he **should have been promoted** by now.*
Type 2 *If you **were** more observant,*	**Type 3** *you **wouldn't have missed** all these clues in the puzzle.*
Type 3 *If I **hadn't missed** the registration deadline,*	**Type 2** *I **would be taking** the exam right now.*
Type 2 *If you **trusted** them,*	**Type 1** *you **may** bitterly regret it.*

'*Will/would*' and '*should*' in *if*-clauses

We do not normally use ***will***, ***would*** or ***should*** in an *if*-clause. However, we can use ***will*** or ***would*** after ***if*** to make a polite request or express insistence or uncertainty (usually with expressions such as ***I don't know***, ***I doubt***, ***I wonder***, etc). In this case, ***if*** means ***whether***. We can also use ***should*** after ***if*** to talk about something which is possible but not very likely to happen. Alternatively, this function can be performed by the structure '***If sb/sth happens/should happen to …***'.

a) *If you **will wait** over there, I will see you in a few minutes.* (Will you please wait … – polite request)
b) *If you **will go on** talking, I will have to ask you to leave.* (If you insist on talking … – insistence)
c) *I **wonder if** she **will** admit to her mistakes.* (I wonder whether … – uncertainty)
d) *If Nancy **should** call, tell her I'm expecting her in my office tomorrow at 2 pm.* (I don't really expect Nancy to call.)
e) *If Nancy **happens/should happen to** call, tell her I'm expecting her in my office tomorrow at 2 pm.*

Note: *If **need be*** (= If it is necessary)*, the loan payment can be adjusted.*

Inversion in *if*-clauses

When there is ***should***, ***were*** or ***had*** in the ***if*-clause**, the subject and the auxiliary verb can be inverted and ***if*** is omitted.

***If she should pass by**, tell her to leave the documents on my desk.*
***Should she pass by**, tell her to leave the documents on my desk.*

***If I were you**, I would purchase it online .*
***Were I you**, I would purchase it online.*

***If I had arrived earlier**, I would have met with your teacher.*
***Had I arrived earlier**, I would have met with your teacher.*

Other phrases with hypothetical meaning

Other phrases/expressions used in place of *if* are the following: ***on condition that***, ***provided*** (***that***), ***providing*** (***that***), ***as/so long as***, ***even if***, ***only if***, ***unless*** (= if not), ***assuming*** (***that***), ***say*** (***that***) (= let's suppose that), ***suppose*** (***that***), ***supposing*** (***that***), ***what if***, ***when***, ***since***, ***as***, ***even though***, ***in case*** + **present tense** (for the present), ***in case*** + **past tense** (for the past), ***but for*** + **gerund/noun/the fact that** (if it weren't for/hadn't been for), ***given that***.

Study the examples:

- ***If*** *the boss attends the meeting, we will go over the sales report.* (The boss may attend or may not.)
- ***Provided (that)/Providing (that)/As long as/So long as*** *the boss attends the meeting, we will go over the sales report.* (We'll only go over the sales report if the boss attends.)
- ***Even if*** *the boss doesn't attend the meeting, we will go over the sales report.* (Whether the boss attends or not doesn't affect the result.)
- ***Only if*** *the boss attends the meeting, will we go over the sales report.* (We'll only go over the sales report if the boss attends.)
- ***Unless*** *the boss attends the meeting, we won't go over the sales report.* (We'll only go over the sales report if the boss attends.)
- ***Assuming (that)*** *the boss attends the meeting, we will go over the sales report.* (We expect the boss to attend, and we'll go over the sales report.)
- ***Say/Suppose/Supposing (that)*** *the boss attends the meeting, shall we go over the sales report?* (It is unlikely that the boss will attend; if he does, would you like us to go over the sales report?)
- ***What if*** *we go over the sales report?* (I suggest that we go over the sales report.)
- ***When*** *the boss attends the meeting, we will go over the sales report.* (The boss will definitely attend.)
- ***Since/As*** *the boss can't attend the meeting, we won't go over the sales report.* (The fact that the boss can't attend means that we can't go over the sales report.)
- ***In case*** *the boss attends the meeting, we will be ready to go over the sales report.* (It is rather unlikely that the boss will attend, but we'd better be prepared.)
- *The boss attended the meeting* ***in case*** *we went over the sales report.* (The boss attended because he was afraid we might go over the sales report without him.)
- ***But for*** *the boss attending* (= If the boss had not attended) *the meeting, we wouldn't have gone over the sales report.* (We only went over the sales report because the boss attended.)
- ***Given that*** *the boss attends the meeting, we'll go over the sales.* (If the boss attends the meeting, we'll go over the sales report.)

Notes

- We can omit the subject and the auxiliary verb ***be*** in conditional clauses.
  If required (= If it is required)*, they will bring their complaints to the CEO of the company.*
- Additionally, we can replace a whole clause with '***if so***' and '***if not***', in order to avoid repetition.
  Are you coming to the party tomorrow? ***If so*** (= If you are coming)*, I'll give you a ride then.* ***If not****, let me know.*

Wishes

We use ***wish/if only*** to express a wish.

Verb tense		Use
I wish/ If only + **past simple/ past continuous**	*I wish I* ***made*** *more money!* *I wish you* ***weren't moving*** *to another city!*	to say that we would like something to be different about a present situation
I wish/ If only + ***could*** + **bare infinitive**	*I wish I* ***could*** *speak French!* (but I can't)	to express regret in the present concerning lack of ability
I wish/ If only + **past perfect**	*I wish I* ***had listened*** *to his suggestions!* (but I didn't) *If only I* ***hadn't lied*** *to my friends!* (but I did)	to express regret about something which happened or didn't happen in the past
I wish/ If only + **subject** + ***would*** + **bare infinitive**	*I wish* ***you would be*** *more specific about what is wrong!* *I wish* ***Tina would stop*** *talking behind my back about me!*	to express: • a polite imperative • a desire for a situation or a person's behaviour to change

Notes

- ***Wish*** can also be followed by a personal pronoun and a noun (*luck*, *success*) or a phrase (*all the best*, *Merry Christmas*, etc). *I want to* ***wish you good luck*** *in your exams.*
- ***If only*** is used in exactly the same way as ***I wish***, but it is more emphatic or more dramatic.
- We can use ***were*** instead of ***was*** after ***wish*** and ***if only*** for all persons. *I wish I* ***were*** *younger!*
- After the subject pronouns ***I*** and ***we***, we usually use ***could*** instead of ***would***. *I wish I* ***could play*** *the piano.*
- ***Wish*** + ***to*-infinitive** = want to (formal)
  I wish ***to make*** *a request.*
- In order to express **hope** about the future, we can't use ***wish***; instead, we use ***I hope*** + **present/future tense.** *I hope you get/you'll get into the university of your choice.* (NOT: ~~*I wish you get into the university of your choice*~~.)

Conditionals

1 ★ **Match the sentences in column A to their uses in column B.**

A	B
1 [ ] When you upgrade your computer, it runs better.	a an imaginary situation contrary to the facts of the present
2 [ ] If we had the wi-fi password, we could use the Internet.	b a general truth
3 [ ] If I change my Internet speed, I can get much faster downloads.	c an imaginary situation contrary to the facts of the past
4 [ ] If technical support had known about your network issues, they would have fixed them.	d a probable situation in the present or future
5 [ ] If I were you, I would look for a better smartphone.	e a regret
6 [ ] If I hadn't been working at the weekend, I could have gone to the computer game expo.	f advice

2 ★★ **Put the verbs in brackets into the correct tense.**

1 A: Unless we .... **(leave)** now, the mobile phone shop .... **(close)** by the time we get there.
B: OK, I'll get my coat.

2 A: We .... **(finish)** the report if we .... **(install)** that new software.
B: Well, there's nothing we can do about that now so we better just get on with it.

3 A: I can't seem to get the Internet to load.
B: If I .... **(be)** you, I .... **(check)** with your wi-fi router and try again.

4 A: If you .... **(raise)** the point at the meeting, you .... **(can/push)** the board for an answer.
B: OK, but when I .... **(do)** that, I .... **(need)** your support.

5 A: Mum, can I upgrade this tablet to a newer model?
B: OK, but only if you .... **(find)** a good deal that isn't too expensive.

Mixed Conditionals

3 ★★ **Rewrite the following as mixed conditionals.**

1 Carol doesn't like online games, so she didn't play with us last night.
....

2 They say the tablet is good, so it should have sold out by now.
....

3 She lost the file, so she is in trouble.
....

4 They changed their electricity provider, so they don't pay as much now.
....

'Will'/'would' – 'should' in *if*-clauses & other phrases with hypothetical meaning

4 ★ **Rewrite the sentences using the words in brackets.**

1 If you will take a seat, the manager will be right with you. **(would)**
....

2 As we don't have any extra resources, we have to continue with the current setup. **(given)**
....

3 If we get the funding, we will update the company's website. **(provided)**
....

4 If we don't find a cheaper alternative, we won't be able to replace the editing suite. **(unless)**
....

5 How about installing a generator to use in the event of a power cut? **(what if)**
....

6 If Jane calls, tell her I'm expecting her in my office tomorrow at 11 am. **(should)**
....

Inversion in *if*-clauses

5 ★★ **Rewrite the sentences using inversion.**

1 If you had told me about the seminar, I would have been there.
....

2 If I were you, I would call IT about the faulty printer.
....

3 If you speak to Adam, can you tell him about the change of supplier?
....

4 If I had saved enough money, I would have bought the new games console.
....

Wishes

6 ★ **Put the verbs in brackets into the correct tense.**

1 A: I wish I .... **(listen)** during Professor Smith's lecture!
B: Don't worry, you can read my notes.

2 A: I wish I .... **(can/go)** with you to the convention next week.
B: Me too. If only you .... **(not/book)** your trip to Bristol that day.

3 A: I wish I .... **(do)** some more research before buying my smartphone.
B: Yes, then you would have got one with the features you wanted. I hope you .... **(get)** it exchanged.

4 A: If only I .... **(be)** younger, I'd understand technology better.
B: I wish you .... **(stop)** talking like that. It's got nothing to do with your age.

7 ★★ **Rewrite the sentences using wishes.**

1 I didn't invest in a new sound system.
....

2 I forgot my password. I can't access my emails.
....

3 I don't know what's wrong with my tablet.
....

4 James plays online games all day.
....

5 Grant doesn't have enough money to buy a computer.
....

8 ★★ **Make sentences using wishes/ conditionals.**

1 *I don't know anything about global marketing. I should have gone to the seminar.*

I wish/If only ....
If ....

2 *We've fallen behind our competitors. We should have branched out years ago.*

I wish/If only ....
If ....

3 *We're paying a lot for electricity. We should have installed solar panels.*

I wish/If only ....
If ....

9 ★★ **Read the text about what happened to Jane. Make sentences as if you were Jane, as in the example. Write your answers in your notebook.**

Jane was anxious about giving her presentation to the committee, so the night before she slept badly. She slept through her alarm so had to get ready quickly. Her car was in the garage so she had to take the bus. Because she was running late, she missed the bus and had to take a taxi. She arrived late and hurried out of the taxi leaving her notes on the back seat. She didn't have a copy of the notes at her desk so she couldn't give the presentation.

1 *I wish I hadn't been anxious about giving the presentation. If I hadn't been so anxious about it, I wouldn't have slept badly.*
2 *I wish I hadn't slept through the alarm…*

Key word transformations

10 ★★ **For questions 1-4, complete the second sentence so that it has a similar meaning to the first sentence using the word given. Do not change the word given. You must use between three and eight words, including the word given.**

1 If I were her, I would not leave my e-book lying around in public. **BETTER**
She ....
lying around in public.

2 Rachel regrets not signing up for the programming workshop. **WISHES**
Rachel ....
for the programming workshop.

3 Zoe would love to start computing classes next week. **ABLE**
Zoe ....
to start computing classes next week.

4 If I were you, I would have returned the phone to the shop. **SHOES**
If ....
have returned the phone to the shop.

5 Should our trip be cancelled, the ticket price will be refunded. **REFUND**
If ....
will be given to ticket holders.

Had better/Would rather/Prefer/Would prefer

Had better (= should/ought to) is used to give strong or urgent advice. ***Had better*** refers only to the present or future. ***Had better*** is more emphatic than ***should/ought to***, but is not as emphatic as ***must***.
*You **must** speak to the police.* (strong advice)
*You **had better** speak to the police.* (less emphatic than 'must')
*You **should/ought to** speak to the police.* (less emphatic than 'had better')

- ***had better*** + **bare infinitive** → future
  *I **had better finish** my homework.*
- ***It would have been better if*** + **past perfect** → past
  ***It would have been better if** you **had asked** for my permission first.*

Would rather/sooner (= would prefer to) expresses preference. When the subject of ***would rather/would sooner*** is also the subject of the following verb, we use the following constructions:

- ***would rather/sooner*** + **present bare infinitive** → present/future *I **would rather/sooner see** a film tonight.*
- ***would rather/sooner*** + **perfect bare infinitive** → past
  ***I'd rather/sooner have gone** for Chinese, but everyone wanted to eat Mexican food.*
- ***would rather/sooner*** + **present bare infinitive** + ***than*** + **present bare infinitive/noun**
  ***I'd rather/sooner go** shopping **than visit** the museum.*
  ***I'd rather/sooner** have **coffee** than **tea**.*

When the subject of ***would rather/would sooner*** is different from the subject of the following verb, we use the following constructions:

- ***would rather/would sooner*** + **different subject** + **past tense** → present/ future
  ***I'd rather/sooner you didn't wear** your shoes in the house.*
- ***would rather/would sooner*** + **different subject** + **past perfect** → past
  ***I'd rather/sooner you had spoken** to me about the problem first.*

Preference can also be expressed by the following constructions:

- ***prefer*** + **full infinitive** + ***rather than*** + **bare infinitive** (general preference) *I prefer **to listen** to classical music **rather than** (listen to) jazz.*
- ***prefer*** + ***-ing*** **form/noun** + ***to*** + ***-ing*** **form/noun** (general preference) *I prefer **running to cycling**. I prefer **theatre to films**.*
- ***would prefer*** + **full infinitive** + ***rather than*** + **bare infinitive** (specific preference) *I would prefer **to go** on the tour in town **rather than sit** by the sea.*
- ***would prefer it if*** + **past tense** (preference in the present) *I would prefer it if you **left** my key in my mailbox.*
- ***would have preferred it if*** + **past perfect** (preference in the past) *They would have preferred it if you **had complained** in person.*
- ***favour sb/sth over sb/sth else*** *I favour **Italian food over Chinese food**.*

- ***would (just) as soon*** + **bare infinitive**
  *I would just as soon **drive** to work this morning.*
- ***would (just) as soon*** + **different subject** + **past tense**
  *I would just as soon you **drove** me to work today.*
- ***be better off*** + ***-ing*** **form** + ***than*** + ***-ing*** **form**
  *You'd be better off **meeting** them at a restaurant than **seeing** them at the office.*

The unreal past

The **past simple** can be used to refer to the **present** when we talk about imaginary, unreal or impossible situations, which are contrary to facts in the **present**.
The **past perfect** can be used to refer to imaginary, unreal or impossible situations, which are contrary to facts in the **past**.

The **past simple** is used with:

- **type 2 conditionals** – *The students would do better on their exam **if** they **studied** more.*
- ***suppose/supposing/imagine*** – ***Suppose/Supposing/ Imagine** you **found** a large sum of money, what would you do?*
- ***wish/if only*** – *I **wish/If only I visited** you more often!*
- ***would rather/sooner*** (present) – ***I'd rather/sooner** you **met** me at the theatre.*
- ***as if/as though*** (for current, future or general hypothetical comparisons) – *He talks **as if** he **were** in charge of the group.*
- **it's (about/high) time** (to express criticism) – ***It's (about/ high) time** you **finished** your work!*

The **past perfect** is used with:

- **type 3 conditionals** – ***If** they **had left** later, they wouldn't have got stuck in traffic.*
- ***suppose/supposing/imagine*** – ***Suppose/Supposing/ Imagine** you **had seen** her at the meeting, what would you have done?*
- ***wish/if only*** – ***I wish/If only I hadn't missed** the party yesterday!*
- ***would rather/sooner*** (past) – ***I'd rather/sooner** you **hadn't discussed** this matter without me.*
- ***as if/as though*** (for past hypothetical comparisons) – *She looked **as if/as though** she **hadn't slept** for days.*

Note: ***It would have been better if*** + **past perfect** (past)
*It would have been better if you **had completed** your project by the deadline.*

Different constructions can be used with ***it's time***, with similar meanings:

- ***It's time*** + ***to*-infinitive** (when time has come to do sth).
  *It's time **to meet** Alice now.*
- ***It's time for*** + **object** + ***to*-infinitive** (to say sth is urgent/ important). *It's time **for us to meet** Alice now.*

Preference/Unreal Past

11 ★ **Choose the correct item.**

1 I'd rather you **had told/would tell** me about the issue with the photocopier.
2 Supposing we **didn't find/hadn't found** the problem, what would you do?
3 It's about time our team **had met/met** with success.
4 It would have been better if we **had seen/saw** an example of his work before we gave him the contract.
5 David acts as though he **were/had been** the only one affected by the merger.
6 I would rather we **went/had gone** on foot today than take our bikes.

12 ★ **Fill in the gaps with the correct word/ phrase.**

• it's high time • as if • imagine • would sooner
• would have been better • it's time for

1 Ralph looked .... he had seen a ghost when he came through the door last night.
2 .... you won the lottery, what would you do?
3 .... the children to get changed.
4 .... Gavin started pulling his weight and took on more responsibility.
5 I .... you hadn't talked to the estate agent without me.
6 It .... if you had created a new password for each client.

13 ★★ **Complete the sentences, as in the example.**

1 Your friend wants to see a western, but you want to see a comedy. What do you say?
I'd prefer *to see a comedy rather than a western*.
2 Your brother has invited you to a technology expo, but you don't want to go. What do you say?
I'd rather ....
3 Your colleague had a problem with his computer and tried to fix it himself. He should have called IT. What do you say?
I'd sooner ....
4 Your friend wants to order pizza. You like Thai food. What do you say?
I favour ....
5 Your colleague has offered to drive you to work tomorrow. You want to drive yourself. What do you say?
I'd just as soon ....

14 ★★ **Fill in the gaps with the correct form of the verbs in brackets.**

REPLY MAIL

To: All staff
From: Managing Director
Subject: Changes to working practices

We are implementing widespread changes in our working practices and I would prefer **1)** .... **(inform)** you of them in writing rather than have you find out about them through word of mouth. Given the extent of the changes, I **2)** .... **(attach)** a list of the business areas that are affected. My only regret is that we did not implement these practices sooner. If we had, we **3)** .... **(not/experience)** our recent troubles.
I wish I **4)** .... **(say)** the transition will be painless, but any change comes with teething problems. Our goal is to improve our practices and make your working life easier. To that end, we would sooner **5)** .... **(hear)** from you directly so feel free to give us your feedback on these new procedures if you **6)** .... **(encounter)** any problems and, if need be, we **7)** .... **(amend)** any issues that may be causing concern. We hope these changes **8)** .... **(make)** the running of our day-to-day services smoother.
Should you need any further information, please **9)** .... **(contact)** your department heads. Provided that all departments work together, we **10)** .... **(anticipate)** seeing positive results in a few months.

Key word transformations

15 ★★ **For questions 1-5, complete the second sentence so that it has a similar meaning to the first sentence using the word given. Do not change the word given. You must use between three and eight words, including the word given.**

1 Why didn't you postpone the meeting? **BETTER**
It .... the meeting.
2 He'd rather work in a team than work alone. **PREFERS**
He .... alone.
3 She prefers to travel by train than travel by car. **SOONER**
She .... by car.
4 If we don't hurry up, we won't make our appointment. **OR**
We'd .... make our appointment.
5 I'd prefer you to do the computer repairs now. **RATHER**
I'd .... now.

Module 5

The passive

Form

We form the passive with the verb ***to be*** in the appropriate tense and the **past participle** of the main verb. Only transitive verbs (verbs which take an object) can be used in the passive.

Use

We use the **passive**:

- when the person or people who do the action are unknown, unimportant or obvious from the context. *A new roundabout **was built** in the centre of town.* (The identity of the builder is obvious.) *Pens and pencils **will be provided** for you.* (It's not important to know who will give you the pens and pencils.)
- when the action itself is more important than the person/people who do it, as in news headlines, newspaper articles, formal notices, advertisements, instructions, processes, etc. *The road **is being cleared**.*
- when we want to avoid taking responsibility for an action, or when we refer to an unpleasant event and we do not want to say who or what is to blame. *I **was held up** in the corridor.*
- in formal academic writing to produce an official impersonal tone. *The hypothesis **was proven** to be incorrect during the study.*

Changing from the active into the passive

- The **object** of the active sentence becomes the **subject** in the passive sentence.
- The active verb remains in the same tense but changes into the passive form.
- The **subject** of the active sentence becomes the agent, and is either introduced with the preposition ***by*** or omitted.

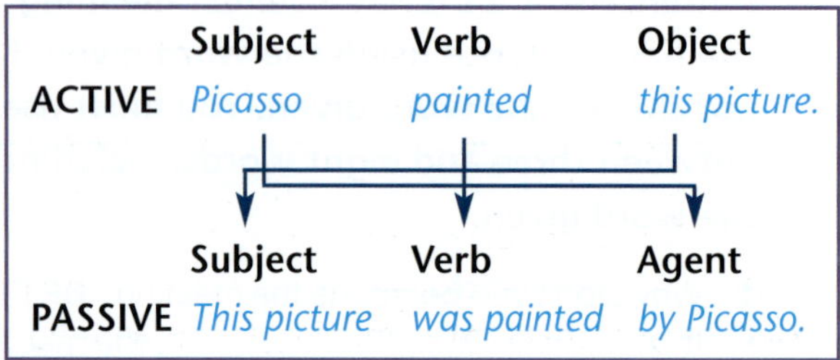

	Subject	Verb	Object
ACTIVE	*Picasso*	*painted*	*this picture.*
	Subject	**Verb**	**Agent**
PASSIVE	*This picture*	*was painted*	*by Picasso.*

- Only transitive verbs (verbs which take an object) can be changed into the passive. **Active:** *He lived in London.* (NOT: ~~He was lived in London~~.)
- Intransitive verbs (verbs not taking an object, e.g. ***arise***, ***be***, ***die***, ***happen***, ***lie***, ***occur***, ***rain***, etc) cannot be changed into the passive. *Difficulties may **occur** over time.*
  Note: Some transitive and stative verbs (***comprise***, ***consist of***, ***fit***, ***have***, ***lack***, ***mean***, ***resemble***, ***suit***, etc) and verbs of measure (***cost***, ***equal***, ***weigh***, etc) cannot be changed into the passive. *I have a terrible headache.* (NOT: ~~A terrible headache is had by me~~.)
  The suit fits me perfectly. (NOT: ~~I am fitted perfectly by the suit~~.) **BUT** *The unit must be fitted by an expert.* ('fit' is not a verb of measure here.)

Passive questions

- In order to ask questions in the passive, we follow the same rules as for statements, keeping in mind that the verb is in the interrogative form. *Did he complete the form? **Was** the form **completed**?*
- When we want to find out who or what performed an action, the passive question form is ***Who/What ... by***? ***Who** was the cake made **by**?*

The agent in the passive

- ***By*** **+ the agent** is used to say who or what carries out an action. ***With*** **+ instrument/material/ingredient** is used to say what the agent uses. *The faulty sink was fixed **by the plumber**. The pothole was filled **with asphalt**.* ***With*** is used after past participles, such as ***covered***, ***crowded***, ***decorated***, ***filled***, ***packed***, ***surrounded***, etc. *The bus was **packed with** people.*
- The agent can be omitted when the subject is ***they***, ***he***, ***someone/somebody***, ***people***, ***one***, etc. ***Someone** drank all the orange juice.* → *All the orange juice was drunk.*
- The agent is not omitted when it is a specific or important person, or when it is essential to the meaning of the sentence. *The telephone was invented **by Alexander Graham Bell**.*

Ditransitive verbs in the passive

- With verbs which can take two objects, such as ***bring***, ***buy***, ***give***, ***lend***, ***offer***, ***promise***, ***read***, ***sell***, ***send***, ***show***, ***teach***, ***tell***, etc, we can form two different passive sentences.
  Grandma sends us letters every week. (active)
  *We **are sent** letters by Grandma every week.*
  *Letters **are sent to** us by Grandma every week.*
- Verbs which take two objects, of which the direct (thing) object is introduced by a preposition, can have only one passive form with the indirect object as subject. *They robbed the old man **of his money**. The old man **was robbed of** his money.* (NOT: ~~His money was robbed of the old man~~.)
  Similarly, the verbs whose indirect object is introduced by a preposition can have only one passive form with the direct (thing) object as subject. *The hotel provides childcare facilities **for the guests**. Childcare facilities **are provided for** the guests (by the hotel).* (NOT: ~~The guests are provided for childcare facilities~~.)

Continuous tenses in the passive

- The present perfect continuous, the future continuous, the past perfect continuous and the future perfect continuous are not used in the passive. Instead, we can make use of various phrases in order to convey their meaning: ***in progress***, ***on display***, ***under arrest***, ***under consideration***, ***under construction***, ***under discussion***, ***under investigation***, ***under review***, ***under scrutiny***, ***under surveillance***, etc.
  They have been reviewing the whole department for two months now.

The whole department ***has been under review*** *for two months now.*

They have been displaying the artwork since January.
The artwork ***has been on display*** *since January.*

This time next week, they will be making the bridge.
This time next week, the bridge ***will be under construction/ will be in progress****.*

By the time I got involved in the project, I had been considering the plan for a long time.
By the time I got involved in the project, the plan ***had been under consideration*** *for a long time.*

By the end of the month, they will have been investigating the case for six weeks.
By the end of the month, the case ***will have been under investigation*** *for six weeks.*

Personal – Impersonal constructions

Verbs such as ***allege***, ***assume***, ***believe***, ***claim***, ***estimate***, ***expect***, ***feel***, ***know***, ***report***, ***rumour***, ***say***, ***think***, ***understand***, etc are commonly used with the following passive constructions: *They* ***think*** *she is a skilled painter.*

a) ***It*** **+ passive verb +** ***that*****-clause (impersonal construction)** ***It is thought that*** *she is a skilled painter.*
b) **Subject + passive verb +** ***to*****-infinitive (personal construction)** ***She is thought to be*** *a skilled painter.*

They ***estimate*** *that there has been a dramatic increase in crime in the city.*

a) ***It is estimated that*** *there has been a dramatic increase in crime in the city.*
b) ***There is estimated to be*** *a dramatic increase in crime in the city.*

Notes

- We can use the verb ***to get*** instead of the verb ***to be*** in everyday speech, when we talk about things that happen by accident or unexpectedly. *His glasses* ***got*** *broken.* (instead of: *His glasses* ***were*** *broken.*)
- If, in an active sentence, a preposition follows a verb, then, in the passive, it is placed immediately after the verb. *The teacher* ***is telling off*** *the students. The students* ***are being told off*** *by the teacher.*
- The verbs ***hear***, ***help***, ***see*** and ***make*** are followed by the **infinitive without** ***to*** in the active, but by the ***to*****-infinitive** in the passive. *They* ***made*** *us* ***carry*** *the boxes from the car. We* ***were made to carry*** *the boxes from the car.*
- ***Let*** becomes ***be allowed to*** in the passive. *Our parents* ***let*** *us stay out a bit later than usual. We* ***were allowed to*** *stay out a bit later than usual.*
- The passive conversion is blocked when there are reflexive pronouns or possessive adjectives in the object of the active sentence. *Tom cut* ***himself*** *shaving.* (NOT: ~~*Himself was cut*~~ ...) *The girl grazed* ***her*** *knee on the gravel.* (NOT: ~~*Her knee was grazed*~~ ...)

Causative form

- We use ***have*** **+ object (thing) + past participle (+ by sb)** to say that we have arranged for someone to do something for us. *She* ***had her hair cut****.* (She didn't cut it herself.)
- Questions and negations of the verb ***have*** are formed with ***do/does*** (present simple) and ***did*** (past simple). ***Did*** *you* ***have*** *your windows cleaned?*
- We can also use ***have something done*** to talk about an unpleasant experience that somebody had. *We* ***had*** *our house* ***broken into*** *last night.* (= Our house was broken into ...)
- We can use the verb ***get*** instead of ***have*** in informal conversation. *I'm going to* ***get*** *my computer serviced on Sunday.*
- ***Get*** **+ object (thing) + past participle** can also be used to mean 'finish doing sth', e.g. *They* ***got the letters typed****.* Another possible usage is to describe something unpleasant. However, this structure may cause ambiguity: *They* ***got*** *their flat* ***foreclosed****.* This could also suggest that they themselves arranged it.
Note: The word order is very important. ***She had her nails polished*** and ***She had polished her nails*** have different meanings. In the first case, she arranged for someone to polish her nails whereas, in the second case, she polished them herself.

Notes

- ***Have*** **+ object (person) + bare infinitive** to give instructions/orders.
The police officer ***had the man pull over*** *his car.*
The teacher ***had the students redo*** *the exercises.*
- ***Have*** **+ object (person) + present participle (-*ing*)** can be used to suggest that somebody experiences something, or causes something to happen.
They usually ***have their grandchildren staying*** *with them at the weekends.*
The fantastic performance ***had the audience crying****.*
- ***Won't have*** **+ object + present participle or past participle** can be used to suggest that we will not allow someone to do something.
I ***won't have you speaking*** *about me like that!*
I ***won't have this project ruined*** *by poor quality work.*
- ***Get*** **+ object (person) +** ***to*****-infinitive**: to persuade somebody to do something.
I ***got my uncle to teach*** *me how to drive.*
- ***Get*** **+ object (person) + present participle (-*ing*)** can be informally used to mean 'make somebody start doing something'. *Once you* ***get her talking*** *about her travels, she never stops.* ALSO: ***get moving***; ***get going*** (without an object).
- ***Make*** **+ object (person) + bare infinitive** is used to express that someone causes someone else to do something.
The teacher ***made us learn*** *the whole unit by heart.* (He insisted that we learnt it by heart.)
- ***Want, prefer, would like*** and ***need*** can be used with an object and a past participle, to indicate that you would like, need or prefer something to be done.
I ***want*** *the door closed.* (= I want the door to be closed.)

The passive

1 ★ **Match the sentences in the passive voice (1-4) to their uses (a-d).**

1 [ ] The fallen branches have been cleared from the road by somebody.

2 [ ] It was found in a recent study that young people benefit emotionally from mentoring programmes.

3 [ ] The plans for a new youth hostel have been approved.

4 [ ] The city centre and surrounding areas were left in disarray after the protest.

a The people who do the action are unknown, unimportant or obvious from the context.

b The action itself is more important than the person/people who do it.

c Referring to an unpleasant event and without saying who or what is to blame.

d Writing in formal academic writing to produce an official impersonal tone.

2 ★★ **Rewrite the sentences in passive voice. In some cases the sentences cannot be changed into the passive.**

1 Critics of the scheme severely underestimated the degree of community support.

....

2 A variety of issues may arise on an intergenerational programme.

....

3 We need to find a new location for the protest meeting due to increased numbers.

....

4 The charity rewarded Billy for his fundraising.

....

5 We will issue tools and safety equipment to all volunteers on the day.

....

6 The crowdfunding platform has raised a phenomenal amount in just one day.

....

7 The lack of funding meant that the outreach programme stalled before it even began.

....

8 They are going to demolish the inner city slums to make way for new housing.

....

9 Jackie has lived in India since she went there to teach English 10 years ago.

....

10 The event cost more to run than the organisers had anticipated.

....

3 ★ **Fill in:** ***by*** **or** ***with*****.**

1 The school houses were built
 a .... volunteers.
 b .... donated supplies.

2 The community garden is maintained
 a .... organic pesticides.
 b .... residents.

3 The posters were created
 a .... school children.
 b .... cardboard and paint.

4 The square was filled
 a .... plants and trees.
 b .... hundreds of protestors.

4 ★★ **Complete the sentences using passive voice.**

1 The council have been considering the plan for the new housing development for 6 months.
The plan ....

2 The authorities have told residents that they should start a neighbourhood watch scheme.
Residents ....

3 Who made the application for the lottery grant?
Who ....?

4 They estimate that more than 100,000 people will attend the march for peace.
It ....

5 The principal let us use the school hall for the charity concert.
We ....

6 Will you have organised the petition by this evening?
Will ....?

7 The police were questioning the suspects for hours.
The suspects ....

8 We will send introductory letters to everyone who signed up to the programme.
Everybody ....

9 The organisers had advised us to wear old clothes at the clean-up day.
We ....

10 The members expect that Ralph will become the next chairman of the committee.
Ralph ....

Causative form

5 ★ **Match the sentences (1-10) to their uses (a-j).**

1 [ ] We would like the funds dispersed to the charity.

2 [ ] The police had the suspect turn out his pockets.

3 [ ] The job will be finished in no time once we get the workmen going.

4 [ ] The scenes of devastation after the disaster had residents crying.

5 [ ] The committee got their application for the grant typed up.

6 [ ] The residents got the council to change their decision about demolishing the playground.

7 [ ] The children had their faces painted at the bazaar.

8 [ ] I won't have this programme derailed because of a lack of funding.

9 [ ] The youth centre had their premises vandalised last night.

10 [ ] The police made the protesters take down their banner.

a to arrange for sb to do sth for us
b to finish doing sth
c to talk about an unpleasant experience
d to give instructions/orders
e to suggest that sb experiences sth
f to not allow sb to do sth
g to persuade sb to do sth
h to make sb start doing sth
i to cause sb else to do sth
j to indicate that you would like sth to be done

6 ★★ **Rephrase the following using *have*, *get* or *make*, as in the example.**

1 Brian asked the volunteers to clear the hall for the meeting.
Brian had the volunteers clear the hall for the meeting.

2 The activists persuaded people to sign the petition.
....

3 Will Rachael ask her sister to cater the event?
....

4 Security insisted that I move my car away from the entrance of the building.
....

5 Tom persuaded me to donate my old toys to charity.
....

6 My teacher insisted that I redo my assignment on political reform.
....

7 ★ **Fill in the gaps with the appropriate forms of the words in brackets.**

Good Samaritans

A couple who **1)** .... **(have/their wallets/steal)** at the airport yesterday while their flight **2)** .... **(prepare)** for departure by the airline, **3)** .... **(pleasantly/surprise)** by the kindness of strangers. After the problem **4)** .... **(draw)** to the airline's attention, the distraught pair **5)** .... **(their/tickets/upgrade)** to business class on the next flight absolutely free. A fellow passenger who **6)** .... **(move)** by their story also gave them $200 cash to ensure that the couple's long-awaited break **7)** ....,.. **(not/ruin)** by the unfortunate incident. When asked about this incredible generosity the passenger simply stated that he **8)** .... **(not have/anyone's holiday/spoil)** by a petty thief. It **9)** .... **(understand)** that an online campaign to track down the good Samaritan **10)** .... **(start)** by the young couple on their return, because he had refused to let them pay him back. They hope to be able to thank him properly soon, as his amazing kindness helped turn a disaster into the holiday of a lifetime after all!

Key word transformations

8 ★★ **For questions 1-4, complete the second sentence so that it has a similar meaning to the first sentence, using the word given. Do not change the word given. You must use between three and eight words, including the word given.**

1 I'm afraid the authorities won't let us use the sports stadium to host the charity concert due to security concerns. **ALLOWED**
Because of security concerns .... the sports stadium to host the charity concert.

2 Don't talk to people in that tone; it isn't polite. **HAVE**
I .... to people in that tone; it isn't polite.

3 Thanks to the auction we have managed to meet our target. **RESULT**
Our target .... the auction.

4 The scheme had been progressing when it was suspended after a couple of months. **PROGRESS**
The scheme .... when it was suspended after a couple of months.

Grammar Bank 5

Reflexive/Emphatic pronouns *(myself, yourself, ..., oneself)*

- **Reflexive pronouns** are used after certain verbs (***behave***, ***burn***, ***cut***, ***enjoy***, ***hurt***, ***kill***, ***look at***, etc) when the subject and the object of the verb are the same. *Can **you** behave **yourself**?* They can also be used after ***be***, ***feel***, ***look*** and ***seem***, to describe emotions or states. ***She** doesn't seem **herself** today.*
- Reflexive pronouns can be used after prepositions, but not after prepositions of place. *I am very proud **of myself**.* **BUT:** *She left her old life behind her.* (NOT: ~~behind herself~~)
- Certain verbs (***dress***, ***get up***, ***meet***, ***relax***, ***rest***, ***shave***, ***sit down***, ***stand up***, ***undress***, ***wake up***, ***wash***, etc) do not normally take a reflexive pronoun. *He lay down and rested.* (NOT: ~~*He lay down and rested himself.*~~) ***Wash***, ***shave*** and ***dress/undress*** can be used with a reflexive pronoun to talk about young children, sick people, etc, in order to indicate some difficulty. *The little boy is trying to **dress himself**. The child is learning to **wash herself**.*
- We use **emphatic pronouns** to give emphasis to the noun, or to the fact that a certain person performs an action. They come after the noun or pronoun they emphasise. ***The actor himself** signed my film poster.* (The actor himself signed the film poster, nobody else did it for him.)
  ***The singer himself** wrote the song.* (The singer wrote the song, not anybody else.)
- We can also use the emphatic pronouns with the preposition ***by***, when we mean ***alone/without company*** or ***without help*** (on one's own).
  *He fixed his bike **by himself**.* (on his own)

  Study these idioms: ***Enjoy yourselves!*** (Have a good time!) ***Behave yourself!*** (Be good!) ***She lives by herself.*** (She lives on her own.) ***Help yourself to tea!*** (You're welcome to take some tea if you want some.) ***Do it yourself!*** (Do it without being helped!) ***Make yourself at home!*** (Feel at ease!) ***Make yourself heard*** (Speak loudly enough to be heard by others) ***Make yourself understood*** (Make what you say clear).

  Note: ***Each other*** is a reciprocal pronoun that means '**one another**'. This cannot be expressed using reflexive pronouns. **Compare:** *Friends should look after **each other**.* (NOT: ~~*Friends should look after themselves*~~, *Each person should look after themselves.*)

Substitution & Ellipsis

Substitution

Substitution is used to **avoid repetition**. The following words can be used to replace a noun phrase or a verb phrase: ***it, there, that, one, do, so, neither, not***.

- *I won a prize in the competition. **It** was a real surprise!*
  (It = the fact that I won a prize)
- *I'm going to watch the match at Carl's house. Will you be **there**?* (there = at Carl's house)
- *– Would you like some free tickets for the gig tomorrow?*
  *– **That** would be amazing!* (That = getting some free tickets)
- *– Are you going to buy a bike?*
  *– No, I've already got **one**.* (one = a bike)
- *– Do you go skiing in the winter?*
  *– No, I **don't**.* (don't = do not go skiing)
- *– Did you say it's going to rain tomorrow?*
  *– Yes, I believe **so**.* (so = that it's going to rain)
- *I'm not on the football team and **neither** is Steven.* (neither = not on the football team)
- *Oscar should be at home when you get there; if **not**, I'll be back by 5.30.* (not = Oscar isn't at home)

Ellipsis

Ellipsis is also used to **avoid repetition** as long as this does not interfere with the meaning which we want to convey. It involves **omitting words** or **phrases** after the conjunctions 'and' and 'but', after the auxiliary and modal verbs (*be, do, have, can, must, will*, etc) and after 'to' in infinitive phrases. *He left rather early but he **shouldn't have** (~~left~~).* (NOT: ~~*He shouldn't.*~~)

- *She looks irritated and* (she looks) *tired.*
- *He feels excited about the opportunity but* (he feels) *nervous about the responsibility.*
- *"Are you going to the theatre this evening?"*
  "I want to (go to the theatre) *but I'm not sure I'll be able to* (go to the theatre)*."*
- *He could have become a film star but he didn't (become a film star).*
- *I'm sorry for stepping on your toe; I didn't mean to (step on your toe).*

Note: In short answers, any adverbs must be placed before the auxiliary or modal verb, despite the rule. *"Philip is being rather petulant today!" "I think he **always is**!"*

Reflexive-Emphatic Pronouns

9 ★ **Fill in:** ***myself***, ***herself***, ***himself***, ***itself***, ***yourself***, ***themselves***, ***yourselves***, ***each other***.

1. A: How does the alarm on this car work? Don't you have to press a button to activate it?
   B: No, it arms .... whenever you lock the door.
2. A: Kate should be proud of .... ; she's achieved a lot in a short space of time.
   B: She loves helping those less fortunate.
3. A: Feel free, all of you, to help .... to something to drink.
   B: Thanks, I think I'll get .... some juice. Anyone else want some?
4. A: This is a great charity gala, everyone seems to be really enjoying ....!
   B: Yes! I still can't believe that George Clooney .... opened the proceedings for us.
5. A: It wasn't much fun going canvassing with Paul. We didn't talk to .... the entire time.
   B: Well, maybe you should go by .... tomorrow.

Substitution & Ellipsis

10 ★ **Fill in the gaps with:** *do so, do, it, there, one, that, so.*

The gift of giving

Do you ever think about volunteering for a worthy cause but don't know which **1)** .... to choose? If you **2)** ...., then worry not. Help is at hand. Numerous websites now match people and skills to open positions and in **3)** .... doing provide charities with much needed support.

Research into volunteering shows that **4)** .... helps the volunteers as much as the causes. Volunteering can bring about benefits **5)** .... can reduce stress and improve our health. So, why not sign up on one of these sites? If you **6)** .... and volunteer for a charity, you can be safe in the knowledge that once you're **7)** .... you'll be helping others and yourself!

11 ★★ **Rewrite the second sentence in each dialogue using ellipsis where possible, as in the example.**

1 A: Are you coming to the rally tonight?
B: I'd like to come to the rally tonight but I'm afraid I can't come.
I'd like to but I'm afraid I can't.

2 A: Adam looks happy he is going to India.
B: He is happy. He feels excited and he feels confident about his trip to India.
....

3 A: Do you volunteer for any charities?
B: No, I don't volunteer for any charities but I'd like to volunteer for a charity.
....

4 A: Did Alfred paint those signs for the rally?
B: No, he didn't paint any signs even though he said he would paint the signs.
....

5 A: Will we see you at the lake for the clean-up?
B: Yes, you will see me there.
....

12 ★★ **Read the sentences and rewrite them using substitution or ellipsis where necessary.**

1 'Do you think we're going to raise a lot of money for the cause tonight?' 'I believe we are going to raise a lot of money tonight.'
....
....
....

2 'Would you like me to bring a spade for you when we go to the tree planting?' 'No thanks, I've already got a spade.'
....
....
....

3 'How about helping me make leaflets and make posters for the fundraiser? Making leaflets and making posters on my own is no fun.' 'Making leaflets and making posters sounds great!'
....
....
....

Key word transformations

13 ★★ **For questions 1-4, complete the second sentence so that it has a similar meaning to the first sentence, using the word given. Do not change the word given. You must use between three and eight words, including the word given.**

1 Bob was happy he had completed the fun run. **HIMSELF**
Bob was happy .... the fun run.

2 The organisation is recruiting volunteers to persuade people to house refugees. **GET**
Volunteers .... refugees.

3 Steven and I both lost out on participating in the demo. **PARTICIPATE**
I didn't .... did Steven.

4 The police have to verify the details of everyone taking part today. **MUST**
Everyone taking part today ....
.... the police.

Module 6

Modals

Can, could, may, might, must, ought to, shall, should, will and ***would:***

- don't take -**s**, -***ing*** or -***ed*** suffixes.
- are followed by the infinitive without '***to***'.
- go before the subject in questions and are followed by '**not**' in negations.
- don't have tenses in the normal sense. When followed by a present infinitive, they refer to the present or future. *We **should leave** in half an hour; we will be there on time.* When followed by a perfect infinitive, they refer to the past. *We **should have arrived** before the performance started.*
- ***have to***, ***need*** and ***dare*** are also considered and used as modals. *You **needn't** come.*

Obligation/Duty/Necessity (*must, have to, should/ought to*)

- ***Must*** expresses a **duty/strong obligation** to do sth, and shows that sth is essential. We generally use ***must*** when the speaker has decided that sth is necessary.
*I **must** start practising my violin more often.* (**The speaker** has decided it is necessary.)
- ***Have to*** expresses **strong necessity/obligation**. We use ***have to*** when somebody other than the speaker has decided that sth is necessary. *The headteacher says that I **have to** try harder with my homework. Mark's mum says that he **has to** go and see his grandmother tomorrow.* (**Somebody else** has decided it is necessary.)
- ***Should/Ought to*** + **present infinitive** express weak **obligation**. *You **should/ought to go** to sleep earlier.* (less emphatic than 'must' – **This is the right thing to do.**)
- ***Have got to*** has the same meaning as ***have to***, and is often used in everyday speech. *I**'ve got to** speak to my sister later.*

Absence of necessity (*don't have to/don't need to, needn't*)

- ***Don't have to/Don't need to/Needn't:*** it isn't necessary to do sth in the present/future.
*Katie has done her work; she **doesn't have to** stay behind late. You **don't need to** buy new shoes yet. You **needn't** buy milk; there's some in the fridge.* (**It isn't necessary.**)

Permission/Prohibition (*can, may, could, mustn't, can't*)

- ***Can/May/Could*** are used to ask for/give **permission**. ***May*** is more formal than ***can***. ***Could*** is the most formal of the three.
***Can/May/Could** I use one of your pens?* (asking for permission – **Is it OK if ...?**) *Yes, you **can/may**.* (NOT: ~~Yes, you could~~.)
- ***Can*** + **present infinitive** expresses the idea that you are allowed to do something. *Jamie **can take** the car if she wants; she's fully insured.* (**She is allowed to.**)
- We use ***can*** and ***be allowed to*** to refer to laws and regulations. *All citizens over the age of 18 **can/are allowed to** vote.* (law)
- ***Mustn't/Can't:*** it is forbidden to do sth; it is against the rules/law; you are not allowed to do sth. *You **mustn't/can't** wear shoes on the bouncy castle.* (**You aren't allowed to; it's forbidden; it's against the rules/law.**)
- ***Shouldn't/Oughtn't to*** can be used to politely advise somebody against doing something or to remind them of public duties and regulations. *You **shouldn't eat** too much saturated fat. You **oughtn't to** park in front of ramps for wheelchair users.*

Note

In formal English, ***should*** is commonly used with emotive verbs (***beg***, ***deplore***, ***prefer***, ***regret***, etc) and phrases (***it's a pity***, ***it's disgraceful***, ***it's unthinkable***, ***it is odd***, ***it worries me***, ***I'm sorry that***, ***I'm surprised that***, etc), to express an idea, a reaction to what we already know, or a judgement, not a fact. ***It's disgraceful that** he **should** abandon his studies.* (the idea of abandonment is disgraceful) **BUT:** *It's disgraceful that he has abandoned his studies.* (the abandonment itself is disgraceful)

Possibility (*can, could, may, might*)

- ***Can*** + **present infinitive: general/theoretical possibility**, not usually used for a specific situation.
*You **can order** extra coursebooks online if you need to.* (general possibility – **It is theoretically possible.**)
- ***Could/May/Might*** + **present infinitive: possibility in a specific situation.**
*We **might watch** a film tonight if you're interested.* (**It is possible; I think it's likely; perhaps** – possibility in a specific situation)
Note: We can use ***can/could/might*** in questions, **BUT** NOT ***may***. *Where **can/could/might** I get some Indian food nearby?* (NOT: Where ~~may I get~~ ...?)

Ability/Inability (*can, can't*)

- ***Can('t)*** expresses **(in)ability** in the present/future.
*Martin **can** sing really well.* (**He is able to.**)
*Norman **can't** ride a motorcycle.* (**He isn't able to.**)

Offers/Suggestions (*can, would, shall, could*)

- ***Can:** **Can** I get you something to drink?* (**Would you like me to ...?** – informal)
- ***Would:** **Would you like** another biscuit?* (**Do you want ...?**)
- ***Shall:** **Shall** I help you bring your bags in?* (**Would you like me to ...?/Do you want me to ...?**)
- ***Can/Could:** We **can** go somewhere to eat later if you want. You **could** visit the Natural History Museum tomorrow.* (**Let's .../Why don't you ...?**)

Probability (*will, should/ought to*)

- ***Will:** Mark **will** be on time; he's never late.* (**It's 100% certain.**)

- ***Should/Ought to:*** *Barbara **should/ought to** pass her Maths exam; she's been revising for three months!* **(It's 90% certain; it's probable.)**

(Asking for) Advice (*should/ought to, shall*)

- ***Should/Ought to* + present infinitive:** general advice. *You **should/ought to eat** more fruit and vegetables.* **(I advise you to; it's a good idea; it's a good thing to do.)**
- ***Shall:*** asking for advice. ***Shall** I **take** any more medicine?* **(Is it a good idea to ... ?)**

Past Modals

Obligation/Duty/Necessity (*had to, should/ought to*)

- ***Had to*** is the past form of both ***must*** and ***have to***.
- ***Should/Ought to* + perfect infinitive** express weak **obligation.** *You really **should/ought to have handed** in this form yesterday.* **(You were supposed to, but you didn't.)**

Absence of necessity (*didn't need to/didn't have to, needn't have + pp*)

- ***Didn't need to/Didn't have to:*** it wasn't necessary to do sth. We don't know if it was done or not.
  *Ben **didn't need to/didn't have to** enrol at the university to attend the lectures.* (We don't know if he enrolled at the university, but **it wasn't necessary** to do so.)
- ***Needn't* + perfect infinitive** expresses the idea that something happened or was done although it was not necessary.
  *I **needn't have saved** him any food – he had already eaten.* (I saved him food, but **it wasn't necessary.**)

Permission/Prohibition (*could, couldn't*)

- ***Could* + present infinitive** expresses the idea that you were allowed to do something in the past.
  *Harry **could eat** pudding only after he had finished his main course when he was a child.* **(He was allowed to.)**
- ***Couldn't* + present infinitive** expresses the idea that you were not allowed to do something in the past.
  *Jerry **couldn't eat** fast food when he was young.*
  (He was not allowed to.)

Criticism (*could, might, should/ought to*)

- ***Could/Might/Should/Ought to* + perfect infinitive** are used to criticise someone's actions, or lack of action, in the past.
  *Isaac **could/might/should/ought to have taken** the bus – it would have been cheaper.* **(It would have been better if ... .)**
  *You **shouldn't have packed** so much luggage!* **(but you did)**

Possibility (*could, may, might, would*)

- ***Could/Might/Would* + perfect infinitive** refer to sth in the past that was possible but didn't happen.
  *You're very lucky; you **could/might have been** seriously hurt! If he hadn't been wearing the red hat, I **would have missed** him!*
- ***May/Might* + perfect infinitive** refer to something that possibly happened in the past.
  *Chris **may/might have started** exercising because of a health scare.* (He **possibly** started for this reason.)

Ability/Inability (*could(n't), was(n't) able to*)

- ***Could* + present infinitive** expresses **general repeated ability** in the past. *Michael **could** run the 100 metres in under 10 seconds as a young athlete.* **(He was able to.)**
- ***Was(n't) able to* + present infinitive** expresses **(in)ability** on a **specific occasion** in the past.
  *Karen **was(n't) able to** finish her homework before bedtime.* **(She managed/didn't manage to ... .)**
- ***Couldn't* + present infinitive** may be used to express any kind of **inability** in the past, repeated or specific.
  *Richard **couldn't** ride a horse until he went on holiday to America.* (repeated inability in the past)
  *Richard **couldn't/wasn't able to** come to the meeting yesterday as he missed the train.* (specific inability in the past)

Note

We normally use ***could*** with the verbs ***feel***, ***guess***, ***hear***, ***remember***, ***see***, ***smell***, ***taste***, ***understand***, and to express ability on a **specific occasion** in the past. *Kate **could see** people starting to gather around the scene of the crime.* (NOT: ... ~~*she was able to see*~~ ...)

Advice (*should/ought to*)

- ***Should/Ought to* + perfect infinitive: general advice.** *You **should/ought to have worn** a warmer jacket.* **(I had advised you to do it, but you didn't.)**

Assumptions (*must, may/might/could, can't/couldn't*)

- ***Must:*** **almost certain** that this is/was **true** (positive logical assumption).
  *I can hear singing; the girls **must be rehearsing** for the musical.* **(I'm almost sure that sth is true.)**
- ***May/Might/Could:*** **maybe, it's possible.**
  *They **may cancel** the flight if conditions don't improve.*
  *The lights aren't on; they **might have gone** to the restaurant already.*
- ***May/Might/Could well:*** **it is highly likely that.**
  *The parcel **may/might/could well be** in the post.* **(it is highly likely that it is in the post.)**
- ***Can't/Couldn't:*** **almost certain** that this is/was **impossible** (negative logical assumption). *Fiona has a broken leg; she **can't/couldn't be playing** volleyball.*
  *Jack **can't/couldn't have ordered** tea; he never drinks tea.*
  (I'm sure that sth wasn't true.)

Notes

- The subjunctive form (bare infinitive for all persons) is

used after certain verbs and expressions to give emphasis. The most common ones are: ***advise***, ***ask***, ***demand***, ***insist***, ***it is essential***, ***it is imperative***, ***it is important***, ***it is necessary***, ***it is vital***, ***propose***, ***recommend***, ***request***, ***suggest***. In British English we normally use ***should*** + **bare infinitive** instead of the subjunctive.
__It is vital (that)__ he __deliver__ the parcel today. (less usual)
__It is vital that he should deliver__ the parcel today. (more usual)

- ***May/might as well*** are used to express resignation, i.e. we agree to do something because there is nothing to do in a situation that we can't change.
We __may/ might as well__ start the meeting without her.

Tenses of the infinitive

The verb tenses corresponding to the tenses of the infinitive are as follows:

Verb tenses	Tenses of the Infinitive
he does/will do	→ (to) do
he is doing/will be doing	→ **(to) be doing**
he did/has done/had done	→ **(to) have done**
he was doing/has been doing/had been doing	→ **(to) have been doing**

• *__Perhaps__ Mike __is__ at the cinema.* • *I'm sure she __practises__ every day.* • *__It's likely__ that I __will see__ Nora tomorrow.*	**present infinitive**	• *Mike __may be__ at the cinema.* • *She __must practise__ every day.* • *I __may see__ Nora tomorrow.*
• *__It's possible__ that Fred __is entering__ the singing contest now.* • *__It's likely__ that I __will be joining__ the scuba diving team next month.*	**present continuous infinitive**	• *Fred __could be entering__ the singing contest now.* • *I __may be joining__ the scuba diving team next month.*
• *__I'm sure__ Sally __didn't eat__ all the cake.* • *__It's likely__ that the ferry __has left__ already.* • *__Perhaps__ Frank __had booked__ a table before we arrived.*	**perfect infinitive**	• *Sally __can't have eaten__ all the cake.* • *The ferry __might have left__ already.* • *Frank __may have booked__ a table before we arrived.*
• *__Perhaps__ they __were packing__ the car when it started to rain.* • *__Maybe__ Glenn __has been training__; he's much fitter than before.* • *I'm __sure__ Henry __had been waiting__ for ages; he looked very annoyed.*	**perfect continuous infinitive**	• *They __may have been packing__ the car when it started to rain.* • *Glenn __may have been training__; he's much fitter than before.* • *Henry __must have been waiting__ for ages; he looks very annoyed.*

Words/Phrases expressing modality

- ***Be supposed to*** + **infinitive** means 'should', but it expresses the idea that someone else expects something to be done.
You__'re supposed to sign__ in every day for attendance.
(Your instructor expects you to.)
- ***Be to*** + **infinitive** means 'must', but it expresses the idea that someone else demands something.
You __are to pay__ your taxes this year. (It's the law so you must obey.)
Be supposed to and ***be to*** are used to express what someone expects about a previously arranged event.
You __are supposed to/are to__ fill out your tax return before the deadline. (It is scheduled.)
- ***Be liable to*** + **infinitive** expresses obligation (often in a legal context).
Offenders __are liable to face__ prosecution.
- ***Be obliged to/Be required to*** + **infinitive** are often used in formal contexts.
Guests __are obliged to dress__ appropriately at the function.
- ***Be likely to*** means 'may' (possibility); it is more emphatic than ***may*** but less emphatic than ***should/ought to***. In order to express possibility in questions, we don't use 'may'. Instead, we use: ***Is he likely to*** ...?, ***Is it likely that he*** ...?, ***Can he*** ...?, ***Could he*** ...?, ***Might he*** ...?
__Is he likely to__ want to go swimming?
__Is it likely that he__ will want to go swimming?
__Could he__ want to go swimming?
- ***Would you mind*** is used to express formal polite requests.
__Would you mind__ helping me move the table?
- ***Let's.../How about...?/Why don't we...?/What about...?*** are used to make suggestions.
__Let's__ meet tomorrow at seven o'clock.
__How about__ meeting tomorrow at seven o'clock?
__Why don't we__ meet tomorrow at seven o'clock?
__What about__ meeting tomorrow at seven o'clock?
- ***Would you like to...?/Would you like me to...?*** (= Shall I ...?) are used when we offer to do something.
__Would you like me to__ carry your bag? (Shall I carry ...?)
- ***Was/Were allowed to*** is used to express permission on a specific occasion in the past.
We __were allowed to__ use our calculators in the test.
(NOT: ~~*We could use*~~ ... .)
- ***Be bound to*** is used to express that it is certain that something will happen, or it is very likely to happen.
You __are bound to__ improve your grades if you study more.

Modals/Past Modals

1 ★ **Match the modal verbs in bold to their meanings (A-J).**

1 ☐ You **oughtn't to** park your car in front of the hospital garage; people need to access it.

2 ☐ Anne **should** get a residency; she's an amazing doctor.

3 ☐ **Shall** I try meditation to help reduce stress?

4 ☐ You **ought to have** read that self-help book that I gave you; it really helps!

5 ☐ If I hadn't been paying attention, I **would have** missed the sign for the clinic.

6 ☐ James **couldn't** join the advanced judo class because he only started the sport last year.

7 ☐ Kurt **wasn't able to** complete his training before the marathon.

8 ☐ Naomi **couldn't have** cooked a steak; she's vegan.

9 ☐ Jack **might have** given up fast food because of the results of his medical.

10 ☐ We **may as well** accept that Hank is never going to improve his diet.

11 ☐ Eating more fruit **will** help you; it's scientifically proven.

12 ☐ I**'ve got to** speak to my personal trainer tonight.

13 ☐ I really **must** start taking better care of my health.

14 ☐ Sam **didn't have to** sign up to the health club to join the aerobics class.

- **a** It wasn't necessary for him to do sth
- **b** I remind you not to
- **c** I have decided that I need to
- **d** It was possible but didn't happen
- **e** It's 100% certain that it's going to
- **f** You were supposed to
- **g** We have to come to terms with the fact
- **h** He possibly did sth
- **i** He wasn't allowed to
- **j** I'm sure that she didn't do sth
- **k** I have to
- **l** He didn't manage to
- **m** It's highly probable that she will
- **n** Is it a good idea for me to

2 ★ **Choose the correct item.**

1 Jodie **has to be/could be/must be** at the physio although I'm not entirely sure.

2 The lights are on in the dance studio; the cast **ought to be practising/must be practising/should be practising** for the show.

3 Where **might/may/shall** I find a pharmacy nearby?

4 Victoria **ought to use/should have used/may have been using** a personal trainer; she's in great shape at the moment.

5 Scott **was able to see/could see/would see** the crowd gathering outside the stadium before kick-off.

6 Thomas **mustn't have ordered/can't have ordered/may not have ordered** a latte; he hates drinking coffee!

7 Karen **needn't have left/can't have left/wouldn't have left** yet for her yoga class; her car is still in the driveway.

8 They **ought to have been preparing/could have been preparing/must have been preparing** for the exam instead of going to the cinema.

3 ★★ **Complete the sentences using the appropriate modal verb.**

1 Stephen .... deadlift a hundred and fifty kilos as a young man. **(general repeated ability in the past)**

2 You .... use multivitamin supplements to boost your nutritional intake. **(offering advice)**

3 We .... try visiting a life coach if you're interested. **(making a suggestion)**

4 You .... use my car so long as you promise to fill up the tank. **(giving permission)**

5 Our trainer says we .... stick to the fitness programme she's set us while we are in the gym. **(expressing obligation)**

6 .... I help you set up the exercise machine that you want to use? **(making an offer)**

7 Your diet plan is flexible; you .... avoid eating cakes all the time. **(absence of necessity)**

8 You .... have ignored your coach's advice; now your injury is worse. **(expressing criticism)**

4 ★ Choose the correct modal verb.

1 You **needn't have brought/oughtn't have brought** a towel with you; the leisure centre provides them for you.
2 Peter **shouldn't have eaten/might not have eaten** much today; he doesn't have any energy at all.
3 I'm not entirely sure but the girls **may have gone/must have gone** to the hospital already.
4 You **ought to have cancelled/must have cancelled** your aerobics class if you weren't feeling well.
5 You **mustn't have seen/can't have seen** Richard at the gym yesterday; he has been in London on a business trip since last week.

5 ★★ Rephrase the sentences using modal verbs.

1 I'm certain Joyce didn't go to the public speaking workshop; she hates standing in front of a crowd.
....
....
2 Now that Henry's a therapist it's likely that he will open his own clinic.
....
....
3 Perhaps he hasn't been feeling well recently; that could explain his absence.
....
....
4 It's possible that she is joining the new health club tomorrow.
....
....
5 I'm sure she's preparing for the marathon at the moment.
....
....
6 It's likely that Ellen has already lost weight; she's been exercising a lot.
....
....
7 It was necessary for us to register for the exercise class before attending.
....
....
8 It was possible for an accident to have occurred if you hadn't been careful.
....
....

6 ★★ Study the situations and write sentences using *mustn't*, *shouldn't*, *must*, *might as well* and *ought to*.

1 Your friend is having difficulty reaching his goals. You think it's a good idea for him to see a life coach to get help. Tell your friend what you think.
....
....
....
2 Your brother wants to use the gym facilities without having an induction first. Tell him that it's not allowed.
....
....
....
3 You believe that everyone has a responsibility to take care of their health and well-being. Express this belief to your friend.
....
....
....
4 It's clear that your friend isn't coming to the concert today after all. You reluctantly agree to go anyway. Tell your friends what you think you should do.
....
....
....
5 You think it's not a good idea for your friend to ignore the doctor's advice.
....
....

7 ★★ Read the sentences and correct the mistakes.

1 Ben didn't need to go to so much trouble cooking; we brought some vegan dishes with us.
....
2 I couldn't have drunk so much coffee last night; I didn't get any sleep at all!
....
3 There are some sports bags on the side of the court but no one else is here; someone might have left them here by accident.
....
4 What are you doing, Bob? You oughtn't drive above the speed limit; it's against the law!
....
5 You really must have checked your therapist's availability yesterday; he probably won't have an appointment at this short notice.
....

Words/Phrases expressing modality

8 ★ **Choose the correct item.**

1 You **are supposed to/are to** scan your membership card when you arrive at the gym; otherwise, you cannot enter.
2 Pharmacists that issue restricted medication without a prescription **are obliged to/are liable to** face prosecution.
3 We **could bring/were allowed to bring** our dog with us on the hike last Friday.
4 **Is she likely to/Is she bound to** have any problems if she forgets to take a dose of her medicine?
5 **Would you mind/How about** going shopping tomorrow if you want something to do?
6 We **are required to/are liable to** check patients' medical history before issuing treatment.

9 ★★ **Fill in the gaps with the modals from the list.**

• might • might/quit • must • can • have to
• don't need to • ought to/take • may/chase

The road to success

For most elite athletes, reaching their goals doesn't come easy and it is likely that they **1)** .... their dream for years. Despite this, they gladly work hard. They set themselves a goal and decide for themselves that they **2)** .... reach it. Top athletes understand that when their trainers tell them that they **3)** .... train hard, it's for their own benefit. What sets a top athlete apart from the rest is that a winner never gives up. They do one more lap even if they **4)** .... do it. They go to the gym even if friends and family are telling them that they **5)** .... the day off. They push themselves even if their goal doesn't materialise; after all, they **6)** .... fall at the last hurdle. Regardless, a winner never gives up even when others **7)** .... already. True athletes know full well that no one **8)** .... be a champion without commitment.

10 ★★ **Replace the modal verbs in bold in the sentences using one of the phrases expressing modality in the list. Make any necessary changes.**

• would you like me to • are supposed to
• are bound to • are obliged to • are to

1 You **must** submit your taxes to the government by April 15th.
....
....
2 **Shall** I get you that book on nutrition that you wanted?
....
....
3 You **will** reach your fitness targets if you work out hard enough.
....
....
4 We **have to** wear formal attire at the presentation ceremony.
....
....
5 You **should** book an appointment before going to the osteopath.
....
....

Key word transformations

11 ★★ **For questions 1-4, complete the second sentence so that is has a similar meaning to the first sentence, using the word given. Do not change the word given. You must use between three and eight words, including the word given.**

1 I'm sure Frank did not forget about his doctor's appointment; he knows how important it was. **FORGOTTEN**
Frank ....
about his doctor's appointment; he knows how important it was.
2 Angela brought more energy bars than was necessary for our training session. **NEED**
Angela ....
so many energy bars for our training session.
3 He'll probably run the marathon with us next week. **LIKELY**
He ....
the marathon with us next week.
4 The fitness studio can accommodate more than twenty exercise stations. **BE**
More than twenty exercise stations ....
.... fitness studio.

Nouns

Nouns are parts of speech which refer to:

- **people** (Ann), **actions** (reading), **objects** (apple), **qualities** (virtue), **places** (Athens), **jobs** (teacher), etc.

There are five kinds of nouns in English. These are:

- **abstract nouns** *(science, peace, anger)*
- **concrete countable nouns** *(car, spoon)*
- **concrete uncountable nouns** *(clothing, glass)*
- **collective nouns** *(group, army, audience)*
- **proper nouns** *(Jacob, Beirut)*

Nouns can be used as the:

a) subject of a verb. *The **plane** took off.*
b) object of a verb. *I saw a **bird**.*
c) object of a preposition. *I saw it in the **park**.*
d) complement of the linking verbs ***be***, ***become***, ***look like***, ***make***, ***remain***, ***seem*** and ***turn***. *Laurie **is** a **singer**. Mary will **become** a great **painter**.*

Most common nouns which refer to jobs, social status, etc have the same form for men and women: *artist, child, cook, doctor, enemy, friend, foreigner, guest, librarian, neighbour, parent, person, servant, student, teacher, writer,* *etc.*

Countable – Uncountable Nouns

- **Countable** nouns are those that can be counted (*one dog, two dogs,* etc). **Uncountable** nouns are those that cannot be counted (*sand, water,* etc). Uncountable nouns take a singular verb and are not used with ***a/an***.

Groups of **uncountable nouns** include:

- **mass nouns** (*meat, flour, air,* etc)
- **nouns ending in *-ics*** (*economics, mathematics,* etc)
  Note: *statistics* + plural verb; *politics* + singular/plural verb
  *The statistics **are** annoying.*
  *Politics **is** an interesting field of study.*
  *What **are** his politics?*
- **sports** (*football, handball, golf,* etc)
- **games ending in *-s*** (*billiards, darts,* etc)
- **languages** (*Welsh, Italian, Maltese,* etc)
- **diseases** (*rubella, influenza,* etc)
- **natural phenomena** (*thunder, snow, rain,* etc)
- **some abstract nouns** (*bravery, hate, shame,* etc)

The most common uncountable nouns are:
accommodation, advice, anger, applause, assistance, baggage, behaviour, business, cardboard, cash, chaos, chess, china, clothing, countryside, courage, damage, difficulty, dirt, education, equipment, evidence, excitement, food, football, footwear, fun, furniture, garbage, glassware, gossip, grass, happiness, harm, health, help, jealousy, jewellery, homework, hospitality, housework, information, knowledge, laughter, leisure, lightning, linen, luck, luggage, machinery, money, moonlight, mud, music, news, nonsense, paper, parking, patience, permission, poetry, produce, progress, research, rubbish, safety, scaffolding, scenery, seaside, soap, steam, strength, stuff, sunshine, thunder, timber, toast, traffic, transport, travel, trouble, understanding, underwear, violence, vocabulary, wealth, weather, work, writing, etc

Many uncountable nouns can be made countable by means of partitives.
a piece of cake/ice/information/baggage/advice/work/equipment/research; **a glass of** water/wine; **a jar of** jam; **a sheet/roll/scrap of** paper; **an item of** news; **a packet of** tea; **a slice of** meat/bread; **a pot/flask of** tea; **a ball of** string; **a lump of** sugar; **a game of** football/chess; **a tube of** toothpaste; **a bar of** soap/chocolate; **a blade of** grass; **a flash of** lightning; **a clap/peal/rumble of** thunder, **a lock of** hair, **a pat of** butter, **a spoonful of** medicine, **a branch of** knowledge, **a fit of** anger, **a spot of** trouble/bother, etc
Note: We can use ***a/an***, ***one/two***, etc with uncountable nouns, such as ***coffee***, ***tea***, etc, when we order something in a restaurant, café, etc. *Would you like **a coffee**?*

The plural of nouns

Nouns are made plural by adding:

- ***-s***, ***-es***, ***-ies***, ***-ves:*** *pencil – pencils, bus – buses, lady – ladies, leaf – leaves,* **BUT** *chiefs, proofs, roofs, cliffs, beliefs, safes, still lifes* (the paintings).
  Note: *wharf – wharves/wharfs, hoof – hooves/hoofs, scarf – scarves/scarfs, handkerchief – handkerchieves/handkerchiefs.*
- Some nouns form their plural irregularly: *child – children, man – men, ox – oxen, penny – pence* (as a collective plural).
- Some nouns remain unchanged in the plural.
  aircraft – aircraft, British – British, Chinese – Chinese, craft – craft, deer – deer, Dutch – Dutch, grouse – grouse, hovercraft – hovercraft, Japanese – Japanese, mackerel – mackerel, means – means, offspring – offspring, plaice – plaice, Portuguese – Portuguese, salmon – salmon, series – series, sheep – sheep, spacecraft – spacecraft, species – species, Swiss – Swiss, trout – trout, etc.
  *The new TV **series is** quite amazing!*
  ***Many** new **series have been cancelled** this year by the television network.*
  *This **sheep is** very small compared to the others.*
  ***There are** 20 **sheep** in the farm.*
- **Some nouns are only plural.** These are:
  a) ***amends, arrears, belongings, cattle, clothes, congratulations, earnings, gentry, goods, greens*** *(vegetables)*, ***groceries, lodgings, oats, odds*** *(chances)*, ***outskirts, particulars, people*** [**ALSO:** peoples (nations)], ***police, premises*** *(building)*, ***proceeds, regards, remains, riches, savings, surroundings, thanks, the Antipodes*** *(Australia and New Zealand)*, ***the Commons, the Lords, the Middle Ages, valuables, vermin, whereabouts***, etc.
  b) garments, tools and instruments consisting of two parts: ***binoculars, braces, brackets, compasses, glasses, jeans, pants, pliers, pyjamas, gloves, scales, scissors, shears, shorts, tights, spectacles, trousers***, etc.

  Note: These nouns can be made singular by using the phrase 'a pair of' in front of them. *Where **are** my **gloves**? The **pair of gloves is** in the cupboard.*

- **Some nouns have different meanings when turned into plural.** These are:
  - ***air*** (atmosphere) – ***airs*** (behaviour)
  - ***arm*** (part of the body) – ***arms*** (weapons)
  - ***brain*** (the organ) – ***brains*** (intellect)
  - ***content*** (what is written or spoken about in a piece of writing, speech, etc)
    contents (the things contained in a box, place, etc)
  - ***custom*** (a traditional event)
    customs (the government department which collects taxes on imported goods)
  - ***damage*** (harm done to something)
    damages (monetary compensation)
  - ***experience*** (knowledge or skill gained over a period)
    experiences (activities/events one has done or lived through)
  - ***fund*** (a sum of money saved for a purpose)
    funds (money)
  - ***glass*** (a drinking receptacle; the material)
    glasses (spectacles)
  - ***hair*** (the hairy part of the head)
    hairs (fine strands growing from the skin)
  - ***look*** (a style; an expression)
    looks (a person's appearance)
  - ***manner*** (the way in which something is done)
    manners (social behaviour; the customs of a social group)
  - ***minute*** (60 seconds)
    minutes (notes taken as a record of a meeting)
  - ***pain*** (the feeling) – ***pains*** (a special effort)
  - ***quarter*** (of an hour, etc)
    quarters (place to live) [**BUT**: a historic quarter of a city]
  - ***regard*** (respect; consideration) – ***regards*** (greetings)
  - ***service*** (a system providing a public need such as healthcare, transport or utilities)
    services (the particular skills sb can offer)
  - ***spectacle*** (an impressive sight; an object of attention)
    spectacles (glasses)
  - ***troop*** (a group of people/animals)
    troops (a group of soldiers)
  - ***tropic*** (each of the two imaginary lines around the globe)
    tropics (the hottest part around the Equator)
  - ***wit*** (saying clever and amusing things)
    wits (the ability to make decisions)
  - ***work*** (employment)
    works (the moving parts of a machine; a place of manufacturing process)
  - *Could I have a **glass** of water?*
    *I can't read without **glasses**.*
  - *There wasn't much **damage** done to the window.*
    *The court awarded her **damages** for her injury.*

Collective nouns

Collective nouns can take either a singular or plural verb, according to the meaning which we want to convey.
*My family **comprises** five members.* (as a whole)
*My family **prefer** different types of holiday.* (each individual)

Some collective nouns are: ***army***, ***aristocracy***, ***audience***, ***clan***, ***choir***, ***class***, ***clergy***, ***club***, ***committee***, ***company***, ***crew***, ***crowd***, ***family***, ***firm***, ***flock***, ***gang***, ***group***, ***government***, ***jury***, ***mob***, ***orchestra***, ***public***, ***staff***, ***team***, ***union***, ***youth***, etc.

Notes:

- With expressions of **duration**, **distance** and **money** meaning 'a whole amount', we use a singular verb. *Three thousand euros **was** what the second-hand car cost.*
- Nouns formed by adjectives preceded by '***the***' always take a plural verb. ***The elderly are** more vulnerable than **the young**.*

Compound nouns

Compound nouns can be formed with:

- **noun + noun**: ***bloodstain***, ***coffee time***, ***hunchback***, ***motorbike***, ***oak tree***, ***snowflake***, ***table leg***, ***tissue paper***, ***toy factory***
  Note: a teacup (= a cup for drinking tea), a cup of tea (= a cup containing tea)
- **noun + verb form or verb form + noun:** ***air-conditioning***, ***babysitter***, ***daydream***, ***haircut***, ***handwriting***, ***sunrise***, ***story teller***, ***chewing gum***, ***dance floor***, ***firing squad***, ***flashlight***, ***swimming pool***

Plural compounds

- Compound nouns form their plural by adding ***-s***/***-es***:
  a) to the noun if the compound noun has only one noun. *passer-by – passer**s**-by, hanger-on – hanger**s**-on* [**BUT** *spoonful – spoonfuls, mouthful – mouthfuls*]
  b) to the second noun if the compound noun consists of two nouns. *cupboard – cupboard**s**, outcast – outcast**s**, greenhouse – greenhouse**s***
  c) to the first noun if the compound noun consists of two nouns connected with a preposition. *mother-in-law – mother**s**-in-law, editor-in-chief – editor**s**-in-chief, man-of-war – **men**-of-war*
  d) at the end of the compound noun if it does not contain any nouns. *breakdown – breakdown**s**, pick-me-up – pick-me-up**s***
  Note: In compound nouns referring to **duration** and **measurement**, the first noun loses its plural form and is always used in the singular. *I had a two-**hour** session and a three-**hour** one last week.*
  (NOT: … ~~a two-hours session and a three-hours one~~ …)
  Such nouns are often used adjectivally:
  a five-day trip (NOT: ~~a five-days trip~~)
  a ten-euro stamp (NOT: ~~a ten-euros stamp~~)

Nominalisation

In order to produce a more varied piece of writing, we can nominalise (= turn into a noun) the verb carrying the main meaning of a construction, making all the necessary transformations, such as turning an adverb into an adjective, or making use of appropriate verbs which collocate with the noun that we derive from the given verb.
*Obesity **is rising** as a result of poor diet.* → *The **rise** in obesity is a result of poor diet.*
*He **ran** quickly around the park.* → *He had a quick **run** around the park.*
*They didn't **explain** why the bus was late.* → *They didn't provide an **explanation** for why the bus was late.*

Nouns

12 ★ Put the nouns in the list in the correct column.

• science • plane • peace • clothing • team
• Jodie • army • committee • car • Jacob
• apple • virtue • audience • spoon • Beirut
• water • group • salt • metal • anger • Athens

Abstract nouns	Concrete countable nouns	Concrete uncountable nouns	Collective nouns	Proper nouns

13 ★ Match the partitives (1-8) with the correct nouns (a-h).

1 ☐	a branch of	a	knowledge
2 ☐	a spot of	b	anger
3 ☐	a flash of	c	trouble
4 ☐	a fit of	d	paper
5 ☐	a game of	e	lightning
6 ☐	a lock of	f	grass
7 ☐	a blade of	g	football
8 ☐	a scrap of	h	hair

14 ★ Write the plural of the following nouns.

1 chief ....
2 series ....
3 economics ....
4 drawback ....
5 offspring ....
6 knife ....
7 editor-in-chief ....
8 bystander ....
9 crutch ....
10 belief ....
11 penny ....
12 fish ....

15 ★ Choose the correct word.

1 a The **custom/customs** office charges taxes on items imported from overseas.
b The festival is an important **custom/customs** that has been held for centuries.

2 a Richard has ten years' **experiences/experience** working in A&E.
b I've had a few bad **experiences/experience** visiting the doctor.

3 a Suzanne lost all her **hair/hairs** because of the treatment but thankfully it will grow back.
b Excuse me, I found some black **hair/hairs** in my soup; can you please prepare me another?

4 a The trainee doctors live together in the student **quarter/quarters**.
b Brian is scheduled for surgery in **a quarter/quarters** of an hour.

5 a The family set up a crowdfunding page to raise **fund/funds** for Callum's hospice care.
b The charity has access to a **fund/funds** for helping the families of patients.

6 a Patrick received **damage/damages** in the amount of £15,000 after he injured himself falling on the broken step.
b Doctors are worried that Amy may have suffered brain **damage/damages** in the accident.

16 ★ Underline the correct item.

1 A: How's your sister doing?
B: She's getting much better; everybody in the family **is/are** confident she will be discharged from hospital soon.

2 A: Have you seen my tool box anywhere?
B: No, sorry. But your pliers **is/are** in the utility room if that helps!

3 A: I'm sorry; members of the public **is/are** not allowed in this part of the hospital.
B: Please excuse me, I didn't realise this wing was staff only.

4 A: The whole committee **was/were** devastated to hear about the closure of the medical clinic.
B: I know, it's terrible that such an essential public service is shutting down.

5 A: The doctors' union **is/are** voting on whether or not to strike over pay.
B: Well, I can understand that. After all, they do deserve more money.

6 A: At this time of year the elderly **is/are** particularly susceptible to the cold.
B: Yes, absolutely. That's why I've made sure that my parents' boiler was recently serviced.

Compound nouns

17 ★★ **Rewrite the sentences using compound nouns making any necessary changes.**

1 I can't understand what the doctor has written by hand; can you make sense of it?
....
....

2 Stanley had a dream during the day that he was a neurosurgeon.
....
....

3 Hayley needs to follow a course of treatment for five days.
....
....

4 Jack lost his licence for driving because he developed a debilitating condition.
....
....

5 A lot of physio work is done in the pool where people go swimming.
....
....

6 Julie went to the hospital with her husband to visit her brother by law .
....
....

18 ★★ **Read the sentences and correct the mistakes.**

1 Unauthorised personal are not allowed on the premises.
....

2 Terry turned down the bar of chocolates because he's trying to cut down on sweets.
....

3 Jake's energy drinks and protein bars are in the cupsboards above the kitchen sink.
....

4 My optician says I need new glass.
....

5 The measles are a disease that can spread from one person to another.
....

6 I think linguistics are a fascinating subject.
....

7 Karen dislikes devices for conditioning of the air as they irritate her skin.
....

Nominalisation

19 ★★ **Finish the sentences using nominalisation. Make any necessary changes.**

1 The council didn't attempt to block the sale of the land.
No ....

2 The two parties have compromised over the ownership of the intellectual rights of the formula.
The two parties ....
....

3 Many scientists and doctors believe that antibiotics will soon become universally ineffective.
Many scientists and doctors are of the ....
....

4 The government needs to prioritise funding for mental health treatment.
There needs to be ....
....

5 The rate of obesity is rapidly increasing and must be dealt with.
There ....
....

20 ★★ **Look at the underlined parts in the sentences and rewrite them using nominalisation.**

1 A local school <u>is attempting</u> to address the poor diet of its pupils.
....
....

2 They have <u>decided</u> to introduce a new lunchtime menu.
....
....

3 They have also <u>announced</u> that they will be launching a breakfast club in the near future.
....
....

4 Members of the school board <u>consulted</u> a local chef on the design of both menus.
....
....

5 <u>Implementing</u> the new menus will make students both healthier and more focused.
....
....

Grammar Bank 6

Determiners

Determiners are: the **indefinite article** (*a/an*), the **definite article** (*the*), **demonstratives** (*this – these/that – those*), **possessive adjectives** *(my, your, his,* etc), **quantifiers** (*some, any, every, no, both, each, either, neither, none, enough, several, all, most, whole,* etc) and **numbers** (*one, two,* etc).

The indefinite article *'a/an'*

- **The indefinite article *a/an*** can be used only with **singular countable nouns**, when we do not define which one we talk about.
- We use ***a/an*** with the verbs ***to be*** and ***have (got)***. *Rufus **has (got) a** cat. It's **a** Persian Longhair.*
- We use ***a/an*** before **Mr/Mrs/Miss/Ms** when we refer to an unknown person. ***A Mr Brown** called you this morning.* (A person that we don't know.)
- A few abstract nouns are used as countable nouns: ***awareness, denial, dislike, distrust, education, fear, hatred, hope, horror, idea, knowledge, love, nuisance, pity, situation, sleep, understanding***. *He has **a** fair **knowledge** of biology. She has **a fear** of heights.*
- ***A/An*** can also be used with: **fractions** (***an**/one eighth*), **measurements** (***a**/one yard*), **weight** (***a**/one ton*), whole **numbers** (***a**/one billion*), **price/weight** (***a**/one cent **a** kilo*), **frequency** (*twice **a** week*), **distance/fuel** (*60 miles **a** gallon*), **speed** (*24 miles **an** hour*), **symptoms** (***a** runny nose*), **jobs** (*work as **a** doctor*).
- ***a/an*** + **noun** (any one) *Could I have **a** bottle of orange juice, please?*
  one + **noun** (when counting) *There was only **one** battery left; I needed two.*
- When we use a **noun** in the **singular number** to represent **a class of things/animals**, ***the*** or ***a/an*** must be used.
  ***The** giraffe can be up to 6 metres tall.*
  ***A** giraffe can be up to 6 metres tall.*
  For **generalisations** we can also use the **plural**.
  ***Sperm whales** can dive deeper than 1,200 metres.*

The definite article *'the'*

We use ***the***:

- with nouns when talking about something **specific**. *Danny has a dog; **the** dog is black and white.*
- with nouns that are **unique** (***the** Earth, **the** sky*, etc).
- with names of **newspapers** (***the** Mail*), **cinemas** (***the** Orpheus*), **theatres** (***the** Old Vic*), **museums/art galleries** (***the** Victoria and Albert Museum*), **ships** (***the** SS Great Britain*), **organisations** (***the** EU*).
- with names of **rivers** (***the** Amazon*), **groups of islands** (***the** Isles of Sicily*), **mountain ranges** (***the** Alps*), **deserts** (***the** Sahara Desert*), **oceans** (***the** Atlantic*), **canals** (***the** Grand Union Canal*), **countries** when they include words such as ***States, Kingdom, Republic*** (***the** United Kingdom, **the** Kingdom of Denmark, **the** Republic of Cuba*), nouns with ***of*** (***the** Chancellor of Germany*), in **geographical terms** such as ***the** Tropic of Capricorn/Cancer, **the** Antarctic, **the** North Pole, **the** north of Scotland, **the** North/South/East/West*.
- with names of **musical instruments/dances** (***the** violin, **the** foxtrot*).
- with names of **families** (***the** Andersons*), **nationalities** ending in ***-ss, -sh, -ch*** or ***-ese*** (***the** Swiss, **the** British, **the** French, **the** Portuguese*).
- with **titles** (***the** Duchess, **the** Prince*) **BUT** NOT with titles including a proper name (*Prince William*).
- with **adjectives/adverbs** in the **superlative form** (***the** worst film ever made*), but when ***most*** is followed by a noun, it doesn't take ***the*** and means 'the majority of' (***Most** people enjoyed the film.*).
- with **adjectives** denoting an abstract quality (*Some people enjoy **the mystical** and **the supernatural** in literature.* – everything that is mystical and supernatural)
- with the words ***day, morning, afternoon*** and ***evening***. *It was early in **the** afternoon.* **BUT** *at night, at noon, at midnight, by day/night.*
- with **historical periods/events** (***the** Regency era*), **BUT** *Crimean War.*
- with the words ***first, last, only, right, same, wrong*** (used as adjectives). *It was **the** wrong key.*
- with the words ***beach, cinema, city, coast, country(side), ground, jungle, library, sea(side), shops, station, theatre, weather, world***. *I prefer living in **the** city.*
- with **group nouns** (***the** jury*).
- with **adjectives** used as **nouns** to **describe groups of people** (***the** wealthy, **the** poor, **the** young*).
- with **inventions** (***the** internal combustion engine, **the** wheel*).

Note: With verbs followed by a prepositional phrase referring to a part of the body or clothes, we cannot use a possessive adjective; instead, we use the article '***the***'. *She is suffering a lot of pain in **the** stomach.* (NOT: ~~her stomach~~)

We do not use ***the***:

- with **uncountable** and **plural nouns** when talking about something **in general**. ***Children** have a different view of the world from **adults**.*
- before **proper nouns**. ***Kim** is in **London** for a training course.*
- before the names of **sports, games, activities, days, months, celebrations, colours** and **drinks**. *I play **rugby** every weekend. Harriet will be here on **Monday**.*
- with names of **languages**, unless they are followed by the word ***language***. *Paul speaks **English, French, Arabic** and **Russian**.* **BUT** ***The Chinese language** is a difficult language to learn.*
- with the names of **countries** which don't include the words ***States, Kingdom*** or ***Republic*** (*Australia, Nepal, Algeria*). **BUT** there are some exceptions: ***the** Netherlands, **the** Gambia.*
- with names of **streets** (*Oxford Street, Sunset Boulevard* **BUT** ***the** M4, **the** A21*), **squares** (*Red Square*), **bridges** (*Tower Bridge,* **BUT** ***the** Clifton Suspension Bridge*), **parks** (*Green Park*), **railway stations** (*King's Cross, Birmingham New Street*), **mountains** (*Everest*), **individual islands** (*Tasmania*), **lakes** (*Lake Superior*) and **continents** (*Europe*).

- with **possessive adjectives** and **the possessive case**. *They're not **my** glasses; they're **my friend's**.*
- with the names of **restaurants**, **shops**, **banks**, **hotels**, etc which are named after the people who started them and end in **-s** or **-'s**. *Mario's,* **BUT** *the Red Lion* (because ***Red*** is not the name of a person or place)
- with the words ***bed***, ***college***, ***court***, ***hospital***, ***prison***, ***school***, ***university***, when we refer to the purpose for which they exist. *He broke his leg and was taken to **hospital**.* **BUT** *Mary works in **the hospital** down the road.*
- with the word ***work*** (= a job/a piece of/place of work). *I start **work** in half an hour.*
- with the word ***home*** when we talk about our own **home**. *I'm going **home**.*
- with ***by*** + **means of transport** (*by bike/train/boat/plane*, etc).
- with names of **illnesses**. *Donald's got **diabetes**.* **BUT** flu/***the*** flu, measles/***the*** measles, mumps/***the*** mumps.
- with names of **meals**. ***Lunch** is my favourite meal of the day.* **BUT** ***The** lunch we had yesterday was rather expensive.* (It's a specific lunch).
- with names of **substances**. ***Sand** is used to make **glass**.*
- with two-word names when the first word is the name of a person or place. *Gatwick Airport*, *Windsor Castle*, **BUT** *the White House* (because '*White*' is not the name of a person or place)
- before **parallel phrases**. *They met **face to face**.* **BUT** *He punched him in **the face**.*

Note: ***Seasons*** can be used with or without ***the***: *We stay here in (the) summer.*

The indefinite article *'a/an'* – The definite article *'the'*

21 ★★ **Fill in:** ***a/an*, *the* or –.**

1 A: Where's .... Adrian?
B: He's got .... cold. He's had .... runny nose and .... cough for .... few days so he's in .... bed.

2 A: What time are you going to .... hospital to visit your .... mum?
B: I'm going to leave in .... hour.

3 A: I didn't realise that .... placebo effect was first discovered during .... WWII.
B: I know. Now it's .... important factor in all drug trials.

4 A: Are you going to take a ferry to .... Greek islands with your .... parents?
B: No, I always get .... travel sick when I'm on .... boat.

5 A: .... Rossini's Restaurant always uses .... freshest ingredients to make their .... dishes.
B: I know, their .... food is delicious! I eat there about twice .... month.

22 ★★ **Choose the correct item.**

1 One of **most significant/the most significant** scientific breakthroughs happened in **Scotland/the Scotland** when colleagues at **University of Edinburgh/the University of Edinburgh** succeeded in cloning Dolly **sheep/the sheep**.

2 Kate is studying **medicine/the medicine** because she wants to become **doctor/a doctor**.

3 **The mineral-rich/Mineral-rich** water of **Dead Sea/the Dead Sea** has **reputation/a reputation** of having healing powers.

4 **Health system/The health system** in **UK/the UK** is known as **NHS/the NHS** and it is free to use for anyone living in **country/the country**.

5 If I could live anywhere in **world/the world**, I would choose to stay on **island/an island** in **Mediterranean/the Mediterranean** where they eat **healthy diet/a healthy diet**.

6 **French/The French** take their food very seriously and believe they have **best/the best** cuisine on **planet/the planet**.

7 **Most/The most** medical terms come from **the Greek/Greek**.

23 ★★ **Fill in** ***a/an*, *the*** **or –.**

Hi Alison,

Sorry I haven't been in touch for **1)** .... while, I know it was very remiss of me to forget to send you **2)** .... message. You see, unfortunately, I've been **3)** .... bit under **4)** .... weather recently. I've had **5)** .... flu since Friday and couldn't get out of **6)** .... bed for **7)** .... week! To be honest it's been **8)** .... worst case of flu I've ever had. I'm starting to feel better slowly, but I'm still confined to **9)** .... house. What bad luck though eh? Right before my **10)** .... holiday to **11)** .... South of France! I couldn't believe it! I was really looking forward to visiting **12)** .... Cannes and swimming in **13)** .... sea. It's really such **14)** .... pity but I guess I can always go next year. Anyway, I hope you are well and I'll see you as soon as **15)** .... doctor says I can!

Bye for now,
Maria

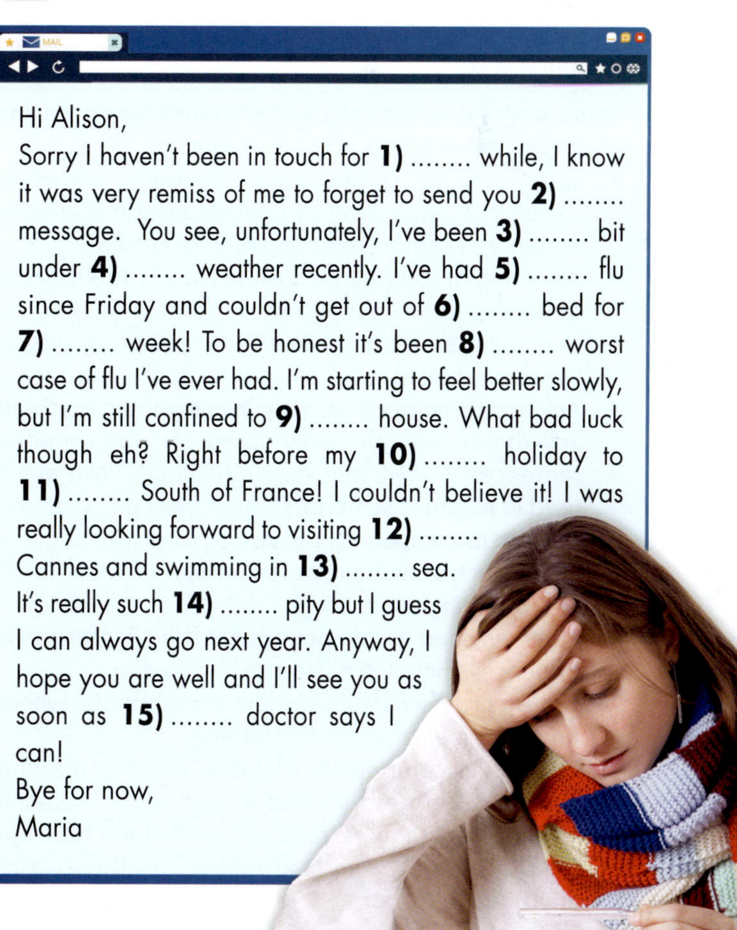

Demonstratives

This – These are used:

- for people or things near us. *These are my cousins.*
- for present/future situations. *I'm seeing a film **this** evening.*
- when the speaker is in or near the place he/she is referring to. ***This** house is beautiful!* (The speaker is inside the house.)
- to introduce people or to identify ourselves on the phone. *Hello, **this** is Carl speaking.*

That – Those are used:

- for people or things not near us. *Look at **those** buildings over there!*
- for past situations. ***That** was a lovely dinner party the other week!*
- to refer back to something mentioned before. *"I won a prize in the competition!" "**That's** great!"*
- when speaking on the phone to ask who the other person is. *Hello? Who's **that**?*

Notes:

- Demonstratives can be used without nouns when the noun they modify is clear from the context. ***These** aren't yours. I'll always remember **this**.*
- Demonstrative adjectives can also be used to point out specific things or people in order to emphasise their importance. ***Those** diets are effective. **That** doctor is highly qualified.*

Quantifiers

Some/Any/No

Some, ***any*** and ***no*** are used with uncountable nouns and plural countable nouns. ***some** ice, **some** tins*

- ***Some*** and its compounds (somebody, someone, something, somewhere) are normally used in affirmative sentences. *There are **some** apples in the basket.*
- ***Some*** and its compounds are also used in interrogative sentences when we expect a positive answer, for example when we make an offer or request. *Would you like **some** cheese?*
- ***Any*** and its compounds (anyone, anybody, anything, anywhere) are normally used in interrogative sentences. *Is there **any** juice in the fridge?* **Not *any*** is used in negative sentences. *There aren**'t any** seats left.* ***Any*** and its compounds can also be used with negative words, such as ***without***, ***never***, ***rarely***, etc. *I have **rarely** seen **anything** so amazing!*
- When ***any*** and its compounds are used in affirmative sentences, there is a difference in meaning. *You can sit **anywhere** you want.* (it doesn't matter where) ***Anything** could happen!* (everything)
- ***No*** and its compounds (nobody, no one, nothing, nowhere) are used instead of ***not any*** in negative sentences. *We have **no** food left.* (= We do**n't** have **any** food left). *There was **nothing** in the box.* (= There was**n't** **anything** in the box.)

Note: We use a singular verb with the compounds of ***some***, ***any*** and ***no***. *No one **is** available this evening.*

- ***Some*** can also be followed by a singular countable noun to indicate somebody or something unknown or extraordinary. *That was **some** performance! I can hear **some** radio playing; is it your neighbour's?*

Every/Each, All, Either, Neither, Whole, etc

Each and ***every*** are used with **singular countable nouns**. We normally use them when we refer to three or more people or things. ***Every** employee in the company has a degree. **Each** employee will receive an electronic clocking-in card.*

- ***Every*** refers to a group of people/things **as a whole**. ***Every** candidate must attend a seminar next week.* (all of them together)
- ***Each*** refers to the members of a group **individually**. ***Each** part of the mechanism must be carefully oiled.* (one at a time)
- ***Each*** is also used to refer to **two** people/things. *He had a gold ring on **each** thumb.*
- The pronouns ***everyone***, ***everybody***, ***everything*** and the adverb ***everywhere*** are used in affirmative, interrogative and negative sentences, and are followed by a **singular verb**.
- We use ***every*** to show how often something happens. *We have rehearsals **every** Wednesday afternoon.*
- We use ***every***, but not ***each***, with words and expressions such as ***almost***, ***nearly***, ***practically*** and ***without exception***. *He's watched **practically every** science-fiction film ever made!*
- ***Both*** refers to two people or things. It has a positive meaning and takes a verb in the plural. It is the opposite of ***neither/not either***. *Food and drinks are free. **Both** food and drinks are free. They are **both** free. **Both of** them are free.*
- ***All*** refers to more than two people or things. It has a positive meaning and takes a verb in the plural. It is the opposite of ***none***. ***All** the children went on the trip. **All of** them went on the trip. They **all** went on the trip. **All** twelve of them went on the trip.*
  All **+ that-clause** (= the only thing that) takes a singular verb. ***All that** I want **is** something to eat.*
- ***None*** refers to more than two people or things. It has a negative meaning and isn't followed by a noun. *"Are there any biscuits left?" "No, **none**."* ***None of*** is used before nouns or object pronouns followed by a verb either in the singular or plural. It is the opposite of ***all***. ***None of** the tourists/them brought water.*
  Note: *no* + noun. *There's **no opera** more beautiful than this one.*
- ***Either*** (= any one of the two) / ***Neither*** (= not one and not the other) refer to two people or things and are used before singular countable nouns. ***Either** dish would be fine. **Neither** road leads to Shrewsbury.*
  Neither of/Either of take a verb either in the singular or plural. ***Neither/Either of them is/are** qualified for the job.*
- ***Whole*** (= complete) is used with countable nouns. We

always use ***a/the/this/my*** etc + ***whole*** + **countable noun**. *the **whole** year*

- ***One/Ones*** are used to avoid repetition of a countable noun. *"Which jacket would you like?" "The grey **one**."*
- ***Both ... and ...*** + **plural verb**. ***Both** Norman **and** Jack **are** on the committee.*
- ***Either ... or ... / Neither ... nor ... / Not only ... but also ...*** + **singular** or **plural verb** depending on the subject which follows ***or/nor/but also***. ***Neither** my father **nor my mother enjoys** war films.*

'Other' constructions:

- ***the other(s)*** = the rest. *I brought this bag in but **the others** are being brought in by Sam.*
- ***others*** = several more apart from the ones already mentioned. *Some students like Maths, but **others** prefer sports.*
- ***each other*** = one another. *Rugby players rely on **each other** to play safely.*
- ***every other*** = alternate. *Olive goes to ballet practice **every other** week.*
- ***the other day*** = a few days ago. *It was raining **the other day** so we had to reschedule the picnic.*
- ***the other one(s)*** = not this/these but sb/sth else. *This hotel is in a good location but **the other one** was cheaper.*
- ***another*** = one more apart from that/those already mentioned. *Shall I put **another** burger on the barbecue?* ***Another*** can be used with expressions of distance, money and time. *It's **another** three years before the next solar eclipse.*

A few/Few – A little/Little

A few and ***few*** are used with **plural countable nouns**. ***A little*** and ***little*** are used with uncountable nouns.

- ***A few*** (= not many but enough) + **countable noun**. *There are **a few** hours left of the flight.*
- ***Few*** (= hardly any, almost none) + **countable noun**. It can be used with ***very*** for emphasis. *There are (very) **few** tickets left for the performance.*
- ***A little*** (= not much but enough) + **uncountable noun**. *I need **a little** time to get ready.*
- ***Little*** (= not much, almost none) + **uncountable noun**. It can be used with ***very*** for emphasis. *There was (very) **little** rain today.*

A lot of/Lots of – Much – Many

- ***A lot of/Lots of*** are used with both plural countable and uncountable nouns. They are normally used in affirmative sentences. The ***of*** is omitted when ***a lot/lots*** are not followed by a **noun**.
  *There are **a lot of/lots of** talented musicians in the orchestra.*
  *Are there **lots of** people in the shop? Yes, there are **lots**.*
- ***Much*** is normally used in negative and interrogative sentences. It is used with uncountable nouns.
  *We don't have **much** space in the car.*
- ***Many*** is used with plural countable nouns. It is used in the negative and interrogative in everyday speech (***lots of/a lot of*** being preferred in affirmative sentences), **except** with nouns of time (hours, days, years, etc), when ***many*** is **always** used in the affirmative too.
  *'Do you know **many** people here?' 'Not **many**, no.'*
  *I've got **lots of/a lot of** things to do today, so don't come over.* (NOT: ... ~~many things to do~~.)
  *I lived in Plymouth for **many** years.* (NOT: ... ~~for lots/a lot of years~~.)
  In formal writing, however, ***many*** is acceptable in all affirmative sentences. *The scan showed that **many** brain cells in the prefrontal cortex were still active.*
- ***How much*** and ***how many*** are used in questions and negations.
  How much + **uncountable noun** → amount
  How many + **countable noun** → number
  ***How much** time is left until the play starts?*
  ***How many** bottles of water should I buy?*
- ***Too much*** is used with uncountable nouns. It has a negative meaning, and shows that there is more of something than wanted or needed. *You put **too much** salt in the soup!*
- ***Too many*** is used with plural countable nouns. It has a negative meaning, and shows that there are more people/things than wanted or needed.
  *You have **too many** items in your shopping basket, sir!*
- We use ***many/much/some/any/most/(a) few/(a) little/several/one/two*** etc + ***of*** followed by ***the/that/this/these/those*** + **noun**, when talking about a specific group. ***Some of the** paintings you've drawn are very nice.* (your paintings) **BUT** ***Some** paintings are very nice.* (paintings in general)

Demonstratives

24 ★★ **Fill in:** *this, these, that* **or** *those.*

1. .... scones here are delicious; they're better than my mum's.
2. I can't believe John said .... about your weight; you definitely don't need to go on a diet.
3. I've always fancied getting one of .... exercise bikes over there.
4. Patricia is sitting her final Science exam .... morning.
5. I'd like to buy .... cake in the window; the one with the chocolate icing, please.
6. .... was an exciting race I took part in the other week. It had to be decided by a photo finish.
7. Hello, ... is Mrs Anderson speaking. Can I talk to the doctor, please?
8. I'm glad Amy is recovering. Really, ... is great.

25 ★ Complete the exchanges using *this*, *these*, *that* or *those*.

1 A: I thought you might like .... book. It's about dealing with high stress levels.
B: .... was very thoughtful of you, thanks.

2 A: .... cast is really uncomfortable.
B: ....'s too bad. I'm sorry it's bothering you.

3 A: What time do you call ....? You should have been home ages ago.
B: Sorry, but I had to fill .... prescription and I couldn't find a chemist open.

4 A: Isn't .... the nurse that was so nice to you in the hospital?
B: You're right. .... was an awful time but she made it a lot easier.

5 A: .... support stockings are a bit expensive but they're better than .... over there by the window.
B: OK. I think I'll take .... ones. I want to make the best recovery.

6 A: Do you want to eat here? I think .... restaurant serves vegan food.
B: I've heard of .... place. It's the one that's recommended on the Internet.

Quantifiers

26 ★★ Complete the sentences using *each* and *every* or a compound of *every*.

1 .... summer I suffer from allergies and I have to take antihistamines and apply drops to .... eye.

2 The organisers informed .... of the candidates that they had passed the medical for the programme.

3 Almost .... time I get a cold .... of my senses are affected and I can't hear, taste or smell properly.

4 This new gym is amazing, it has practically .... type of exercise machine you could imagine!

5 My grandfather has to wear a hearing aid in .... ear because he doesn't catch .... that is being said without it.

6 .... patient will be treated by the doctor but it may take some time.

7 Caitlin goes to the gym .... Wednesday without exception.

8 It felt like .... single bone in my body hurt after the accident; I had aches .... for days!

27 ★★ Fill in the gaps with *some*, *any*, *every*, *no* or one of their compounds.

MAIL

Hi Julia,

I went to an amazing seminar yesterday and the speaker gave us **1)** .... fantastic advice! He was really inspiring and motivational. I mean, I know a lot of people scoff at life coaches, but in my opinion there's **2)** .... wrong with it. Why not seek expert help, especially if you haven't got **3)** .... else to turn to? Life coaches are professionals after all, and can point you in the right direction when you feel like you're getting **4)** .... by yourself. Like the speaker said to us, coaches just provide that extra little push, **5)** .... actually comes from within the client themselves. Most life coaches don't tell us **6)** .... that we don't already know. It's just the way they help us see it. Anyway, it was fascinating, you should definitely read into it!

Have a great weekend, and when I see you on Monday I'll tell you all about it!

Amanda

HISTORY • BOOKMARKS

28 ★★ Fill in: *all*, *every*, *both*, *whole*, *either*, *none*.

1 A: I need to speak to a doctor.
B: Unfortunately, ... Dr Gregory and Dr Scott are busy at the moment.

2 A: .... of the exercises seem to be helping me.
B: Come on, Steve! .... that you need to do is be patient, things will get better.

3 A: Excuse me. Do .... the lasagne or the cannelloni come with a side salad?
B: They .... do. In fact .... the pasta dishes are served with .... salad and a portion of chips.

4 A: Can you believe that no one from my class visited me the .... time I was in hospital?
B: What? .... of them?

5 A: Remember you have to warm up .... time you start working out.
B: I know. .... the trainer and the instructor told me that already.

6 A: The .... department went through the first-aid course and they .... did very well.
B: They did. I was really surprised that .... of them had done any first-aid training before.

29 ★★ **Rewrite the sentences using the words in brackets.**

1 You can speak to your doctor or the chemist about your medication. **(either ... or)**

....

2 Alexander is allergic to shellfish and so is Chris. **(both ... and)**

....

3 You can use a walking stick or you can use a crutch until your foot is fully healed. **(either ... or)**

....

4 Jessica and I have never had chickenpox. **(neither ... nor)**

....

5 You need calcium and vitamin D for healthy bones. **(not only ... but also)**

....

30 ★★ **Fill in the gaps with a word/phrase from the list.**

• the other one • others • the others • another • each other • every other • the other day

1 Raymond and Kyle motivate .... when they're at the gym.
2 I saw the doctor .... and he said I was on the mend.
3 Some patients make a quick recovery but .... take months.
4 This burger is ready but .... aren't cooked yet; they'll take .... five minutes at least.
5 This orthopaedic slipper is cheap but .... is more comfortable.
6 You should really go to the gym .... day if you want to see results quickly.

31 ★ **Choose the correct item.**

1 There were very **little/much/few** people in the waiting room so I didn't have to wait long to see the dentist.
2 **Lots of/Much/A little** people take vitamins as a supplement to their diet.
3 Can I have **a few/little/a little** milk in my coffee, please?
4 **How many/How much/Very few** times do you have to attend physiotherapy?
5 **Too much/Too many/Lots** people don't follow the rules and leave their towels lying around when they use the health club.

32 ★★ **Choose the correct item.**

Loneliness: the silent affliction

When recuperating from an illness or injury, **1) a lot/lots of** people find themselves confined to the house with not **2) much/many** to do and **3) few/little** in the way of company. This can have a big impact on well-being, as the recovery process depends on a person's state of mind. **4) Few/A few** people might be able to cope but **5) many/much** will be badly affected by spending **6) lots/a lot of** time on their own. This is easily remedied, however, by friends and family taking **7) a little/little** time out of their day to visit with them. It doesn't have to be for long and the simple gesture of stopping by for a **8) little/few** minutes can do the world of good!

Key word transformations

33 ★★ **For questions 1-5, complete the second sentence so that it has a similar meaning to the first sentence, using the word given. Do not change the word given. You must use between three and eight words, including the word given.**

1 You can't do anything about a cold except wait for it to pass. **IS**
There ....
a cold except wait for it to pass.

2 Both chicken and duck were on the menu. **OR**
You could order ....
duck.

3 The clinic provides holistic treatments as well as counselling. **BUT**
The clinic ....
counselling.

4 There are not many plasters left in this box. **ONLY**
There are ....
left in this box.

5 Sandra couldn't decide what to have for dinner and Tina couldn't either. **NOR**
Neither ....
what to have for dinner.

Module 7

Reported Speech

Reported speech is the exact meaning of what someone said, but not the exact words. We do not use quotation marks. The word ***that*** can either be used or omitted after the introductory verb (say, tell, suggest, etc).
*He said **(that) he saw Michael yesterday**.*

Say – Tell

- ***say*** **+ no personal object** – *He **said** he was excited.*
- ***say*** **+ to + personal object** – *He **said to us** he was excited.*
- ***tell*** **+ personal object** – *He **told us** he was excited.*

Note: We cannot use ***say about***. We can use ***tell sb/speak/ talk about*** instead.
*He **told us/spoke/talked about** his new job in finance.*

Expressions used with ***say***, ***tell*** and ***ask***.

Say	hello, good morning/afternoon etc, something/ nothing, so, a prayer, a few words, no more, for certain/sure, etc
Tell	the truth, a lie, a story, a secret, a joke, the time, the difference, one from another, someone's fortune, etc
Ask	a question, a favour, the price, after somebody, the time, around, for something/someone, etc

Reported statements

- In reported speech, **personal/possessive pronouns** and **possessive adjectives** change according to the meaning of the sentence.
  Sally said, 'I'm going to the shop round the corner.'
  *Sally said (that) **she** was going to the shop round the corner.*
- We can report someone's words either a long time after they were said (out-of-date reporting), or a short time after they were said (up-to-date reporting).

Up-to-date reporting
The tenses can either change or remain the same in reported speech.
Direct speech: *Barry said, 'I haven't watched the film yet.'*
Reported speech: *Barry said (that) he **hasn't/hadn't watched** the film yet.*

Out-of-date reporting
The introductory verb is in the past simple, and the tenses change as follows:

Direct speech	Reported speech
Present Simple → Past Simple	
*'He **is** tired.'*	*He said (that) he **was** tired.*
Present Continuous → Past Continuous	
*'I **am walking** the dog now.'*	*He said (that) he **was walking** the dog at that moment.*
Present Perfect → Past Perfect	
*'I **have been** to Canada.'*	*He said (that) he **had been** to Canada.*
Past Simple → Past Simple or Past Perfect	
*'They **sold** the old house.'*	*They said (that) they **(had) sold** the old house.*
Past Continuous → Past Continuous or Past Perfect Continuous	
*'I **was watching** TV at 6 pm yesterday evening.'*	*She said that she **was watching/ had been watching** TV at 6 pm the previous evening.*
Future (*will*) → *would*	
*'I **will take** the rubbish out tonight.'*	*He said (that) he **would take** the rubbish **out** that night.*

- Certain words and time expressions change according to the meaning, as follows:
  tonight → that night
  now → then, immediately, at that moment
  today → that day
  yesterday → the day before, the previous day
  tomorrow → the next/following day
  this week → that week
  last week → the week before, the previous week
  next week → the week after, the following week
  ago → before
  here → there
  come → go
  bring → take

Note

- When ***this/these*** are used in time expressions, they change to ***that/those***. *this week – that week, these days – those days*
  When ***this/these/that/those*** are not used in time expressions, they change as follows:
  a) they change to ***the*** when used as adjectives, i.e. when they are followed by a noun. *'**This car** looks very expensive,' Derek told me. – Derek told me (that) **the car** looked very expensive.*
  b) they change to ***it*** or ***they/them*** when used as pronouns, i.e. when they are not followed by a noun. *'**This is** a complicated idea,' the professor said. – The professor said (that) **it** was a complicated idea.*

Changes in verb tenses in reported speech

The verb tenses remain the same:

- when the introductory verb is in the present, future or present perfect.
  *Peter **says**, 'I'm ecstatic.' Peter **says** (that) he **is** ecstatic.*
  The introductory verb is in the present tense:
  a) when we pass on messages. *Fiona **says** she wants the keys for the front door.*
  b) when we report the content of a letter, article, etc while reading it. *The letter **says** that they'll be here next week!*

c) when we refer to something someone says very often. *Dad often **says** that I should work harder at school.*

- when the verb of the direct sentence is in the **unreal past** or in **Type 3 Conditionals**.
  *He said, 'I would rather you **ate** more quietly.'*
  *He said (that) he would rather I **ate** more quietly.*
  *She said, 'It's about time we **went** home.'*
  *She said (that) it was about time they **went** home.*
  *He said, 'If you **had tried** harder, you **would have passed** the test.'*
  *He said (that) if I **had tried** harder, I **would have passed** the test.*
- when the following verbs/verb phrases are used: ***had better***, ***could***, ***would***, ***used to***, ***needn't have***, ***should***, ***might*** and ***ought to***.
  *They said, 'We **used to swim** in the lake in the summer.'*
  *They said (that) they **used to swim** in the lake in the summer.*
  *She said,' I **had better recharge** my phone.'*
  *She said (that) she **had better recharge** her phone.*
- when there is a **past simple** or a **past continuous** in a time clause.
  *She said, 'When I **was cooking**, I **heard** a strange noise.'*
  *She said (that) when she **was cooking**, she **heard** a strange noise.*
- when the time of the information being reported is not over yet.
  *He said, 'I'**ll** be there tomorrow.' He said (that) he **will** be there tomorrow.* (It's still the same day).

The verb tenses can either change or remain the same in reported speech when reporting a general truth or law of nature.
*The old man said, 'This lake **freezes/froze** in winter.'*
*The old man said (that) this lake **freezes/froze** in winter.*

Reported/Indirect Questions

Reported questions

- Reported questions are usually introduced with the verbs ***ask***, ***inquire***, ***wonder***, or the expression ***want to know***.
- When the direct question begins with a question word (***who***, ***where***, ***how***, ***when***, ***what***, etc), then the reported question is introduced with the same question word.
  'Where are you going?' she asked him. (direct question)
  She asked him where he was going. (reported question)
  She inquired where he was going. (reported question)
  She wanted to know where he was going. (reported question)
- When the direct question begins with an auxiliary verb (***be***, ***do***, ***have***), or a modal verb (***can***, ***may***, etc), then the reported question is introduced with ***if*** or ***whether***.
  'Do you speak to Isaac often?' (direct question)
  *He asked me **if/whether** I spoke to Isaac often.* (reported question)

Note: In reported questions, the verb is in the **affirmative**. The **question mark** and words/expressions such as ***please***, ***well***, ***oh***, etc are omitted. The **verb tenses**, **pronouns** and **time expressions change** as in **statements**.
'Can I have a ticket, please?' (direct question)
He asked me if he could have a ticket. (reported question)

Indirect questions

- **Indirect questions** are used to ask for **advice** or **information**. They are introduced with: ***Could you tell me ... ?, Do you know ... ?, I wonder ..., I'd like to know ..., I want to know ...***, etc, and the verb is in the **affirmative**. If the indirect question starts with ***I want to know*** ... or ***I wonder*** ..., the question mark is omitted.
  'Where is the post office?' (direct question)
  'I'd like to know where the post office is.' (indirect question)
  'Are the banks open tomorrow?' (direct question)
  'Could you tell me if the banks are open tomorrow?' (indirect question)
  Question words (***what***, ***where***, ***who***, etc) or ***whether***, **BUT NOT *why***, can be followed by an **infinitive** in reported speech if the subject of the question is the speaker.
  'Where can I find fresh eggs?' he asked me. → *He wanted to know **where to find** fresh eggs.*

Note: Sometimes reported and indirect questions look similar. However, changing from direct to indirect question does not involve the changes required when using reported speech.
*How **will** climate change affect **my** city?* (direct question)
*I wonder how climate change **will** affect **my** city.* (indirect question)
*'How **will** climate change affect **my** city?' he asked himself.* (question – direct speech)
*He wondered how climate change **would** affect **his** city.* (reported question)

Reported exclamations

- We use the verbs ***exclaim*** and ***say/tell*** to report **exclamations** which begin with '***What a/an*** ...!' or '***How*** ...!' in direct speech. *'What an unusual design!' he said. – He exclaimed/said/told them that it was an unusual design. He exclaimed/said/told them that the design was unusual.*
  But with exclamations such as '***Splendid!***', '***Great!***', '***Excellent!***', '***Oh!***', '***Oh dear!***', etc, we use the expressions **give an exclamation of delight/disgust/ relief/surprise**, etc. *'Wow!' he said as he unwrapped his gift. He gave an exclamation of surprise as he unwrapped his gift.*

Yes/No short answers in Reported speech

- ***Yes/No*** **short answers** are expressed in reported speech with **subject + appropriate auxiliary verb** OR **subject + appropriate introductory verb.**
  'Will you eat your pudding?' he asked. 'No,' she said. → *He asked her if she would eat her pudding, but she said she **wouldn't**.* OR *He asked her if she would eat her pudding but she refused.*

Reported question tags

- **Question tags** are omitted in reported speech. However, we can use the verb ***remind*** as a suitable introductory verb, in order to retain their effect.
  'This isn't the first time we've been to Paris, is it?' she said.
  *She **reminded** him (that) it wasn't the first time they had been to Paris.*

Reported commands, requests, suggestions, etc

To report **commands, requests, suggestions, instructions**, etc, we use a special introductory verb followed by a ***to*-infinitive**, ***-ing* form** or ***that*-clause**, depending on the introductory verb. *'Turn off the radio, please,' Tom asked Ellen.* → *Tom asked Ellen to **turn off** the radio.*
In order to report orders, we use the introductory verbs ***order*** or ***tell*** **+ sb + (not) *to*-infinitive**.
'Stop the vehicle!' (direct order)
*The security guard **ordered them** to stop the vehicle.* (reported order)
'Stop running!' (direct order)
*The teacher **told us** to stop running.* (reported order)

Reported Speech

1 ★ **Fill in the gaps with the correct form of *say*, *tell* or *ask*.**

1 She .... us about her life in New York.
2 I can't .... the difference between the two products; they look the same!
3 She .... me a favour when she needed help after her move.
4 At the press conference, the mayor .... a few words about the new government policy.
5 The volunteer .... for some help soliciting support for the new nature reserve.
6 It's OK, ... no more, Jeff, I totally understand your problem.
7 Should you see Jenny, please .... after Jackie; I haven't seen her for years.

2 ★ **Underline the correct item.**

1 The citizen group said that they would hold a meeting later **this/that/next** week.
2 Tim told us that 10 years **ago/before/now** he had lived in that neighbourhood.
3 She told me that we should drive to the city centre **herself/ourselves/myself** instead of taking the train.
4 Kevin said that he had got stuck in terrible traffic **before/the day before/at that moment**.
5 The environmental commissioner said they hadn't measured pollution levels since the **previous/last/following** year.

Reported statements

3 ★★ **Report what the people said.**

1 'We will save a lot of resources with the new recycling scheme,' Jim told the community group.
....
2 'City engineers are surveying the area where the new motorway will be built,' the councillor explained to the mayor.
....
3 'The city's energy plan was devised with the target of sustainability in mind,' the city official said in the press conference.
....
4 'I have never seen so much rubbish,' Kelly told us.
....
5 'Yesterday morning at 9 am, I was waiting in traffic and finally arrived at work an hour later,' Julia complained.
....
6 'I want to go to the Citizen's Action meeting next week,' Paul said to us.
....

4 ★★ **Tick (✓) the sentences whose tenses can change, then turn them all into reported speech.**

1 Mike said 'I used to live in a small town before moving to the city.' ☐
....
2 'I would rather we moved to the suburbs,' Tim told his mother. ☐
....
3 'I'm shopping on high street now,' Gloria says. ☐
....
4 'I want to attend the class about composting,' Jeannie says. ☐
....
5 'I will call the police about the noise!' Gordon told his neighbour. ☐
....
6 'You had better find a way to reduce the stress that living in the city causes you,' Max said to George. ☐
....
7 Jack always says, 'If everyone would just recycle, what a difference it would make!' ☐
....
8 'I was travelling on the underground during the power cut,' she said. ☐
....

Reported/Indirect questions – Exclamations – Yes/No short answers – Question tags

5 ★★ **Report the following sentences using the verbs in brackets.**

1 'Leave this area at once,' the security officer told us. **(commanded)**
....
....

2 'What an incredible view!' Tina said. **(exclaimed)**
....

3 'Have you managed to find yourself a new apartment yet?' he said. **(asked)**
....
....

4 'This isn't the first time you've volunteered for a charity, is it?' Anita said. **(reminded)**
....
....

5 'Sort out the rubbish for recycling, please,' Jean told her brother. **(asked)**
....
....

6 'Why don't we join the march on parliament against the new superhighway?' Jackie said. **(suggested)**
....
....

7 'Will you take the rubbish to the recycling centre today?' Ethan asked. 'No,' Jane said. **(asked/refused)**
....
....

6 ★★ **Rewrite the following questions as indirect questions.**

1 Have they started to charge for plastic bags at the supermarket?
Do you know ....?

2 'Is the youth centre next to the train station?'
Can you tell me ....?

3 'How much is all this air pollution affecting our health?'
I wonder ....

4 'Will the government really reach its targets for reducing crime this year?'
I want to know ....

5 'How can we contact the mayor about the rubbish problem on high street?
I'd like to know ....

6 'Is there any way to arrange for the council to deliver compost bins?'
Could you tell me ....?

7 ★ **Choose the option (a or b) which shows how the sentence was in direct speech.**

1 She said she would join the rally supporting the nature reserve the next day.
a 'I would like to join the rally supporting the nature reserve the next day.'
b 'I will join the rally supporting the nature reserve tomorrow.'

2 The reporter asked if a representative had been chosen for the residents' side for the dispute.
a 'Who has been chosen as a representative of the residents' side for the dispute?'
b 'Has a representative been chosen for the residents' side of the dispute?'

3 She told us that she had attended the energy conference the previous week.'
a 'I've attended the energy conference the week before.
b 'I attended the energy conference last week.'

4 The mayor said the city had been implementing alternative energy schemes the last few months.
a 'The city has been implementing alternative energy schemes the last few months.'
b 'The city was implementing alternative energy schemes a few months ago.'

5 He said that it was the cleanest city he had ever seen.
a 'This is the cleanest city I have ever seen.'
b 'This city is cleanest city I have ever seen!'

8 ★★ **An earthquake hit a large city a short while ago. Report what some of the people living in the city said about it.**

1 'I've experienced an earthquake before but this one was much larger. Some people are afraid more aftershocks will follow but I don't think they will.' **(Alexa)**
....
....
....

2 'I've never witnessed anything like it in my life. My office building was literally shaking. I thought for sure it would collapse. I'm still looking for some of my friends. If I don't find them soon, I'll contact search and rescue teams tomorrow.' **(Mark)**
....
....
....

Modal verbs in reported speech

The following modal verbs change in reported speech when the reported sentence is out-of-date.

will	***would***
can	***could*** (present reference) ***would be able to*** (future reference)
may	***might/could***
shall	***should*** (asking for advice) ***would*** (asking for information) ***offer*** (expressing offers)
must	***must*** (expressing possibility or assumption) ***had to*** (expressing obligation)
needn't	***didn't need to*** (present reference) ***didn't have to*** (present reference) ***wouldn't have to*** (future reference)

Direct speech	Reported speech
*He said, "I **will** try my best to be on time."*	*He said (that) he **would** try his best to be on time*
*He said, "I **can't** find my car keys."* *He said, "We **can** grab some coffee later."*	*He said (that) he **couldn't** find his car keys.* (present reference) *He said (that) we **would be able to** grab some coffee later.* (future reference)
*He said, "It **may** snow tomorrow."*	*He said (that) it **might/could** snow the next day.*
*He said, "**Shall** I buy the tickets?"* *He said, "When **shall** we go to the restaurant?"* *He said, "**Shall** I make some dinner?"*	*He asked (me) if he **should** buy the tickets.* (advice) *He asked when we **would** go to the restaurant.* (information) *He **offered** to make some dinner.* (offer)
*He said, "They **must** have won the game."* *He said, "You **must** stay off the grass."*	*He said (that) they **must** have won the game.* (assumption) *He said (that) we **had to** stay off the grass.* (obligation)
*He said, "You **needn't** panic."* *He said, "You **needn't** book a table in advance."*	*He said (that) I **didn't need to/didn't have to** panic.* (present reference) *He said (that) I **wouldn't have to** book a table in advance.* (future reference)

Reporting nouns instead of verbs

Besides reporting verbs, one can make use of corresponding noun phrases, in order to better report the meaning of the utterance in direct speech:

- ***advise sb that*** → give sb advice on/about sth
- ***announce that*** → make an announcement about sb/sth
- ***answer that*** → give an answer to sb/about sth
- ***apologise for sth*** → make/issue an apology for sth
- ***claim that*** → make a claim that
- ***comment that*** → make a comment on/about sb/sth
- ***complain that*** → make/submit/lodge/file a complaint about sth
- ***deny that*** → issue a denial of sth
- ***explain that*** → provide/give an explanation of/for sth
- ***not respond*** → make no response
- ***predict that*** → make predictions about sb/sth
- ***promise that*** → make a promise that
- ***recommend that*** → make a recommendation that
- ***remark that*** → make a remark about sb/sth
- ***suggest that*** → make a suggestion that
- ***state that*** → make/issue/give a statement about/on sb/sth
- ***threaten sb*** → make/issue a threat against sb
- ***warn sb*** → give sb a warning/issue a warning

or similar constructions including the nouns mentioned above.

'You've made no progress, so you should retake the class,' she remarked.
She made a remark about the student's progress, advising him to retake the class.

Subjunctive

- In formal written English and especially in American English, certain reporting verbs and verb phrases can also be followed by the subjunctive (the base form of the verb in all persons): ***advise***, ***ask***, ***command***, ***decide***, ***decree***, ***demand***, ***insist***, ***move*** (= make an official proposal), ***order***, ***persist***, ***propose***, ***recommend***, ***request***, ***require***, ***suggest***, ***it is essential***, ***it is imperative***, ***it is important***, ***it is necessary***, ***it is vital***, etc.
  In British English, a subordinate clause with ***should*** + **bare infinitive** is preferable.
  'The meeting could be adjourned until next Monday,' moved one of the delegates.
  *One of the delegates **moved** that the meeting **be adjourned/should be adjourned** until next Monday.*
  'You ought to wear warm clothing.'
  It is essential *(that) you **wear** warm clothing.*
  It is essential *that you **should wear** warm clothing.*

Special introductory verbs

To report commands, requests, suggestions, instructions, etc, we use an appropriate introductory verb (***advise***, ***ask***, ***order***, ***suggest***, etc) and the ***to*-infinitive**, ***-ing*** form or ***that*-clause**, depending on the introductory verb.
(see the table of introductory verbs p. GR33)

- The verbs marked with an asterisk (*) can also be followed by a ***that*-clause** in reported speech.
  *Mark **denied that he had eaten** the last piece of cake.*
  Note: In order to report negative commands and requests, we usually use ***not*** + ***to*-infinitive**.
  Direct speech: *Mother said, 'Don't bring mud into the house!'*
  Reported speech: *Mother told us **not to bring** mud into the house.*

SPECIAL INTRODUCTORY VERBS			
Introductory verb	**Direct speech**		**Reported speech**
+ ***to*-inf**			
agree	*'You're right! We should get a takeaway.'*	→	*She **agreed to get** a takeaway.*
* claim	*'It is mine; I bought it!'*	→	*She **claimed to have bought** it.*
* demand	*'I want a refund!'*	→	*He **demanded to get** a refund.*
offer	*'I can lend you some money.'*	→	*He **offered to lend** me some money.*
* promise	*'I will be back in three hours.'*	→	*She **promised to be back** in three hours.*
refuse	*'I won't pay the fine!'*	→	*He **refused to pay** the fine.*
* threaten	*'We're going to leave if our food doesn't arrive soon.'*	→	*They **threatened to leave** if their food didn't arrive soon.*
+ sb + *to*-inf			
advise	*'If I were you, I'd leave straightaway.'*	→	*She **advised him to leave** straightaway.*
allow	*'You may have some pudding as long as you eat your greens.'*	→	*They **allowed me to have** some pudding as long as I ate my greens.*
ask	*'I need you to send these emails.'*	→	*He **asked me to send** the emails.*
beg	*'Please don't go!'*	→	*She **begged him not to go**.*
command	*'Clean the ship!'*	→	*The captain **commanded them to clean** the ship.*
encourage	*'I think you should start singing in public.'*	→	*My mother **encouraged me to start** singing in public.*
forbid	*'You mustn't go out on your own at night.'*	→	*Dad **forbade us to go out** on our own at night.*
invite	*'Would you like to go to the cinema?'*	→	*He **invited me to go** to the cinema.*
order	*'Stay where you are!'*	→	*The detective **ordered us to stay** where we were.*
* remind	*'Don't forget to take your umbrella.'*	→	*She **reminded him to take** his umbrella.*
* warn	*'Drive carefully! It's raining heavily!'*	→	*Our father **warned us to drive carefully** because it was raining heavily.*
***-ing* form**			
accuse sb of	*'I know you broke the window!'*	→	*He **accused her of breaking** the window.*
* admit (to)	*'To be honest, I don't know anything about physics.'*	→	*She **admitted (to) not knowing** anything about physics.*
apologise for	*'I'm sorry I was late.'*	→	*He **apologised for being** late.*
boast about	*'My daughter is very clever!'*	→	*He **boasted about** his daughter **being** very clever.*
* complain (to sb) about	*'Your music is too loud!'*	→	*She **complained (to us) about** our music **being** too loud.*
* deny	*'I didn't see the sign.'*	→	*He **denied seeing** the sign.*
insist on	*'I'm sure I'm right!'*	→	*Sam **insisted on being** right.*
* suggest	*'Why don't we buy an ice-cream?'*	→	*She **suggested buying** an ice-cream.*
+ ***that*-clause**			
complain	*'It's too cold here!'*	→	*She **complained that** it was too cold there.*
exclaim/remark	*'What a lovely day!'*	→	*She **exclaimed/remarked** that it was a lovely day.*
inform sb	*'Your tickets have been booked.'*	→	*He **informed us that** our tickets had been booked.*
think	*'It was a long route to take.'*	→	*The guide **thought that** it had been a long route to take.*
***explain to sb how* + *to*-infinitive/ clause**	*'That's how you change the fuse in a plug.'*	→	*He **explained to me how to change** the fuse in a plug./ He **explained to me how I should change** the fuse in a plug.*
***wonder where/ what/why/how* + clause**	*'Why is Jack here?' Mary asked herself.*	→	*Mary **wondered why** Jack was there.*
***wonder where/ what/how* + *to*-infinitive** (when the subject of the infinitive is the **same** as the subject of the verb)	*'What shall I have for my dinner?' he asked himself.*	→	*He **wondered what to have** for his dinner.*

- In conversation, we use a mixture of statements, commands and questions. When we turn them into reported speech, we use ***and*, *as*, *adding that*, *and he/she added that*, *because*, *but*, *since***, etc. Words/ Expressions such as ***oh*, *oh dear*, *well***, etc are omitted in reported speech.

Direct speech: *'I can't meet you at the airport,' said Ned, 'you see, my car is at the garage.'*
Reported speech: *Ned said that he couldn't meet me at the airport **because** his car is/was at the garage.*

Modal verbs in reported speech

9 ★★ **Turn the following sentences into reported speech.**

1 'I can help you with the new design of the community centre,' said Carl.

....

....

2 'There may be a rally in the city centre tomorrow so you should leave a little earlier in the morning,' Holly said.

....

....

3 'The mayor can speak to you soon,' said the secretary.

....

....

4 'What time shall we meet for the park clean-up?' said Vicky.

....

....

5 'You needn't come to the city council meeting next week,' Gerald told me.

....

....

6 'Shall I pick you up from the train station?' Suzy said.

....

....

Reporting nouns instead of verbs

10 ★★ **Rewrite the sentences using the correct noun phrases from the list below. Make any necessary changes.**

- issue a denial • make a recommendation
- give a statement • make a remark
- issue a warning

1 I thought what you recommended in order to reduce traffic in the city was a great idea.

....

2 I thought it was inappropriate how he remarked on the politician's personal life.

....

3 The fact that the company denied dumping waste in the lake was unbelievable given that there were so many witnesses present.

....

4 The government warned the developers not to encroach onto protected land.

....

5 It was ridiculous when he stated that CO_2 emissions have been drastically reduced.

....

Subjunctive

11 ★★ **Look at the underlined parts in the sentences below and rewrite the sentences using the subjunctive. Make any necessary changes.**

1 The refuse service requires that all rubbish is separated into its appropriate categories before collection.

....

....

2 The environmental groups advised the city to use the undeveloped land as a nature reserve.

....

....

3 The transport minister proposed to ban all diesel buses.

....

....

4 Neighbourhood watch groups have demanded cameras are installed in public areas to discourage crime.

....

....

Special introductory verbs

12 ★★ **Match the sentences (1-6) to the correct introductory verb (a-f). Then report the sentences.**

1 ☐ 'I'm sorry I forgot to take out the recycling,' he told me.

2 ☐ 'Should I get a hybrid car?' she asked herself.

3 ☐ 'I'm sure that I turned off the lights before we left!' he said to me.

4 ☐ 'Your accommodation has been arranged,' the organiser told us.

5 ☐ 'Be careful in the city centre. It's dangerous,' Dave told them.

6 ☐ 'I think you should run for mayor,' Jane told Bill.

a	inform	c	wonder	e	encourage
b	apologise	d	warn	f	insist

1 ....

2 ....

3 ....

4 ....

5 ....

6 ....

13 ★★ **Put the verbs in brackets into the correct form.**

1 Kevin advised me .... **(install)** solar panels on my house.
2 The mayor wondered what .... **(cover)** in his speech tomorrow.
3 The residents accused the property developer of .... **(try)** to devalue property in their area.
4 Tim's neighbours invited him .... **(join)** them for a dinner party.
5 The police advised residents .... **(keep)** an eye out for suspicious activity.
6 She insisted on .... **(make)** the building more energy efficient.

14 ★★ **Report the sentences using the appropriate introductory verbs.**

1 'You are right, we should start composting.' Jill said.
....
....
2 'I'm sorry, I didn't tell you the truth about it,' she told us.
....
....
3 'If I were you, I'd move to a smaller city,' Joe told me.
....
....
4 'That's how you purify your own water,' said the professor.
....
....
5 'Our city is the safest in the country,' she said proudly.
....
....
6 'My neighbourhood has way too much traffic,' she said to me.
....
....

Key word transformations

15 ★★ **For questions 1-10, complete the second sentence so that it has a similar meaning to the first sentence, using the word given. You must use between three and eight words, including the word given.**

1 'There is no residential parking around in this area of town,' he complained to the city transit authority. **MADE**
He .... the lack of residential parking in that area of town.
2 'Your flat is wonderful,' Jeanie told Ken. **COMPLIMENTED**
Jeanie .... flat.
3 'I'm really sorry to have missed your talk about global warming,' Ann told me. **FOR**
Ann .... talk about global warming.
4 'I would move to the suburbs if I were you,' Heather told Jim. **ADVISED**
Heather .... the suburbs.
5 'I haven't got enough money to rent a flat near the high street,' Julie told us. **AFFORD**
Julie .... rent a flat near the high street.
6 'The cost of living is so high in the city,' Murial said. **REMARKED**
Murial .... high in the city.
7 'You can't volunteer until you fill out all the necessary forms,' the director told me. **LET**
The director refused .... out all the necessary forms.
8 'You should not live in such a dangerous neighbourhood,' Frank said to Gordon. **AGAINST**
Frank .... in such a dangerous neighbourhood.
9 'Yes, I did see the man dumping waste into the river,' said the witness. **CONFIRMED**
The witness .... waste into the river.
10 'I know you falsified the budget for the development,' the lawyer told Martin. **ACCUSED**
The lawyer .... the budget for the development.

Module 8

Subordinate clauses

Sentences can consist of main and subordinate clauses. Subordinate clauses can be: **a) relative clauses** (*I saw a film **which/that** was directed by Steven Spielberg.*) and **b) adverbial clauses**: time clauses, clauses of purpose/ result/concession/reason/place/manner. (*The castaway had to wait five years **until** she was rescued.*)
They may function grammatically as a **subject**, **object** or **adverb** in a **sentence**:

- **clauses as subjects**
  ***Whoever completes the race** will win a prize.*
- **clauses as objects**
  *He informed us **(that) the bus was on its way**.*
- **clauses as adverbs**
  *I enjoyed the director's latest film **although it received bad reviews**.*

Relative clauses

Relative clauses are introduced with either a **relative pronoun** or a **relative adverb**.

Relative pronouns

We use:
a) ***who(m)/that*** to refer to people,
b) ***which/that*** to refer to things,
c) ***whose*** with people, animals and objects to show possession (instead of a possessive adjective).

- ***Who***, ***which*** and ***that*** can be omitted when they are the **object of the relative clause**. *This is my friend (**who**) I met at university.*
- ***Whom*** can be used instead of ***who*** when it is the object of the relative clause. ***Whom*** is always used instead of ***who*** or ***that*** **after a preposition**. *Dave is the person **to whom** the letter was addressed.*
- ***Who***, ***which*** and ***that*** are not omitted when they are the **subject of the relative clause**. *The artist **who** won the prize really deserved it.*
- ***Whose*** is never omitted. *This is the person **whose** grandfather comes from France.*

Relative adverbs

We use:
a) ***when*** to refer to time, usually after nouns such as ***time***, ***period***, ***moment***, ***day***, ***year***, ***season***, ***summer***, ***occasion***, etc. It can either be replaced by ***that*** or can be omitted.
*That was the summer (**when/that**) we holidayed in Switzerland.*
b) ***where*** to refer to places, usually after nouns such as ***place***, ***house***, ***village***, ***city***, ***street***, ***town***, ***country***, etc. It can be replaced by ***which/that*** + **clause** + **preposition** and, in this case, ***which/that*** can be omitted.
*This is the town **where** I grew up.*
*This is the town (**which/that**) I grew up **in**.*
c) ***why*** to give a reason, after the word ***reason***. It can either be replaced by ***that*** or can be omitted.
*That's the reason **why** I don't talk to her anymore.*
*That's the reason (**that**) she no longer works there.*

Defining/Non-defining relative clauses

A **defining relative clause** gives necessary information, essential to the meaning of the main sentence. It is not put between commas, and is introduced with ***who***, ***whom***, ***which***, ***that***, ***whose***, ***where***, ***when*** or **the reason** (***why***). *I'm really annoyed by the person **who** sits next to me.*

A **non-defining relative clause** gives extra information, and is not essential to the meaning of the main sentence. It is put between commas, and is introduced with ***who***, ***whom***, ***which***, ***whose***, ***where*** or ***when***. *My car, **which** is in the garage at the moment, keeps breaking down.*
We cannot omit the relative pronoun or replace it with ***that***. *Ned, **whom** we all respect for his hard work, is retiring this year.* (NOT: ~~Ned, we all respect for his hard work~~, .../ ~~Ned, that we all respect for his hard work~~, ...)

Notes:
- When ***that*** replaces ***where***, it can be omitted after the words ***somewhere***, ***anywhere***, ***nowhere***, ***everywhere*** and ***place***, without using any prepositions.
  *Is there **nowhere** (that) I can find a sandwich?*
  *Is there **anywhere** (that) I can sit down?*
- ***That*** is never used after a comma or prepositions.
  *That's the house **in which** I was born.* (NOT: *That's the house ~~in that~~ I was born.*)
- We use ***that*** with words such as ***all***, ***anything***, ***everything***, ***few***, ***little***, ***much***, ***none***, ***nothing***, ***only***, ***something***, and with the superlative form. *Is this **all that** you can do for me?* (more natural than ... *all which you can do ...*) *The **only** thing **that** is important to me is my family. It's **the best** song **that** I've ever heard.*
- In non-defining relative clauses, we can use ***each***, ***part***, ***some***, ***very little/few***, ***a number***, ***both***, ***all***, ***one***, ***either***, ***neither***, ***most***, ***none***, etc + ***of which/whom***, to refer to a term in the main clause.
  *I have two laptops, **neither of which** works properly.*
  *I have seven cousins, **all of whom** live in Seattle.*
- ***At which point/ in which case/ in which event/ during which/ despite which/ which is why*** can also be used to introduce a comment on the main clause.
  *There were roadworks, **which is why** I'm running late.*
- Besides the relative pronouns, ***'what'(ever)*** is also used as a relative pronoun and a determiner.
  *We should all be accountable for **what(ever)** we do.* (pronoun) (= all the things which we do)
  *We should all be accountable for **what(ever)** decisions we make.* (determiner) (= all the decisions which we make)

Relatives with prepositions

The preposition is put in front of ***whom*** or ***which*** (formal English). It can also be put at the end of the relative clause, in which case ***whom*** becomes ***who***. In such instances, however, ***that*** (less formal) is more commonly used instead of ***who/which***. In everyday speech, it is also common for ***who/which/that*** to be omitted altogether.
*That's the colleague **with whom** I completed my last project.* (formal)
*That's the colleague **who** I completed my last project **with**.* (less formal)
*That's the colleague (**that**) I completed my last project **with**.* (informal)

Where can be replaced by:
a) **preposition + *which***
b) ***which/that* + clause + preposition**
c) **clause + preposition** (no relative)
*That's the shop **where** I bought my trousers.*
*a) That's the shop **in which** I bought my trousers.*
*b) That's the shop **which/that** I bought my trousers **in**.*
*c) That's the shop I bought my trousers **in**.*

When can be replaced by:
a) **preposition + *which***
b) ***that* + clause + preposition**
*1996 is the year **when** I started school.*
*a) 1996 is the year **in which** I started school.*
*b) 1996 is the year **that** I started school **in**.*
c) It can also be omitted.
1996 is the year I started school.

Reduced relative clauses

Relative clauses can be replaced by **present** and **past participles**: the ***-ing*** participles are used in place of active verbs, and the ***-ed*/past participles** in place of passive verbs.
*We're going to travel on the boat **docking*** (= which is docking) *now at the port.*
*The definition **found*** (= which is found) *on this site is not trustworthy.*
***Coughing** loudly, the man reached for a glass of water.*
(= the man who was coughing)
***Dressed** in red, the women proceeded to the party.*
(= the women who were dressed in red)
Note: *~~**Rambling** through the island lanes, the sun started setting idly.~~* This structure is impossible because the subjects of the participle and the main verb are different: obviously tourists/people were those who were rambling through the streets, not the sun.

Time clauses

Time clauses are introduced with time conjunctions or expressions such as: ***after*, *as*, *as soon as*, *before*, *by*, *by the time*, *hardly ... when*, *no sooner ... than*, *now that*, *once*, (*ever*) *since*, *the minute* (*that*), *the moment* (*that*), *then*, *the sooner ... the sooner*, *till/until*, *on/upon*, *when*, *whenever*, *while*.**
*I went down to the shop **as soon as** it opened.*
Time clauses follow the rule of the sequence of tenses; that is, when the verb of the **main clause** is in a **present** or **future form**, the verb of the time clause must be in a **present form**, and when the verb of the main clause is in a **past form**, the verb of the time clause must be in a **past form** too.
*I'**ll put on** my shoes before I **go** outside.*
*They **arrived** after the show **had started**.*
We **never** use a **future tense** in a **future time clause**; instead, we use a **present tense**.
Exams will start in July. You'll have lots of work to do.
*You'll have lots of work to do **when** exams **start** in July.*
(NOT: ~~will start~~)

Compare:
when (time conjunction) + **present tense**
***When** I **finish** my dinner, I will give him a call.*
when (question word) + **present tense** or **future tense**
*When **does** the bus **arrive**?*
*When **will** he **collect** his books?*

Relative clauses

1 ★ **Fill in** *who*, *which*, *whose*, *when*, *where* **or** *why*. **Say whether they can be omitted or not.**

1 A: My friend, ... is performing in a concert this weekend, sent me tickets for the show. Would you like to go?
B: Sure, I don't have any plans.

2 A: Do you know .... Andrew dropped out of drama school?
B: He said it just wasn't right for him.

3 A: I didn't like the book .... Rachel recommended.
B: Really? I thought it was great!

4 A: Do you want to see the location .... they shot the *Harry Potter* films?
B: I'd love to.

5 A: Benedict Cumberbatch is in a new film that's coming out this week.
B: I still remember .... he was a struggling actor looking for his big break.

6 A: Ewan McGregor, ... uncle is also in the business, is one of my favourite actors.
B: Me too, and both he and his uncle have been in *Star Wars* films.

2 ★★ **Use the information in brackets and join the sentences, as in the example.**

1 The leading actor dropped out of the production. **(No one knows the reason.)**
No one knows the reason why the leading actor dropped out of the production.

2 Our annual concert is to be held on the school grounds. **(It will raise funds for charity.)**
....

3 The actor David Jones is the guest speaker at the film festival. **(He grew up in the area.)**
....

4 Mr Allen is looking for some fresh-faced talent. **(His films are famous for being improvised.)**
....

5 He still remembers the moment with great pride. **(He won the award.)**
....

6 The actress in the film is the director's sister. **(She plays the lead role.)**
....

7 The area in the Louvre museum is always packed with tourists. **(*The Mona Lisa* hangs there.)**
....

8 Their latest play has just opened. **(It has sold out.)**
....

3 ★★ **Fill in the correct relative pronoun or adverb. Put commas where necessary. Write *D* (for defining) or *ND* (for non-defining) and say whether the relative can be omitted.**

1 Nina .... was the understudy for the principal ballerina forgot her steps last night.
....
2 I don't know .... the group dropped out at the last minute.
....
3 This blog is written by the author .... book was turned into my favourite TV show.
....
4 The cast all of .... were under 16 had to adhere to strict working regulations.
....
5 The painting .... the artist is best remembered for is up for sale in the auction.
....
6 This is the festival .... he first performed so he always comes back.
....
7 The film is set in a period .... people didn't have electricity.
....
8 He won an award .... was very prestigious for his first significant role.
....
9 Is there somewhere .... John can store his guitar after his recital?
....
10 Mr Michaels .... we all love working for has said this play is to be his last production.
....

4 ★ **Fill in the gaps with the correct phrase from the list below.**

• most of whom • nothing that • the best that
• at which point • some of which

1 The director started yelling at the actress .... she walked off the set.
2 They called a wrap on the scene because there was .... could be done about the bad weather.
3 They used 300 extras in the film, ... were students from the nearby university.
4 The props in the play, ... had come from a local museum, were all authentic to the period it was set in.
5 This song is .... the group has ever written.

Relatives with prepositions

5 ★★ **Rewrite the sentences.**

1 This is the theatre where I first performed.
....
....
2 He and the actor he is appearing with have had a long-standing partnership.
....
....
3 That is the bestselling book which this film is based on.
....
....
4 This is the song for which the artist received his Grammy.
....
....
5 2010 is the year when the theatre opened.
....
....

Reduced relative clauses

6 ★★ **Join the two sentences to form a reduced relative clause. Make any necessary changes.**

1 The film is a true story. It is based on a book.
Based on a book, the film is a true story.
2 The film was set in an abandoned castle. It needed an authentic location.
....
....
3 The location scout was seeking a suitable castle for the shoot. He stumbled upon the perfect site.
....
....
4 The location is surrounded by a beautiful park. It is in a wildlife reserve.
....
....
5 The reserve contains a number of protected species. It has limited accessibility.
....
....
6 The director was poised to begin shooting. He was informed that the location was unavailable.
....
....

Time clauses

7 ★ **Underline the correct item.**

1 **The time/The moment** the director yelled action, it started raining and the crew had to stop shooting.
2 The cast will go on a press junket **as/after** they wrap up the production.
3 **When/Whenever** are they making the sequel to last summer's blockbuster?
4 You can borrow the book for **as soon as/as long as** you like.
5 The actress was allowed to keep some of her costumes **when/while** the play finished its run.
6 This was one of those whodunnits where you don't find out who the villain is **upon/until** the very end of the book.
7 The reporter had never interviewed a film star **after/before** so he was a little star struck.
8 My sister has wanted to be an actress ever **since/once** she was little.
9 **The sooner/No sooner** we leave **than/the sooner** we will get to the theatre.
10 I find it really annoying when people talk **while/during** films at the cinema.

8 ★★ **Choose the correct item and put the verbs in brackets into the correct tense.**

1 They are expecting the tickets to sell out **when/as** the film .... **(open)** in July.
2 He was commissioned to create the statue for the company **till/after** the managing director .... **(see)** his work in a gallery.
3 **As long as/As soon as** the actor arrived at the premier, he .... **(greet)** by his adoring fans.
4 Can you call me **the minute/the time** you .... **(complete)** the final edit of the film?
5 The ballerina has more time to devote to her dance school **once/now that** she .... **(retire)** from the ballet.
6 The volunteers will have to be on site one hour **before/after** the guests .... **(arrive)** for the screening.
7 **By the time/Every time** the auction finished, they .... **(raise)** over £20,000 for charity.
8 The director has promised to give a masterclass **the moment/the next time** he .... **(visit)** the city.
9 **No sooner/Hardly** had we found our seats **when/than** the play .... **(start)**.

9 ★★ **Choose the correct item and fill in the gaps with the words/phrases below.**

• ever since • during • after • till • the moment

FOCUS on Film

The new drama from acclaimed director Josh Adams, **1) whose/who** repertoire includes such hits as *Courage and Under the Blue Moon*, is in cinemas now. It is yet another collaboration between the director and his favourite actress, Eve Hart, **2) whom/who** finally received an award for their last production **3)** .... years of missing out on a prize. The film is set **4)** .... the great depression **5) when/which** may seem like a heavy topic to tackle, but the way **6) in that/in which** it is dealt with is delicate and heart-warming. **7)** .... his debut film 20 years ago, **8) where/when** he confronted the topic of homelessness, Adams has been pushing the boundaries with his subject matter. The film is refreshingly honest and keeps the audience glued to the screen throughout from **9)** .... it starts **10)** .... the credits roll.

Key word transformations

10 ★★ **For questions 1-5, complete the second sentence so that it has a similar meaning to the first sentence, using the word given. Do not change the word given. You must use between three and eight words, including the word given.**

1 The reason I missed the beginning of the film is that I was stuck in traffic. **IS**
I was stuck in traffic, ... I missed the beginning of the film.
2 The guests will leave the special screening and then the caterer will start serving immediately. **SOON**
The caterer will start serving .... the special screening.
3 Dressed in period costumes, the extras gathered on set. **WHO**
The extras, ... period costumes, gathered on set.
4 The stars in this production are new actors and they have never appeared on stage before. **NONE**
This production stars new actors, ... on stage before.
5 I was performing in *A Midsummer Night's Dream* when I was spotted and given my big break. **IN**
A Midsummer Night's Dream .... when I was spotted and given my big break.

Clauses of purpose

To*-infinitive** is commonly used to express **purpose**. We can also use ***in order to and ***so as to***. ***In order to*** and ***so as to*** are more **emphatic** and more **formal**.
*We had to wear warm clothing **in order to/so as to** endure the Arctic temperatures.*
Clauses of purpose are introduced with ***so that/in order that*** in the following way:

so that/in order that + ***will/can*** (present/future reference) ***so that/in order that*** + ***would/could*** (past reference)	(common structures)

*Martha goes swimming every day **so that she will/can improve**. The students listened in class **so that they would/could learn**.*

so that/in order that + ***may/should*** (present/future reference) ***so that/in order that*** + ***might/should*** (past reference)	(formal structures)

*He wrote his instructions down **in order that** he **might/should** be understood better.*
Note: We use ***so that***, but NOT: the ***to*-infinitive** structure, when the main and the subordinate clauses have different subjects. ***We** left early in the morning **so that Karl** could get to his practice on time.*

We can also introduce clauses of purpose with:

- ***for*** + **noun** (to express the purpose of an action)
  *I went to the shops **for** some **milk**.*
  for + **gerund** (to express the general use of a thing)
  *Glasses are devices used **for improving** your sight.*
- ***in case*** + **present tense/*should*** (present/future reference)
  in case + **past tense/*should*** (past reference)
  *Buy your tickets now **in case** they **sell/should sell** out.*
  *He took some earplugs **in case** the music **was/should be** too loud.*
  Note: ***Will/Would*** are never used with ***in case***.
  *Try to be on time **in case** the bus leaves early.*
  (NOT: ... ~~*in case the bus will leave*~~.)

Negative purpose is expressed with:

- ***so as not/in order not*** + ***to*-infinitive** (only when the subject of the verb is also the subject of the infinitive)
  *I left the window open **so as not/in order not to get** too warm.*
- ***so that*** + ***won't/can't*** (present/future reference)
  so that + ***wouldn't/couldn't*** (past reference)
  *We put an extra lock on the door **so that burglars won't/can't** get in. I wore a reflective jacket **so that I wouldn't** be hit by cars.*
- ***for fear (that)*** + ***might/should/would*** (very formal)
  for fear of sth/doing sth
  lest (+ **subject** + ***might/should***) + **bare infinitive** (very formal)
  *He saved the address on his phone **for fear (that)** he **might/should/would** get lost.*
  *He didn't put down his keys **for fear of losing** them.*
  *Running by the pod is forbidden **lest** one **(might/should) have** an accident.*
- ***prevent*** + **noun/pronoun** (+ **from**) + ***-ing*** **form** *The coach couldn't **prevent the team (from) conceding** the goal.*
- ***avoid*** + ***-ing*** **form** *You should **avoid drinking** fizzy drinks if you're sick.*

Clauses of result

They are introduced with the following words/phrases:

- ***as a result/therefore/consequently/as a consequence***
  *The bus is late, **as a result/therefore/consequently/as a consequence** we'll be late for the meeting.*
- ***such a(n)*** + **adjective** + **singular countable noun** + ***that***
  *It was **such a cold day that** I couldn't stop shivering.*
- ***such*** + **adjective** + **plural/uncountable noun** + ***that***
  *There are **such beautiful forests in Canada that** I took a lot of photos.*
- ***such*** + ***a lot of*** + **plural/uncountable noun** + ***that***
  *Mother made **such a lot of cake that** we couldn't finish it all.*
- ***so*** + **adjective/adverb** + ***that***
  *The weather was **so bad that** everyone stayed inside.*
- ***so*** + **adjective** + ***a(n)*** + **singular noun** + ***that*** (not usual)
  *He was **so fast a runner that** no one could beat him.*
- ***so*** + ***many/few*** + **plural noun** + ***that***
  *There are **so many cars** on the road **that** we have constant traffic jams.*
- ***so*** + ***much/little*** + **uncountable noun** + ***that***
  *There was **so much rain that** the town flooded.*

Note: Clauses of result follow the rule of the sequence of tenses.
*The weightlifter **is** so strong that he **can** lift up a piano.*
*Our neighbour **was** such a nice person that everyone **loved** her.*

Clauses of purpose

11 ★ **Underline the correct item.**

1. I watch the news everyday **so as to/for** keep up to date on current affairs.
2. We should get to the theatre early **so that/in case** there's a long queue for tickets.
3. Age ratings on films are there to **avoid/prevent** vulnerable children from watching something inappropriate.
4. A good review doesn't include spoilers **so as not to/so that** give away the plot of the film.
5. The director worked with the actors individually in rehearsal **so that/so as** their performances would be flawless when they all got on stage.

12 ★ **Match column A with column B using a clause of purpose from the list below to form sentences.**

• in case • for • to prevent • so that • to avoid • lest

	A		B
1	A number of people use opera glasses	a	... their show might be a failure.
2	I'd book your tickets online	b	... the rush of everyone leaving at the end.
3	People are asked to turn their phones off	c	... they can see what is happening on stage.
4	Theatre folks are superstitious and follow traditions	d	... them from ringing during the performance.
5	We left the theatre before the encore	e	... amusement and are not supposed to be deep.
6	Comedies and sitcoms are made primarily	f	... they sell out.

Clauses of result

13 ★ **Fill in:** *so, such* **or** *such a/an.*

1 We had .... exciting time at the festival we're planning to go again next year.
2 There were .... few people at the concert that the organisers decided to cancel and give everyone their money back.
3 The actors have .... little time to change between scenes that I'm surprised they don't miss their cues.
4 There were .... many of the actor's fans outside the stage door that he was signing autographs for an hour.
5 He's made .... lot of hits that he's always in the charts.
6 He is .... talented a singer that he was signed immediately by a record label.
7 There are .... beautiful pieces of art in the gallery that I could spend days looking round.
8 The film was .... bad that the audience walked out before it even finished.
9 It was .... clear night that you could see the stars above the open-air theatre.
10 The audience were creating .... much noise that we couldn't hear the artist perform.

14 ★★ **Join the sentences using the words in brackets.**

1 It's difficult to succeed as an actor. A lot of people don't make it. **(so ... that)**
....
2 My friends and I joined the cinema club. Members get discounts on tickets. **(so as to)**
....
3 The artist moved his artwork himself. He was worried someone else might damage it. **(for fear that)**
....
4 There were hardly any parking spaces. We couldn't find anywhere to park outside the museum. **(so few ... that)**
....
5 There isn't much time left to rehearse. The play might not be ready. **(so little ... that)**
....
6 They put up barriers. They don't want the crowd climbing on stage. **(prevent)**
....
7 The actor was a really nice person. I forgot he was famous. **(such a ... that)**
....

Key word transformations

15 ★★ **For questions 1-4, complete the second sentence so that it has a similar meaning to the first sentence, using the word given. Do not change the word given. You must use between three and eight words, including the word given.**

1 The film was so boring that I couldn't stay awake till the end. **SUCH**
It was ....
.... I couldn't stay awake till the end.
2 Ralph was worried that he would sleep in and miss his audition so he set three alarm clocks. **FOR**
Ralph set three alarm clocks ....
.... sleep in and miss his audition.
3 There are not many jobs for costume designers which makes the field very competitive. **FEW**
There ....
is a very competitive field.
4 The producers didn't even tell the actors the ending of the film to keep it a surprise. **NOT**
The producers didn't even tell the actors how
.... ruin the surprise.

Clauses of concession

Clauses of concession are used to express contrast. They are introduced with the following words/phrases:

- ***but*** – *Oscar was tired **but** he had work to do.*
- ***although/even though/though*** **+ clause**
  Even though is more emphatic than ***although***.
  Though is informal and is often used in everyday speech. It can also be put at the end of a sentence.
  ***Although/Even though/Though** it was late, we decided to go for a walk.*
  *We decided to go for a walk **although/even though/though** it was late.*
  *It was late; we decided to go for a walk, **though**.*
- ***however/nevertheless*** (a comma is always used after ***however/nevertheless***). *He can't swim very well. **However/Nevertheless,** she wants to learn.*
- ***yet*** (formal)/***still*** (when ***yet*** joins the main clause and the clause of concession, it is preceded by a comma. When ***yet/still*** are at the beginning of a sentence, they are followed by a comma).
  *The singer said he'd be here at nine, **yet** I'm not sure if he will.*
  *The marathon was very tough. **Yet/Still,** I'm glad that I took part.*
- ***while/whereas/whilst*** (very formal)
  *My mother is a sculptor **while/whereas/whilst** my father works in finance.*
  ***While** he wants to go to the show, the tickets are very expensive.*
- ***in spite of/despite*** **+ noun/*-ing* form/*the fact that* + clause**
  ***In spite of/Despite** the long delay, the plane journey was relatively hassle-free.*
  ***In spite of/Despite** leaving ahead of schedule, we missed our connection.*
  ***In spite of/Despite the fact that** I had just eaten, I was starting to get hungry again.*
- ***however/no matter how*** **+ adjective/adverb + subject (+ *may*) + verb**
  ***No matter how** hard I try, I can never solve crosswords.*
  ***However** difficult a challenge is/may be, we can find ways to succeed.*
- ***whatever/no matter what*** **+ clause**
  ***No matter what/Whatever** you want to do when you grow up, you should study at university.*
- ***even if*** **+ present tense/past tense/*should*** (unlikely to happen)
  ***Even if it rains/should rain,** I'm going to the beach!*
- **adjective/adverb + *though* + subject + *may* + verb**
  ***Fast though he is/may be,** he won't win the race.*
  ***Strong though it is,** the bracket won't take the weight of that shelf.*
- **adjective/adverb + *as* + subject + verb**
  ***Famous as he is,** he always makes time for his fans.*
  ***Hard as he looked,** he couldn't find his phone anywhere.*
- **infinitive form + *as* + subject + *may/might***
  ***Try as you may/might,** you won't persuade Jim; he's very stubborn.*
- ***for all*** **+ noun (= despite + noun)**
  ***For all his hard work,** Joel failed the exam.*

Note: Clauses of concession follow the rule of the sequence of tenses.
*Much as **I like** this software, it **isn't** the right program for the job.*
*Gifted as the singer **is**, he **has made** some rather average records.*
*Even though Mark **was** in pain, he **got** on stage and **sang** the song.*

Clauses of reason

They are introduced with the following words/phrases:

- ***because*** – *I bought a sandwich **because** I was hungry. **Because** I was hungry, I bought a sandwich.*
- ***for*** (= because; in a formal written style) – a clause of reason introduced with ***for*** always comes after the main clause. *I didn't open the door, **for** I didn't know who it was.*
  Note: *Because* and ***for*** can both be used to introduce a clause of reason. However, ***for*** can't be used at the beginning of a sentence, or as an answer to a ***why***-question. When used, there is always a comma before it in written speech, or a pause in oral speech.
  ***Because** I can't swim, I didn't want to go canoeing.*
  *I didn't want to go canoeing **because** I can't swim.*
  *I didn't want to go canoeing, **for** I can't swim.*
- ***as/since*** (= because) – *I bought the first coat I saw **as/since** it was cheap. **As/Since** the first coat I saw was cheap, I bought it.*
- ***the reason for*** **+ noun/*-ing* form** – ***The reason for** her **applying** was that she'd always wanted to work in advertising. The fact that she had always wanted to work in advertising was **the reason** for her **applying**.*
- ***the reason why*** **+ clause** – ***The reason why** she was **angry** was (the fact) that Clive had lost her purse.*
- ***now (that)*** **+ clause** – ***Now (that)** she has finished **university**, she will start looking for a job.*
- ***because of/on account of/due to*** **+ noun** *The skydive was cancelled **because of/on account of/due to** bad **weather**.*
- ***because of/on account of/due to the fact that*** **+ clause**
  *The skydive was cancelled **because of/on account of/due to the fact that there was bad weather**.*
- ***in view of*** **+ noun/*-ing* form/*the fact that***
  *The film's release was delayed **in view of it not being ready/the fact that** it wasn't ready.*
- ***out of*** **+ noun** (to express the motive for an action)
  *We went round to their house **out of sympathy**.*
- ***considering/seeing that/given that***.
  ***Considering/Seeing that/Given that** the plane leaves in four hours, we've left the house very early.*

Note: Clauses of reason follow the rule of the sequence of tenses.
*Since he **has lost** his skis, he **can't** come on the trip.*
*Everyone **celebrated because** the winter **had ended**.*

Clauses of concession

16 ★ **Circle the correct item.**

1 **Despite/However/While** the actor's inexperience, he managed to get the lead part.
2 Joe can't sing very well. **Nevertheless,/Although/ Whereas** he wants to learn how to.
3 **No matter/Whatever/Even though** what the author writes, it becomes a best seller.
4 Even **though/if/as** it rains, I'm not going to miss the outdoor concert.
5 Smart **so/as/even** he was, he couldn't solve the puzzle.
6 **No matter/However/For** all the film's praise, it failed to get nominated for an award.

17 ★★ **Rephrase the sentences with the words in brackets.**

1 She is talented. She is too shy to perform in front of an audience. **(although, despite)**
....
....
2 *Star Wars* is his favourite film series. He hasn't seen the latest film. **(though/yet)**
....
....
3 The performers spoke loudly on stage. They could not make themselves heard. **(Even though/however)**
....
....
4 He tries hard. He cannot pass the audition for the talent show. **(no matter/still)**
....
....
5 He wants to order the cable TV service. The subscription is rather expensive. **(while/but)**
....
....

Clauses of reason

18 ★ **Fill in:** ***the reason why, because, due to, now that, since.***

1 The director yelled at the actor .... of the fact that he was late for rehearsal.
2 The musical was extended for three extra weeks .... its overwhelming success.
3 .... the film director is disenchanted is because he didn't receive an award nomination.
4 .... all her guests have arrived, she will serve dinner.
5 She can't go to the festival with her friends .... she has to work overtime.

19 ★★ **Join the sentences using the words in brackets.**

1 He missed the meeting about the play. He had a car accident. **(because)**
....
2 The band had a lot of rehearsals. They were planning a world tour. **(as)**
....
3 The TV series was cut. It had low ratings. **(due to)**
....
4 The award nominee didn't attend the ceremony. He was out of the country. **(the reason why)**
....
5 The lead actor is sixty. He's still remarkably fit. **(considering)**
....
6 The singer cancelled her appearance. She was feeling unwell. **(on account of)**
....

Key word transformations

20 ★★ **For questions 1-6, complete the second sentence so that it has a similar meaning to the first sentence, using the word given. Do not change the word given. You must use between three and eight words, including the word given.**

1 He wanted to sell his electric guitar so he put an advert on social media. **SINCE**
He put an advert on social media ....
.... his electric guitar.
2 The outdoor concert was cancelled on account of the thunderstorm. **REASON**
The thunderstorm ....
.... was cancelled.
3 He can't sing in the musical because he has a sore throat. **ACCOUNT**
He can't sing in the musical ....
.... sore throat.
4 The film star was queasy because she read the tabloid report about her. **FOR**
The ....
was the tabloid report about her.
5 Since her acting classes are over she can go to theatre auditions. **NOW**
She can go to theatre auditions ....
.... are over.
6 If it hadn't been for the director's efforts, the film wouldn't have been so successful. **DUE**
The success of the film ....
.... the director's efforts.

Clauses of place

Clauses of place are introduced with ***where***, ***wherever***, ***as far as***, ***as high as***, ***as low as***, ***as near as***, etc as follows:

where *wherever* *as far as* *as high as* *as low as* *as near as*	**+ present tense/*may***	present/ future reference	*As far as he **travels**, he always comes home.*
	+ past tense/*might*	past reference	*Wherever he **went**, he's back now.*

Note: A future tense is not normally used in clauses of place. *Boris will follow his favourite singer no matter **where he performs**.* (NOT: ~~no matter where he will perform~~.)

Clauses of manner

Clauses of manner are introduced with ***as***, ***exactly as***, ***just as***, ***in the way that***, and express how someone does/should do something. They are also introduced with ***as if*** and ***as though***.

- We mostly use ***as if/as though*** after verbs such as ***act***, ***appear***, ***be***, ***behave***, ***feel***, ***look***, ***seem***, ***smell***, ***sound*** and ***taste***, to say how someone or something acts, appears, etc. *She's behaving **as if/as though** she knew everything.*
- We use ***as if/as though*** + **past tense** when we are talking about an unreal present situation. ***Were*** can replace ***was*** in the first and third persons singular. *He walks around **as if/as though** he **was/were** really important.* (but he isn't) *It tastes **as if/as though** it **contained** sugar.* (but it doesn't.)

Note: We can use ***like*** instead of ***as if/as though*** in spoken English. *He looks **like** he's about to cry.*

Participle clauses

We can replace a subordinate clause with a participle clause when the subject of the main clause and the subject of the subordinate clause are the same.

Present participles (*writing, telling, playing*, etc)

Present participles can be used in place of clauses in the present or past tense, when the action of the participle happens at the same time as that of the main verb. They can be used to replace:

- **relative clauses** – *The man **mowing (= who is mowing)** the lawn is my uncle.*
- **time clauses** (introduced with *before*, *since*, *when*, *while*) – *Karen tidied up the house **while waiting (= while she was waiting)** for her guests to arrive.*
- **clauses of concession** (introduced with *although*, *even though*, *though*, *while*) – *While **playing (= I play)** several instruments, I'm not very good at any one of them.*
- **conditional clauses** – *If **arriving (= you arrive)** by car, you must pay for parking.*
- **clauses of reason** – ***Wondering (= Because he was wondering)** where everyone was, Joe went to look for them.*

Note: The present participle ***being*** may be used in place of ***is/are/was/were***, but this is only used in formal writing. ***Being (= As we were)** on a tight schedule, we decided not to visit the Louvre.*

Past participles (*written, told, played*, etc)

Past participles can be used in place of clauses in the present or past tense that have a passive meaning. They can be used to replace:

- **relative clauses** – *The saw **used (= which was used)** to cut this wood was blunt.*
- **time clauses** – *When **heard (= it is heard)** on a good sound system, the music sounds even more amazing!*
- **clauses of concession** – *Although **interested (= he was interested)**, Dan decided not to attend the conference.*
- **conditional clauses** – *If **released (= it is released)** before December, the film will make more money.*

Notes:

- Sometimes, the past participle can be used without a conjunction in front of it. ***Heard** on a good sound system, the music sounds even more amazing.*
- Time clauses introduced with ***after***, ***before***, ***since***, ***on*** cannot be followed directly by a past participle, but require **being + past participle**. *Since **being hired (= he was hired)** at the company, Kurt has consistently proved himself.* (NOT: ~~Since hired~~...)

Perfect participles (*having written, having told, having played*, etc)

Perfect participles can be used in place of clauses in the present perfect, past perfect and simple past tenses, when the action of the participle happened before that of the main verb of the sentence. They can be used in active and passive sentences.

- **Active**

  ***We have eaten** dinner, so we should go straight to the cinema. = **Having eaten** dinner, we should go straight to the cinema.*

  ***Because we had eaten** dinner, we went straight to the cinema. = **Having eaten** dinner, we went straight to the cinema.*

  ***We ate** dinner then we went straight to the cinema. = **Having eaten** dinner, we then went straight to the cinema.*
- **Passive**

  ***I had been sold** the wrong item, so I went back to the shop. = **Having been sold** the wrong item, I went back to the shop.*

  ***Since I have been sold** the wrong item, I am going back to the shop. = **Having been sold** the wrong item, I am going back to the shop.*

  ***I was sold** the wrong item and then I went back to the shop. = **Having been sold** the wrong item, I then went back to the shop.*

Note carefully: If the subject of the participle is different from the subject of the main verb, we cannot omit it. In this case, we put the subject of the participle in front of its participle. ***The pie** being ready, **Mum** took it out of the oven.* (NOT: ~~Being ready, Mum took the pie out of the oven.~~)
We can also introduce the subject of the participle with the preposition ***'with'***. ***With the teacher** assigning no homework for the holidays, the students felt excited!*

Clauses of place

21 ★ **Fill in:** ***where, as high as, wherever, as far as*** **or** ***as near as*.**

1 .... Peter goes, he always manages to have a good time.
2 Did you see .... I put my guitar case?
3 John lives only two blocks from the cinema and .... it is, he still takes a taxi.
4 Groups from .... Asia participate in the annual European music competition.
5 .... the ceiling is, the architectural acoustics still affect the sound.

Clauses of manner

22 ★★ **Put the verbs in brackets into the correct tense.**

1 She talked about the celebrity as though she .... **(meet)** him, but I knew she hadn't.
2 The sky is cloudy. It looks as if it .... **(rain)** during the festival.
3 When she saw her idol up close, she looked like she .... **(be)** about to faint.
4 He behaves as if he .... **(own)** the place because his friend is the manager.
5 It smells as though something .... **(burn)** in the restaurant's kitchen.
6 When she was given only a small role in the film she acted as if she .... **(get)** bad news.

Participle clauses

23 ★★ **Put the verbs below in the correct participle form (present/past/perfect) to complete the sentences below.**

1 The artifacts .... **(display)** at the museum arrived from overseas.
2 If .... **(write)** in the first person, a story has a more personal note.
3 .... **(buy)** the tickets online, we didn't have to queue at the box-office.
4 While .... **(sing)** folk songs well, I'm not very good at opera.
5 The wooden props .... **(use)** in the play were handmade.
6 .... **(renovate)** recently, the art gallery will open to the public next month.
7 The cinema closure .... **(announce)** yesterday has provoked criticism in the community.

24 ★★ **Rewrite the following sentences using participle clauses as in the example.**

1 He read the bestseller. It reminded him of a happy time in his childhood.
Reading the bestseller, reminded him of a happy time in his childhood.
2 Tina told me about the concert dates so I decided to book the tickets online.
....
....
3 While he was stuck in traffic, John missed the start of the play.
....
....
4 When she stepped on stage, Liz smiled at the audience with enthusiasm.
....
....
5 Because he had never been to the opera, Sean sat in his seat in awe.
....
....
6 If you buy a ticket at the door, you should go to the theatre early.
....
....
7 Keith studied choreography and then he got a job in a ballet production.
....
....

25 ★★ **Complete the text with an appropriate participle form of the verbs in brackets.**

Though first **1)** .... **(create)** in the 1970s, computer animation in the film industry didn't truly come into its own until 1993. At least, that is what some film buffs maintain. After the release of *Jurassic Park*, **2)** .... **(witness)** a spectacular moment in computer-generated film history, fans and industry players alike realised that animated films would never be the same again. This film was the first physically textured CGI film, **3)** .... **(mean)** the dinosaurs appeared incredibly realistic on screen. Though the effects were unprecedented, they were not easy to achieve. After **4)** .... **(sketch)** by hand, the dinosaurs were scanned into a computer and animation software was used to control arm and leg movements. If **5)** .... **(invest)** so many months of work into a few minutes of footage seems extreme, remember that the results were truly remarkable!

Emphasis

Cleft sentences

We can emphasise particular information in a sentence by means of **cleft structures**:

- ***It is/was*** **(*not*) + noun/noun phrase/pronoun + relative clause**
  Alistair extols his wife's virtues.
  It is Alistair who/that *extols his wife's virtues.*
  It is his wife's virtues that *Alistair extols.*
  Claire isn't late. ***It isn't Claire who*** *is late.*
- ***Is/Was it*** **+ noun/noun phrase/pronoun + relative clause ...?**
  Was it a gold ring that *you lost on the ferry?*
  Was it Dave who *met his wife at university?*
- ***What*** **+ subject + verb +** ***is/was***
  What Harriet wants *most is to visit New York.*
- ***What happens/happened*** **+** ***is/was*** **+** ***that*** **clause**
  What happened was that *no one saw the man leave the house.*
- ***What*** **+ subject +** ***do/does*** (emphasis on the verb)
  a) *Sharon* ***designs*** *clothes.* ***What*** *Sharon does is (to) design clothes.* **b)** *Greg* ***updated*** *the files.* ***What*** *Greg did was (to) update the files.*
- **question word +** ***ever*** (to show surprise)
  Who ever *told you I was getting married?*
  Where ever *did you find this old map?*
  Note: The question words and '***ever***' in this structure are written as two separate words in order to avoid confusion with the pronouns and adverbs in clauses of concession:
  whoever = no matter who, ***whomever*** = no matter whom, ***whatever*** = no matter what, ***wherever*** = no matter where, ***whenever*** = no matter when, ***however*** = no matter how.
  Which and ***whose*** are not used in this function.
  Whose *idea was it?* (NOT: ~~*Whose ever idea*~~ ...)
- ***The place where/The day when/The reason why/The person/people who*** **+ clause +** ***is/was***
  The person who *wrote this song* ***is*** *my uncle!*
- ***The (only/first) thing that*** **+ clause +** ***is/was***
  The first thing that *he did was (to) replace the windows.*
- ***All*** **(*that*) + clause +** ***is/was***
  All (that) *my brother does* ***is*** *(to) play computer games.*

Note: We can also use the auxiliary ***do/does/did*** + **bare infinitive** in the present simple, past simple or the imperative to give emphasis. **a)** *She* ***works*** *in show business. She* ***does work*** *in show business.* **b)** *She* ***went*** *to the ceremony. She* ***did go*** *to the ceremony.* **c)** ***Come*** *around later!* ***Do come*** *around later!*

Inversion

Inversion involves putting the verb before the subject in an affirmative sentence. It is used after certain expressions which are placed first in the sentence in order to give emphasis.

Inversion with auxiliary verbs:

- with **negative**, **restrictive** or **emphatic expressions**.
  No sooner had I *arrived at the house* ***than*** *the arguments started.*

The most common adverbs and adverbial phrases with negative, restrictive or emphatic meaning which are followed by inversion are: ***Seldom***, ***Rarely***, ***Little***, ***Nowhere***, ***Not even once***, ***In no way***, ***Scarcely ... when***, ***Hardly ... when***, ***Barely ... when***, ***No sooner ... than***, ***Not only ... but (also)***, ***On no occasion/account/condition***, ***In/Under no circumstances***, ***Only in this way***, ***Only then***, ***Never***, ***Never before***, ***Neither/Nor/So***, ***Well*** (formal), etc.

"I'm going to the conference." ***"So am I."***
Nowhere had I *seen such a tall man!*
On no occasion did my father *ever shout at me.*
On no condition should *you open this box.*

- with **clauses of result.**
  Such a *long performance* ***was it*** *that most of the audience fell asleep.*
- **in the main clause after the phrases: *Only after, Only by, Only if, Only when, Not until/till, Not since.***
  Only after *it started to pour with rain* ***did we*** *move inside.*
  Only by *turning up the volume* ***could I*** *hear the lyrics of the song.*
  Not until *we received the letter* ***did we*** *find out what had happened.*
- with **conditionals**: ***Should I*** ... (type 1), ***Were I*** ... (type 2), ***Had I*** ... (type 3).
  Were I *a richer man, I would have bought the house.*

Inversion without auxiliary verbs:

- with verbs of movement and adverbial expressions of place when they come at the beginning of a sentence.
  Outside the shop ***was a motorbike****. At the bus stop* ***stood a teenager****. Here* ***comes my friend****! There* ***go the marathon runners****!*
  If the subject is a pronoun, there is no inversion. *Here* ***he comes****!* (NOT: ~~Here comes he~~.) *Down* ***you get****!* (NOT: ~~Down get you~~.)
- after direct speech when the subject of the reporting verb is a noun, **NOT** a pronoun! *"I will be late," said Henry.* (OR: ... *Henry said.*)
  "The library closes at seven," said the librarian. (OR: ... *the librarian said.*)
  BUT: *"What can I do for you?" she asked.* (NOT: ... *asked she*, because the subject of the introductory verb is a pronoun.)

Fronting

Another means of achieving emphasis is **fronting**, i.e. placing the item that conveys the emphasis at the beginning of a sentence.

The music he likes most is ***rock****.*
Rock *is the music he likes the most.*
The Lord of the Rings *is* ***Tolkien's most famous work****.*
Tolkien's most famous work *is* The Lord of the Rings.
The artist's message is ***even more relevant*** *today than it was in the past.*

***Even more relevant** today is the artist's message than it was in the past.*

***Though she was irritated**, the singer answered the interviewer's question.*

***Irritated though she was**, the singer answered the interviewer's question.*

Emphasis

Cleft sentences

26 ★★ **Use the words in brackets to form a cleft sentence.**

1 John leads the graphic design team. **(does)**
....
2 An amateur songwriter wrote the number-one single. **(it)**
....
3 The film company fired the lead actor. **(happened)**
....
4 My sister only watches DVDs all day. **(all)**
....
5 Who thought up this cartoon character? **(who ever)**
....

Inversion

27 ★★ **Look at the following text and write inverted sentences in your notebooks using the words/phrases in bold.**

HARRY POTTER

J. K.Rowling, the author of the Harry Potter children's book series, could **barely** make ends meet as a single mother before she started writing. It was **only after** the release of her first book *Harry Potter and the Sorcerer's Stone* that she started to obtain some recognition. However, she could **in no way** imagine she would one day become an international literary sensation. She had **no sooner** written her first three instalments of *Harry Potter* **than** they went on the New York Time's bestseller list. It was **not until** the series had sold more than 450 million copies that it was converted into a multi-million dollar film franchise. There has **seldom** been an author so highly paid before. J. K. Rowling has become one of the wealthiest in the world!

Fronting

28 ★★ **Look at the words in italics and rewrite the sentences using fronting.**

1 The actor's performance is *even more gripping* on stage than on screen.
....
....
2 The band was *so popular* that some dedicated fans followed them everywhere.
....
....
3 The books he enjoys most are *science-fiction* novels.
....
....
4 It proved impossible *to get* the celebrity to open up during the interview.
....
....
5 The *Mona Lisa* is *Leonardo da Vinci's* most distinguished painting.
....
....
6 Listening to live music is *much more invigorating* for audiences than listening to CDs.
....
....

29 ★★ **Rewrite the sentences using different emphatic structures and the word given.**

1 My sister uses the Internet and nothing else to chat with her friends.
All ....
2 I will never watch that film again no matter what happens.
Under ....
3 It was such a wonderful performance that the audience called for an encore.
Such ....
4 The singer sang another set even though he was tired.
Tired ....
5 The actor stood alone on stage performing his soliloquy.
Alone ....
6 The director didn't insist that the lead actress stay in character; she made that decision herself.
It ....
7 The actor is not known for appearing in comedies.
Comedies ....
8 Abigail really wants to star in a musical on Broadway.
What ....

Listening

Section 1: *Questions 1-10*

Questions 1-6

Complete the table below.
*Write **NO MORE THAN ONE WORD AND/OR A NUMBER** for each answer.*

Community College Literature Classes				
Class	**Time**	**Where**	**Topic**	**Notes**
20th Century English Literature	*Example:* at *6:30 pm*	West Hall, room **1**	covers both **2** .... and novelists	scheduling changes
Modern Irish Literature	at 8 pm	Douglas **3**	includes Irish history	**4** .... is excellent
Introduction to English Literature	Friday class: at **5**	West Hall, room 180	focuses on **6** .... stories	held twice a week

Questions 7-10

Complete the sentences below.
*Write **ONE WORD ONLY** for each answer.*

7 Registering online is a .... change for students and staff.

8 Students may begin registering on the third of ....

9 It is important to enrol early because .... classes can rapidly reach capacity.

10 To find out about getting a student ID card, contact Ms ....

Section 2: *Questions 11-20*

Questions 11-14

What does the guide say about each of the following activities?

A It is allowed. **B** It is sometimes allowed. **C** It is not allowed.

*Write the correct letter **A**, **B** or **C**, next to questions 11-14.*
You may choose any letter more than once.

11 eating and drinking ....
12 touching items ....
13 talking ....
14 taking photographs ....

Questions 15-20

Label the plan below.
*Choose **SIX** answers from the box and write the correct letters **A-I**, next to questions 15-20.*

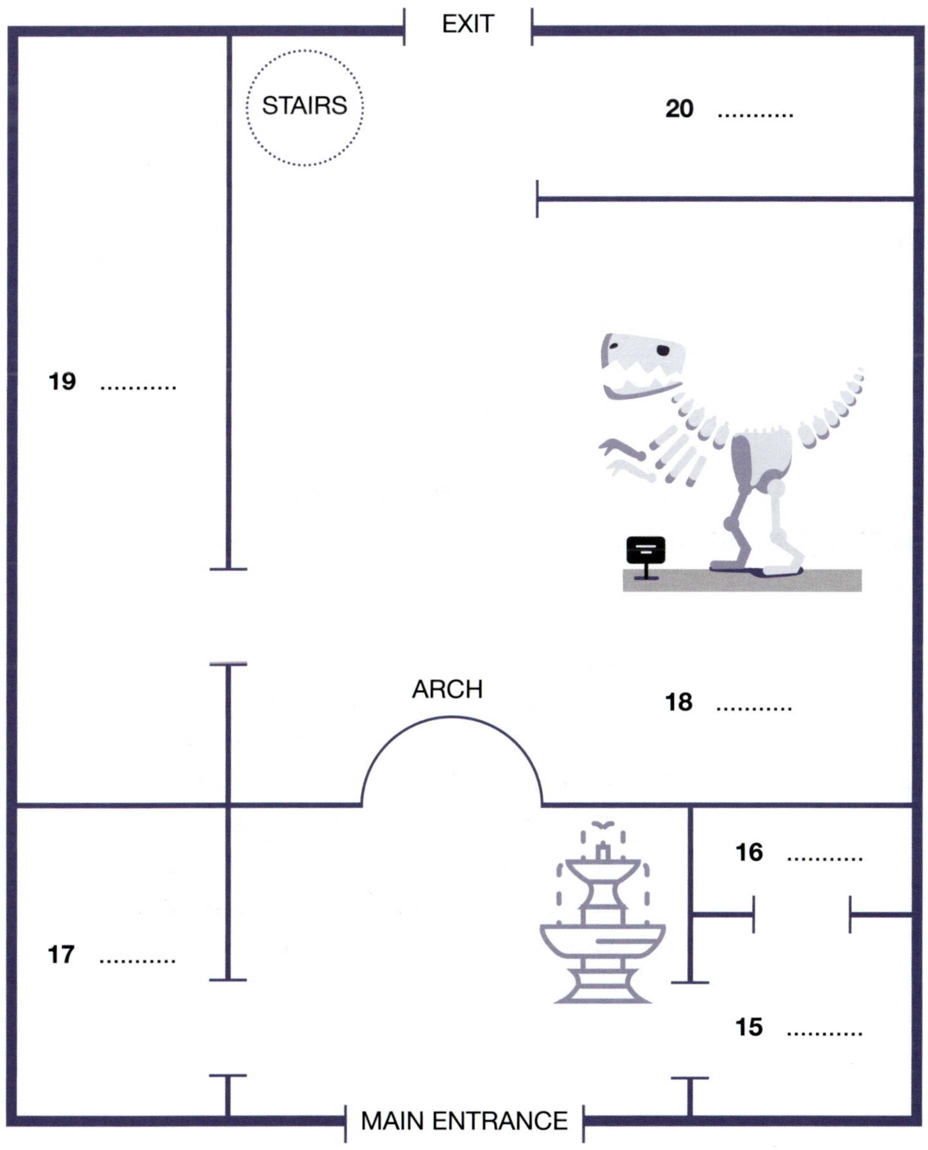

A Fossils exhibit
B Biodiversity Hall
C Night Forest exhibit
D Rocks and Minerals exhibit
E Deep Ocean exhibit
F Store room
G Hands-on Science Lab
H Café
I Gift shop

Section 3: *Questions 21-30*

Questions 21-25

*Choose the correct letter **A**, **B** or **C**.*

21 So far, Alan has focused his research on
- **A** the extent of global transport.
- **B** how far food products are shipped.
- **C** where different foods are produced.

22 What point does Alan make about the air transport of food?
- **A** It is the most damaging method.
- **B** It is less harmful than rail transport.
- **C** There is not a completely safe alternative.

23 The speakers agree that some sources of information
- **A** do not provide facts to strengthen their views.
- **B** provide too much data to mislead people.
- **C** ignore data because they don't understand it.

24 Where did their instructor tell them to get their information?
- **A** reliable information sites
- **B** research papers
- **C** popular blogs

25 Jen and Alan decide to focus their presentation on
- **A** conflicting viewpoints in the field.
- **B** positive actions individuals can take.
- **C** an in-depth discussion of food miles.

Questions 26-30

What benefits do the speakers identify for each of the following choices?
*Choose **FIVE** answers from the box and write the correct letter, **A-G**, next to the Questions 26-30.*

Choices

26 eat locally grown, seasonal food ....
27 buy from small farms ....
28 eat environmentally friendly protein ....
29 eat organic food ....
30 avoid packaged food ....

Benefits

- **A** Fewer dangerous chemicals will be used.
- **B** People will have more nutritious food.
- **C** There will be more space in landfills.
- **D** Agriculture will be more efficient.
- **E** The cost of many foods will be reduced.
- **F** Factory farming will be discouraged.
- **G** Pollution from transport will decrease.

Section 4: *Questions 31-40*

Complete the notes below.
*Write **ONE WORD** for each answer.*

Marine Biology 101 – **Cephalopods**

The octopus:

- All octopuses have eight **31** ....
- There are many **32** .... species of octopus.
- Some octopuses have probably not been **33** .... by anyone yet.

Intelligence:

- Octopuses' **34** .... is an indication of their cleverness.
- An octopus can remember a hidden exit and find it **35** .... with practice.
- Octopuses can open things as complicated as a **36** .... bottle.
- Octopuses use **37** .... ; one example is carrying a coconut shell for shelter.

Traits:

- Octopuses can survive low temperatures because their **38** .... is efficient at carrying oxygen.
- Releasing ink gives octopuses an opportunity to **39** .... from predators.
- Octopuses can also alter their **40** .... to hide or to frighten predators.

Reading

PASSAGE 1

*You should spend about 20 minutes on **Questions 1-13**, which are based on Reading Passage 1 below.*

Where is Air Travel Going?

New innovations are expanding our concept of flight

Between 2006 and 2016, the number of airline passengers worldwide went up by around a billion and a half, to nearly four billion. Given the environmental impact of air travel, it is imperative that the industry develop aircraft that produce less noise and fewer carbon emissions than those of the past. Fortunately we have a number of new technologies and new, lightweight building materials at our disposal.

Electricity could be key to the future of air travel. Just as electric, driverless cars are set to revolutionise personal transport, battery-powered automated flying machines could soon replace traditional taxis. A number of companies worldwide are working on them, convinced that they will take off both literally and metaphorically. One of the things that make the concept of 'sky taxis' suitable for dense urban environments is the ability to start and end journeys vertically, with no runway required.

A number of inventors have also shown that it is possible to build flying machines for personal use on both the roads and in the air, proving that motor pioneer Henry Ford was right when he predicted the appearance of flying cars back in 1940. The problem is that these vehicles have very complicated designs, are very expensive and are subject to very strict regulations about where they can be used; they cannot land just anywhere. They are likely to remain something of a wealthy person's toy for some time yet.

However, some passenger planes on scheduled routes could soon be electric, as long as we find ways of making batteries lighter and more efficient. The most advanced electric aeroplanes today do not carry passengers and have a maximum range of around 100 km, but at least one company is hoping to introduce a commercial, battery-powered electric aircraft within a decade. Its plan is for a nine-seat aeroplane with a range of around 500 km.

Since electric aeroplanes need to fly more slowly and at lower altitudes than those with jet engines, it seems unlikely they will ever be used for long-distance journeys. A mix of fuel and battery power is certainly possible, however. In fact, this is a very sensible arrangement, as aeroplanes are required to fly with 45 minutes of reserve power available at all times in case an emergency arises.

In the near future, even the passengers themselves could generate at least some of the power an aircraft needs to fly. Seats that have the ability to turn body heat into electrical energy are under development. If you feel uncomfortable about the idea of becoming a human battery, the seats might also have plenty of features to help you relax. It has been suggested that aeroplane seats – which are notoriously lacking in comfort – could one day change shape to match an individual body. Massage or acupuncture treatments could even be built in. Such luxuries would be provided to passengers who are willing to pay the top fares, anyway.

Other design innovations seem to be aimed at helping people who find flying unpleasant or frightening. If you wish you were somewhere else every time you board an aircraft, how would you like to use a virtual-reality helmet to transport yourself to a different environment? There is a good chance that 'sensory headsets' will be fitted to the headrests of aeroplane seats before long. A more outlandish virtual-reality idea is to make the plane walls seem invisible. By covering them with special materials that give off light, airlines will be able to show passengers images of the sky outside the plane. Of course, that is not everyone's idea of a relaxing experience – so some people might be very grateful for the sensory headset option!

For those who do enjoy flying, however, a new kind of holiday that puts the plane at the centre of the experience has already become available – but it does not come cheap. You can fly around the world in a luxury Boeing 777 aircraft, spending time in ten of the world's most exciting cities, for around $160,000. The 'air cruise', as the name suggests, is an attempt to recreate in the air the experience of travelling by sea for pleasure. The aeroplane has lounge seating, beds, fine dining, a bar and even butlers, and is used exclusively for air cruises lasting between two weeks and a month.

Clearly, standard aircraft are not likely to become so luxurious, but ordinary flyers can at least expect to get more room for themselves. That is because the shape of commercial aircraft is expected to change quite fundamentally in the future, as today's designs are not ideal for fuel efficiency and smooth movement. Future aircraft will likely be more triangular in shape, with larger wings that blend into the middle of the plane rather than sticking out from it. These aeroplanes will be less noisy and they will have more interior space, but there will also be fewer windows. Indeed, if you think about how much cars have changed since their early days, it is hard to believe that the basic design of aircraft has stayed the same for as long as it has.

Questions 1-8

Do the following statements agree with the information given in Reading Passage 1?
For questions 1-8, write:

TRUE	if the statement agrees with the information
FALSE	if the statement contradicts the information
NOT GIVEN	if there is no information on this

1 The popularity of air travel is threatening the environment. ....

2 Electric power is unlikely to be used in the flight industry. ....

3 Sky taxis are viewed by some as an opportunity for profit. ....

4 Sky taxis are not a good idea for crowded, big city locations. ....

5 Henry Ford designed a prototype flying car. ....

6 It is illegal to land a flying car on a roadway. ....

7 There are still technical limitations which electric planes must overcome. ....

8 In the next decade, electric planes are expected to almost double their range. ....

Questions 9-13

*Choose the correct letter **A**, **B**, **C** or **D**.*

9 What is the writer doing in the fifth paragraph?

A describing why electric planes are not widely used
B pointing out the advantages of battery power
C discussing future applications of battery technology
D warning of potential risks associated with electric planes

10 What are we told about innovations in seats in the sixth paragraph?

A They will benefit the airlines more than the passengers.
B They will each make flying a more relaxing experience.
C They will do little to ease the discomfort of current seats.
D They are unlikely to be made available to everyone.

11 Future virtual reality innovations could affect anxious passengers

A minimally, as there will be little change.
B in several different ways.
C by obscuring the flight experience completely.
D because the thrills of flight are emphasised.

12 An air cruise seeks to make

A round-the-world travel attainable for those with little time.
B luxury travel accessible to people from all walks of life.
C the destination more important than the journey.
D air travel emulate a more traditional holiday experience.

13 What is the main point that the writer makes about change in aircraft in the final paragraph?

A It is long overdue.
B It will be mostly cosmetic.
C It will be at the expense of comfort.
D It is unlikely to actually take place.

PASSAGE 2

*You should spend about 20 minutes on **Questions 14-26**, which are based on Reading Passage 2 below.*

TITANIUM

A marvellous metal

One of the most useful substances in modern industry – titanium – is the ninth most common element found in the Earth's crust. Despite its abundance, titanium wasn't discovered until 1791. More than a century went by before anybody found a way to extract the metal titanium from titanium ore, and it wasn't until the mid-20th century that a method of doing this was invented that made it possible to use titanium metal commercially. Since then, it's been used in everything from bicycles and hockey sticks to ships and aeroplane engines. It's an ideal material for anything that needs to be hard-wearing yet light – titanium is, in fact, as strong as steel, but only 45% as heavy, and it's highly resistant to corrosion. It was seen as such a valuable material in the 1950s and 1960s that attempts were made to monopolise the world titanium market and prevent access to it. This didn't work though, as it was accessed secretly via overseas companies which agreed to cover up the transactions.

Titanium metal, however, makes up only a small percentage of titanium usage. The vast majority of titanium that is mined remains in its naturally occurring oxide form. Known as titanium dioxide, it provides a white pigment that is often used in paints and as a covering for plastics. Because of its ability to absorb ultraviolet rays, titanium dioxide is a component of many sunscreens. It's also used, controversially, to whiten toothpastes and food products such as chewing gum, marshmallows and sweets. Although small amounts of titanium occur naturally in the human body, there are concerns that titanium dioxide could be harmful if ingested in large quantities by people with certain health conditions relating to their digestive systems. We know that titanium dioxide can damage the intestines of mice and, although there's no evidence humans are similarly affected by it, people who have existing problems in that area should probably avoid products containing titanium dioxide.

A newer form of titanium has appeared which has been designed especially for use in the treatment of bone injuries. Known as TiFoam, it is made by covering a foam structure with titanium powder. Once the titanium has stuck to the whole of the material, the foam is destroyed, leaving behind a strong titanium mesh. TiFoam is used to create implants which stabilise broken bones while they heal. Titanium rods have been used to repair bones for some time, but the foam form is a significant advancement because it encourages the bone to grow into, rather than rely on, the implant. Because solid titanium implants are stiffer than the surrounding bone, they tend to take over when the patient gets active. This means the bone can fail to regain its original strength, or even become weaker. TiFoam implants, on the other hand, are as flexible as human bone, and allow bone cells and blood vessels to grow into them.

One of the main reasons titanium has become common in surgery is its compatibility with the human body. It doesn't cause any kind of irritation to human tissue, and it combines well with bone. Titanium – in non-foam form – is even helping to make one of the most complex types of surgery – brain surgery – more effective and safe via 3D printing technology. In the past, brain surgery patients who needed to have part of their skull replaced with a piece of metal were given a plate which was hammered and cut to something approximately the right shape, and then adjusted during the procedure. These plates never produced a perfect fit and one in ten people who were given them developed an infection. Now, however, it's possible to scan a person's head and then produce titanium plate which will fit their skull perfectly. A 3D printer produces the plates by gradually building up layers of very fine titanium powder. These 3D-printed titanium skull plates are both faster and more economical to produce than hand-made ones.

Titanium is perhaps even more ideal for dentistry. Because it's lightweight and doesn't react with chemicals or other metals, it's practical and perfectly safe for installing in a mouth. It's also much cheaper, of course, than the likes of gold for tooth crowns and, unlike gold, its price stays stable rather than fluctuating according to demand and world markets. Artificial teeth made of titanium fuse very well to the jaw, and, as with the skull plates, reduce the risk of infection compared with traditionally used materials. Teeth-straightening braces are far more comfortable when made out of titanium than heavy steel – and much less likely to break.

Given its range of qualities, it seems fitting that Titanium was named after the Titans, part of the family of Greek gods. It may not have supernatural powers, but it certainly is a super-useful material.

Questions 14-17

Do the following statements agree with the claims of the writer in Reading Passage 2?
In boxes 14-17, write

YES	if the statement agrees with the claims of the writer
NO	if the statement contradicts the claims of the writer
NOT GIVEN	if it is impossible to say what the writer thinks about this

14 The conversion of titanium dioxide to metal is an expensive process.
15 The consumption of titanium dioxide is considered perfectly safe.
16 TiFoam technology was designed with medical applications in mind.
17 The strength of solid titanium implants is actually detrimental to bones.

Questions 18-22

*Choose **ONE WORD ONLY** from the passage for each answer.*

18 Previous plates which were shaped by hand were only .... fitted.
19 It is an unexpected bonus when technological advancements are .... rather than more costly.
20 For the field of .... , titanium seems to be a perfect material.
21 Titanium teeth .... easily with the bones that support them.
22 The lightness of titanium makes braces more .... than they used to be.

Questions 23-26

Complete the summary below.
*Choose **ONE WORD ONLY** from the passage for each answer.*

The history of the exploitation of titanium as a resource

Titanium is a(n) **23** .... that is not at all rare, yet it was discovered relatively late. Many decades went by after its discovery before it became **24** .... available. Titanium was considered so important that attempts were made to **25** .... its use. These attempts failed, however, because of secret **26** .... between countries.

PASSAGE 3

*You should spend about 20 minutes on **Questions 27-40**, which are based on Reading Passage 3 below.*

The Mystery of Sleep

Sleep takes up precious time and leaves us vulnerable, so why do we do it?

A The question of why we sleep has been on people's minds at least since the time of Aristotle, who believed that the warming and cooling of the body as a result of digestion caused sleep. Though we know this is incorrect today, other early theories have held up better. The possibility of a 'sleep toxin' – a substance that built up during the day, causing drowsiness, and was subsequently relieved by sleep – was put forward by Henri Pieron in the early 1900s, and this concept is not unlike some contemporary ideas about sleep that researchers are pursuing today. It was not until 1953 that Nathaniel Kleitman and his colleagues identified two different kinds of sleep; REM and non-REM sleep. Many say that this breakthrough paved the way for modern sleep research. But since then, despite the great deal of effort that has been made to better understand sleep, it is still largely a mysterious phenomenon.

B Among living things, sleep is practically universal. Even jellyfish, which have no brains, experience something called sleep pressure – the need to rest longer after being kept awake. Tiny worms, with only a few neurons, spend time in a sleep-like state and die more quickly when exposed to stress if this state is prevented. Sharks and dolphins, which must keep moving at all times in order to breathe, have the ability to sleep with one hemisphere of the brain at a time. Yet, when an animal sleeps, it cannot protect itself from danger, it cannot eat or reproduce. Sleep is high-risk and costly, so why is it such a universal phenomenon? Clearly it must be important.

C One theory about the reason for sleep is that it arose simply as a way to save energy. If there were times when it was difficult or hazardous for an animal to move around, then it might make sense for them to simply enter a sleep state when all of their physical systems slow down. That way, they would require less food, and could hide away from danger. The observation that animals with few natural predators, lions for example, sleep up to 15 hours a day, while small prey animals seldom sleep more than 5 hours a day, seems to contradict this, however. In addition, the objection has been raised that sleep only lowers the metabolism by 10-15 percent, so not much energy is, in fact, saved. According to Serge Daan, a researcher who studied arctic ground squirrels, something else must be taking place. He found that the ground squirrels would periodically come out of their suspended-animation-like state of hibernation in order to sleep. For these animals, sleep was actually energetically expensive, so it must serve some other essential purpose.

D It is well established that the act of sleeping is important for essential brain functions such as memory and learning. A rapidly increasing body of cognitive research suggests that sleep allows us to consolidate and process information that has been acquired during the day. Sleep scientist Matthew Walker used MRI scans to visualise activity in the brains of people who were learning a series of finger movements. One group was allowed to sleep and the other was not. He found differences in the areas of the brain that were activated when they recalled the movements; the group that had slept showed less activity in the brain, and better recollection of the task. In other words, the way the memory was stored had become more efficient. Walker believes that this could explain why toddlers, who are constantly learning new motor skills, require so much more sleep than adults. Furthermore, Ted Abel, while assistant professor at the University of Pennsylvania, found that mice deprived of sleep for the first five hours after learning did not remember their physical surroundings, while their memory of facts and events was not affected. This result allowed him to specify that sleep regulates memory in a specific part of the brain, the hippocampus, which is responsible for memories related to spatial and contextual information. But despite numerous studies, there are still more questions than answers on the role of sleep in memory and learning

E Another theory about the role of sleep is that it is essential for cleanup and repair in the brain and body. Support for this theory is provided by research that shows periods of REM sleep increase following periods of sleep deprivation and strenuous physical activity. During sleep, the body also increases its rate of cell division and protein synthesis, further suggesting that repair and restoration occurs during sleeping periods. Recently, new evidence supporting the repair and restoration theory has been uncovered. Research has shown that the cellular structure of the brain is altered during sleep, and more space forms between cells. This allows fluid to move between the cells and flush out toxic waste products. It is believed that these toxins increase in the central nervous system during waking times, and the restorative function of sleep is a consequence of their removal.

F It may seem that all of this new evidence is not making the question of why we sleep any clearer; indeed, the evidence seems to point to different explanations. In this context it seems important to remember that there may not be one correct answer, but instead it could be a combination. While the idea that sleep is a method of energy conservation seems to be falling out of favour, it seems more and more likely that benefits for memory and learning, the cleanup of the brain and the repair of the body can all be attributed to a good night's sleep.

Glossary

REM sleep: the period of sleep when we dream

non-REM sleep: also called slow-wave sleep, when we do not dream and sleep very deeply

metabolism: the process by which the body uses food to make energy

Questions 27-32

Reading passage 3 has six paragraphs, ***A-F****.*
Which paragraph contains the following information?

Write the correct letter, ***A-F****, in boxes 27-32.*
NB *You may use any letter more than once.*

27 how researchers can see what is happening inside the brain
28 how many reasons for sleep there might realistically be
29 an example of lack of sleep being deadly
30 a particular discovery that was essential for how we view sleep today
31 how sleep might have arisen from threatening conditions
32 how the brain physically changes during sleep

Questions 33-36

Look at the following statements (Questions 33-36) and the list of researchers below.
Match each statement with the correct researcher, ***A-E****.*

A Henri Pieron
B Nathaniel Kleitman
C Serge Daan
D Matthew Walker
E Ted Abel

33 Sleep is essential for the recollection only of certain types of memory. ....
34 The fact that sleep requirements vary with age alludes to its role. ....
35 A chemical that promotes sleep accumulates throughout the day. ....
36 An example in the natural world contradicts the concept that sleep arose to save energy. ....

Questions 37-38

*Choose **TWO** letters, **A-E**.*
Write the correct letters in boxes 37 and 38.
*Which **TWO** theories does the writer question the validity of?*

37 ☐ **38** ☐

A Sleep pressure is proof of the necessity of sleep.
B Animals' sleeping habits are related to their place on the food chain.
C Sleep is related to changes in body temperature.
D Sleep prevents the unnecessary burning of calories.
E There are different types of sleep with different functions.

Questions 39-40

*Choose **TWO** letters, **A-E**.*
Write the correct letters in boxes 39 and 40.
*Which **TWO** points does the writer mention in support of the importance of sleep for memory?*

39 ☐ **40** ☐

A During sleep, unimportant memories are removed.
B Sleep makes recollection more effortless.
C Sleep results in more activity throughout the brain.
D The function of a specific brain region is affected by sleep.
E Sleep duration modifies learning.

Writing

WRITING TASK 1

You should spend about 20 minutes on this task.

The graph below gives information about mobile phone ownership as a percentage of the population in the city of Westforth in the years 2012, 2014 and 2016.

Summarise the information by selecting and reporting the main features, and make comparisons where relevant.

Write at least 150 words.

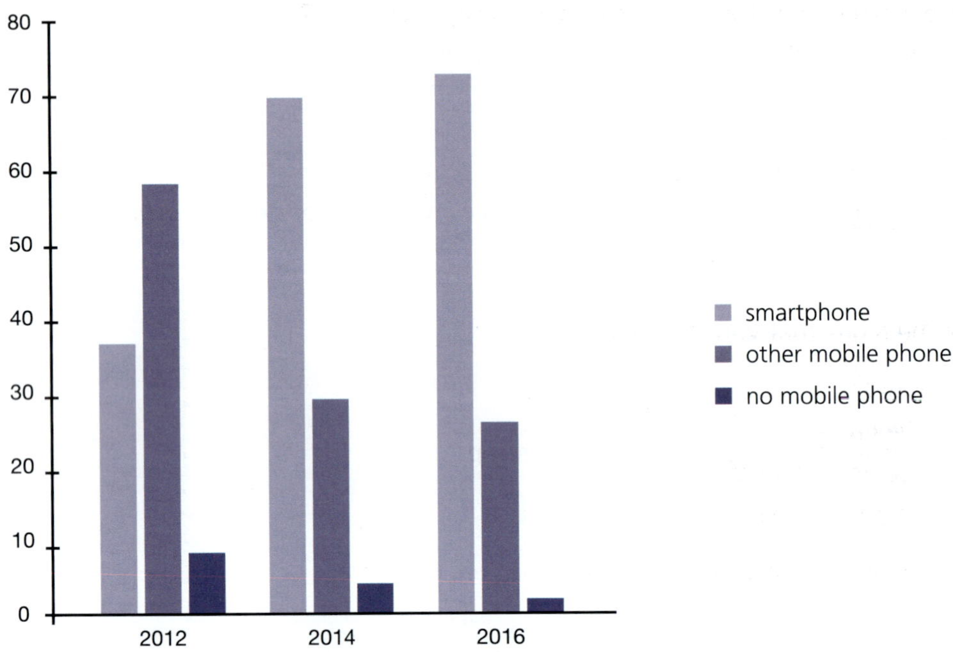

WRITING TASK 2

You should spend about 40 minutes on this task.

Due to the popularity of photo sharing websites it's no longer necessary to have framed pictures or printed photo albums.

To what extent do you agree or disagree with this opinion?

Give reasons for your answer and include any relevant examples from your own knowledge or experience.

Write at least 250 words.

PART 1 – Introduction and interview

Let's talk about your hobbies and interests.

- What's your main hobby outside school?
- How long have you been doing this/interested in this for?
- How did you get interested in it?
- Would you say it is a good hobby/interest to have? Why?

Let's move on to talk about your future.

- Do you plan to continue studying? Why/why not?
- What sort of job would you like to do?
- Do you think you'll stay in this area, or move away? Why?
- How important is it to you to have a family? (Why?)

PART 2 – Individual long turn

Candidate task card:

Describe a gift that you received.

You should say:
what the gift was
what the occasion was
why the gift made an impression on you

and explain how you felt when you received this gift.

Rounding-off questions

- Is it something you might have bought for yourself?
- How well did the person who gave you the gift know you?

PART 3 – Two-way discussion

The importance of possessions in society

- Which possessions do people use to show wealth in your society?
- Is it possible to have too many material possessions?
- Would you rather own a material possession or enjoy an experience?

Spending money

- Does spending money make people happy?
- Do you think people are less careful with money now than they used to be in the past?
- Is there anything governments can do to make sure everyone has enough money to buy what they need?

Practice Test 2 IELTS Listening

Section 1: *Questions 1-10*

Questions 1-6

Complete the form below.
*Write **NO MORE THAN THREE WORDS AND/OR A NUMBER** for each answer.*

Belvedere Hotel
Booking amendment

Example	
Reason for amendment:	*wrong dates*
Customer's name:	Helena **1** ....
Original dates:	27th April to 4th May
New dates:	**2** .... to 3rd May
Amendment charge:	**3** ....
Customer's address:	**4** .... , Coventry, CV4 5GW
Dietary requirements:	One guest is **5** ....
Arrival time:	**6** ....

Questions 7-10

Complete the sentences below.
*Write **NO MORE THAN THREE WORDS AND/OR A NUMBER** for each answer.*

7 You can reach the hotel on foot in .... an hour.
8 For a taxi, expect to pay around .... pounds
9 There is a bus stop .... to the station.
10 Bus number .... goes directly past the hotel.

Section 2: *Questions 11-20*

Questions 11-15

Complete the table below.
Write ***NO MORE THAN TWO WORDS*** *for each answer.*

Building:	Advantages	Disadvantages
Regent Tower	**11** .... location, close to **12**	Unaffordable **13** ....
Newbridge Business Park	Would lower **14** .... bill	Reduced **15** .... at night

Questions 16-20

Label the map below.
Write the correct letter, ***A-H****, next to questions 16-20.*

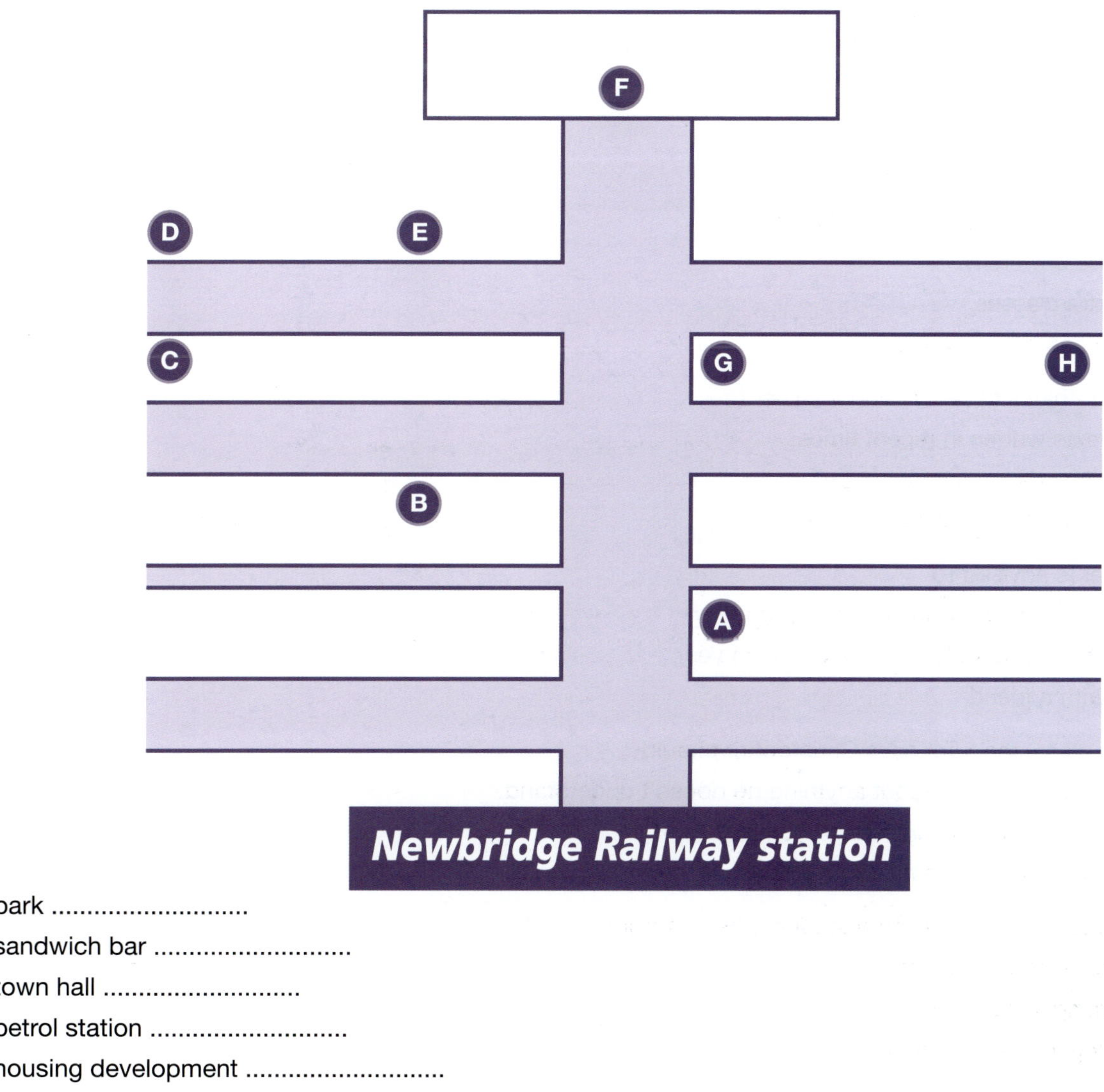

16 park ....
17 sandwich bar ....
18 town hall ....
19 petrol station ....
20 housing development ....

Section 3: *Questions 21-30*

Questions 21-24

Use ***NO MORE THAN THREE WORDS AND/OR A NUMBER*** *for each answer.*

TUTOR'S ADVICE TO CHRISTOPHER

It's not unusual to find your early weeks at university **21** .... A good way to make friends is to get involved with **22** .... There's a film society that might appeal to you and you should take the opportunity to **23** .... a sport you used to enjoy. It's important to know how to **24** .... and have fun, too.

Questions 25-30

Choose the correct letter, ***A, B*** *or* ***C****.*

25 Christopher says his main problem with the coursework relates to

A remembering to write essays.

B his reading comprehension.

C finding printed copies of the plays.

26 The tutor tells Christopher one option is to

A leave the university.

B take extra classes.

C choose another area of study.

27 Christopher thinks he would find it easier to

A study texts written in recent times.

B specialise in a foreign language.

C do something more creative.

28 Christopher is advised to

A read more than the books he must study.

B think about what he'd like to study next year.

C study with a friend.

29 After each class, the tutor says Christopher should

A speak to the lecturer about anything he doesn't understand.

B do some studying on university premises.

C spend time doing something he enjoys.

30 According to the tutor, literature students benefit from

A attempting to write drama.

B performing writers' work.

C attending live performances.

Section 4: *Questions 31-40*

Questions 31-36

Complete the summary below.
*Write **ONE WORD ONLY** for each answer.*

Fanny Mendelssohn's early life

In the opinion of the young Felix, Fanny was the **31** .... pianist of the two. However, only Felix was seen by their parents as someone who might one day have a career in music. Their father's opinions on this are an example of the **32** .... of the period. He told Fanny that her life could include music, but it couldn't be her **33** .... Felix also didn't like the idea of Fanny publishing her music or playing it in public, even though he valued her **34** .... about his own. Felix showed his respect for her, however, by publishing her musical **35** .... as his own, though he did admit to Queen Victoria that they were hers because he was a **36** .... person.

Questions 37-38

*Choose **TWO** letters, **A-E**.*
*Which **TWO** things, according to the Mendelssohns, made Wilhelm an unsuitable husband for Fanny?*

37 ☐ **38** ☐

A He was an artist.
B He was poor.
C He insisted Fanny write music.
D He spent time working abroad.
E They did not believe he was clever.

Questions 39-40

*Choose **TWO** letters, **A-E**.*
*In which **TWO** situations did Fanny perform?*

39 ☐ **40** ☐

A with a full orchestra
B while staying in Rome
C at an event to help people
D with the musician Franz Liszt
E at her home for guests

PASSAGE 1

You should spend about 20 minutes on ***Questions 1-13****, which are based on Reading Passage 1 below.*

THE UNREST BEHIND THE ROMANCE

According to Sydney Waterlow, the era of the Romantic movement was a turbulent time in Britain, politically and socially.

The greatest of Britain's lyric poets, the culmination of the Romantic movement in English literature, appeared in an age which, following on from a series of successful military campaigns that had established British power all over the world, was one of the gloomiest in the country's history. If in some ways the Britain of 1800-20 was ahead of the rest of Europe, in others it lagged far behind. The Industrial Revolution, which in time transformed a nation of peasants and traders into a nation of manufacturers, had begun; but its chief fruits as yet were increased materialism and greed, and politically the period was far from calm.

Alone of European peoples, the British had been untouched by the tide of Napoleon's conquests, which, when it receded from the Continent, at least left behind a framework of enlightened institutions, while Britain's success in the Napoleonic wars only confirmed the grip of ruling aristocratic families on the nation which they had governed since the reign of Queen Anne. This despotism crushed the humble and stimulated the high-spirited to violence, and is the reason why poets such as Byron, Landor, and Shelley, though by birth and fortune members of the ruling class, were pioneers of political, as much as of spiritual, rebellion. Unable to breathe the atmosphere of England, they were driven by their sensibilities to live in exile.

In their home country there was exhaustion after war; workmen being thrown out of employment; high taxes, rents and corn prices; and a sense of fear arising from the French Revolution, which had sent a wave of panic through the country which would last until about 1830. Suspicion of republican principles – which, it seemed, led straight to organised slaughter – frightened many good men, who would otherwise have been reformers, into supporting the establishment. The elder generation of poets had been republicans in their youth. Wordsworth, for example, had said of the revolution that it was "bliss to be alive" in that dawn; Southey and Coleridge had even planned to found a communist-style society in the New World. Now all three were committed to the defence of order and property, as well as the Church and the throne. From their seclusion in the Lake District, Southey and Wordsworth praised the royal family and celebrated England as the home of freedom.

However, England had ruthlessly stamped out the Irish rebellion of 1798, forced Ireland by fraud into the union of 1800 and was strangling that island's industry and commerce. Catholics could neither vote nor hold office. In fact, at a time when the population of the United Kingdom was some 30 million, the right to vote was possessed by no more than a million, and the majority of the seats in parliament were the private property of rich men. Representative government did not exist, and whoever agitated for some measure of it was deported to Australia or forced to flee to America. Glasgow and Manchester weavers starved and rioted, but anyone not directly involved in such incidents didn't necessarily hear about them, as news publishers were tightly controlled. In 1812, bands of poor people were driven by hunger to steal to feed themselves, placing themselves in mortal danger, for death was still the punishment for the theft of a loaf or a sheep. The social organism had come to a deadlock - on the one hand a starved and angry populace, on the other a vast, powerful Church-and-king party, made up of all who had a stake in the country.

In 1820 Shelley wrote what might be described as a not quite successful piece of satirical drama, *Oedipus Tyrannus or Swellfoot The Tyrant*, inspired by the quarrel between the Prince Regent and his wife. When the Princess of Wales, Caroline of Brunswick-Wolfenbuttel, after having left her husband to live in Italy, returned soon after the prince became George IV to claim her position as queen, the royal differences became an affair of high national importance. The divorce case which followed encapsulated the distempers of the age. Shelley felt that sort of disgust which makes a man rave and curse under the attacks of some oppressive disease; if he laughs, it is the laugh of frenzy. In the play, which was suppressed soon after publication, he represents the men of England as starving pigs content to lap up whatever scraps their tyrant, the priests, and the soldiers will allow them. At the end, when the pigs, rallying around the triumphant princess, hunt down their oppressors, the reader cannot help feeling a little sorry that Shelley does not permit a gentler mood into the work: there is an unrelentingly cruel quality in his humour, even if it is justified.

Questions 1-3

Choose the correct letter, A, B, C or D.

1 According to the text, in the early 19th century, people in Britain began doing what?

A making goods

B joining the army

C growing food

D travelling abroad

2 The poets Byron, Landor, and Shelley

A supported Napoleon.

B came from poor backgrounds.

C received an order to leave Britain.

D were members of powerful families.

3 Why did Wordsworth, Southey and Coleridge change their political views?

A because of ordinary people's poverty

B because they were losing money

C because they feared the rise of violence

D because of their experiences overseas

Questions 4-7

Do the following statements agree with the information given in Reading Passage 1?
For questions 4-7, write:

TRUE	if the statement agrees with the information
FALSE	if the statement contradicts the information
NOT GIVEN	if there is no information on this

4 Ireland and Britain agreed to a temporary union. ....

5 The British population was decreasing. ....

6 Newspapers made unrest seem more frequent than it was. ....

7 Stealing bread could lead to someone's execution. ....

Questions 8-13

Complete the summary below.
*Choose **NO MORE THAN TWO WORDS** from the text for each answer.*

The Subject of a Satirical Drama

Oedipus Tyrannus was **8** .... a disagreement between the Prince Regent and the Princess of Wales which drew the attention of the nation. Although the couple had been living apart, Caroline came back to England to **9** .... her place as the queen. This soon led to their divorce. Shelley felt extreme **10** .... in response to the events, which he expressed in the play. The play was not successful; it didn't have a chance because it was **11** .... right away. This was not surprising since he portrayed the English as pigs who finally rose up against their **12** .... It has been suggested that the play would have benefited from a **13** .... and less cruelty in its style of satire.

PASSAGE 2

You should spend about 20 minutes on **Questions 14-26**, *which are based on Reading Passage 2 below.*

Questions 14-20

Reading Passage 2 has seven paragraphs, ***A-G****.*
Choose the correct heading for each paragraph from the list of headings below.
Write the correct number, ***i-x****, next to Questions 14-20.*

List of Headings

i	Elevating every drinker
ii	Its discovery by the wider world
iii	A better way to judge a culture
iv	A cause of military conflict
v	Present in all the arts
vi	Society's suspicions disappeared
vii	Tea's effects on the body
viii	A forgivable obsession
ix	Representing higher things
x	How tea united nations

14 Paragraph A ....
15 Paragraph B ....
16 Paragraph C ....
17 Paragraph D ....
18 Paragraph E ....
19 Paragraph F ....
20 Paragraph G ....

TEA FROM A JAPANESE PERSPECTIVE

In an excerpt from ***The Book of Tea****, Okakura Kakuzo addresses the significance of tea in Japanese aesthetics and culture.*

A Tea began as a medicine and grew into a beverage. In China, in the 8th century, it entered the realm of poetry as one of the polite amusements. The 15th century saw Japan ennoble it into a religion of aestheticism – Teaism. Teaism is a cult founded on the adoration of the beautiful among the sordid facts of everyday existence. It demonstrates purity and harmony, the mystery of mutual charity, the romanticism of the social order. It is essentially a worship of the imperfect, as it is a tender attempt to accomplish something possible in this impossible thing we know as life.

B What we might call the philosophy of tea expresses a whole point of view about humankind and nature. It is hygiene, for it enforces cleanliness; it is economics, for it shows comfort in simplicity rather than in the complex and costly; it is moral geometry, inasmuch as it defines our sense of proportion to the universe. It represents the true spirit of Eastern democracy by making all its participants aristocrats in taste.

C The long isolation of Japan from the rest of the world, so conducive to introspection, has been highly favourable to the development of Teaism. Our home and habits, costume and cuisine, porcelain, painting – our very literature – all have been subject to its influence. No student of Japanese culture could ever ignore its presence. It has permeated the elegance of noble boudoirs, and entered the abode of the humble.

D We speak of those who seem unnaturally unmoved by life's dramas as having 'no tea in them'. Conversely, we suggest those who allow their emotions to run riot as having 'too much tea in them'. The outsider may indeed wonder at this. But when we consider how small, after all, the cup of human enjoyment is, how soon overflowed with tears, how easily frustrated is our thirst for infinity, we shall not blame ourselves for making so much of the tea cup. Mankind has done worse.

E The average Westerner might see in the tea ceremony just another instance of the 1,001 oddities which constitute the quaintness of the East to him. He tended to regard Japan as barbarous while she indulged in the gentle arts of peace: he called her civilised when she took to battlefields. Much comment has been given lately to the code of the Samurai - the 'Art of Death' which makes our soldiers glory in self-sacrifice; but scarcely any attention has been drawn to Teaism, which represents so much of our art of life. A claim to civilisation must never be based on the gruesome glory of war; due respect should be paid instead to our art and ideals.

F The earliest record of tea in European writing is said to be found in the statement of an Arabian traveller that after the year 879 the main sources of revenue in Canton were the taxes on salt and tea. Marco Polo records the words of a Chinese minister of finance who raised tea taxes in 1285. At the end of the 16th century the Dutch brought the news that a pleasant drink was made in the East from the leaves of a bush. The travellers Giovanni Batista Ramusio, L. Almeida, Maffeno and Tareira, also mentioned tea. Then, in 1610, ships of the Dutch East India Company brought the first tea into Europe. It was known in France in 1636, and reached Russia in 1638. England welcomed it in 1650 and spoke of it as 'that excellent, and by all physicians approved, China drink, called by the people of China "tcha", and by other nations "tay", alias "tee".'

G As with all good things, the propaganda of tea met with opposition. Detractors like Henry Saville denounced drinking it as a filthy custom. Jonas Hanway wrote in 1756 that men seemed to lose their stature and comeliness, and women their beauty, through the use of tea. Its cost in this period forbade popular consumption and made it more a drink for special celebrations and wealthy people, yet tea-drinking spread with rapidity. The coffee houses of London in the early half of the 18th century became, in fact, teahouses visited by the great wits of the day, who amused each other over their 'dish of tea'. The beverage soon became a necessity of life – a taxable matter. It even played an important role in history. Colonial America resigned herself to oppression until human endurance was pushed too far by the heavy duties laid on tea. American independence dates from the throwing of tea chests into Boston's harbour.

Questions 21-26

Complete the flow-chart below.
*Choose **ONE WORD ONLY** from the text for each answer.*

A Timeline of Tea in Europe

879: The first historical mention of tea in Europe was a **21** .... about items that were taxed in Canton after this year.

↓

1285: Marco Polo left an account of Chinese bureaucrats who **22** .... funds by taxing tea in this year.

↓

Late 16th century: Explorers returned home with **23** .... of a beverage they admired.

↓

1610: The first tea arrives in Europe on **24** ....

↓

1630s: Tea becomes more widely **25** .... in the countries of Europe.

↓

Early 18th century: In London, **26** .... become popular meeting places for intellectuals.

PASSAGE 3

*You should spend about 20 minutes on **Questions 27-40**, which are based on Reading Passage 3 below.*

Life on the Mississippi

Mark Twain describes the people and places encountered on a trip on the river.

The scenery from St. Louis to Cairo – two hundred miles – is varied and beautiful. The hills were clothed in the fresh foliage of spring now, and were a gracious and worthy setting for the broad river flowing between. Our trip began with a perfect day which we took as a good omen, and our boat seemed to cover the miles with ease.

At Chester, Illinois, we found a railway taking shape. Chester has also a prison now, and is developing well in other ways. At Grand Tower, too, there was a railway, and another at Cape Girardeau. The former town gets its name from a huge, squat pillar of rock, which stands up out of the water on the Missouri side of the river – a piece of nature's fanciful handiwork, and one of the most picturesque features of that region.

The Town of Grand Tower was evidently a busier place than it had been in old times, but it seemed to need some repairs here and there, and a new coat of whitewash[1] all over. 'Uncle' Mumford, our second officer, said the place had been suffering from flooding, and consequently was not looking its best now. But he said it was not strange that it didn't waste whitewash on itself, for more lime was made there, and of a better quality, than anywhere in the West. He added, "On a dairy farm you never can get any milk for your coffee, nor any sugar for it on a sugar plantation; and it is against sense to go to a lime town to hunt for whitewash." From my own experience I knew the first two assertions to be true; and also that people who sell candy don't care for candy; therefore there was plausibility in Uncle Mumford's final observation that "people who make lime run more to religion than whitewash". Uncle Mumford said, further, that Grand Tower was a great coal-mining center and a prospering place.

Cape Girardeau is situated on a hillside, and makes for a handsome sight. There is a school for boys at the foot of the town by the river. Uncle Mumford said it had as high a reputation for thoroughness as any similar institution in Missouri! There was another college higher up on an airy summit – a bright new facade, with peculiar towers. Uncle Mumford said that Cape Girardeau was the Athens of Missouri, and contained several colleges besides those already mentioned; and all of them on a religious basis of one kind or another. He directed my attention to what he called the "strong and pervasive religious look of the town," but I could not perceive an atmosphere any more religious than the other hill towns with the same slope and built of the same kind of bricks. Prior knowledge often makes people see more than really exists.

Uncle Mumford has been thirty years a mate on the river. He is a man of a practical sensibility and a level head. He has observed much of the world and had much experience of one sort or another. He has plenty of opinions and also just a dash of poetry in his expression of them, gifted as he is with easy-flowing speech and a thick growl in his voice. He is a sailor of the old-fashioned kind, who doesn't hesitate to insult his subordinates if he thinks they deserve it, or in order to make them work harder. "Get up there, you!" He might say "Going to be all day? Why didn't you say your legs failed you when on water before you came on board?!"

Although he is firm, the crew like him because he is fair and just; men tend to give him their loyalty. His clothing is still the scruffy sort of the old generation of mates; but by his next trip the Anchor Line will have him in uniform – a smart blue naval one, with brass buttons, along with all the officers of the line.

Uniforms on the Mississippi! It beats all the other changes put together for surprise. Still, perhaps it's more surprising that this didn't come to pass fifty years ago. The sheer common sense of the move makes you wonder why it wasn't thought of earlier. For decades innocent passengers in need of help and information have been mistaking mates for cooks, and captains for barbers – and been responded to harshly for it, too. Their troubles are ended now, and the greatly improved appearance of the boat staff is a bonus.

Glossary

whitewash: a solution of lime and water used for painting walls etc.

Questions 27-31

Look at the following features (Questions 27-31) and the list of towns below.
Match each feature with the town in which it is found.
*Write the correct letter **A, B** or **C**, next to Questions 27-31.*

NB *You may use any letter more than once.*

27 successful industries ....
28 a natural landmark ....
29 modern architecture ....
30 a place of punishment ....
31 educational establishments ....

Towns along the Mississippi River

A Chester
B Grand Tower
C Cape Girardeau

Questions 32-36

Complete the summary below.
*Choose **NO MORE THAN TWO WORDS** from the text for each answer.*

UNCLE MUMFORD

Uncle Mumford expresses his **32** .... quite poetically, and speaks with a **33** .... He's old-fashioned enough to consider it acceptable to **34** .... those under his command if he thinks it necessary. In spite of this, he earns people's **35** .... because he is fair and well-liked. His clothing identifies him as one of the older generation of ship's mates, but that's about to change as a **36** .... is being introduced.

Questions 37-40

Do the following statements reflect the claims of the writer in Reading Passage 3?
For questions 37-40, write:

TRUE if the statement agrees with the information
FALSE if the statement contradicts the information
NOT GIVEN if there is no information on this

37 The thought of officers on boats on the Mississippi wearing uniforms is quite shocking. ....
38 The officers have wanted uniforms for a long time. ....
39 The uniforms will make things easier for passengers. ....
40 The uniforms will probably not look very smart. ....

Writing

WRITING TASK 1

You should spend about 20 minutes on this task.

The graph below gives information about drinks sales at Freda's Cafe on two different days of the week.

Summarise the information by selecting and reporting the main features. Make comparisons if relevant.

Write at least 150 words.

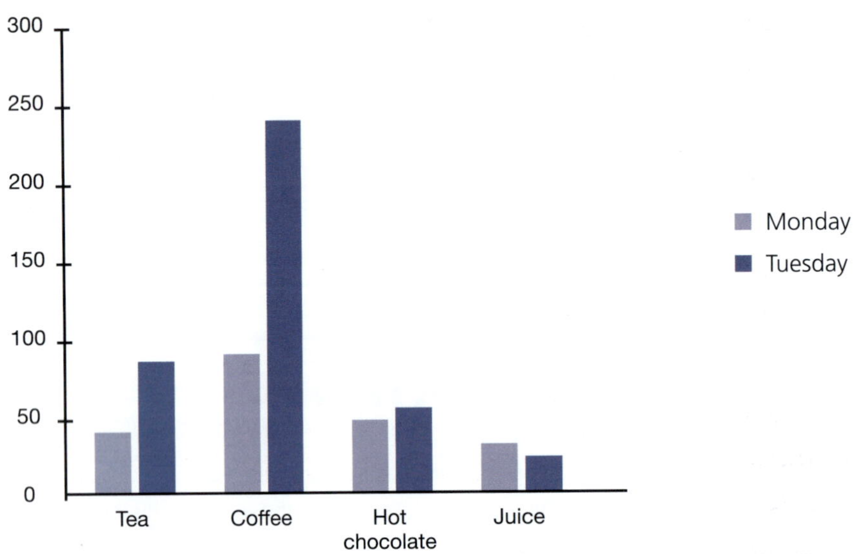

WRITING TASK 2

You should spend about 40 minutes on this task.

It is a perfectly valid choice for parents to educate their children at home; home education is just as valuable as formal education, and perhaps even more so.

How far do you agree with this statement?

Do you think the advantages of home education outweigh the disadvantages?

Give reasons for your answer and include any relevant examples from your own knowledge or experience.

Write at least 250 words.

PART 1 – Introduction and interview

Let's talk about where you live.

- What do you like about your village/town/city?
- What kind of industries are important in your village/town/city?
- How has your village/town/city changed in the last 20 years?
- What would you like to change about your village/town/city?

Now let's talk about your particular neighbourhood.

- What kind of building do you live in?
- Can you describe your street?
- What kind of things can you do in your neighbourhood?
- Would you recommend living in your area?

PART 2 – Individual long turn

Candidate task card:

Describe the importance of music in your life.

You should say:
what kind of music you listen to
if you play an instrument, or whether you'd like to
what music means to you

and describe a particular piece of music that affects you.

Rounding-off questions

- Do you enjoy attending concerts?
- Is there any kind of music you dislike?

PART 3 – Two-way discussion

The importance of music in education and wider culture
• How important is it that music is taught in schools? • Should public money be used to help train musicians? • How does music enrich our lives?
The future of music
• How do you think music will sound in the future? • How is the consumption of music changing? • Do you think it will be easier or more difficult to earn a living as a musician?

Glossary

Abbreviations	(adj)	adjective	(n)	noun	(pp)	past participle	(sb)	somebody
	(adv)	adverb	(phr)	phrase	(prep)	preposition	(sth)	something
	(conj)	conjunction	(phr v)	phrasal verb	(pron)	pronoun		
	(idm)	idiom	(pl n)	plural noun	(v)	verb		

1a (pp. 4-5)

astounded (adj) = astonished
bland (adj) = having very little flavour
dorm (n) = a large room at a hostel, an institution, etc where a number of individuals can sleep
edible (adj) = that can be eaten
gush (about sth) (v) = to talk about sth enthusiastically
hunchback (n) = an abnormal curve on sb's back
intimidating (adj) = daunting
mumble (v) = to mutter
squash sth down (phr v) = to suppress sth
suffocate (v) = to cause difficulty in breathing
swap (v) = to share
tentacle (n) = a part of an animal such as an octopus, a squid, etc that is long and used for grabbing things

1b (pp. 6-7)

assert (v) = to state categorically
boast (v) = (of a place) to have sth extraordinary
brag (v) = to talk too proudly about yourself
close escape (phr) = a narrow escape
close shave (phr) = a narrow escape
damage (n) = physical or emotional harm
decisive effect (phr) = a result that strongly affects a situation
desirable effect (phr) = a wanted outcome
devastation (n) = destruction
diminish (v) = to reduce
disgruntled (adj) = very disappointed and annoyed
dissipate (v) = to decrease sth gradually
drain (sth of sth) (v) = to make all the liquid in sth get used up
dramatic effect (phr) = a great and impressive influence
drive sb out (phr v) = to make sb leave a place
dwindle (v) = to decrease gradually
embark (v) = to get onto a ship or plane
embed (v) = to insert sth deeply and firmly into sth else
embody (v) = to represent
excellent example (phr) = a very good example
exemplify (v) = to constitute a typical example of sth
exertion (n) = the use of a great deal of physical effort
fair chance (phr) = a reasonable possibility
financial gain (phr) = profit
fine example (phr) = a good example
fine print (phr) = the small print in a contract
gloat (v) = to express immense satisfaction because of you own success
it dawns on sb (phr) = sb starts to realise sth
likely chance (phr) = the fact that sth seems quite probable to happen
lucky escape (phr) = the fact that you are lucky enough to avoid injury or death
mass tourism (phr) = tourism involving large numbers of people
microclimate (n) = the specific weather patterns in a particular area
microcosm (n) = a small society or place which has all the features of sth larger
microscope (n) = an instrument for magnifying items
microscopy (n) = examining sth through a microscope
narrow escape (phr) = the fact that one barely avoids danger or problems
outcome (n) = a result
package tour (phr) = a holiday with visits to several places, which has been organised by an agency at an all-inclusive price
prime example (phr) = the most typical example of sth
repercussions (pl n) = consequences
seasonal job (phr) = a job available only for a certain period of time within a year
set out (phr v) = to explain thoroughly
sheer luck (phr) = pure luck
sth goes off (phr v) = sth occurs as expected
strong chance (phr) = a strong possibility
tourism sector (phr) = the part of the economy relating to tourism
tourist destination (phr) = a place popular with tourists
wildlife conservation (phr) = the protection of animals and plants in their natural habitat
wipe out (phr v) = to destroy completely
working conditions (phr) = the place and situation in which one works

1c (pp. 8-9)

desolate (adj) = empty and deserted
fortune favours the bold (idm) = luck helps those who are brave
procrastinate (v) = to postpone sth without justification
threshold (n) = a lower limit

1d (p. 10)

immersion course (n) = a series of foreign language lessons conducted only in the target language
policyholder (n) = sb who has insurance

1e (p. 11)

comfort zone (n) = a situation in which you feel at ease
exceed (v) = to go beyond sth
strike up a conversation (idm) = to enter into a discussion with sb
unwind (v) = to relax

1f (p. 12)

consensus (n) = an agreement
holistay (n) = staying at home during holidays and taking part in local leisure activities
lodging expenses (phr) = accommodation costs
reinforcement (n) = strengthening sth
self-assurance (n) = self-confidence

Skills Work 1 (p. 13)

arrondissement (n) = (in the French language) a district within a big city
ashlar-stone (phr) = made of squared stone blocks
boulevard (n) = a wide city road with trees
dweller (n) = a resident
eclectic (adj) = wide-ranging
étage noble (phr) = (in the French language) (of a building) the second floor with higher ceilings and balconies
garret (n) = a small attic
menu plaisir (n) = a small pleasure
notorious (adj) = infamous for sth
ornate (adj) = highly decorated

refined (adj) = elegant
salle (n) = a hall; a big room
shabby (adj) = in bad condition
tailored tour (phr) = a customised sightseeing excursion
the cradle of sth (phr) = the birthplace of sth
the beau monde (n) = the members of a specific society that are wealthy and fashionable
wistfully (adv) = in a sad and longing way
wrought-iron (adj) = made from iron formed into shapes

Language Knowledge 1
(pp. 14-15)

announcement (n) = a public statement
aspire (to do sth) (v) = to have a strong desire to achieve sth
at short notice (idm) = having little time before sth occurs
bask (in sth) (v) = to enjoy exposing yourself to sth (e.g. sunlight)
be aware of sth (phr) = to have knowledge of sth
be familiar with sth (phr) = to be acquainted with sth
be specialised in sth (phr) = to know a great deal about sth and be an expert in it
be accustomed to sth (phr) = to be used to doing sth
be short of funds (phr) = to have little money
be entitled to an allowance (phr) = to be eligible for financial support
come across (phr v) = to find sth accidentally
confront (v) = to tackle sth
deal (with sth) (v) = to handle sth
encounter (v) = to face problems, difficulties, etc
end up (doing sth) (phr v) = to eventually have to do sth
experience (v) = to go through sth
extra (n) = a bonus
facilities (pl n) = equipment, buildings, services, etc provided for a specific purpose
feature (n) = a characteristic
go on (phr v) = to continue doing sth
have in common (phr) = to share the same interests, etc with sb else
have money to burn (idm) = to have a lot of money to spend on unnecessary things
in response to sth (phr) = in answer to sth
inspire (v) = to fill sb with a desire to do sth
live beyond your means (idm) = to spend more money than you are able to afford
mutual (adj) = reciprocal
overcome (v) = to get over sth
parallel (to sth) (adj) = corresponding to sth; concurrent with sth
peak (n) = the highest point of sth
perk (n) = a benefit
pursue (v) = to work towards sth
resources (pl n) = supplies; reserves
retire (v) = to stop working and receive a pension
risk (n) = a possibility of danger
service (n) = provision of assistance or work, either paid or unpaid
stagger (v) = to walk unsteadily
sth bears a relation to sth else (phr) = sth appears to be similar to sth else
stumble upon (phr v) = to discover sth accidentally
surpass (v) = to exceed sth
trip over (phr v) = to fall by catching your foot on sth
tumble out (phr v) = to fall off of sth
turn out (phr v) = to prove to be in the end
undo (v) = to reverse sth
without warning (phr) = without any prior notice
withstand (v) = to hold out against sth

2a (pp. 16-17)

accomplished (adj) = highly skilled
decipher (v) = to manage to make sense of sth
denominator (n) = the number at the bottom of a fraction
equation (n) = a mathematical statement showing that two totals are the same
fraction (n) = a number that indicates a part of a whole
inhibition (n) = an inability to act due to a lack of confidence
intrinsic motivation (phr) = an incentive to do sth that comes from within an individual
liken (sth to sth else) (v) = to show the resemblance between two things
maxim (n) = an established principle
numerator (n) = the number at the top of a fraction
nurture (v) = to encourage and support the gradual growth of sth
pertain to (phr v) = to relate to sth
ratio (n) = proportion
teem with (phr v) = to be filled with
trait (n) = a characteristic

2b (pp. 18-19)

a pat on the back (idm) = favourable comments about sth good you have done
achieve (v) = to be successful in obtaining sth
articulate (adj) = able to express yourself clearly and accurately
aspiration (n) = an ambition
be in awe of sb/sth (phr) = to greatly admire and deeply respect sb/sth
be sucked in (phr) = to get involved in sth bad unwillingly
cognitive conditioning (phr) = a process of learning based on behavioural patterns
competent (adj) = adequately skilled for a job
dedicated (to sth) (adj) = committed to sth
diligent (adj) = careful and hard-working
drive (sb to do sth) (v) = to inspire and influence sb to do sth
encounter (v) = to face sth difficult
focused (adj) = clear on your goals
humble (adj) = not conceited
inspiration (n) = a sudden clever idea that prompts sb to do sth
knowledgeable (adj) = well-informed
leap at an opportunity (phr) = to take advantage of a chance
on impulse (phr) = spontaneously
overcome (v) = to manage to deal with difficulties successfully
passive (adj) = not taking an active part (in an interview)
pick up the pieces (idm) = to try to get back to normal after facing difficulties
pin one's hopes on sth (idm) = to base all your plans on sth that you hope will happen
pluck up the courage (to do sth) (idm) = to finally dare do sth that you were afraid to do
predecessor (n) = sb who did the same job as you before you started
set one's sights on sth (idm) = to decide to accomplish sth
set out (to do sth) (phr v) = to start doing sth that you've planned to do
stimulation (n) = encouragement
the sky's the limit (idm) = there is no limit to what one can do
think ahead (phr v) = to make plans and get prepared for the future
upsurge (n) = a sudden increase

2c (pp. 20-21)

delegate pack (n) = a folder containing information on a conference or event
flagship store (n) = the main shop of a chain
merger (n) = the joining of two or more corporations into one
one-dimensional (adj) = narrow and limited
refurbishment (n) = a renovation
reimburse (v) = to repay sb

Glossary

2d (p. 22)

gravity (n) = seriousness
salient (adj) = the most important

Skills Work 2 (p. 25)

compliance (n) = demand for obedience
demotivating (adj) = discouraging
fervour (n) = passion
integrity (n) = being honest and moral
lump (people together) (v) = to put different people together
mediocre (adj) = not particularly good
reap (v) = to receive sth good as a reward for doing sth
zeal (n) = enthusiasm

Language Knowledge 2 (pp. 26-27)

accept liability for sth (phr) = to take responsibility for sth
admit your guilt about/over sth (phr) = to confess to having done sth wrong
barricade (n) = a makeshift structure across a route to prevent people/vehicles from passing
barrier (to doing sth) (n) = a hindrance that prevents sb from doing sth
be consumed with guilt (phr) = to be overcome by regret
be obsessed by/with sth (phr) = to be unable to get sth out of your mind
beyond the scope of sth (phr) = outside the range of sth
beyond/out of/outside the realms of sth (phr) = beyond the limits of an area of activity
blockade (n) = a situation where movement of goods or people into or out of a country is restricted
blur (v) = to make sth less clear and more difficult to see
border (v) = (of a country) to be next to another country
bring up (phr v) = to raise a subject
cloud sb's judgement/mind (idm) = to make sb unable to think clearly
clutch at straws (idm) = to desperately try to do anything to get out of trouble, however unlikely it seems
conflate (v) = to condense sth
conquer my fear (phr) = to manage to control my fear
contend (v) = to claim that sth is true
contort (v) = to twist sth
contract (v) = to catch all illness
current (adj) = happening now
difference (n) = the way in which two things are not the same
discredited (adj) = with damaged reputation
discrepancy (n) = inconsistency
disgraced (adj) = humiliated
disqualified (from sth) (pp) = barred from sth
disregarded (pp) = ignored
distort (v) = to convey information in an inaccurate way
disturbance (n) = trouble; annoyance
divergence (n) = a deviation
encase (v) = to put sth in sth else for protection
encircle (v) = to form a circle around sb/sth
engulfed (pp) = strongly affected (by an emotion)
essentially (adv) = primarily
exhume (v) = to remove a corpse (for medical investigation)
existing (adj) = being present at the time of speaking
furnish (sb with sth) (v) = to give sth to sb that they need
genuinely (adv) = really
gimmick (n) = a clever trick to attract people's attention
grab sb's attention (idm) = to attract and hold sb's attention
have a/some/little bearing on sth (phr) = to affect sth in a way
have pertinence to sth (phr) = to be directly relevant to sth
honestly (adv) = truthfully
hopefully (adv) = it is hoped that
instigate (v) = to cause sth bad to happen
invest (time/money in sth) (v) = to spend time/money on sth
it's all/entirely my (own) fault (phr) = to be totally responsible for doing sth wrong
launch (v) = to introduce sth new
lay blame (on sb/sth for sth) (phr) = to hold sb/sth responsible for sth
marginally (adv) = slightly
mental block (phr) = a temporary inability to think
modern (adj) = contemporary
muddle (up) (v) = to confuse; to mix up
on a large/small, etc scale (phr) = at a high/low, etc level
open up (phr v) = to create and offer opportunities
outside the arena of sth (phr) = outside the range of a field of activity
participate (in sth) (v) = to take part in sth
peptide (n) = a chemical compound of two or more amino acids
play a role (phr) = to have influence on a situation
potential (adj) = possible
present (adj) = not absent
project yourself as sth (phr) = to give a particular impression of yourself to others
propel (sb to/into sth) (v) = to prompt sb to do sth
provide sth for sb/provide sb with sth (phr) = to offer sb sth that they need
purely (adv) = merely
put sth up for sale (phr) = to make sth available for purchase
reliable (adj) = trustworthy
respectively (adv) = correspondingly
set up (phr v) = i) to establish a business; ii) to organise (an event)
settled (in sth) (adj) = having a permanent job or residence somewhere
squeeze sb/sth in (phr v) = to be able to see sb or do sth in a short time frame
staunch (adj) = (of a supporter) very loyal to sb/sth
steady (adj) = (of a person) reliable and trustworthy
sth poses a threat/danger/risk (phr) = sth is likely to cause a problem or danger
sth presents a problem/difficulty (phr) = sth is the cause of a problem/difficulty
substantially (adv) = considerably
supply (sb with sth/sth to sb) (v) = to provide sth for sb that they need
surround (v) = to be all around sb/sth
tentative (adj) = provisional
transformative (adj) = able to make a significant change
unsettled (adj) = unresolved, feeling uncertain
verbally (adv) = orally

3a (pp. 28-29)

affiliation (n) = a connection with others in a social group
be affiliated with (phr) = to be associated with sb/sth
by-product (n) = an additional result of a different action
civic movement (n) = a campaign for sth by the citizens of a place
derive (sth from sth else) (v) = to obtain sth from sth else
disorientating (adj) = that causes sb to lose sense of place or time
enduring (adj) = lasting
euphoria (n) = great joy
familial bonds (pl n) = family ties
immune function (phr) = the condition in which the body recognises foreign elements in it and produces or activates cells to fight them off
inconsequential (adj) = unimportant

psyche (n) = the human mind and feelings
self-preservation (n) = the natural desire to protect yourself from harm
soothing (adj) = calming
substantial (adj) = considerable
surge (v) = to increase rapidly and suddenly
testosterone (n) = a male hormone responsible for the development of male characteristics

3b (pp. 30-31)

a lack of sth (phr) = an absence of sth
at the drop of a hat (idm) = impulsively, on the spot
be out of pocket (idm) = to end up with less money because of your actions
blemish free (phr) = (of skin) without any spots
bony (adj) = extremely thin
burly (adj) = big and strong
coax (sb into doing sth) (v) = to persuade sb to do sth that they don't want to do
cosmetic enhancement (phr) = the improvement of the appearance of a body part, especially the face, through medical procedures
distorted (adj) = not depicting reality
enhance (v) = to improve
frown upon sth (phr v) = to disapprove of sth
gaze at sth in awe (phr) = to stare at sth because you admire it and long to have it
get hot under the collar (idm) = to become irritated about sth trivial
grubby (adj) = rather dirty
have sth under your belt (idm) = to have achieved sth important
hunched position (phr) = the posture in which the body curves forward
in close proximity to sth (phr) = very close to sth
involuntarily (adv) – without being able to control yourself
manipulation (n) = the process of altering sth in the way you want
out of style (phr) = out of fashion
photoshop (v) = to alter a picture on a computer using the appropriate software
pull your socks up (idm) = to try to become better
puny (adj) = (of a person) very small and weak
reflection of reality (phr) = a representation of what is considered to be a fact
rise in sth (phr) = an increase in a number or amount
scrawny (adj) = skinny
scruffy (adj) = dirty and untidy
shabby (adj) = (of clothes) worn-out and untidy
short-lived trend (phr) = a fashion lasting for only a short period of time
shrink (v) = to make sth smaller
skimpy (adj) = (of clothes) made with little material
skin flaws (pl n) = marks that spoil the appearance of the skin
smugness (n) = self-satisfaction
sth fits sb like a glove (idm) = sth is the perfect size for sb
stocky (adj) = short and strong
stubby (adj) = short and thick
sturdy (adj) = strong and healthy
tangled (adj) = twisted
unblemished (adj) = without any marks; spotless
unimpaired (adj) = not weakened
untarnished (adj) = (of sb's reputation) undamaged
unvarnished (adj) = plain and straightforward
winning smile (phr) = an attractive smile
your eyes glaze over (phr) = you feel bored

3c (pp. 32-33)

abundantly (adv) = completely
aghast (adj) = shocked
ajar (adj) = slightly open
atrium (n) = a courtyard inside a building with a glass roof
cordial (adj) = friendly
explicitly (adv) = categorically
mortified (adj) = embarrassed
waffle on (about sth) (phr v) = to keep talking without saying anything important

3f (p. 36)

acronym (n) = an abbreviation formed by the first letters of other words
a host of (phr) = a large number of sth
diminish (v) = to reduce, to weaken
impairment (n) = damage to a part of the body
lingo (n) = jargon
prominent (adj) = leading, distinguished
verbalise (v) = to say sth in words

Skills Work 3 (p. 37)

allegiance (n) = commitment to sth
be dripping with people or things (phr) = to have a lot of people or things
conformist (adj) = following established customs
erode (v) = to wear sth away
geek (n) = a technology enthusiast who is socially awkward
gravitate (v) = to be drawn to sb
judgemental (adj) = critical
mohawk (n) = a hairstyle with both sides of the head shaven and a strip of hair sticking up on top
nerd (n) = sb only interested in computers and socially inept
nuanced (adj) = subtle and sophisticated
pariah (n) = a social outcast
persona (n) = a character that an artist presents in a performance
pimply (adj) = covering the face with spots
restrictive (adj) = oppressive, limiting
shut-in (n) = (in North American English) sb who is confined in a place
subdued (adj) = restrained
tartan (adj) = with a pattern of coloured squares and crossed lines
validation (n) = confirmation
vinyl (n) = records that were played on a record player
wannabe yuppy (phr) = a would-be young professional with a well-paid job

Language Knowledge 3 (pp. 38-39)

abundant (adj) = plentiful
activate (v) = to put sth in motion
adverse (adj) = unfavourable
adverse effects (phr) = unfavourable results
against sth (phr) = contrary to sth
anonymity (n) = the state of being unknown
apply (v) = to put sth to use
as opposed to sth (phr) = in contrast to/with sth
at no point (phr) = not at any time
be in favour of sb (phr) = to support sb
be under no illusion about sth (phr) = to be fully aware of sth
be under the impression that (phr) = to believe sth, often incorrectly
capitalise (v) = to take advantage of sth
contain one's excitement (phr) = to not show one's enthusiasm
contrary (adj) = contradictory
contrary to popular belief (phr) = in opposition to what is widely believed
deception (n) = an act of deceit
declare (v) = to state without doubt that sth is true
disguise (v) = to conceal sth
enclose (v) = to put sth inside sth else
enormous (adj) = huge
exert an influence on sb (phr) = to play a part in changing sb's opinion in relation to sth
exhaustive (adj) = thorough
expel (sb from school, etc) (v) = to force sb to leave a school, etc

extravagant (adj) = spending more than necessary
exuberant (adj) = full of joy and energy
fragrant (adj) = scented
gratification (n) = satisfaction
have a great/deep admiration for sb (phr) = to have great respect for sb
have an appreciation for sth (phr) = to acknowledge and enjoy the good aspects of sth
hint (at sth) (v) = to insinuate sth
hypnotise (v) = to greatly fascinate sb
identity (n) = who or what sb is
imply (v) = to suggest sth indirectly
innocuous (adj) = not intended to offend; harmless
in preference to sb/sth (phr) = rather than sb/sth
in support of (a claim, an argument, etc) (phr) = in a way that shows you approve of sth
intimidation (n) = frightening sb
it occurs to sb that (phr) = it comes to sb's mind all of a sudden that
it strikes sb as odd that (phr) = it seems strange to sb that
mesmerise (v) = to fascinate sb completely
misconception (about sth) (n) = a mistaken belief about sth
mutate (v) = to change into sth
not for a moment (idm) = not at all; never
not for an instant (idm) = not even for a short amount of time
off the mark/wide of the mark (idm) = inaccurate
opposing (adj) = conflicting
overwhelming (adj) = overpowering
personality (n) = sb's character and behaviour
pervasive (adj) = widespread
propel (v) = to move sth forwards
redeem (v) = to compensate for sth
refine (v) = to improve sth
refresh (v) = to renew
repurpose (v) = to change sth so as to suit a new function
reversible (adj) = that can be changed to what it was previously
revitalise (v) = to revive sb/sth
security (n) = protection from risk
sling (v) = to throw sth in a careless way with force
soothe (v) = to reduce (pain)
show one's recognition of sth (phr) = to express one's appreciation of sth
sth catches sb by surprise (phr) = sth catches sb off-guard
sth hits sb unexpectedly (phr) = sth takes sb by surprise
tame (v) = to make sth less intense and control it
trigger a response (phr) = to cause a reaction
unceasing (adj) = never-ending
utilise (v) = to make use of sth
vigil (n) = the act of watching sth intently for a long time
with sb's approval (phr) = with sb's permission

4a (pp. 40-41)

commodity (n) = a product to be bought or sold
entrepreneur (n) = a self-made businessman
forefather (n) = an ancestor
gizmo (n) = a gadget
thrive (v) = to prosper
scam (n) = a fraud
transaction (n) = buying or selling products or services

4b (pp. 42-43)

appreciation (n) = high regard for sth/sb
articulacy (n) = the ability to speak and pronounce sth clearly
attribute (sth to sth else) (v) = to indicate that sth is caused by sth else
bear fruit (idm) = to have good results
behind the times (idm) = out-of-date
break new ground (idm) = to pioneer sth
budge (v) = to make sth move a little
by default (phr) = due to lack of a better alternative
come about (v) = to occur
computer literacy (n) = the ability to use computers effectively
controversial application (phr) = the implementation of sth that causes differences of opinion
convey (v) = to communicate sth
depict (v) = to describe sth; to represent sth with words
dexterity (n) = the skilfulness in doing sth with your hands
dislocate (v) = to put sth out of place
dislodge (v) = to knock sb/sth out of the position they previously held
divulge (sth to sb) (v) = to disclose sth to sb
early adoption (phr) = a new idea/product accepted/used by some people before most others
efficiency (n) = the skilfulness in doing sth without wasting money, time or effort
envisage (v) = to imagine sth is likely to happen
eschew (v) = to intentionally avoid sth
expose (v) = to uncover sth
generic design (phr) = a plan of sth that is not distinctive in any way
get sth off the ground (idm) = to make a successful start with sth
go the whole hog (idm) = to do sth with full determination
have the world at one's fingertips (idm) = to have information readily available for immediate use
industrial application (phr) = the implementation of sth for manufacturing purposes
integration (n) = incorporation
intelligence (n) = cleverness
long-lasting concept (phr) = an idea that can exist or does exist for a long time; an enduring idea
long-standing concept (phr) = an idea that has existed for a long time; an established and traditional idea
long-winded (adj) = (of written or oral speech) lengthy
meme (n) = a cultural idea, image, video, etc that is transmitted virally on the Internet
minimalist design (phr) = an arrangement of elements that is very simple
move with the times (idm) = to change the way you do things as society changes
objective (adj) = impartial
point of reference (n) = a fact that provides the framework by which sth else is determined; a criterion
relocate (v) = to move to a different place
start the ball rolling (idm) = to put sth into operation
think outside the box (idm) = to think of sth from a new perspective
turn the clock back (idm) = to go back to an earlier period of time
unveil (v) = to reveal sth for the first time
vague (adj) = unclear
validate (v) = to confirm sth
vigilant (adj) = alert
widespread adoption (phr) = a new idea/product accepted/used by most people

4e (p. 47)

alumni (pl n) = graduates of a specific school, college or university
daunting (adj) = intimidating
diddle (v) = to play with (a device, a gadget, etc)
establishment (n) = an organisation or institution
journal (n) = a serious magazine about a specific subject
social media detox (phr) = a period during which you stop using social media applications

4f (p. 48)

cryptocurrency (n) = an entirely digital currency
encryption (n) = using a code to secure important data
escalate (v) = to rise rapidly
fluctuation (n) = variation
instantaneous (adj) = instant, immediate
monetary (adj) = relating to money
volatile (adj) = unstable

Skills Work 4 (p. 49)

Aboriginal (adj) = relating to the first inhabitants of Australia
collective genius (n) = shared intelligence
demise (n) = the fact that sth has stopped existing
genocide (n) = the systematic and complete destruction of sth
hideously (adv) = thoroughly unpleasantly
oppression (n) = suppression

Language Knowledge 4 (pp. 50-51)

adapt (v) = to alter sth in order to suit a new purpose
adjust (v) = to suit your needs
archaic (adj) = belonging to ancient times
be consumed with sth (phr) = to be strongly affected by a feeling, an idea, etc
be inundated with sth (phr) = to be overwhelmed with sth
consult (sb about sth) (v) = to ask advice about sth from sb
earn (sb sth) (v) = sb deserves to have sth
excessive (adj) = over the top; too much
gain (v) = to acquire sth
have a/some/no etc bearing on sth (phr) = to affect/not affect sth
immerse myself in sth (phr) = to get involved in sth to a great extent
impede (v) = to be an obstacle to sb's doing sth
implant (sth in/into sth) (v) = to place sth in/into sth else
implement (v) = to put sth into effect
implicate (v) = to say sb is responsible for a crime, etc
impose (sth on sb) (v) = to enforce sth on sb
incur (v) = to bring sth unpleasant upon oneself
instigate (v) = to bring sth about
Internet sensation (n) = sb/sth that becomes very popular on the Web
intersect (v) = (of roads, etc) to cross one another
invade (a place) (v) = to enter a place with force
manner (n) = a way of doing things
marvel (n) = a wondrous thing
miracle (n) = a supernatural event
miscalculate (v) = to judge sth incorrectly
misconstrue (v) = to interpret sth incorrectly
negotiate (sth with sb) (v) = to have a formal discussion with sb in order to reach an agreement about sth
nil (n) = zero, nothing
obsolete (adj) = out-of-date, old-fashioned
outspread (adj) = fully extended in width
point of view (on sth) (n) = the way one considers sth
primitive (adj) = unsophisticated; basic
stance on sth (phr) = an opinion about sth
sweeping (adj) = having a profound effect on sth
tune (v) = to adjust an engine so that it will work at its best
turn (v) = to rotate sth
underestimate (v) = to misjudge the worth of sth
undermine (v) = to gradually make sb/sth less strong
vast (adj) = huge
virtual (adj) = that can be done electronically using a computer
visual (adj) = i) relating to sight; ii) that can be seen
voluminous (adj) = (of a container) very large
widespread (adj) = occurring among many people and in many places
wonder (n) = sth that causes admiration
zero tolerance (n) = harsh punishment even for the slightest violation of the law

5a (pp. 52-53)

adversity (n) = a period of misfortune and hardship
advocacy (n) = support for a course of action
catalyst (for sth) (n) = sb/sth that makes sth happen
ceaselessly (adv) = continuously
charisma (n) = a person's natural power to influence and motivate others
custodian (n) = sb who bears the responsibility for looking after sb else
delinquency (n) = illegal behaviour especially of young people
faculty (n) = the body of teachers at school, at a university department, etc
faze (v) = to upset and deter sb
forfeit (n) = losing a game as a result of breaking a rule or not meeting an obligation
hostility (n) = showing aggression against sb/sth
mentoring (n) = provision of guidance and advice to younger and less experienced people
odds (pl n) = chances
on the cusp (of sth) (idm) = at a point in time that marks the change of sth
outcry (n) = public disapproval of a current event
overwhelming (adj) = hard to fight against
prompt (v) = to cause sth
rally against sb (idm) = to gather in numbers and speak out against sb
realise one's power (phr) = to manifest one's abilities
scout (n) = sb whose job is to discover and recruit new talents in sports
seize (v) = to take full advantage of sth
strike a chord (idm) = to have an emotional impact on sb
tenacity (n) = persistence
unorthodox (adj) = unconventional
verbal abuse (n) = insulting language aimed at sb
write sb off (phr v) = to disregard sb

5b (pp. 54-55)

aisle (n) = a passageway between rows of seats in a train, plane, supermarket, etc
autarchy (n) = a country's self-sufficiency
authority (n) = power
autocracy (n) = the political system in which a single individual governs
back down (phr v) = to admit being wrong about sth
bill of rights (phr) = an official list of the most essential human rights
blunt (adj) = straightforward
bring about (phr v) = to cause sth to happen
carte blanche (n) = complete freedom to do as you wish
condone (v) = to accept or allow wrong behaviour
conflict resolution (phr) = the solution of disputes between sides
constituent (n) = a voter in a certain area
constitutional crisis (phr) = a serious situation relating to the government of a country
dominate (v) = to control
elbow room (phr) = freedom to act
emancipation (n) = the act of giving sb political rights

embrace (v) = to accept a new stance, suggestion, etc
extrication (n) = the act of helping sb to get out of a difficulty
franchise (n) = the right to vote in elections
freedom of the press (phr) = the right of newspapers and magazines to publish what they want without being censored
free will (phr) = the fact that every individual can act in the way they want
get up to (phr v) = to be busy doing sth rather bad
hallway (n) = an entrance hall; an enclosed passageway
intervene (v) = to get involved in a difficult situation in order to help
intimidate (v) = to frighten sb
keep on (phr v) = to continue to do sth
landing (n) = the area at the top of a staircase
latitude (n) = freedom to say/do what you want
legislation (n) = a set of laws
mammoth (adj) = enormous, lengthy
political autonomy (phr) = political self-rule
ratify (v) = to officially approve a treaty, a bill, etc and sign it
reform (n) = a set of changes in a system
refurbishment (n) = improvement in an area
reprisal (n) = retaliation
revoke (v) = to officially end a law, agreement, etc
rife (adj) = (of sth bad) widespread
rule out (phr v) = to say that sth is unlikely to happen
scope (n) = room for action
self-government (n) = political independence
self-regulation (n) = exercising control of yourself
self-sufficiency (n) = the quality of being able to provide the essentials needed for survival without the help of others
self-support (n) = the state of maintaining yourself without outside assistance
single out (phr v) = to treat sb unfairly differently from others
testify (v) = to say what you know about a case in a court of law
the corridors of power (idm) = the higher positions of government
vassal state (n) = a protectorate
war-torn country (phr) = a country devastated by war
wield power (phr) = to have power and rule a country

5d (p. 58)

all walks of life (idm) = all ethnic, social and economic groups
anecdote (n) = an entertaining short story
apprehension (n) = anxiety
at a loose end (idm) = with nothing to do
dubious (adj) = uncertain
echo (v) = to repeat sth
engage (v) = to become involved in sth
excursion (n) = a short journey made for pleasure
eye-opener (n) = a revelation
font of knowledge (idm) = a wise person
gratifying (adj) = satisfying; rewarding
guidance counsellor (n) = sb whose job is to provide advice about career choices
inception (n) = the start of sth
intergenerational (adj) = involving groups of people that were born at different time periods
keep your hand in (idm) = to remain involved in sth
magnanimous (adj) = generous
mix things up (idm) = to add variety to a particular situation
notion (n) = a concept
pilot (v) = to test sth such as a new concept, plan, etc
prospect (n) = a view of the future
rejuvenate (v) = to revive sth
respectful (adj) = showing consideration for sb/sth
retiree (n) = a pensioner
sentiment (n) = a feeling
settle in (phr v) = to begin to feel at home
take a back seat (idm) = to have a subordinate position
tap into (phr v) = to make use of sth
two-way street (idm) = a reciprocal situation
wealth (n) = a great deal of sth
while away the hours (phr) = to spend your time in an unproductive but pleasant way

Skills Work 5 (p. 61)

ambiguity (n) = vagueness
attuned (to sth) (adj) = familiar with sth
avert (v) = to stop sth bad from happening
brainchild (n) = sb's own idea, creation, etc
concede (v) = to admit that sth is correct
content (adj) = satisfied
doom (n) = sth very bad that will happen

formidable (adj) = challenging
friction (n) = tension
frustrated (adj) = very annoyed and upset
interlocking (adj) = interconnecting
proliferate (v) = to grow and spread rapidly
prosperity (n) = the fact that one is well-off and successful
saboteur (n) = sb who intentionally causes harm to sb/sth else
seasoned (adj) = experienced
simulation (n) = a condition created to look like a real one in order to study and solve problems

Language Knowledge 5 (pp. 62-63)

a feather in your cap (idm) = an accomplishment that you take pride in
accomplish (v) = to achieve sth; to reach sth
account for (phr v) = to be the reason for sth; to explain sth
activist (n) = sb who struggles for political or social change
advocate (n) = a supporter of sth
alleviate (v) = to relieve sth
an isolated incident (phr) = a single occurrence
at the end of the day (idm) = ultimately
challenge (v) = to dispute sth
combat (v) = to fight against sth
complaint (n) = a way of expressing displeasure
concern (n) = a worry
condition (n) = a situation; a requirement
consequence (n) = a result of sth
contend (with sb) (v) = to compete against sb
contest (v) = to call an action/theory into question
go the extra mile (idm) = to make a greater effort
hem (n) = a folded and sewn edge of a garment
inevitable (adj) = unavoidable
inexcusable (adj) = unforgivable
inflexible (adj) = reluctant to make any changes
invariable (adj) = unchanging
on the margin (of sth) (phr) = on the fringes (of sth)
on the verge of extinction (phr) = on the brink of a species' disappearance
pay the price (idm) = to suffer the consequences of your actions
placate (v) = to make sb calm
promoter (n) = sb who organises and finances sporting or musical events

read sb the riot act (idm) = to reprimand sb strongly
reappraise (v) = to assess sth again
receive (v) = to get sth
sponsor (n) = sb who donates money to an organisation, charity, etc for a specific cause
sth brings a lump to your throat (idm) = sth makes you feel very sad and unable to speak
succeed (in sth) (v) = to reach the desired goal in sth
take stock of your life, etc (idm) = to evaluate your life, etc
teller (n) = a vote counter, especially in a parliament
temper (sth with sth) (v) = to counterbalance sth with sth else
the downtrodden (pl n) = ill-treated people by those in power
there is no time like the present (idm) = there is no better moment to do sth than now
unanimous (adj) = (of an opinion, decision, etc) shared by everyone involved
undertake (v) = to promise to do sth
undivided (adj) = complete; not separated into parts
undoubted (adj) = unquestioned
united (adj) = unified; joined together
wet behind the ears (idm) = inexperienced
widespread concern (phr) = the fact that many people and in many places worry about sth
within limits (phr) = to a reasonable extent
you can't judge a book by its cover (idm) = you can't form an opinion on sth based only on its appearance

6a (pp. 64-65)

attainment (n) = the act of achieving sth
attribute (n) = a characteristic
extrinsic (adj) = external
instinctual (adj) = instinctive
intrinsic (adj) = internal
overrated (adj) = considered better than sth actually is
oversaturation (n) the act of providing too much coverage for sth
pit sb against sb else (phr v) = to get sb to compete against sb else
plethora (n) = an extremely large number of sth
reinforcement (n) = sth that influences behaviour
shore up (phr v) = to reinforce sth/sb

6b (pp. 66-67)

absorb (v) = to soak sth up; to take sth in
absorption (n) = the act of taking sth in
acute condition (phr) = a health problem that quickly becomes very serious
adjust (v) = to modify sth
be descended from sb (phr) = to have sb as an ancestor
bounce back (phr v) = to get well again
calculable risk (phr) = a source of danger that can be estimated
chronic pain (phr) = pain caused by an illness that lasts for a long time
convalesce (v) = to recuperate
convalescence (n) = recuperation; recovery from an illness
degenerative (adj) = (of a disease) gradually getting worse
diagnose (v) = to identify the exact cause of an illness
diagnosis (n) = a judgement of the condition of sb's health
die back (phr v) = (of a plant) to suffer from an illness that destroys the part of a plant above the ground but leaves the roots alive
die down (phr v) = to fade slowly
die off (phr v) = (of a group) each member dies until the group disappears
discredit (v) = to ruin the reputation of sb
dispute (v) = to claim that a fact, theory, etc is not true
disqualify (v) = to exclude sb from sth
gland (n) = a body organ that produces necessary liquids
hand (sth) back (to sb) (phr v) = to return sth to its owner with your hand
hand (sth) down (to sb) (phr v) = to pass sth down to a successor
hand (sth) over (to sb) (phr v) = to give sth to sb in a formal manner
health insurance (n) = an arrangement with a company to cover your medical expenses in case of an illness
hereditary illness (phr) = an inherited disorder
hostile reception (phr) = a negative response to sth
implicate (v) = to suggest sth indirectly; to imply sth
implication (n) = an indirect suggestion of sth
informed debate (phr) = a discussion about the various points of a topic after being aware of all the facts
irrelevant (to sb/sth) (phr) = having no connection with sb/sth
irrespective of sth (phr) = regardless of sth
it is irresponsible of sb to do sth (phr) = it is thoughtless of sb to do sth
legitimacy (n) = the validity of sth
live through (phr v) = to endure sth
makeshift sling (phr) = a bandage worn around the neck for temporary support of a broken or injured arm
observable difference (phr) = a noticeable distinction
placebo effect (n) = the fact that sb's health improves after they take medication without any active ingredients in it, only thanks to its psychological influence
presume (v) = to assume sth
presumption (n) = an assumption
regulate (v) = to control sth with rules and restrictions
reprisal (n) = an action that you take against sb as a punishment for sth
strike (sb) down (phr v) = to make sb critically ill or kill them
strike back (at/against sb) (phr v) = to retaliate
strike out (at sb/sth) (phr v) = to attack sb/sth physically or verbally
trigger (v) = to cause sth to happen
unintended (adj) = not planned
variety (n) = a range of sth
vary (v) = to range

6c (pp. 68-69)

complementary therapy (n) = treatment that is used in addition to conventional medication
manipulation (n) = the skilful use of your hands for the treatment of sth as part of a therapy
musculoskeletal framework (n) = the structure of the body in relation to its muscles and skeleton
osteopathic (adj) = relating to osteopathy (a type of alternative medical treatment for bone and muscle injuries that involves massaging the skeleton and the muscles of the body)
proponent (n) = a supporter of an idea, a theory, etc

6d (p. 70)

assess knowledge (phr) = to evaluate what sb has learnt
cognitive ability (phr) = the skill to acquire knowledge
burn the candle at both ends (idm) = to become tired after working extremely hard, by staying up late at night and getting up early the next morning
detrimental (adj) = damaging
energise (v) = to fill sb with energy
function (v) = (of the brain) to work

gauge (v) = to assess sth
genius (n) = a highly intelligent person
go overboard (on sth) (idm) = to exaggerate sth
grab (v) to get sth to eat quickly
have a laugh (phr) = to joke
hit the books (idm) = to study hard
keep sth straight (in your head) (idm) = to keep information about sth clear in your mind
need your head examined (idm) = said about sb who believes sth that is completely crazy
recuperation (n) = recovery
regime (n) = a fitness plan
regurgitate (v) = to repeat sb else's ideas, etc after memorising them without understanding them
wholesome (adj) = good for your health

6e (p. 71)

abdominal muscle (n) = each of the muscles located where the belly is
chiropractor (n) = sb whose job is to treat injured joints and the spine with their hands
fatigue (n) = tiredness
plague (v) = to cause sb to suffer for a long period of time
sciatica (n) = a medical condition characterised by pain in the back, hips and thighs

6f (p. 72)

aspiration (n) = an ambition
commission (v) = to order sb to do a project for you
constraint (n) = a restriction
replicate (v) = to make an exact copy of sth
sedentary (adj) = (of a person) engaging in very little physical activity

Skills Work 6 (p. 73)

anchor (n) = what prevents sb from doing sth they want
cheerleader (n) = sb who supports and encourages people
endorsement (n) = a formal approval
equation (n) = a mathematical statement showing that two totals are the same
falter (v) = to get weaker
glitchy (adj) = (of a device) malfunctioning often and unexpectedly
janitor (n) = a caretaker
snippet (n) = a small amount of information
splash photo (n) = a photo used to capture the user's attention as part of a lead-in to a website
unbridled (adj) = full; undivided

Language Knowledge 6 (pp. 74-75)

affiliate (sth with sth else) (v) = to associate (sth with sth else)
allegations (pl n) = unproven accusations
as a last resort (phr) = after everything else has failed
association (n) = a link between two theories, ideas, etc
at risk (phr) = more likely to suffer from sth
carry (v) = to possess sth within the body
churn out (phr v) = to produce sth in large quantities
circle (v) = to draw a circle around sth
combine (sth with sth) (v) = to blend two different things harmoniously
sth is concerned with (phr) = sth has to do with sth else
connect (sth with sth) (v) = to link sth to sth else
consequently (adv) = as a result
convey (v) = to communicate information, a message, etc
correspondingly (adv) = at the same rate as sth else happening before
draw back (phr v) = to withdraw from sth
embellished (adj) = (of a story) having details added to make it more interesting
enhanced (adj) = improved
enlarged (adj) = having increased in size
enriched (adj) = having improved the quality
exceed (v) = to prove better than expected
express (v) = to say or show what you think or feel
finite (adj) = having a limit
harbour (v) = to keep hopes, ambitions, fears, etc in your mind
implications (pl n) = effects
implicitly (adv) = indirectly
in danger (phr) = likely to be harmed
in fear (phr) = being afraid
indicate (v) = to show that sth is true
inherently (adv) = naturally
insinuation (n) = an indirect suggestion of sth unpleasant
internally (adv) = within the body
intimately (adv) = in a very familiar manner
it is understood that (phr) = people are all agreed that
link (sth to/with sth) (v) = to relate sth to sth else
manipulation (n) = making others behave the way you want them to
mark (v) = to draw a sign on sth to make it noticeable
motion (v) = to signal to sb to do sth
move out (phr v) = to leave your place in order to move into a new one
obviously (adv) = clearly
outline (n) = a summary of the main facts about sth
outline (v) = to give the main points of sth
path (n) = a series of actions to achieve sth
pattern (n) = a regularly repeated way of behaviour
pinpoint (v) = to discover the exact details or facts about sth
place (v) = to put sth somewhere
proceed (v) = to carry on; to go towards a place
programme (n) = a schedule
programming (n) = producing computer programs
put across (phr v) = to manage to communicate information, thoughts, etc clearly
put apart (phr v) = to place sth apart from other things
put aside (phr v) = to keep a certain amount of time free for yourself
put away (phr v) = to put and keep sth in its place
reach (v) = to arrive at a particular decision, conclusion, etc
recede (v) = (of a feeling, a sound, etc) to fade
recourse (n) = using sb/sth as a way of getting help with hardship
respectively (adv) in the same order as items have been mentioned before
sceptical (adj) = doubtful
scout (v) = to look for good athletes, musicians, etc in order to recruit them
screening (n) = medical tests to verify sb's suitability for a purpose
sedately (adv) = calmly and slowly
selection (n) = a choice
serenity (n) = peacefulness
seriously (adv) = with a lot of attention and thought
soberly (adv) = in a calm manner
solemnly (adv) = in a sombre manner
sth is involved with sth else (phr) = sth is part of an event, an activity, etc
sth is regarded as (phr) = sth is considered to be
stir up (phr v) = to cause problems, arguments, etc
stopgap (n) = a temporary solution
subjectable (adj) = that can be, or must be, controlled or examined by sb/sth
succeed (in sth/in doing sth) (v) = to manage to achieve what you wanted (to do)
suggestible (adj) = easily influenced by others

surrogate (n) = sb/sth that substitutes for sb/sth else
susceptible (to sth) (adj) = easily affected by sth
swing (v) = (of opinions/emotions) to change to the opposite
trace sth back (to sth else) (phr v) = to find the origins of sth in sth else
unaccustomed (to sth/to doing sth) (adj) = not used to sth/to doing sth
unacquainted (with sth) (adj) = not knowing about sth
unaware (of sth) (adj) = not informed about sth
under threat (phr) = at risk of sth
unfamiliar (with sth) (adj) = having no experience of sth
voice your concern (phr) = to openly express your worry about sb/sth
waver (v) = to be between two opinions
work up (enthusiasm, an appetite, etc) (phr v) = to become more and more enthusiastic, hungry, etc

7a (pp. 76-77)

benchmark (n) = a standard which sth can be measured against
bunk bed (n) = a bed on top or below another one
camaraderie (n) = a feeling of friendship among members of a group who have shared an experience
Census Bureau (n) = the agency that collects and produces demographic information about the population of the USA
controversial (adj) = causing differences of opinion
flat-pack (v) = to package in a box in a way similar to how a ready-to-assemble furniture is packed
monetary (adj) = relating to money
petition (n) = a document signed by many people requesting sth from the government or the authorities
pint-sized (adj) = small
stringent (adj) = strict
subdivision (n) = an urban area divided into plots for housing development
sublet (v) = to sublease property that you rent from sb else
substantial (adj) = fairly large; significant
surging (adj) = increasing
take a stand (phr) = to state your position on sth

7b (pp. 78-79)

a turn of events (phr) = a change in a situation
adapt (v) = to change in order to fit in with a new situation
adaptation (n) = a change in order to fit in with a new situation
anemone (n) = a colourful marine animal attached to rocks that looks like a plant
auction (n) = a public sale in which items are sold to the person who offers the highest price
be headed for sth (phr) = to be likely to experience sth bad
colonisation (n) = the action of an animal establishing itself in a location
colonise (v) = (of animals/plants) to start living in an area in large numbers
corrosion (n) = the slow destruction of metal caused by water or chemicals
criticise sb for sth (phr) = to strongly disapprove of sth that sb says/does
disrupt (v) = to disturb a process or activity
disruption (n) = interrupting the normal way that sth works or functions
encroachment (n) = an illegal advance beyond proper limits
endurance (n) = the ability to keep existing
endure (v) = to continue to exist despite difficulties
equilibrium (n) = a state of balance between opposing things
erosion (n) = the slow destruction of soil by rain, wind, fire, etc
experiment on sth (phr) = to carry out tests on sth
flora and fauna (phr) = all the plants and animals in a place
jeopardise (v) = to put sth in danger
jeopardy (n) = danger
natural (adj) = produced by nature
organic (adj) = produced from living organisms
poaching (n) = illegal hunting
predator (n) = an animal that kills and eats other animals
protect sb/sth from sth (phr) = to keep sb/sth safe from sth dangerous
stability (n) = the condition in which sth is unlikely to change
sth is wearing thin (idm) = sth is getting boring and rather annoying
sth takes a turn for the worse (phr) = sth worsens
survival (n) = the continuation of life
survive (v) = to continue to live after several problems
the turn of the century (phr) = the beginning of a new century
tunicate (n) = a type of marine invertebrate animals like corals
turn a profit (phr) = to earn money
ward off (phr v) = to keep danger away from yourself

7c (pp. 80-81)

demolition (n) = the deliberate destruction of a building
diligent (adj) = thorough
wry (adj) = (of a smile) = humorously sarcastic

7d (p. 82)

delve into (phr v) = to thoroughly explore sth
rally (n) = a large gathering of people to protest against sth

7e (p. 83)

shrub (n) = a bush

7f (p. 84)

ameliorate (v) = to make sth better
exacerbate (v) = to make sth worse
unprecedented (adj) = having never occurred before

Skills Work 7 (p. 85)

combat (v) = to prevent sth from happening
groundbreaking (adj) = innovative
hail (v) = to commend sth
laud (v) = to praise sth
revenue (n) = money earned
stacking (n) = the act of putting one thing on top of another
tolls (pl n) = money paid to use a road, a tunnel, etc
vault (n) = an underground car park

Language Knowledge 7 (pp. 86-87)

accordingly (adv) = in accordance with sth
adhere to sth (phr v) = to abide by a rule or agreement
adversely (adv) = unfavourably
algorithm (n) = a set of instructions in a specific order for writing computer programs
altercation (n) = a noisy argument
anticipation (n) = an expectation of sth
backlash (n) = a negative reaction you get after you do sth
be under intense pressure (phr) = to be forced to do sth
be under the impression that (phr) = to believe that sth is true
biophilic (adj) = loving humanity and nature
commissioner (n) = a government representative in a local community
condemn (v) = to strongly disapprove of sth
confound (v) = to shock and confuse sb

convict sb of sth (phr) = (of a court) to announce that a defendant is guilty of a crime
crowdfunding (n) = the practice of raising money for a cause through the Internet
designate sth as sth (phr) = to choose sth for a specific use
dire (adj) = awful
discharge your duties/ responsibilities (phr) = to do what you are expected to do
dismiss an idea/opinion (phr) = to not consider an idea, opinion, etc
drastic (adj) = radical and effective
embroilment (n) = a complex interpersonal or political situation
essentially (adv) = basically
established (adj) = existing for a long time
follow (v) = to do what you are asked or advised to
generate (v) = to create (excitement, support, etc)
green belt (n) = a protected area of green land near a town or city
growing concern over sth (phr) = worry about sth that keeps increasing
harsh (adj) = severe
imminently (adv) = very soon
impertinently (adv) = rudely
impulsively (adv) = without thinking about the possible dangers before doing sth
in the aftermath of sth (phr) = during the period after an accident, a war, etc
incinerate (v) = to get rid of sth by burning it
intrinsic (adj) = innate
magnitude (n) = importance
municipality (n) = the local government of a city or town
obey (v) = to do what laws, rules and people in authority say
observe (v) = to obey laws and rules
outcome (n) = a result
outlook on life (phr) = sb's general attitude towards the world
paramount (adj) = the most important
prevalent (adj) = common
prospect (n) = likelihood
purpose (of sth/of doing sth) (n) = what sth is intended for
raise awareness (phr) = to help people realise sth
reference (n) = the act of mentioning sb/sth
regard (n) = consideration
repercussions (pl n) = consequences
rigorous (adj) = strict and intense
rigorous (adj) = very thorough and exact
sanctuary (n) = an area for the protection of animals and birds
significantly (adv) = to an important degree
sth carries weight (phr) = sth is important
terminate (v) = to end sth
the bulk of sth (phr) = the biggest part of sth
the fact of the matter is that (phr) = it is true that
trail (n) = a path in the countryside
urbanite (n) = a city dweller
urgently (adv) = in a way that indicates sth must be done immediately

8a (pp. 88-89)

adaptation (n) = a TV programme based on a film
behemoth (n) = an organisation with massive power in an industry
critically acclaimed (phr) = praised by critics
demographic (n) = a group of customers of a similar age or social standing
dismissive (adj) = considering sth unworthy of your attention
feature (v) = (of a film) to include actors in important parts
heavyweight (n) = a significant/ influential person
intricate (adj) = complex and detailed
stirring (adj) = that arouses particular emotions
story arc (n) = a storyline in a TV series
swap (sth for sth else) (v) = to exchange sth for sth else

8b (pp. 90-91)

adhere to sth (phr v) = to abide by sth
air your views (phr) = to make your opinions publicly known
arbiter (n) = sb who makes a judgement about sth and is accountable for their decisions
blurt out (phr v) = to say sth spontaneously
budding (adj) = (of an artist, athlete, etc) making a promising first appearance
cite (v) = to state sth as a reason for doing sth
code of conduct (phr) = a code of behaviour
come in for (criticism, blame, etc) (phr v) = to be criticised, blamed, etc for sth
come on to (an issue, a question, etc) (phr v) = to start dealing with an issue, a question, etc
come up for (discussion, examination, etc) (phr v) = (of a topic) to be discussed, examined, etc
credible (adj) = that can be believed
debut (n) = the first appearance of an artist, athlete, etc
defamation of character (phr) = damage to sb's character by saying/writing false bad things about them
discreet (adj) = careful in what you say/do in order to keep sth confidential or not to offend
discrete (adj) = separate; distinct
dry out (phr v) = to become completely dry
dry up (phr v) = to come to an end
dry yourself off (phr v) = to remove wetness from your body
extent (n) = how far you are willing to go in order to attain sth
feasible (adj) = (of a solution, etc) possible to be successful
get around (phr v) = (of news, information, etc) to circulate
get away (phr v) = to manage to leave a place
get on with (sth) (phr v) = to carry on doing sth
grace the screen (phr) = (of a film) to appear on screen to the delight of audiences
impartiality (n) = freedom from bias
in droves (phr) = en masse
in tune with sb/sth (phr) = fully understanding sb/sth
infighting (n) = a difference of opinion within a group
issue a statement (phr) = to write and publicise your opinion about sth
libel (n) = writing and publicising untrue things that damage sb's reputation
muckraking (n) = writing false bad things about famous people's private lives
quote (v) = to mention the exact words that sb has said/written
scoop (n) = a piece of news exclusively presented by one of the media before others
scurrilous (adj) = insulting
slander (n) = saying untrue things that damage sb's reputation
sublime (adj) = exquisite
tabloid (n) = a small-sized newspaper with sensational stories
the proof is in the pudding (idm) = only when one starts acting can we know how good/bad they are
wry (adj) = showing that sth bad has also a funny side

8c (pp. 92-93)

artisan (n) = an artist
commission (n) = the act of formally asking an artist to create a painting, etc for a client

consign sth to history (phr) = to stop making use of sth from this moment onwards

8d (p. 94)

allure (n) = attraction
chance encounter (n) = the act of getting together with sb by accident
familial (adj) = relating to family
intricacy (n) = complexity
unjust (adj) = unfair

8e (p. 95)

narcissistic (adj) = admiring yourself excessively
nerdy (adj) = only interested in gadgets and thus unpopular
obnoxious (adj) = very rude and thus unpleasant
quirky (adj) = eccentric
tribulation (n) = a hardship

8f (p. 96)

testimonial (n) = a written recommendation for sth

Skills Work 8 (p. 97)

deviate (from sth) (v) = to do sth differently from what you are expected to do
emblematic (adj) = being symbolic or representative of sth
enthral (v) = to captivate sb
genesis (n) = the birth of sth
iconic (adj) = vary famous and representative
laconic (adj) = (of speech) brief
mannerism (n) = a gesture
meticulously (adv) = carefully; thoroughly
plunge sb into sth (phr v) = to immerse sb in sth, especially a fictional world or setting
prerogative (n) = a privilege
soliloquy (n) = a monologue where the character is speaking to himself/herself or the audience
spontaneity (n) = acting without prior consideration

Language Knowledge 8 (pp. 98-99)

accentuate (v) = to render sth easy to notice
accordingly (adv) = in a way that is suitable
account for (phr v) = to explain sth
adjustment (n) = a minor change to make sth better
admittedly (adv) = one has to accept that sth is true
alteration (to/in sth) (n) = a modification to/in sth
amendment (to sth) (n) = a change **in** sth for improvement
apply (sth to sth else) (v) = to make a law, a method, etc effective in a situation
assign (sb to do sth) (v) = to officially give sb a specific task
assuredly (adv) = definitely
attribute (sth to sth else) (v) = to ascribe sth to sth else
backdrop (n) = the background to a story
be in the right place at the right time (phr) = to happen to be in a position to seize an opportunity that becomes available
be rooted in sth (phr) = to have sth as an origin
boost (v) = to lift sth up
circulation (n) = the act of handing newspapers, magazines, etc out
conceivably (adv) = it can be believed
correspondingly (adv) = in a similar way
digitally enhanced (phr) = (of a film/ photo) that has been changed in a digital form so that it looks better
embedded (adj) = (of an idea, opinion, etc) being an important part of sb/sth
emphasize (v) = to stress sth
emulate (v) = to imitate sb you admire
enduring (adj) = existing for a long time
entail (v) = to involve sth
entrenched (adj) = (of sth bad) firmly fixed
excusable (adj) = forgivable
exemplar (n) = a typical example
fault (n) = a weakness; a bad part of sb/sth
feature (v) = to present as an artist
film distribution (n) = supplying cinemas with films
flaw (n) = a problem in a system, plan, project, etc
implanted (pp) = (of an idea, opinion, etc) deeply fixed into sb's mind
impose (v) = to officially force people to accept a law, a tax, etc
impress (v) = to make sb admire sb/sth
improved (adj) = made better
inclination (n) = a tendency to do sth
inexorably (adv) = unstoppably
lingering (adj) = lasting longer than appropriate
norm (n) = the usual and acceptable way of doing sth
notice (v) = to see/hear that sth exists
pardonable (adj) = forgivable
pathetic (adj) = pitiful
pitch (n) = the act of persuading sb to accept or buy sth
placement (n) = the process by which an agency helps sb find a suitable job, a place to live, etc
plain (adj) = obvious
plausible (adj) = believable
poignant (adj) = emotionally upsetting
precise (adj) = accurate
predictable (adj) = that can be foretold
predominantly (adv) = mainly
proportionately (adv) = in a way suitable for the scale of sth
pungent (adj) = strongly critical
read (v) = to interpret sth
reason (v) = to think logically
reinforced (adj) = strengthened
sense (v) = to realise sth without being told
shocking (adj) = appalling
simulate (v) = to mimic
snag (n) = a minor problem that no-one expected
staggering (adj) = extremely great
standard (n) = an acceptable level
startling (adj) = very unusual
stunning (adj) = exceptionally attractive
tenable (adj) = (of an idea, opinion, etc) that you can support; reasonable
ultimately (adv) = finally
unabating (adj) = continuing without losing intensity
unceasing (adj) = never stopping
well-prepared (adj) = suitably made ready
well-rehearsed (adj) = (of a speech, a theatrical performance, etc) adequately practised till sb has perfected it
well-schooled (adj) = well-educated
well-seasoned (adj) = experienced

Irregular Verbs

Infinitive	Past	Past Participle
be /biː/	was /wɒz/	been /biːn/
bear /beə/	bore /bɔː/	born(e) /bɔːn/
beat /biːt/	beat /biːt/	beaten /biːtən/
become /bɪ'kʌm/	became /bɪ'keɪm/	become /bɪ'kʌm/
begin /bɪ'gɪn/	began /bɪ'gæn/	begun /bɪ'gʌn/
bite /baɪt/	bit /bɪt/	bitten /'bɪtən/
blow /bləʊ/	blew /bluː/	blown /bləʊn/
break /breɪk/	broke /brəʊk/	broken /'brəʊkən/
bring /brɪŋ/	brought /brɔːt/	brought /brɔːt/
build /bɪld/	built /bɪlt/	built /bɪlt/
burn /bɜːn/	burnt (burned) /bɜːnt (bɜːndɻ/	burnt (burned) /bɜːnt (bɜːndɻ/
burst /bɜːst/	burst /bɜːst/	burst /bɜːst/
buy /baɪ/	bought /bɔːt/	bought /bɔːt/
can /kæn/	could /kʊd/	(been able to /bɪn 'eɪbəl tə/)
catch /kætʃ/	caught /kɔːt/	caught /kɔːt/
choose /tʃuːz/	chose /tʃəʊz/	chosen /tʃəʊzən/
come /kʌm/	came /keɪm/	come /kʌm/
cost /kɒst/	cost /kɒst/	cost /kɒst/
cut /kʌt/	cut /kʌt/	cut /kʌt/
deal /diːl/	dealt /delt/	dealt /delt/
dig /dɪg/	dug /dʌg/	dug /dʌg/
do /duː/	did /dɪd/	done /dʌn/
draw /drɔː/	drew /druː/	drawn /drɔːn/
dream /driːm/	dreamt (dreamed) /dremt (driːmdɻ/	dreamt (dreamed) /dremt (driːmdɻ/
drink /drɪŋk/	drank /dræŋk/	drunk /drʌŋk/
drive /draɪv/	drove /drəʊv/	driven /drɪvən/
eat /iːt/	ate /eɪt/	eaten /iːtən/
fall /fɔːl/	fell /fel/	fallen /fɔːlən/
feed /fiːd/	fed /fed/	fed /fed/
feel /fiːl/	felt /felt/	felt /felt/
fight /faɪt/	fought /fɔːt/	fought /fɔːt/
find /faɪnd/	found /faʊnd/	found /faʊnd/
fly /flaɪ/	flew /fluː/	flown /fləʊn/
forbid /fə'bɪd/	forbade /fə'beɪd/	forbidden /fə'bɪdən/
forget /fə'get/	forgot /fə'gɒt/	forgotten /fə'gɒtən/
forgive /fə'gɪv/	forgave /fə'geɪv/	forgiven /fə'gɪvən/
freeze /friːz/	froze /frəʊz/	frozen /'frəʊzən/
get /get/	got /gɒt/	got /gɒt/
give /gɪv/	gave /geɪv/	given /'gɪvən/
go /gəʊ/	went /went/	gone /gɒn/
grow /grəʊ/	grew /gruː/	grown /grəʊn/
hang /hæŋ/	hung (hanged) /hʌŋ (hæŋdɻ/	hung (hanged) /hʌŋ (hæŋdɻ/
have /hæv/	had /hæd/	had /hæd/
hear /hɪə/	heard /hɜːd/	heard /hɜːd/
hide /haɪd/	hid /hɪd/	hidden /hɪdən/
hit /hɪt/	hit /hɪt/	hit /hɪt/
hold /həʊld/	held /held/	held /held/
hurt /hɜːt/	hurt /hɜːt/	hurt /hɜːt/
keep /kiːp/	kept /kept/	kept /kept/
know /nəʊ/	knew /njuː/	known /nəʊn/
lay /leɪ/	laid /leɪd/	laid /leɪd/
lead /liːd/	led /led/	led /led/
learn /lɜːn/	learnt (learned) /lɜːnt (lɜːndɻ/	learnt (learned) /lɜːnt (lɜːndɻ/

Infinitive	Past	Past Participle
leave /liːv/	left /left/	left /left/
lend /lend/	lent /lent/	lent /lent/
let /let/	let /let/	let /let/
lie /laɪ/	lay /leɪ/	lain /leɪn/
light /laɪt/	lit /lɪt/	lit /lɪt/
lose /luːz/	lost /lɒst/	lost /lɒst/
make /meɪk/	made /meɪd/	made /meɪd/
mean /miːn/	meant /ment/	meant /ment/
meet /miːt/	met /met/	met /met/
pay /peɪ/	paid /peɪd/	paid /peɪd/
put /pʊt/	put /pʊt/	put /pʊt/
read /riːd/	read /red/	read /red/
ride /raɪd/	rode /rəʊd/	ridden /'rɪdən/
ring /rɪŋ/	rang /ræŋ/	rung /rʌŋ/
rise /raɪz/	rose /rəʊz/	risen /'rɪzən/
run /rʌn/	ran /ræn/	run /rʌn/
say /seɪ/	said /sed/	said /sed/
see /siː/	saw /sɔː/	seen /siːn/
sell /sel/	sold /səʊld/	sold /səʊld/
send /send/	sent /sent/	sent /sent/
set /set/	set /set/	set /set/
sew /səʊ/	sewed /səʊd/	sewn /səʊn/
shake /ʃeɪk/	shook /ʃʊk/	shaken /'ʃeɪkən/
shine /ʃaɪn/	shone /ʃɒn/	shone /ʃɒn/
shoot /ʃuːt/	shot /ʃɒt/	shot /ʃɒt/
show /ʃəʊ/	showed /ʃəʊd/	shown /ʃəʊn/
shut /ʃʌt/	shut /ʃʌt/	shut /ʃʌt/
sing /sɪŋ/	sang /sæŋ/	sung /sʌŋ/
sit /sɪt/	sat /sæt/	sat /sæt/
sleep /sliːp/	slept /slept/	slept /slept/
smell /smel/	smelt (smelled) /smelt (smeldɻ/	smelt (smelled) /smelt (smeldɻ/
speak /spiːk/	spoke /spəʊk/	spoken /'spəʊkən/
spell /spel/	spelt (spelled) /spelt (speldɻ/	spelt (spelled) /spelt (speldɻ/
spend /spend/	spent /spent/	spent /spent/
stand /stænd/	stood /stʊd/	stood /stʊd/
steal /stiːl/	stole /stəʊl/	stolen /'stəʊlən/
stick /stɪk/	stuck /stʌk/	stuck /stʌk/
sting /stɪŋ/	stung /stʌŋ/	stung /stʌŋ/
swear /sweə/	swore /swɔː/	sworn /swɔːn/
sweep /swiːp/	swept /swept/	swept /swept/
swim /swɪm/	swam /swæm/	swum /swʌm/
take /teɪk/	took /tʊk/	taken /teɪkən/
teach /tiːtʃ/	taught /tɔːt/	taught /tɔːt/
tear /teə/	tore /tɔː/	torn /tɔːn/
tell /tel/	told /təʊld/	told /təʊld/
think /θɪŋk/	thought /θɔːt/	thought /θɔːt/
throw /θrəʊ/	threw /θruː/	thrown /θrəʊn/
understand /ʌndə'stænd/	understood /ʌndə'stʊd/	understood /ʌndə'stʊd/
wake /weɪk/	woke /wəʊk/	woken /'wəʊkən/
wear /weə/	wore /wɔː/	worn /wɔːn/
win /wɪn/	won /wʌn/	won /wʌn/
write /raɪt/	wrote /rəʊt/	written /'rɪtən/